The Calculus of Computation

Aaron R. Bradley · Zohar Manna

The Calculus
of Computation

Decision Procedures
with Applications to Verification

With 60 Figures

 Springer

Authors

Aaron R. Bradley
Zohar Manna

Gates Building, Room 481
Stanford University
Stanford, CA 94305
USA

arbrad@cs.stanford.edu
manna@cs.stanford.edu

ACM Computing Classification (1998): B.8, D.1, D.2, E.1, F.1, F.3, F.4, G.2, I.1, I.2

ISBN 978-3-642-09347-0   e-ISBN 978-3-540-74113-8

Springer is a part of Springer Science+Business Media

springer.com

© Springer-Verlag Berlin Heidelberg 2010

Cover design: KünkelLopka Werbeagentur, Heidelberg

Printed on acid-free paper   45/3180/YL - 5 4 3 2 1 0

To my wife,

Sarah

A.R.B.

To my grandchildren,

Itai
Maya
Ori

Z.M.

Preface

Logic is the calculus of computation. Forty-five years ago, John McCarthy predicted in *A Basis for a Mathematical Theory of Computation* that "the relationship between computation and mathematical logic will be as fruitful in the next century as that between analysis and physics in the last". The field of *computational logic* emerged over the past few decades in partial fulfillment of that vision. Focusing on producing efficient and powerful algorithms for deciding the satisfiability of formulae in logical theories and fragments, it continues to push the frontiers of general computer science.

This book is about computational logic and its applications to *program verification*. Program verification is the task of analyzing the correctness of a program. It encompasses the formal specification of what a program should do and the formal proof that the program meets this specification. The reasoning power that computational logic offers revolutionized the field of verification. Ongoing research will make verification standard practice in software and hardware engineering in the next few decades. This acceptance into everyday engineering cannot come too soon: software and hardware are becoming ever more ubiquitous and thus ever more the source of failure.

We wrote this book with an undergraduate and beginning graduate audience in mind. However, any computer scientist or engineer who would like to enter the field of computational logic or apply its products should find this book useful.

Content

The book has two parts. Part I, *Foundations*, presents first-order logic, induction, and program verification. The methods are general. For example, Chapter 2 presents a complete proof system for first-order logic, while Chapter 5 describes a relatively complete verification methodology. Part II, *Algorithmic Reasoning*, focuses on specialized algorithms for reasoning about fragments of first-order logic and for deducing facts about programs. Part II trades generality for decidability and efficiency.

The first three chapters of Part I introduce first-order logic. Chapters 1 and 2 begin our presentation with a review of propositional and predicate logic. Much of the material will be familiar to the reader who previously studied logic. However, Chapter 3 on first-order theories will be new to many readers. It axiomatically defines the various first-order theories and fragments that we study and apply throughout the rest of the book. Chapter 4 reviews induction, introducing some forms of induction that may be new to the reader. Induction provides the mathematical basis for analyzing program correctness.

Chapter 5 turns to the primary motivating application of computational logic in this book, the task of verifying programs. It discusses *specification*, in which the programmer formalizes in logic the (sometimes surprisingly vague) understanding that he has about what functions should do; *partial correctness*, which requires proving that a program or function meets a given specification if it halts; and *total correctness*, which requires proving additionally that a program or function always halts. The presentation uses the simple programming language pi and is supported by the verifying compiler πVC (see **The πVC System**, below, for more information on πVC). Chapter 6 suggests strategies for applying the verification methodology.

Part II on *Algorithmic Reasoning* begins in Chapter 7 with quantifier-elimination methods for limited integer and rational arithmetic. It describes an algorithm for reducing a quantified formula in integer or rational arithmetic to an equivalent formula without quantifiers.

Chapter 8 begins a sequence of chapters on decision procedures for quantifier-free and other fragments of theories. These fragments of first-order theories are interesting for three reasons. First, they are sometimes decidable when the full theory is not (see Chapters 9, 10, and 11). Second, they are sometimes efficiently decidable when the full theory is not (compare Chapters 7 and 8). Finally, they are often useful; for example, proving the verification conditions that arise in the examples of Chapters 5 and 6 requires just the fragments of theories studied in Chapters 8–11. The simplex method for linear programming is presented in Chapter 8 as a decision procedure for deciding satisfiability in rational and real arithmetic without multiplication.

Chapters 9 and 11 turn to decision procedures for non-arithmetical theories. Chapter 9 discusses the classic congruence closure algorithm for equality with uninterpreted functions and extends it to reason about data structures like lists, trees, and arrays. These decision procedures are for quantifier-free fragments only. Chapter 11 presents decision procedures for larger fragments of theories that formalize array-like data structures.

Decision procedures are most useful when they are combined. For example, in program verification one must reason about arithmetic and data structures simultaneously. Chapter 10 presents the Nelson-Oppen method for combining decision procedures for quantifier-free fragments. The decision procedures of Chapters 8, 9, and 11 are all combinable using the Nelson-Oppen method.

Chapter 12 presents a methodology for constructing *invariant generation procedures*. These procedures reason inductively about programs to aid in

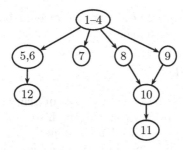

Verification   Decision procedures

Fig. 0.1. The chapter dependency graph

verification. They relieve some of the burden on the programmer to provide program annotations for verification purposes. For now, developing a static analysis is one of the easiest ways of bringing formal methods into general usage, as a typical static analysis requires little or no input from the programmer. The chapter presents a general methodology and two instances of the method for deducing arithmetical properties of programs.

Finally, Chapter 13 suggests directions for further reading and research.

Teaching

This book can be used in various ways and taught at multiple levels. Figure 0.1 presents a dependency graph for the chapters. There are two main tracks: the *verification track*, which focuses on Chapters 1–4, 5, 6, and 12; and the *decision procedures track*, which focuses on Chapters 1–4 and 7–11. Within the decision procedures track, the reader can focus on the *quantifier-free decision procedures track*, which skips Chapters 7 and 11. The reader interested in quickly obtaining an understanding of modern combination decision procedures would prefer this final track.

We have annotated several sections with a ★ to indicate that they provide additional depth that is unnecessary for understanding subsequent material. Additionally, all proofs may be skipped without preventing a general understanding of the material.

Each chapter ends with a set of exercises. Some require just a mechanical understanding of the material, while others require a conceptual understanding or ask the reader to think beyond what is presented in the book. These latter exercises are annotated with a ★. For certain audiences, additional exercises might include implementing decision procedures or invariant generation procedures and exploring certain topics in greater depth (see Chapter 13).

In our courses, we assign program verification exercises from Chapters 5 and 6 throughout the term to give students time to develop this important skill. Learning to verify programs is about as difficult for students as learning to program in the first place. Specifying and verifying programs also strengthens the students' facility with logic.

Bibliographic Remarks

Each chapter ends with a section entitled **Bibliographic Remarks** in which we attempt to provide a brief account of the historical context and development of the chapter's material. We have undoubtedly missed some important contributions, for which we apologize. We welcome corrections, comments, and historical anecdotes.

The πVC System

We implemented a *verifying compiler* called πVC to accompany this text. It allows users to write and verify annotated programs in the pi programming language. The system and a set of examples, including the programs listed in this book, are available for download from http://theory.stanford.edu/~arbrad/pivc. We plan to update this website regularly and welcome readers' comments, questions, and suggestions about πVC and the text.

Acknowledgments

This material is based upon work supported by the National Science Foundation under Grant Nos. CSR-0615449 and CNS-0411363 and by Navy/ONR contract N00014-03-1-0939. Any opinions, findings, and conclusions or recommendations expressed in this material are those of the authors and do not necessarily reflect the views of the National Science Foundation or the Navy/ONR. The first author received additional support from a Sang Samuel Wang Stanford Graduate Fellowship.

We thank the following people for their comments throughout the writing of this book: Miquel Bertran, Andrew Bradley, Susan Bradley, Chang-Seo Park, Caryn Sedloff, Henny Sipma, Matteo Slanina, Sarah Solter, Fabio Somenzi, Tomás Uribe, the students of CS156, and Alfred Hofmann and the reviewers and editors at Springer. Their suggestions helped us to improve the presentation substantially. Remaining errors and shortcomings are our responsibility.

Stanford University,   *Aaron R. Bradley*
June 2007   *Zohar Manna*

Contents

Part II Algorithmic Reasoning

Part I

Foundations

Everything is vague to a degree you do not realize till you have tried to make it precise.

— Bertrand Russell
Philosophy of Logical Atomism, 1918

Modern design and implementation of software and hardware systems lacks precision. Design documents written in a natural language admit misinterpretation. Informal arguments about why a system works miss crucial weaknesses. The resulting systems are fragile. Part I of this book presents an alternative approach to system design and implementation based on using a formal language to specify and reason about software systems.

Chapters 1 and 2 introduce the (first-order) predicate calculus. Chapter 1 presents the propositional calculus, and Chapter 2 presents the full predicate calculus. A central task is determining whether formulae of the calculus are valid. Chapter 3 formalizes common data types of software in the predicate calculus. It also introduces the concepts of decidability and complexity of deciding validity of formulae.

The final three chapters of Part I discuss applications of the predicate calculus. Chapter 4 formalizes mathematical induction in the predicate calculus, in the process introducing several forms of induction that may be new to the reader. Chapters 5 and 6 then apply the predicate calculus and mathematical induction to the specification and verification of software. Specification consists of asserting facts about software. Verification applies mathematical induction to prove that each assertion evaluates to true when program control reaches it; and to prove that program control eventually reaches specific program locations.

Part I thus provides the mathematical foundations for precise engineering. Part II will investigate algorithmic aspects of applying these foundations.

1

Propositional Logic

A deduction is speech in which, certain things having been supposed, something different from the things supposed results of necessity because of their being so.

— Aristotle
Prior Analytics, 4th century BC

A calculus is a set of symbols and a system of rules for manipulating the symbols. In an interesting calculus, the symbols and rules have meaning in some domain that matters. For example, the differential calculus defines rules for manipulating the integral symbol over a polynomial to compute the area under the curve that the polynomial defines. Area has meaning outside of the calculus; the calculus provides the tool for computing such quantities. The domain of the differential calculus, loosely speaking, consists of real numbers and functions over those numbers.

Computer scientists are interested in a different domain and thus require a different calculus. The behavior of programs, or computation, is a computer scientist's chief concern. What is an appropriate domain for studying computation? The basic entity of the domain is *state*: roughly, the assignment of values (for example, Booleans, integers, or addresses) to variables. Pairs of states comprise *transitions*. A *computation* is a sequence of states, each adjacent pair of which is a transition. A program defines the form of its states, the set of transitions between states, and the set of computations that it can produce. A program's set of computations characterizes the program itself as precisely as its source code. Chapter 5 studies these ideas in depth.

With a domain in mind, a computer scientist can now ask questions. Does this program that accepts an array of integers produce a sorted array? In other words, does each of the program's computations have a state in which a sorted array is returned? Does this program ever access unallocated memory? Does this function always halt? To answer such questions, we need a calculus to reason about computations.

This chapter and the next introduce the calculus that will be the basis for studying computation in this book. In this chapter, we cover **propositional logic (PL)**; in the next chapter, we build on the presentation to define **first-order logic (FOL)**. PL and FOL are also known as **propositional calculus** and **predicate calculus**, respectively, because they are calculi for reasoning about propositions ("the sky is blue", "this comment references itself") and predicates ("x is blue", "y references z"), respectively. Propositions are either true or false, while predicates evaluate to true or false depending on the values given to their parameters (x, y, and z).

Just as differential calculus has a set of symbols, a set of rules, and a mapping to reality that provides its meaning, propositional logic has its own symbols, rules of inference, and meaning. Sections 1.1 and 1.2 introduce the *syntax* and *semantics* (meaning) of PL formulae. Then Section 1.3 discusses two concepts that are fundamental throughout this book, *satisfiability* (Is this formula ever true?) and *validity* (Is this formula always true?), and the rules for computing whether a PL formula is satisfiable or valid. Rules for manipulating PL formulae, some of which preserve satisfiability and validity, are discussed in Section 1.5 and applied in Section 1.6.

1.1 Syntax

In this section, we introduce the syntax of PL. The **syntax** of a logical language consists of a set of symbols and rules for combining them to form "sentences" (in this case, **formulae**) of the language.

The basic elements of PL are the **truth symbols** $\top$ ("true") and $\bot$ ("false") and the **propositional variables**, usually denoted by P, Q, R, P_1, P_2,.... A countably infinite set of propositional variable symbols exists. **Logical connectives**, also called **Boolean connectives**, provide the expressive power of PL. A **formula** is simply $\top$, $\bot$, or a propositional variable P; or the application of one of the following connectives to formulae F, F_1, or F_2:

- $\neg F$: negation, pronounced "not";
- $F_1 \wedge F_2$: conjunction, pronounced "and";
- $F_1 \vee F_2$: disjunction, pronounced "or";
- $F_1 \rightarrow F_2$: implication, pronounced "implies";
- $F_1 \leftrightarrow F_2$: iff, pronounced "if and only if".

Each connective has an **arity** (the number of arguments that it takes): negation is **unary** (it takes one argument), while the other connectives are **binary** (they take two arguments). The left and right arguments of $\rightarrow$ are called the **antecedent** and **consequent**, respectively.

Some common terminology is useful. An **atom** is a truth symbol $\top$, $\bot$ or propositional variable P, Q, ... A **literal** is an atom α or its negation $\neg\alpha$. A **formula** is a literal or the application of a logical connective to a formula or formulae.

Formula G is a **subformula** of formula F if it occurs syntactically within G. More precisely,

- the only subformula of P is P;
- the subformulae of $\neg F$ are $\neg F$ and the subformulae of F;
- and the subformulae of $F_1 \wedge F_2$, $F_1 \vee F_2$, $F_1 \rightarrow F_2$, $F_1 \leftrightarrow F_2$ are the formula itself and the subformulae of F_1 and F_2.

Notice that every formula is a subformula of itself. The **strict subformulae** of a formula are all its subformulae except itself.

Example 1.1. Consider the formula

$$F : (P \wedge Q) \rightarrow (P \vee \neg Q) .$$

It contains two propositional variables, P and Q. Each instance of P and Q is an atom and a literal. $\neg Q$ is a literal, but not an atom. F has six distinct subformulae:

$$F , \quad P \vee \neg Q , \quad \neg Q , \quad P \wedge Q , \quad P , \quad Q .$$

Its strict subformulae are all of its subformulae except F itself.   ■

Parentheses are cumbersome. We define the relative precedence of the logical connectives from highest to lowest as follows: $\neg$, $\wedge$, $\vee$, $\rightarrow$, $\leftrightarrow$. Additionally, let $\rightarrow$ and $\leftrightarrow$ associate to the right, so that $P \rightarrow Q \rightarrow R$ is the same formula as $P \rightarrow (Q \rightarrow R)$.

Example 1.2. Abbreviate F of Example 1.1 as

$$F' : P \wedge Q \rightarrow P \vee \neg Q .$$

Also,

$$P_1 \wedge \neg P_2 \wedge \top \vee \neg P_1 \wedge P_2$$

stands for

$$(P_1 \wedge ((\neg P_2) \wedge \top)) \vee ((\neg P_1) \wedge P_2) .$$

Finally,

$$P_1 \rightarrow P_2 \rightarrow P_3$$

abbreviates

$$P_1 \rightarrow (P_2 \rightarrow P_3) .$$

■

1.2 Semantics

So far, we have considered the syntax of PL. The **semantics** of a logic provides its meaning. What exactly is meaning? In PL, meaning is given by the **truth values** true and false, where true $\neq$ false. Our objective is to define how to give meaning to formulae.

The first step in defining the semantics of PL is to provide a mechanism for evaluating the propositional variables. An **interpretation** I assigns to every propositional variable exactly one truth value. For example,

$$I : \{P \mapsto \text{true}, \ Q \mapsto \text{false}, \ \ldots\}$$

is an interpretation assigning true to P and false to Q, where ... elides the (countably infinitely many) assignments that are not relevant to us. That is, I assigns to every propositional variable available to us (and there are countably infinitely many) a value. We usually do not write the elision. Clearly, many interpretations exist.

Now given a PL formula F and an interpretation I, the truth value of F can be computed. The simplest manner of computing the truth value of F is via a **truth table**. Let us first examine truth tables that indicate how to evaluate each logical connective in terms of its arguments. First, a propositional variable gets its truth value immediately from I. Now consider the possible evaluations of F: it is either true or false. How is $\neg F$ evaluated? The following table summarizes the possibilities, where 0 corresponds to the value false, and 1 corresponds to true:

F	$\neg F$
0	1
1	0

The other connective can be defined similarly given values of F_1 and F_2:

F_1	F_2	$F_1 \wedge F_2$	$F_1 \vee F_2$	$F_1 \rightarrow F_2$	$F_1 \leftrightarrow F_2$
0	0	0	0	1	1
0	1	0	1	1	0
1	0	0	1	0	0
1	1	1	1	1	1

In particular, $F_1 \rightarrow F_2$ is false iff F_1 is true and F_2 is false. (Throughout the book, we use the word "iff" to abbreviate the phrase "if and only if"; one can also read it as "precisely when".)

Example 1.3. Consider the formula

$$F : \ P \wedge Q \ \rightarrow \ P \vee \neg Q$$

and the interpretation

$I:\ \{P \mapsto \mathsf{true},\ Q \mapsto \mathsf{false}\}$.

To evaluate the truth value of F under I, construct the following table:

P	Q	$\neg Q$	$P \wedge Q$	$P \vee \neg Q$	F
1	0	1	0	1	1

The top row is given by the subformulae of F. I provides values for the first two columns; then the semantics of PL provide the values for the remainder of the table. Hence, F evaluates to true under I. ∎

This tabular notation is convenient, but it is unsuitable for the predicate logic of Chapter 2. Instead, we introduce an **inductive definition** of PL's semantics that will extend to Chapter 2. An inductive definition defines the meaning of basic elements first, which in the case of PL are atoms. Then it assumes that the meaning of a set of elements is fixed and defines a more complex element in terms of these elements. For example, in PL, $F_1 \wedge F_2$ is a more complex formula than either of the formulae F_1 or F_2.

Recall that we want to compute whether F has value true under interpretation I. We write $I \models F$ if F evaluates to true under I and $I \not\models F$ if F evaluates to false. To start our inductive definition, define the meaning of truth symbols:

$$I \models \top$$
$$I \not\models \bot$$

Under any interpretation I, $\top$ has value true, and $\bot$ has value false. Next, define the truth value of propositional variables:

$$I \models P \quad \text{iff } I[P] = \mathsf{true}$$

P has value true iff the interpretation I assigns P to have value true.

Since an interpretation assigns a truth value to every propositional variable, I assigns false to P when I does not assign true to P. Thus, we can instead define the truth values of propositional variables as follows:

$$I \not\models P \quad \text{iff } I[P] = \mathsf{false}$$

Since true $\neq$ false, both definitions yield the same (unique) truth values.

Having completed the base cases of our inductive definition, we turn to the inductive step. Assume that formulae F, F_1, and F_2 have truth values. From these formulae, evaluate the semantics of more complex formulae:

$$
\begin{aligned}
I &\models \neg F & &\text{iff } I \not\models F \\
I &\models F_1 \wedge F_2 & &\text{iff } I \models F_1 \text{ and } I \models F_2 \\
I &\models F_1 \vee F_2 & &\text{iff } I \models F_1 \text{ or } I \models F_2 \\
I &\models F_1 \rightarrow F_2 & &\text{iff, if } I \models F_1 \text{ then } I \models F_2 \\
I &\models F_1 \leftrightarrow F_2 & &\text{iff } I \models F_1 \text{ and } I \models F_2, \text{ or } I \not\models F_1 \text{ and } I \not\models F_2
\end{aligned}
$$

In studying these definitions, it is useful to recall the earlier definitions given by the truth tables, which are free of English ambiguities.

For implication, consider also the equivalent formulation

$$I \not\models F_1 \rightarrow F_2 \qquad \text{iff } I \models F_1 \text{ and } I \not\models F_2$$

The formula $F_1 \rightarrow F_2$ has truth value true under I when either F_1 is false or F_2 is true. It is false only when F_1 is true and F_2 is false. Our inductive definition of the semantics of PL is complete.

Example 1.4. Consider the formula

$$F : P \wedge Q \rightarrow P \vee \neg Q$$

and the interpretation

$$I : \{P \mapsto \text{true}, \ Q \mapsto \text{false}\} \ .$$

Compute the truth value of F as follows:

1.	$I \models P$	since $I[P] = \text{true}$
2.	$I \not\models Q$	since $I[Q] = \text{false}$
3.	$I \models \neg Q$	by 2 and semantics of $\neg$
4.	$I \not\models P \wedge Q$	by 2 and semantics of $\wedge$
5.	$I \models P \vee \neg Q$	by 1 and semantics of $\vee$
6.	$I \models F$	by 4 and semantics of $\rightarrow$

We considered the distinct subformulae of F according to the **subformula ordering**: F_1 precedes F_2 if F_1 is a subformula of F_2. In that order, we computed the truth value of F from its simplest subformulae to its most complex subformula (F itself).

The final line of the calculation deserves some explanation. According to the semantics for implication,

$$I \models F_1 \rightarrow F_2 \qquad \text{iff, if } I \models F_1 \text{ then } I \models F_2$$

the implication $F_1 \rightarrow F_2$ has value true when $I \not\models F_1$. Thus, line 5 is unnecessary for establishing the truth value of F. ∎

1.3 Satisfiability and Validity

We now consider a fundamental characterization of PL formulae.

A formula F is **satisfiable** iff there exists an interpretation I such that $I \models F$. A formula F is **valid** iff for all interpretations I, $I \models F$. Determining satisfiability and validity of formulae are important tasks in logic.

Satisfiability and validity are dual concepts, and switching from one to the other is easy. F is valid iff $\neg F$ is unsatisfiable. For suppose that F is valid;

then for any interpretation I, $I \models F$. By the semantics of negation, $I \not\models \neg F$, so $\neg F$ is unsatisfiable. Conversely, suppose that $\neg F$ is unsatisfiable. For any interpretation I, $I \not\models \neg F$, so that $I \models F$ by the semantics of negation. Thus, F is valid.

Because of this duality between satisfiability and validity, we are free to focus on either one or the other in the text, depending on which is more convenient for the discussion. The reader should realize that statements about one are also statements about the other.

In this section, we present several methods of determining validity and satisfiability of PL formulae.

1.3.1 Truth Tables

Our first approach to checking the validity of a PL formula is the **truth-table method**. We exhibit this method by example.

Example 1.5. Consider the formula

$$F : P \wedge Q \ \rightarrow \ P \vee \neg Q .$$

Is it valid? Construct a table in which the first row is a list of the subformulae of F ordered according to the subformula ordering. Fill columns of propositional variables with all possible combinations of truth values. Then apply the semantics of PL to fill the rest of the table:

P	Q	$P \wedge Q$	$\neg Q$	$P \vee \neg Q$	F
0	0	0	1	1	1
0	1	0	0	0	1
1	0	0	1	1	1
1	1	1	0	1	1

The final column, which represents the truth value of F under the possible interpretations, is filled entirely with true. F is valid. ∎

Example 1.6. Consider the formula

$$F : P \vee Q \ \rightarrow \ P \wedge Q .$$

Construct the truth table:

P	Q	$P \vee Q$	$P \wedge Q$	F
0	0	0	0	1
0	1	1	0	0
1	0	1	0	0
1	1	1	1	1

Because the second and third rows show that F can be false, F is invalid. ∎

1.3.2 Semantic Arguments

Our next approach to validity checking is the **semantic argument method**. While more complicated than the truth-table method, we introduce it and emphasize it throughout the remainder of the chapter because it is our only method of evaluating the satisfiability and validity of formulae in Chapter 2.

A proof based on the semantic method begins by assuming that the given formula F is invalid: hence, there is a **falsifying interpretation** I such that $I \not\models F$. The proof proceeds by applying the semantic definitions of the logical connectives in the form of **proof rules**. A proof rule has one or more **premises** (assumed facts) and one or more **deductions** (deduced facts). An application of a proof rule requires matching the premises to facts already existing in the semantic argument and then forming the deductions. The proof rules are the following:

- According to the semantics of negation, from $I \models \neg F$, deduce $I \not\models F$; and from $I \not\models \neg F$, deduce $I \models F$:

$$\frac{I \models \neg F}{I \not\models F} \qquad \frac{I \not\models \neg F}{I \models F}$$

- According to the semantics of conjunction, from $I \models F \wedge G$, deduce both $I \models F$ and $I \models G$; and from $I \not\models F \wedge G$, deduce $I \not\models F$ or $I \not\models G$. The latter deduction results in a fork in the proof; each case must be considered separately.

$$\frac{I \models F \wedge G}{\begin{array}{l} I \models F \\ I \models G \end{array}} \qquad \frac{I \not\models F \wedge G}{I \not\models F \mid I \not\models G}$$

- According to the semantics of disjunction, from $I \models F \vee G$, deduce $I \models F$ or $I \models G$; and from $I \not\models F \vee G$, deduce both $I \not\models F$ and $I \not\models G$. The former deduction requires a case analysis in the proof.

$$\frac{I \models F \vee G}{I \models F \mid I \models G} \qquad \frac{I \not\models F \vee G}{\begin{array}{l} I \not\models F \\ I \not\models G \end{array}}$$

- According to the semantics of implication, from $I \models F \rightarrow G$, deduce $I \not\models F$ or $I \models G$; and from $I \not\models F \rightarrow G$, deduce both $I \models F$ and $I \not\models G$. The former deduction requires a case analysis in the proof.

$$\frac{I \models F \rightarrow G}{I \not\models F \mid I \models G} \qquad \frac{I \not\models F \rightarrow G}{\begin{array}{l} I \models F \\ I \not\models G \end{array}}$$

- According to the semantics of iff, from $I \models F \leftrightarrow G$, deduce $I \models F \wedge G$ or $I \not\models F \vee G$; and from $I \not\models F \leftrightarrow G$, deduce $I \models F \wedge \neg G$ or $I \models \neg F \wedge G$. Both deductions require considering multiple cases.

$$\frac{I \models F \leftrightarrow G}{I \models F \wedge G \mid I \not\models F \vee G} \qquad \frac{I \not\models F \leftrightarrow G}{I \models F \wedge \neg G \mid I \models \neg F \wedge G}$$

- Finally, a contradiction occurs when following the above proof rules results in the claim that an interpretation I both satisfies a formula F and does not satisfy F.

$$\frac{I \models F}{I \not\models F}$$
$$\frac{}{I \models \bot}$$

Before explaining proofs in more detail, let us see several examples.

Example 1.7. To prove that the formula

$$F : \quad P \wedge Q \;\rightarrow\; P \vee \neg Q$$

is valid, assume that it is invalid and derive a contradiction. Thus, assume that there is a falsifying interpretation I of F (such that $I \not\models F$). Then,

1.	$I \not\models P \wedge Q \rightarrow P \vee \neg Q$	assumption
2.	$I \models P \wedge Q$	by 1 and semantics of $\rightarrow$
3.	$I \not\models P \vee \neg Q$	by 1 and semantics of $\rightarrow$
4.	$I \models P$	by 2 and semantics of $\wedge$
5.	$I \models Q$	by 2 and semantics of $\wedge$
6.	$I \not\models P$	by 3 and semantics of $\vee$
7.	$I \not\models \neg Q$	by 3 and semantics of $\vee$
8.	$I \models Q$	by 7 and semantics of $\neg$

Lines 4 and 6 contradict each other, so that our assumption must be wrong: F is actually valid.

We can end the proof as soon as we have a contradiction. For example,

1.	$I \not\models P \wedge Q \rightarrow P \vee \neg Q$	assumption
2.	$I \models P \wedge Q$	by 1 and semantics of $\rightarrow$
3.	$I \not\models P \vee \neg Q$	by 1 and semantics of $\rightarrow$
4.	$I \models P$	by 2 and semantics of $\wedge$
5.	$I \not\models P$	by 3 and semantics of $\vee$

This argument is sufficient because a contradiction already exists. In other words, the discovered contradiction closes the one branch of the proof. We sometimes note the contradiction explicitly in the proof:

6.	$I \models \bot$	4 and 5 are contradictory

■

Example 1.8. To prove that the formula

$$F : (P \to Q) \land (Q \to R) \ \to \ (P \to R)$$

is valid, assume otherwise and derive a contradiction:

1.	$I \not\models F$	assumption
2.	$I \models (P \to Q) \land (Q \to R)$	by 1 and semantics of $\to$
3.	$I \not\models P \to R$	by 1 and semantics of $\to$
4.	$I \models P$	by 3 and semantics of $\to$
5.	$I \not\models R$	by 3 and semantics of $\to$
6.	$I \models P \to Q$	by 2 and semantics of $\land$
7.	$I \models Q \to R$	by 2 and semantics of $\land$

There are two cases to consider from 6. In the first case,

8a.	$I \not\models P$	by 6 and semantics of $\to$
9a.	$I \models \bot$	4 and 8a are contradictory

In the second case,

8b.	$I \models Q$	by 6 and semantics of $\to$

Now there are two more cases from 7. In the first case,

9ba.	$I \not\models Q$	by 7 and semantics of $\to$
10ba.	$I \models \bot$	8b and 9ba are contradictory

In the second case,

9bb.	$I \models R$	by 7 and semantics of $\to$
10bb.	$I \models \bot$	5 and 9bb are contradictory

All three branches of the proof are closed: F is valid. ∎

    We introduce vocabulary for discussing semantic proofs. The reader need not memorize these terms now; just refer to them as they are used. A **line** $L : I \models F$ or $L : I \not\models F$ is a single statement in the proof, sometimes labeled as in the examples. A line L is a **direct descendant** of a **parent** M if L is directly below M in the proof. L is a **descendant** of M if M is L itself, if L is a direct descendant of M, or if the parent of L is a descendant of M (in other words, *descendant* is the reflexive and transitive closure of *direct descendant*). M is an **ancestor** of L if L is a descendant of M. Several proof rules — the second conjunction rule, the first disjunction rule, the first implication rule, and both rules for iff — produce a fork in the argument, as the last example shows. A proof thus evolves as a tree rather than linearly. A **branch** of the tree is a sequence of lines descending from the root. A branch is **closed** if it contains a contradiction, either explicitly as $I \models \bot$ or implicitly as $I \models G$

and $I \not\models G$ for some formula G. Otherwise, the branch is **open**. A semantic argument is **finished** when no more proof rules are applicable. It is a proof of the validity of F if every branch is closed; otherwise, each open branch describes a falsifying interpretation of F.

While the given proof rules are (theoretically) sufficient, **derived** proof rules can make proofs more concise.

Example 1.9. The derived rule of **modus ponens** simplifies the proof of Example 1.8. The rule is the following:

$$\frac{\begin{array}{l} I \models F \\ I \models F \to G \end{array}}{I \models G}$$

In words, from $I \models F$ and $I \models F \to G$, deduce $I \models G$.

Using this rule, let us simplify the proof of the validity of

$$F : (P \to Q) \wedge (Q \to R) \ \to \ (P \to R) \ .$$

We assume that it is invalid and try to derive a contradiction.

1.	$I \not\models F$		assumption
2.	$I \models (P \to Q) \wedge (Q \to R)$		by 1 and semantics of $\to$
3.	$I \not\models P \to R$		by 1 and semantics of $\to$
4.	$I \models P$		by 3 and semantics of $\to$
5.	$I \not\models R$		by 3 and semantics of $\to$
6.	$I \models P \to Q$		by 2 and semantics of $\wedge$
7.	$I \models Q \to R$		by 2 and semantics of $\wedge$
8.	$I \models Q$		by 4, 6, and *modus ponens*
9.	$I \models R$		by 8, 7, and *modus ponens*
10.	$I \models \bot$		5 and 9 are contradictory

This proof has only one branch.   ∎

The truth-table and semantic methods can be used to check satisfiability. For example, the truth table of Example 1.6 can be extended to show that

$$\neg F : \ \neg(P \vee Q \ \to \ P \wedge Q)$$

is satisfiable:

P	Q	$P \vee Q$	$P \wedge Q$	F	$\neg F$
0	0	0	0	1	0
0	1	1	0	0	1
1	0	1	0	0	1
1	1	1	1	1	0

The second and third rows represent satisfying interpretations of $\neg F$. Additionally, the semantic argument in the following example shows that

$$G: \neg(P \vee Q \rightarrow P \wedge Q)$$

is satisfied by the discovered interpretation I, and thus that G is satisfiable.

Example 1.10. To prove that the formula

$$F: P \vee Q \rightarrow P \wedge Q$$

is valid, assume that F is invalid; then there is an interpretation I such that $I \models \neg F$:

1. $I \not\models P \vee Q \rightarrow P \wedge Q$ assumption
2. $I \models P \vee Q$ by 1 and semantics of $\rightarrow$
3. $I \not\models P \wedge Q$ by 1 and semantics of $\rightarrow$

We have two choices to make. By 2 and the semantics of disjunction, either P or Q must be true. By 3 and the semantics of conjunction, either P or Q must be false. So there are two options: either P is true and Q is false, or P is false and Q is true. We choose P to be true and Q to be false. Then,

4a. $I \models P$ by 2 and semantics of $\vee$
5a. $I \not\models Q$ by 3 and semantics of $\wedge$

The only subformulae of P and Q are themselves, so the table is complete. Yet we did not derive a contradiction. In fact, we found the interpretation

$$I: \{P \mapsto \text{true}, \ Q \mapsto \text{false}\}$$

for which $I \models \neg F$. Therefore, F is actually invalid. The interpretation $I: \{P \mapsto \text{true}, \ Q \mapsto \text{false}\}$ is a falsifying interpretation.

If our choice had resulted in a contradiction, then we would have had to try the other choice for P and Q, in which P is false and Q is true. In general, we stop either when we have found an interpretation or when we have closed every branch.   ∎

1.4 Equivalence and Implication

Just as satisfiability and validity are important properties of PL formulae, **equivalence** and **implication** are important properties of pairs of formulae. Two formulae F_1 and F_2 are **equivalent** if they evaluate to the same truth value under all interpretations I. That is, for all interpretations I, $I \models F_1$ iff $I \models F_2$. Another way to state the equivalence of F_1 and F_2 is to assert the validity of the formula $F_1 \leftrightarrow F_2$. We write $F_1 \Leftrightarrow F_2$ when F_1 and F_2 are equivalent. $F_1 \Leftrightarrow F_2$ is *not* a formula; it simply abbreviates the statement "F_1 and F_2 are equivalent."

We use the last characterization to prove that two formulae are equivalent.

Example 1.11. To prove that

$$P \Leftrightarrow \neg\neg P \,,$$

we prove that

$$P \leftrightarrow \neg\neg P$$

is valid via a truth table:

P	$\neg P$	$\neg\neg P$	$P \leftrightarrow \neg\neg P$
0	1	0	1
1	0	1	1

∎

Example 1.12. To prove

$$P \rightarrow Q \Leftrightarrow \neg P \vee Q \,,$$

we prove that

$$F: \ P \rightarrow Q \ \leftrightarrow \ \neg P \vee Q$$

is valid via a truth table:

P	Q	$P \rightarrow Q$	$\neg P$	$\neg P \vee Q$	F
0	0	1	1	1	1
0	1	1	1	1	1
1	0	0	0	0	1
1	1	1	0	1	1

∎

Formula F_1 **implies** formula F_2 if $I \models F_2$ for every interpretation I such that $I \models F_1$. Another way to state that F_1 implies F_2 is to assert the validity of the formula $F_1 \rightarrow F_2$. We write $F_1 \Rightarrow F_2$ when F_1 implies F_2. Do not confuse the *implication* $F_1 \Rightarrow F_2$, which asserts the validity of $F_1 \rightarrow F_2$, with the *PL formula* $F_1 \rightarrow F_2$, which is constructed using the logical operator $\rightarrow$. $F_1 \Rightarrow F_2$ is *not* a formula.

As with equivalences, we use the validity characterization to prove implications.

Example 1.13. To prove that

$$R \wedge (\neg R \vee P) \ \Rightarrow \ P \,,$$

we prove that

$$F : \ R \wedge (\neg R \vee P) \ \rightarrow \ P$$

is valid via a semantic argument. Suppose F is not valid; then there exists an interpretation I such that $I \not\models F$:

1. $I \not\models F$ assumption
2. $I \models R \wedge (\neg R \vee P)$ by 1 and semantics of $\rightarrow$
3. $I \not\models P$ by 1 and semantics of $\rightarrow$
4. $I \models R$ by 2 and semantics of $\wedge$
5. $I \models \neg R \vee P$ by 2 and semantics of $\wedge$

There are two cases to consider. In the first case,

6a. $I \models \neg R$ by 5 and semantics of $\vee$
7a. $I \models \bot$ 4 and 6a are contradictory

In the second case,

6b. $I \models P$ by 5 and semantics of $\vee$
7b. $I \models \bot$ 3 and 6b are contradictory

Thus, our assumption that $I \not\models F$ is wrong, and F is valid.   ∎

1.5 Substitution

Substitution is a syntactic operation on formulae with significant semantic consequences. It allows us to prove the validity of entire sets of formulae via **formula templates**. It is also an essential tool for manipulating formulae throughout the text.

A **substitution** σ is a mapping from formulae to formulae:

$$\sigma : \ \{F_1 \mapsto G_1, \ \dots, \ F_n \mapsto G_n\} \ .$$

The **domain** of σ, domain(σ), is

$$\text{domain}(\sigma) : \ \{F_1, \dots, F_n\} \ ,$$

while the **range** range(σ) is

$$\text{range}(\sigma) : \ \{G_1, \dots, G_n\} \ .$$

The application of a substitution σ to a formula F, $F\sigma$, replaces each occurrence of a formula F_i in the domain of σ with its corresponding formula G_i in the range of σ. Replacements occur all at once. We remove any ambiguity by establishing that when both subformulae F_j and F_k are in the domain of σ, and F_k is a strict subformula of F_j, then the larger subformula F_j is replaced by the corresponding formula G_j. An example clarifies this statement.

Example 1.14. Consider formula

$$F : \ P \wedge Q \ \rightarrow \ P \vee \neg Q$$

and substitution

$$\sigma : \ \{P \ \mapsto \ R, \quad P \wedge Q \ \mapsto \ P \rightarrow Q\} \ .$$

Then

$$F\sigma : \ (P \rightarrow Q) \ \rightarrow \ R \vee \neg Q \ ,$$

where the antecedent $P \wedge Q$ of F is replaced by $P \rightarrow Q$, and the P of the consequent is replaced by R. Moreover,

$$F\sigma \ \neq \ R \wedge Q \ \rightarrow \ R \vee \neg Q$$

by our convention.   ■

A **variable substitution** is a substitution in which the domain consists only of propositional variables.

One notation is useful when working with substitutions. When we write $F[F_1, \ldots, F_n]$, we mean that formula F can have formulae F_i, $i = 1, \ldots, n$, as subformulae. If σ is $\{F_1 \mapsto G_1, \ldots, F_n \mapsto G_n\}$, then

$$F[F_1, \ldots, F_n]\sigma : \ F[G_1, \ldots, G_n] \ .$$

In the formula of Example 1.14, writing

$$F[P, \ P \wedge Q]\sigma : \ F[R, \ P \rightarrow Q]$$

emphasizes that subformulae P and $P \wedge Q$ of F are replaced by formulae R and $P \rightarrow Q$, respectively.

Two interesting semantic consequences can be derived from substitution. Proposition 1.15 states that substituting subformulae F_i of F with corresponding equivalent subformulae G_i results in an equivalent formula F'.

Proposition 1.15 (Substitution of Equivalent Formulae). *Consider substitution*

$$\sigma : \ \{F_1 \mapsto G_1, \ldots, F_n \mapsto G_n\}$$

such that for each i, $F_i \Leftrightarrow G_i$. Then $F \Leftrightarrow F\sigma$.

Example 1.16. Consider applying substitution

$$\sigma : \ \{P \rightarrow Q \ \mapsto \ \neg P \vee Q\}$$

to

$$F : (P \to Q) \; \to \; R \, .$$

Since $P \to Q \Leftrightarrow \neg P \vee Q$, the formula

$$F\sigma : (\neg P \vee Q) \; \to \; R$$

is equivalent to F. ∎

Proposition 1.17 asserts that proving the validity of a PL formula F actually proves the validity of an infinite set of formulae: those formulae that can be derived from F via variable substitutions.

Proposition 1.17 (Valid Template). *If F is valid and $G = F\sigma$ for some variable substitution σ, then G is valid.*

Example 1.18. In Example 1.12, we proved that $P \to Q$ is equivalent to $\neg P \vee Q$:

$$F : (P \to Q) \; \leftrightarrow \; (\neg P \vee Q)$$

is valid. The validity of F implies that every formula of the form $F_1 \to F_2$ is equivalent to $\neg F_1 \vee F_2$, for arbitrary subformulae F_1 and F_2. ∎

Finally, it is often useful to compute the **composition** of substitutions. Given substitutions σ_1 and σ_2, the idea is to compute substitution σ such that $F\sigma_1\sigma_2 = F\sigma$ for any F. Compute $\sigma_1\sigma_2$ as follows:

1. apply σ_2 to each formula of the range of σ_1, and add the results to σ;
2. if F_i of $F_i \mapsto G_i$ appears in the domain of σ_2 but *not* in the domain of σ_1, then add $F_i \mapsto G_i$ to σ.

Example 1.19. Compute the composition of substitutions

$$\sigma_1\sigma_2 : \{P \mapsto R, \; P \wedge Q \mapsto P \to Q\}\{P \mapsto S, \; S \mapsto Q\}$$

as follows:

$$\{P \mapsto R\sigma_2, \; P \wedge Q \mapsto (P \to Q)\sigma_2, \; S \mapsto Q\}$$
$$= \{P \mapsto R, \; P \wedge Q \mapsto S \to Q, \; S \mapsto Q\}$$

∎

1.6 Normal Forms

A **normal form** of formulae is a syntactic restriction such that for every formula of the logic, there is an equivalent formula in the normal form. Three normal forms are particularly important for PL.

Negation normal form (NNF) requires that $\neg$, $\wedge$, and $\vee$ be the only connectives and that negations appear only in literals. Transforming a formula F to equivalent formula F' in NNF can be computed recursively using the following list of template equivalences:

$$\neg\neg F_1 \;\Leftrightarrow\; F_1$$
$$\neg\top \;\Leftrightarrow\; \bot$$
$$\neg\bot \;\Leftrightarrow\; \top$$
$$\neg(F_1 \wedge F_2) \;\Leftrightarrow\; \neg F_1 \vee \neg F_2$$
$$\neg(F_1 \vee F_2) \;\Leftrightarrow\; \neg F_1 \wedge \neg F_2$$
$$F_1 \to F_2 \;\Leftrightarrow\; \neg F_1 \vee F_2$$
$$F_1 \leftrightarrow F_2 \;\Leftrightarrow\; (F_1 \to F_2) \wedge (F_2 \to F_1)$$

When implementing the transformation, the equivalences should be applied left-to-right. The equivalences

$$\neg(F_1 \wedge F_2) \;\Leftrightarrow\; \neg F_1 \vee \neg F_2 \qquad \neg(F_1 \vee F_2) \;\Leftrightarrow\; \neg F_1 \wedge \neg F_2$$

are known as **De Morgan's Law**.

Propositions 1.15 and 1.17 justify that the result of applying the template equivalences to a formula produces an equivalent formula. The transitivity of equivalence justifies that this equivalence holds over any number of transformations: if $F \Leftrightarrow G$ and $G \Leftrightarrow H$, then $F \Leftrightarrow H$.

Example 1.20. To convert the formula

$$F : \neg(P \to \neg(P \wedge Q))$$

into NNF, apply the template equivalence

$$F_1 \to F_2 \;\Leftrightarrow\; \neg F_1 \vee F_2 \tag{1.1}$$

to produce

$$F' : \neg(\neg P \vee \neg(P \wedge Q)) \,.$$

Let us understand this "application" of the template equivalence in detail. First, apply variable substitution

$$\sigma_1 : \{F_1 \mapsto P, \; F_2 \mapsto \neg(P \wedge Q)\}$$

to the valid template formula of equivalence (1.1):

$$(F_1 \to F_2 \;\leftrightarrow\; \neg F_1 \vee F_2)\sigma_1 : \; P \to \neg(P \wedge Q) \;\leftrightarrow\; \neg P \vee \neg(P \wedge Q) \,.$$

Proposition 1.17 implies that the result is valid. Then construct substitution

$$\sigma_2 : \{P \to \neg(P \wedge Q) \;\mapsto\; \neg P \vee \neg(P \wedge Q)\} \,,$$

and apply Proposition 1.15 to $F\sigma_2$ to yield that

$$F' : \ \neg(\neg P \vee \neg(P \wedge Q))$$

is equivalent to F. Subsequently, we shall not provide these details.
Continuing with the conversion to NNF, apply De Morgan's law

$$\neg(F_1 \vee F_2) \ \Leftrightarrow \ \neg F_1 \wedge \neg F_2$$

to produce

$$F'' : \ \neg\neg P \wedge \neg\neg(P \wedge Q) \ .$$

Apply

$$\neg\neg F_1 \ \Leftrightarrow \ F_1$$

twice to produce

$$F''' : \ P \wedge P \wedge Q \ ,$$

which is in NNF and equivalent to F. ∎

A formula is in **disjunctive normal form (DNF)** if it is a disjunction
of conjunctions of literals:

$$\bigvee_i \bigwedge_j \ell_{i,j} \quad \text{for literals } \ell_{i,j} \ .$$

To convert a formula F into an equivalent formula in DNF, transform F into
NNF and then use the following table of template equivalences:

$$(F_1 \vee F_2) \wedge F_3 \ \Leftrightarrow \ (F_1 \wedge F_3) \vee (F_2 \wedge F_3)$$
$$F_1 \wedge (F_2 \vee F_3) \ \Leftrightarrow \ (F_1 \wedge F_2) \vee (F_1 \wedge F_3)$$

Again, when implementing the transformation, the equivalences should be
applied left-to-right. The equivalences simply say that conjunction distributes
over disjunction.

Example 1.21. To convert

$$F : \ (Q_1 \vee \neg\neg Q_2) \ \wedge \ (\neg R_1 \rightarrow R_2)$$

into DNF, first transform it into NNF

$$F' : \ (Q_1 \vee Q_2) \ \wedge \ (R_1 \vee R_2) \ ,$$

and then apply distributivity to obtain

$$F'' : \ (Q_1 \wedge (R_1 \vee R_2)) \ \vee \ (Q_2 \wedge (R_1 \vee R_2)) \ ,$$

and then distributivity twice again to produce

$$F''' : \ (Q_1 \wedge R_1) \ \vee \ (Q_1 \wedge R_2) \ \vee \ (Q_2 \wedge R_1) \ \vee \ (Q_2 \wedge R_2) \ .$$

F''' is in DNF and is equivalent to F. ∎

The dual of DNF is **conjunctive normal form (CNF)**. A formula in CNF is a conjunction of disjunctions of literals:

$$\bigwedge_i \bigvee_j \ell_{i,j} \quad \text{for literals } \ell_{i,j} .$$

Each inner block of disjunctions is called a **clause**. To convert a formula F into an equivalent formula in CNF, transform F into NNF and then use the following table of template equivalences:

$$(F_1 \wedge F_2) \vee F_3 \;\Leftrightarrow\; (F_1 \vee F_3) \wedge (F_2 \vee F_3)$$
$$F_1 \vee (F_2 \wedge F_3) \;\Leftrightarrow\; (F_1 \vee F_2) \wedge (F_1 \vee F_3)$$

Example 1.22. To convert

$$F : \; (Q_1 \wedge \neg\neg Q_2) \vee (\neg R_1 \to R_2)$$

into CNF, first transform F into NNF:

$$F' : \; (Q_1 \wedge Q_2) \vee (R_1 \vee R_2) .$$

Then apply distributivity to obtain

$$F'' : \; (Q_1 \vee R_1 \vee R_2) \wedge (Q_2 \vee R_1 \vee R_2) ,$$

which is in CNF and equivalent to F. ■

1.7 Decision Procedures for Satisfiability

Section 1.3 introduced the truth-table and semantic argument methods for determining the satisfiability of PL formulae. In this section, we study algorithms for *deciding* satisfiability (see Section 2.6 for a formal discussion of decidability). A **decision procedure** for satisfiability of PL formulae reports, after some finite amount of computation, whether a given PL formula F is satisfiable.

1.7.1 Simple Decision Procedures

The truth-table method immediately suggests a decision procedure: construct the full table, which has 2^n rows when F has n variables, and report whether the final column, representing F, has value 1 in any row.

The semantic argument method also suggests a decision procedure. The basic idea is to make sure that a proof rule is only applied to each line in the argument at most once. Because each deduction is simpler in construction than its premise, the constructed proof is of finite size (see Chapter 4 for a formal approach to proving this point). When the semantic argument is finished, report whether any branch is still open.

This simple description leaves out many details. Most importantly, when many lines exist to which one can apply proof rules, which line should be considered next? Different implementations of this decision, called **proof tactics**, result in different proof shapes and sizes. For example, one basic tactic is to apply proof rules with only one deduction before proof rules with multiple deductions to delay forks in the proof as long as possible.

Subsequent sections consider more sophisticated procedures that are the basis for modern satisfiability solvers.

1.7.2 Reconsidering the Truth-Table Method

In the naive decision procedure based on the truth-table method, the entire table is constructed. Actually, only one row need be considered at a time, making for a space efficient procedure. This idea is implemented in the following recursive algorithm for deciding the satisfiability of a PL formula F:

```
let rec SAT F =
   if F = ⊤ then true
   else if F = ⊥ then false
   else
      let P = CHOOSE vars(F) in
      (SAT F{P ↦ ⊤}) ∨ (SAT F{P ↦ ⊥})
```

The notation "`let rec SAT F =`" declares SAT as a recursive function that takes one argument, a formula F. The notation "`let P = CHOOSE vars(F) in`" means that P's value in the subsequent text is the variable returned by the CHOOSE function. When applying the substitutions $F\{P \mapsto \top\}$ or $F\{P \mapsto \bot\}$, the template equivalences of Exercise 1.2 should be applied to simplify the result. Then the comparisons $F = \top$ and $F = \bot$ can be implemented as purely syntactic operations.

At each recursive step, if F is not yet $\top$ or $\bot$, a variable is chosen on which to branch. Each possibility for P is attempted if necessary. This algorithm returns **true** immediately upon finding a satisfying interpretation. Otherwise, if F is unsatisfiable, it eventually returns $\bot$. SAT may save branching on certain variables by simplifying intermediate formulae.

Example 1.23. Consider the formula

$$F : (P \rightarrow Q) \wedge P \wedge \neg Q .$$

To compute SAT F, choose a variable, say P, and recurse on the first case,

$$F\{P \mapsto \top\} : (\top \rightarrow Q) \wedge \top \wedge \neg Q ,$$

which simplifies to

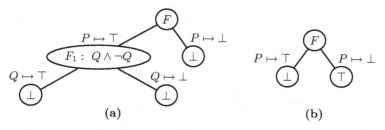

Fig. 1.1. Visualizing runs of SAT

$F_1 : Q \wedge \neg Q$.

Now try each of

$F_1\{Q \mapsto \top\}$ and $F_1\{Q \mapsto \bot\}$.

Both simplify to $\bot$, so this branch ends without finding a satisfying interpretation.

Now try the other branch for P in F:

$F\{P \mapsto \bot\} : (\bot \rightarrow Q) \wedge \bot \wedge \neg Q$,

which simplifies to $\bot$. Thus, this branch also ends without finding a satisfying interpretation. Thus, F is unsatisfiable.

The run of SAT on F is visualized in Figure 1.1(a).   ■

Example 1.24. Consider the formula

$F : (P \rightarrow Q) \wedge \neg P$.

To compute SAT F, choose a variable, say P, and recurse on the first case,

$F\{P \mapsto \top\} : (\top \rightarrow Q) \wedge \neg\top$,

which simplifies to $\bot$. Therefore, try

$F\{P \mapsto \bot\} : (\bot \rightarrow Q) \wedge \neg\bot$

instead, which simplifies to $\top$. Arbitrarily assigning a value to Q produces the following satisfying interpretation:

$I : \{P \mapsto \text{false}, Q \mapsto \text{true}\}$.

The run of SAT on F is visualized in Figure 1.1(b).   ■

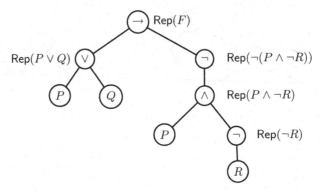

Fig. 1.2. Parse tree of $F : P \vee Q \rightarrow \neg(P \wedge \neg R)$ with representatives for subformulae

1.7.3 Conversion to an Equisatisfiable Formula in CNF

The next two decision procedures operate on PL formulae in CNF. The transformation suggested in Section 1.6 produces an equivalent formula that can be exponentially larger than the original formula: consider converting a formula in DNF into CNF. However, to decide the satisfiability of F, we need only examine a formula F' such that F and F' are **equisatisfiable**. F and F' are equisatisfiable when F is satisfiable iff F' is satisfiable.

We define a method for converting PL formula F to equisatisfiable PL formula F' in CNF that is at most a constant factor larger than F. The main idea is to introduce new propositional variables to represent the subformulae of F. The constructed formula F' includes extra clauses that assert that these new variables are equivalent to the subformulae that they represent.

Figure 1.2 visualizes the idea of the procedure. Each node of the "parse tree" of F represents a subformula G of F. With each node G is associated a representative propositional variable $\mathsf{Rep}(G)$. In the constructed formula F', each representative $\mathsf{Rep}(G)$ is asserted to be equivalent to the subformula G that it represents in such a way that the conjunction of all such assertions is in CNF. Finally, the representative $\mathsf{Rep}(F)$ of F is asserted to be true.

To obtain a small formula in CNF, each assertion of equivalence between $\mathsf{Rep}(G)$ and G refers at most to the children of G in the parse tree. How is this possible when a subformula may be arbitrarily large? The main trick is to refer to the representatives of G's children rather than the children themselves.

Let the "representative" function $\mathsf{Rep} : \mathsf{PL} \rightarrow \mathcal{V} \cup \{\top, \bot\}$ map PL formulae to propositional variables $\mathcal{V}$, $\top$, or $\bot$. In the general case, it is intended to map a formula F to its representative propositional variable P_F such that the truth value of P_F is the same as that of F. In other words, P_F provides a compact way of referring to F.

Let the "encoding" function $\mathsf{En} : \mathsf{PL} \rightarrow \mathsf{PL}$ map PL formulae to PL formulae. En is intended to map a PL formula F to a PL formula F' in CNF that asserts that F's representative, P_F, is equivalent to F: "$\mathsf{Rep}(F) \leftrightarrow F$".

As the base cases for defining Rep and En, define their behavior on $\top$, $\bot$, and propositional variables P:

$$\text{Rep}(\top) = \top \qquad \text{En}(\top) = \top$$
$$\text{Rep}(\bot) = \bot \qquad \text{En}(\bot) = \top$$
$$\text{Rep}(P) = P \qquad \text{En}(P) = \top$$

The representative of $\top$ is $\top$ itself, and the representative of $\bot$ is $\bot$ itself. Thus, $\text{Rep}(\top) \leftrightarrow \top$ and $\text{Rep}(\bot) \leftrightarrow \bot$ are both trivially valid, so $\text{En}(\top)$ and $\text{En}(\bot)$ are both $\top$. Finally, the representative of a propositional variable P is P itself; and again, $\text{Rep}(P) \leftrightarrow P$ is trivially valid so that $\text{En}(P)$ is $\top$.

For the inductive case, F is a formula other than an atom, so define its representative as a unique propositional variable P_F:

$$\text{Rep}(F) = P_F \ .$$

En then asserts the equivalence of F and P_F as a CNF formula. On conjunction, define

$\text{En}(F_1 \wedge F_2) =$
    `let` $P = \text{Rep}(F_1 \wedge F_2)$ `in`
    $(\neg P \vee \text{Rep}(F_1)) \ \wedge \ (\neg P \vee \text{Rep}(F_2)) \ \wedge \ (\neg\text{Rep}(F_1) \vee \neg\text{Rep}(F_2) \vee P)$

The returned formula

$$(\neg P \vee \text{Rep}(F_1)) \ \wedge \ (\neg P \vee \text{Rep}(F_2)) \ \wedge \ (\neg\text{Rep}(F_1) \vee \neg\text{Rep}(F_2) \vee P)$$

is in CNF and is equivalent to

$$\text{Rep}(F_1 \wedge F_2) \ \leftrightarrow \ \text{Rep}(F_1) \wedge \text{Rep}(F_2) \ .$$

In detail, the first two clauses

$$(\neg P \vee \text{Rep}(F_1)) \ \wedge \ (\neg P \vee \text{Rep}(F_2))$$

together assert

$$P \ \rightarrow \ \text{Rep}(F_1) \wedge \text{Rep}(F_2)$$

(since, for example, $\neg P \vee \text{Rep}(F_1)$ is equivalent to $P \rightarrow \text{Rep}(F_1)$), while the final clause asserts

$$\text{Rep}(F_1) \wedge \text{Rep}(F_2) \ \rightarrow \ P \ .$$

Notice the application of Rep to F_1 and F_2. As mentioned above, it is the trick to producing a small CNF formula.

On negation, $\text{En}(\neg F)$ returns a formula equivalent to $\text{Rep}(\neg F) \leftrightarrow \neg\text{Rep}(F)$:

$\text{En}(\neg F) =$
    `let` $P = \text{Rep}(\neg F)$ `in`
    $(\neg P \vee \neg\text{Rep}(F)) \ \wedge \ (P \vee \text{Rep}(F))$

En is defined for $\vee$, $\rightarrow$, and $\leftrightarrow$ as well:

$\mathsf{En}(F_1 \vee F_2) =$
 let $P = \mathsf{Rep}(F_1 \vee F_2)$ in
 $(\neg P \vee \mathsf{Rep}(F_1) \vee \mathsf{Rep}(F_2)) \wedge (\neg \mathsf{Rep}(F_1) \vee P) \wedge (\neg \mathsf{Rep}(F_2) \vee P)$

$\mathsf{En}(F_1 \rightarrow F_2) =$
 let $P = \mathsf{Rep}(F_1 \rightarrow F_2)$ in
 $(\neg P \vee \neg \mathsf{Rep}(F_1) \vee \mathsf{Rep}(F_2)) \wedge (\mathsf{Rep}(F_1) \vee P) \wedge (\neg \mathsf{Rep}(F_2) \vee P)$

$\mathsf{En}(F_1 \leftrightarrow F_2) =$
 let $P = \mathsf{Rep}(F_1 \leftrightarrow F_2)$ in
 $(\neg P \vee \neg \mathsf{Rep}(F_1) \vee \mathsf{Rep}(F_2)) \wedge (\neg P \vee \mathsf{Rep}(F_1) \vee \neg \mathsf{Rep}(F_2))$
 $\wedge (P \vee \neg \mathsf{Rep}(F_1) \vee \neg \mathsf{Rep}(F_2)) \wedge (P \vee \mathsf{Rep}(F_1) \vee \mathsf{Rep}(F_2))$

Having defined En, let us construct the full CNF formula that is equisatisfiable to F. If S_F is the set of all subformulae of F (including F itself), then

$$F' : \ \mathsf{Rep}(F) \wedge \bigwedge_{G \in S_F} \mathsf{En}(G)$$

is in CNF and is equisatisfiable to F. The second main conjunct asserts the equivalences between all subformulae of F and their corresponding representatives. $\mathsf{Rep}(F)$ asserts that F's representative, and thus F itself (according to the second conjunct), is true.

If F has size n, where each instance of a logical connective or a propositional variable contributes one unit of size, then F' has size at most $30n + 2$. The size of F' is thus linear in the size of F. The number of symbols in the formula returned by $\mathsf{En}(F_1 \leftrightarrow F_2)$, which incurs the largest expansion, is 29. Up to one additional conjunction is also required per symbol of F. Finally, two extra symbols are required for asserting that $\mathsf{Rep}(F)$ is true.

Example 1.25. Consider formula

$$F : \ (Q_1 \wedge Q_2) \vee (R_1 \wedge R_2) \, ,$$

which is in DNF. To convert it to CNF, we collect its subformulae

$$S_F : \ \{Q_1, \ Q_2, \ Q_1 \wedge Q_2, \ R_1, \ R_2, \ R_1 \wedge R_2, \ F\}$$

and compute

$$\mathsf{En}(Q_1) = \top$$
$$\mathsf{En}(Q_2) = \top$$
$$\mathsf{En}(Q_1 \wedge Q_2) = (\neg P_{(Q_1 \wedge Q_2)} \vee Q_1) \wedge (\neg P_{(Q_1 \wedge Q_2)} \vee Q_2)$$
$$\wedge (\neg Q_1 \vee \neg Q_2 \vee P_{(Q_1 \wedge Q_2)})$$

$$\mathsf{En}(R_1) = \top$$
$$\mathsf{En}(R_2) = \top$$
$$\mathsf{En}(R_1 \wedge R_2) = (\neg P_{(R_1 \wedge R_2)} \vee R_1) \wedge (\neg P_{(R_1 \wedge R_2)} \vee R_2)$$
$$\wedge (\neg R_1 \vee \neg R_2 \vee P_{(R_1 \wedge R_2)})$$

$$\mathsf{En}(F) = (\neg P_{(F)} \vee P_{(Q_1 \wedge Q_2)} \vee P_{(R_1 \wedge R_2)})$$
$$\wedge (\neg P_{(Q_1 \wedge Q_2)} \vee P_{(F)})$$
$$\wedge (\neg P_{(R_1 \wedge R_2)} \vee P_{(F)})$$

Then

$$F' : P_{(F)} \wedge \bigwedge_{G \in S_F} \mathsf{En}(G)$$

is equisatisfiable to F and is in CNF.   ∎

1.7.4 The Resolution Procedure

The next decision procedure that we consider is based on **resolution** and applies only to PL formulae in CNF. Therefore, the procedure of Section 1.7.3 must first be applied to the given PL formula if it is not already in CNF.

Resolution follows from the following observation of any PL formula F in CNF: to satisfy clauses $C_1[P]$ and $C_2[\neg P]$ that share variable P but disagree on its value, either the rest of C_1 or the rest of C_2 must be satisfied. Why? If P is true, then a literal other than $\neg P$ in C_2 must be satisfied; while if P is false, then a literal other than P in C_1 must be satisfied. Therefore, the clause $C_1[\bot] \vee C_2[\bot]$, simplified according to the template equivalences of Exercise 1.2, can be added as a conjunction to F to produce an equivalent formula still in CNF.

Clausal resolution is stated as the following proof rule:

$$\frac{C_1[P] \qquad C_2[\neg P]}{C_1[\bot] \vee C_2[\bot]}$$

From the two clauses of the premise, deduce the new clause, called the **resolvent**.

If ever $\bot$ is deduced via resolution, F must be unsatisfiable since $F \wedge \bot$ is unsatisfiable. Otherwise, if every possible resolution produces a clause that is already known, then F must be satisfiable.

Example 1.26. The CNF of $(P \rightarrow Q) \wedge P \wedge \neg Q$ is the following:

$$F : (\neg P \vee Q) \wedge P \wedge \neg Q .$$

From resolution

$$\frac{(\neg P \vee Q) \qquad P}{Q} ,$$

construct

$$F_1 : (\neg P \vee Q) \wedge P \wedge \neg Q \wedge Q .$$

From resolution

$$\frac{\neg Q \qquad Q}{\bot} \, ,$$

deduce that F, and thus the original formula, is unsatisfiable. ■

Example 1.27. Consider the formula

$$F : (\neg P \vee Q) \wedge \neg Q .$$

The one possible resolution

$$\frac{(\neg P \vee Q) \qquad \neg Q}{\neg P}$$

yields

$$F_1 : (\neg P \vee Q) \wedge \neg Q \wedge \neg P .$$

Since no further resolutions are possible, F is satisfiable. Indeed,

$$I : \{P \mapsto \mathsf{false}, \ Q \mapsto \mathsf{false}\}$$

is a satisfying interpretation. A CNF formula that does not contain the clause $\bot$ and to which no more resolutions can be applied represents all possible satisfying interpretations. ■

1.7.5 DPLL

Modern satisfiability procedures for propositional logic are based on the Davis-Putnam-Logemann-Loveland algorithm (**DPLL**), which combines the space-efficient procedure of Section 1.7.2 with a restricted form of resolution. We review in this section the basic algorithm. Much research in the past decade has advanced the state-of-the-art considerably.

Like the resolution procedure, DPLL operates on PL formulae in CNF. But again, as the procedure decides satisfiability, we can apply the conversion procedure of Section 1.7.3 to produce a small equisatisfiable CNF formula.

As in the procedure SAT, DPLL attempts to construct an interpretation of F; failing to do so, it reports that the given formula is unsatisfiable. Rather than relying solely on enumerating possibilities, however, DPLL applies a restricted form of resolution to gain some deductive power. The process of applying this restricted resolution as much as possible is called **Boolean constraint propagation (BCP)**.

BCP is based on **unit resolution**. Unit resolution operates on two clauses. One clause, called the **unit clause**, consists of a single literal ℓ ($\ell = P$ or $\ell = \neg P$ for some propositional variable P). The second clause contains the negation of ℓ: $C[\neg\ell]$. Then unit resolution is the deduction

$$\frac{\ell \qquad C[\neg\ell]}{C[\bot]} \ .$$

Unlike with full resolution, the literals of the resolvent are a subset of the literals of the second clause. Hence, the resolvent replaces the second clause.

Example 1.28. In the formula

$$F : \ (P) \ \wedge \ (\neg P \vee Q) \ \wedge \ (R \vee \neg Q \vee S) \ ,$$

(P) is a unit clause. Therefore, applying unit resolution

$$\frac{P \qquad (\neg P \vee Q)}{Q}$$

produces

$$F' : \ (Q) \ \wedge \ (R \vee \neg Q \vee S) \ .$$

Applying unit resolution again

$$\frac{Q \qquad R \vee \neg Q \vee S}{R \vee S}$$

produces

$$F'' : \ (R \vee S) \ ,$$

ending this round of BCP.   ■

The implementation of DPLL is structurally similar to SAT, except that it begins by applying BCP:

```
let rec DPLL F =
    let F' = BCP F in
    if F' = ⊤ then true
    else if F' = ⊥ then false
    else
        let P = CHOOSE vars(F') in
        (DPLL F'{P ↦ ⊤}) ∨ (DPLL F'{P ↦ ⊥})
```

As in SAT, intermediate formulae are simplified according to the template equivalences of Exercise 1.2.

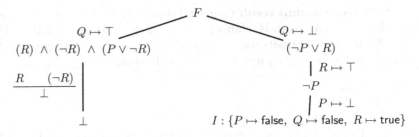

Fig. 1.3. Visualization of Example 1.30

One easy optimization is the following: if variable P appears only positively or only negatively in F, it should not be chosen by CHOOSE vars(F'). P appears only positively when every P-literal is just P; P appears only negatively when every P-literal is $\neg P$. In both cases, F is equisatisfiable to the formula F' constructed by removing all clauses containing an instance of P. Therefore, these clauses do not contribute to BCP. When only such variables remain, the formula must be satisfiable: a full interpretation can be constructed by setting each variable's value based on whether it appears only positively (true) or only negatively (false).

The values to which propositional variables are set on the path to a solution can be recorded so that DPLL can return a satisfying interpretation if one exists, rather than just true.

Example 1.29. Consider the formula

$$F : (P) \wedge (\neg P \vee Q) \wedge (R \vee \neg Q \vee S) .$$

On the first level of recursion, DPLL recognizes the unit clause (P) and applies the BCP steps from Example 1.28, resulting in the formula

$$F'' : R \vee S .$$

The unit resolutions correspond to the partial interpretation

$$\{P \mapsto \text{true}, \ Q \mapsto \text{true}\} .$$

Only positively occurring variables remain, so F is satisfiable. In particular,

$$\{P \mapsto \text{true}, \ Q \mapsto \text{true}, \ R \mapsto \text{true}, \ S \mapsto \text{true}\}$$

is a satisfying interpretation of F.

Branching was not required in this example.   ∎

Example 1.30. Consider the formula

$$F : (\neg P \vee Q \vee R) \wedge (\neg Q \vee R) \wedge (\neg Q \vee \neg R) \wedge (P \vee \neg Q \vee \neg R) .$$

On the first level of recursion, DPLL must branch. Branching on Q or R will result in unit clauses; choose Q.

Then

$$F\{Q \mapsto \top\}:\ (R) \wedge (\neg R) \wedge (P \vee \neg R)\ .$$

The unit resolution

$$\frac{R \qquad (\neg R)}{\bot}$$

finishes this branch.

On the other branch,

$$F\{Q \mapsto \bot\}:\ (\neg P \vee R)\ .$$

P appears only negatively, and R appears only positively, so the formula is satisfiable. In particular, F is satisfied by interpretation

$$I:\ \{P \mapsto \mathsf{false},\ Q \mapsto \mathsf{false},\ R \mapsto \mathsf{true}\}\ .$$

This run of DPLL is visualized in Figure 1.3.   ∎

1.8 Summary

This chapter introduces propositional logic (PL). It covers:

- Its *syntax*. How one constructs a PL formula. Propositional variables, atoms, literals, logical connectives.
- Its *semantics*. What a PL formula means. Truth values true and false. Interpretations. Truth-table definition, inductive definition.
- *Satisfiability* and *validity*. Whether a PL formula evaluates to true under any or all interpretations. Duality of satisfiability and validity, truth-table method, semantic argument method.
- *Equivalence* and *implication*. Whether two formulae always evaluate to the same truth value under every interpretation. Whether under any interpretation, if one formula evaluates to true, the other also evaluates to true. Reduction to validity.
- *Substitution*, which is a tool for manipulating formulae and making general claims. Substitution of equivalent formulae. Valid templates.
- *Normal forms*. A normal form is a set of syntactically restricted formulae such that every PL formula is equivalent to some member of the set.
- *Decision procedures for satisfiability*. Truth-table method, SAT, resolution procedure, DPLL. Transformation to equisatisfiable CNF formula.

PL is an important logic with applications in software and hardware design and analysis, knowledge representation, combinatorial optimization, and complexity theory, to name a few. Although relatively simple, the Boolean structure that is central to PL is often a main source of complexity in applications of the algorithmic reasoning that is the focus of Part II. Exercise 8.1 explores this point in more depth.

Besides being an important logic in its own right, PL serves to introduce the main concepts that are important throughout the book, in particular syntax, semantics, and satisfiability and validity. Chapter 2 presents first-order logic by building on the concepts of this chapter.

Bibliographic Remarks

For a complete and concise presentation of propositional logic, see Smullyan's text *First-Order Logic* [87]. The semantic argument method is similar to Smullyan's tableau method.

The DPLL algorithm is based on work by Davis and Putnam, presented in [26], and by Davis, Logemann, and Loveland, presented in [25].

Exercises

1.1 (PL validity & satisfiability). For each of the following PL formulae, identify whether it is valid or not. If it is valid, prove it with a truth table or semantic argument; otherwise, identify a falsifying interpretation. Recall our conventions for operator precedence and associativity from Section 1.1.

(a) $P \wedge Q \ \rightarrow \ P \ \rightarrow \ Q$
(b) $(P \ \rightarrow \ Q) \vee P \wedge \neg Q$
(c) $(P \ \rightarrow \ Q \ \rightarrow \ R) \ \rightarrow \ P \ \rightarrow \ R$
(d) $(P \ \rightarrow \ Q \vee R) \ \rightarrow \ P \ \rightarrow \ R$
(e) $\neg(P \wedge Q) \ \rightarrow \ R \ \rightarrow \ \neg R \ \rightarrow \ Q$
(f) $P \wedge Q \vee \neg P \vee (\neg Q \ \rightarrow \ \neg P)$
(g) $(P \ \rightarrow \ Q \ \rightarrow \ R) \ \rightarrow \ \neg R \ \rightarrow \ \neg Q \ \rightarrow \ \neg P$
(h) $(\neg R \ \rightarrow \ \neg Q \ \rightarrow \ \neg P) \ \rightarrow \ P \ \rightarrow \ Q \ \rightarrow \ R$

1.2 (Template equivalences). Use the truth table or semantic argument method to prove the following template equivalences.

(a) $\top \ \Leftrightarrow \ \neg\bot$
(b) $\bot \ \Leftrightarrow \ \neg\top$
(c) $\neg\neg F \ \Leftrightarrow \ F$
(d) $F \wedge \top \ \Leftrightarrow \ F$
(e) $F \wedge \bot \ \Leftrightarrow \ \bot$
(f) $F \wedge F \ \Leftrightarrow \ F$

(g) $F \vee \top \Leftrightarrow \top$
(h) $F \vee \bot \Leftrightarrow F$
(i) $F \vee F \Leftrightarrow F$
(j) $F \rightarrow \top \Leftrightarrow \top$
(k) $F \rightarrow \bot \Leftrightarrow \neg F$
(l) $\top \rightarrow F \Leftrightarrow F$
(m) $\bot \rightarrow F \Leftrightarrow \top$
(n) $\top \leftrightarrow F \Leftrightarrow F$
(o) $\bot \leftrightarrow F \Leftrightarrow \neg F$
(p) $\neg(F_1 \wedge F_2) \Leftrightarrow \neg F_1 \vee \neg F_2$
(q) $\neg(F_1 \vee F_2) \Leftrightarrow \neg F_1 \wedge \neg F_2$
(r) $F_1 \rightarrow F_2 \Leftrightarrow \neg F_1 \vee F_2$
(s) $F_1 \rightarrow F_2 \Leftrightarrow \neg F_2 \rightarrow \neg F_1$
(t) $\neg(F_1 \rightarrow F_2) \Leftrightarrow F_1 \wedge \neg F_2$
(u) $(F_1 \vee F_2) \wedge F_3 \Leftrightarrow (F_1 \wedge F_3) \vee (F_2 \wedge F_3)$
(v) $(F_1 \wedge F_2) \vee F_3 \Leftrightarrow (F_1 \vee F_3) \wedge (F_2 \vee F_3)$
(w) $(F_1 \rightarrow F_3) \wedge (F_2 \rightarrow F_3) \Leftrightarrow F_1 \vee F_2 \rightarrow F_3$
(x) $(F_1 \rightarrow F_2) \wedge (F_1 \rightarrow F_3) \Leftrightarrow F_1 \rightarrow F_2 \wedge F_3$
(y) $F_1 \rightarrow F_2 \rightarrow F_3 \Leftrightarrow F_1 \wedge F_2 \rightarrow F_3$
(z) $(F_1 \leftrightarrow F_2) \wedge (F_2 \leftrightarrow F_3) \Rightarrow (F_1 \leftrightarrow F_3)$

1.3 (Redundant logical connectives). Given $\top$, $\wedge$, and $\neg$, prove that $\bot$, $\vee$, $\rightarrow$, and $\leftrightarrow$ are redundant logical connectives. That is, show that each of $\bot$, $F_1 \vee F_2$, $F_1 \rightarrow F_2$, and $F_1 \leftrightarrow F_2$ is equivalent to a formula that uses only F_1, F_2, $\top$, $\vee$, and $\neg$.

1.4 (The nand connective). Let the logical connective $\overline{\wedge}$ (pronounced "nand") be defined according to the following truth table:

F_1	F_2	$F_1 \overline{\wedge} F_2$
0	0	1
0	1	1
1	0	1
1	1	0

Show that all standard logical connectives can be defined in terms of $\overline{\wedge}$.

1.5 (Normal forms). Convert the following PL formulae to NNF, DNF, and CNF via the transformations of Section 1.6.

(a) $\neg(P \rightarrow Q)$
(b) $\neg(\neg(P \wedge Q) \rightarrow \neg R)$
(c) $(Q \wedge R \rightarrow (P \vee \neg Q)) \wedge (P \vee R)$
(d) $\neg(Q \rightarrow R) \wedge P \wedge (Q \vee \neg(P \wedge R))$

1.6 (Graph coloring). A solution to a **graph coloring** problem is an assignment of colors to vertices such that no two adjacent vertices have the same color. Formally, a finite graph $G = \langle V, E \rangle$ consists of vertices $V = \{v_1, \ldots, v_n\}$ and edges $E = \{\langle v_{i_1}, w_{i_1} \rangle, \ldots, \langle v_{i_k}, w_{i_k} \rangle\}$. The finite set of colors is given by $C = \{c_1, \ldots, c_m\}$. A problem instance is given by a graph and a set of colors: the problem is to assign each vertex $v \in V$ a color$(v) \in C$ such that for every edge $\langle v, w \rangle \in E$, color$(v) \neq$ color(w). Clearly, not all instances have solutions.

Show how to encode an instance of a graph coloring problem into a PL formula F. F should be satisfiable iff a graph coloring exists.

(a) Describe a set of constraints in PL asserting that every vertex is colored. Since the sets of vertices, edges, and colors are all finite, use notation such as "color$(v) = c$" to indicate that vertex v has color c. Realize that such an assertion is encodeable as a single propositional variable P_v^c.

(b) Describe a set of constraints in PL asserting that every vertex has at most one color.

(c) Describe a set of constraints in PL asserting that no two connected vertices have the same color.

(d) Identify a significant optimization in this encoding. *Hint*: Can any constraints be dropped? Why?

(e) If the constraints are not already in CNF, specify them in CNF now. For N vertices, K edges, and M colors, how many variables does the optimized encoding require? How many clauses?

1.7 (CNF). Example 1.25 constructs a CNF formula that is equisatisfiable to a given small formula in DNF.

(a) If distribution of disjunction over conjunction (described in Section 1.6) were used, how many clauses would the resulting formula have?

(b) Consider the formulae

$$F_n : \bigvee_{i=1}^{n} (Q_i \wedge R_i)$$

for positive integers n. As a function of n, how many clauses are in

(i) the formula F' constructed based on distribution of disjunction over conjunction?

(ii) the formula

$$F' : \text{Rep}(F_n) \wedge \bigwedge_{G \in S_{F_n}} \text{En}(G) ?$$

(iii) For which n is the distribution approach better?

1.8 (DPLL). Describe the execution of DPLL on the following formulae.

(a) $(P \vee \neg Q \vee \neg R) \wedge (Q \vee \neg P \vee R) \wedge (R \vee \neg Q)$

(b) $(P \vee Q \vee R) \wedge (\neg P \vee \neg Q \vee \neg R) \wedge (\neg P \vee Q \vee R) \wedge (\neg Q \vee R) \wedge (Q \vee \neg R)$

First-Order Logic

One task we logicians are interested in is that of analyzing the notion of "proof" — to make it as rigorous as any other notion in mathematics.

— Raymond Smullyan
The Lady or the Tiger?, 1982

This chapter extends the machinery of propositional logic to **first-order logic (FOL)**, also called both **predicate logic** and the first-order **predicate calculus**. While first-order logic enjoys a degree of expressiveness that makes it suitable for reasoning about computation, it does not admit completely automated reasoning.

FOL extends PL with predicates, functions, and quantifiers. As in our discussion of PL, we first introduce the syntax of FOL and its semantics. We then build on the semantic argument method of PL to provide a method of proving first-order validity.

Section 2.6 reviews *decidability* and *complexity*. A decidable problem has an algorithm, which is a procedure that always finishes with a correct answer on every instance of the problem. While validity of PL formulae is decidable, validity of FOL formulae is not. Complexity is the study of the intrinsic hardness of a decidable problem.

The optional Section 2.7 proves the soundness and completeness of the semantic argument method. It also presents two classic theorems that are applied in Chapter 10.

2.1 Syntax

All formulae of PL evaluate to true or false. FOL is not so simple. In FOL, **terms** evaluate to values other than truth values such as integers, people, or cards of a deck. However, we are getting ahead of ourselves: just as in PL,

the syntax of FOL is independent of its meaning. The most basic terms are
variables x, y, z, x_1, x_2, ... and **constants** a, b, c, a_1, a_2, ...

More complicated terms are constructed using **functions**. An n-ary function f takes n terms as arguments. Notationally, we represent generic FOL
functions by symbols f, g, h, f_1, f_2, ... A constant can also be viewed as a
0-ary function.

Example 2.1. The following are all terms:

- a, a constant (or 0-ary function);
- x, a variable;
- $f(a)$, a unary function f applied to a constant;
- $g(x, b)$, a binary function g applied to a variable x and a constant b;
- $f(g(x, f(b)))$.

∎

The propositional variables of PL are generalized to **predicates**, denoted
p, q, r, p_1, p_2, ... An n-ary predicate takes n terms as arguments. A **FOL
propositional variable** is a 0-ary predicate, which we write P, Q, R, P_1,
P_2, ...

Countably infinitely many constant, function, and predicate symbols are
available.

An **atom** is $\top$, $\bot$, or an n-ary predicate applied to n terms. A **literal** is
an atom or its negation.

Example 2.2. The following are all literals:

- P, a propositional variable (or 0-ary predicate);
- $p(f(x), g(x, f(x)))$, a binary predicate applied to two terms;
- $\neg p(f(x), g(x, f(x)))$.

The first two literals are also atoms.

∎

A **FOL formula** is a literal, the application of a logical connective $\neg$, $\wedge$,
$\vee$, $\rightarrow$, or $\leftrightarrow$ to a formula or formulae, or the application of a **quantifier** to a
formula. There are two FOL quantifiers:

- the **existential quantifier** $\exists x.\ F[x]$, read "there exists an x such that
  $F[x]$";
- and the **universal quantifier** $\forall x.\ F[x]$, read "for all x, $F[x]$".

In $\forall x.\ F[x]$, x is the **quantified variable**, and $F[x]$ is the **scope** of the
quantifier $\forall x$. For convenience, we sometimes refer informally to the scope
of the quantifier $\forall x$ as the scope of the quantified variable x itself. The case
is similar for $\exists x.\ F[x]$. Also, x in $F[x]$ is **bound** (by the quantifier). By
convention, the period in ". $F[x]$" indicates that the scope of the quantified
variable x extends as far as possible. We often abbreviate $\forall x.\ \forall y.\ F[x, y]$ by
$\forall x, y.\ F[x, y]$.

Example 2.3. In

$$\forall x.\ p(f(x), x)\ \to\ (\exists y.\ \underbrace{p(f(g(x,y)), g(x,y)))}_{G} \land\ q(x, f(x)))\ ,$$

$$\underbrace{}_{F}$$

the scope of x is F, and the scope of y is G. This formula is read: "for all x, if $p(f(x), x)$ then there exists a y such that $p(f(g(x,y)), g(x,y))$ and $q(x, f(x))$".   ∎

A variable is **free** in formula $F[x]$ if there is an occurrence of x that is not bound by any quantifier. Denote by free(F) the set of free variables of a formula F. A variable is **bound** in formula $F[x]$ if there is an occurrence of x in the scope of a binding quantifier $\forall x$ or $\exists x$. Denote by bound(F) the set of bound variables of a formula F. In general, it is possible that free(F) $\cap$ bound(F) $\neq \emptyset$, as a variable x can have both free and bound occurrences.

A formula F is **closed** if it does not contain any free variables.

Example 2.4. In

$$F:\ \forall x.\ p(f(x), y)\ \to\ \forall y.\ p(f(x), y)\ ,$$

x only occurs bound, while y appears both free (in the antecedent) and bound (in the consequent). Thus, free(F) $= \{y\}$ and bound(F) $= \{x, y\}$.   ∎

If free(F) $= \{x_1, \ldots, x_n\}$, then its **universal closure** is

$$\forall x_1.\ \ldots \forall x_n.\ F\ ,$$

and its **existential closure** is

$$\exists x_1.\ \ldots \exists x_n.\ F\ .$$

We usually write the universal and existential closures as $\forall *.\ F$ and $\exists *.\ F$, respectively.

The **subformulae** of a FOL formula are defined according to an extension of the PL definition of subformula:

- the only subformula of $p(t_1, \ldots, t_n)$, where the t_i are terms, is $p(t_1, \ldots, t_n)$;
- the subformulae of $\neg F$ are $\neg F$ and the subformulae of F;
- the subformulae of $F_1 \land F_2$, $F_1 \lor F_2$, $F_1 \to F_2$, $F_1 \leftrightarrow F_2$ are the formula itself and the subformulae of F_1 and F_2;
- and the subformulae of $\exists x.\ F$ and $\forall x.\ F$ are the formula itself and the subformulae of F.

The **strict subformulae** of a formula excludes the formula itself.

The **subterms** of a FOL term are defined as follows:

- the only subterm of constant a or variable x is a or x itself, respectively;

- and the subterms of $f(t_1, \ldots, t_n)$ are the term itself and the subterms of $t_1, \ldots, t_n$.

The **strict subterms** of a term excludes the term itself.

Example 2.5. In

$$F : \ \forall x. \ p(f(x), y) \ \rightarrow \ \forall y. \ p(f(x), y) \ ,$$

the subformulae of F are

$$F \ , \ p(f(x), y) \ \rightarrow \ \forall y. \ p(f(x), y) \ , \ \forall y. \ p(f(x), y) \ , \ p(f(x), y) \ .$$

The subterms of $g(f(x), f(h(f(x))))$ are

$$g(f(x), f(h(f(x)))) \ , \ f(x) \ , \ f(h(f(x))) \ , \ h(f(x)) \ , \ x \ .$$

$f(x)$ occurs twice in $g(f(x), f(h(f(x))))$. ∎

Example 2.6. Before discussing the formal semantics for FOL, we suggest translations of English sentences into FOL. The names of the constants, functions, and predicates are chosen to provide some intuition for the meaning of the FOL formulae.

- Every dog has its day.

$$\forall x. \ dog(x) \ \rightarrow \ \exists y. \ day(y) \ \land \ itsDay(x, y)$$

- Some dogs have more days than others.

$$\exists x, y. \ dog(x) \ \land \ dog(y) \ \land \ \#days(x) > \#days(y)$$

- All cats have more days than dogs.

$$\forall x, y. \ dog(x) \ \land \ cat(y) \ \rightarrow \ \#days(y) > \#days(x)$$

- Fido is a dog. Furrball is a cat. Fido has fewer days than does Furrball.

$$dog(Fido) \ \land \ cat(Furrball) \ \land \ \#days(Fido) < \#days(Furrball)$$

- The length of one side of a triangle is less than the sum of the lengths of the other two sides.

$$\forall x, y, z. \ triangle(x, y, z) \ \rightarrow \ length(x) < length(y) + length(z)$$

- Fermat's Last Theorem.

$$\forall n. \ integer(n) \ \land \ n > 2$$
$$\rightarrow \ \forall x, y, z.$$
$$integer(x) \ \land \ integer(y) \ \land \ integer(z) \ \land \ x > 0 \ \land \ y > 0 \ \land \ z > 0$$
$$\rightarrow \ x^n + y^n \neq z^n$$

∎

2.2 Semantics

Having defined the syntax of FOL, we now define its **semantics**. Formulae of FOL evaluate to the truth values true and false as in PL. However, terms of FOL formulae evaluate to values from a specified domain. We extend the concept of interpretations to this more complex setting and then define the semantics of FOL in terms of interpretations.

First, we define a FOL **interpretation** I. The **domain** D_I of an interpretation I is a nonempty set of values or objects, such as integers, real numbers, dogs, people, or merely abstract objects. $|D_I|$ denotes the **cardinality**, or size, of D_I. Domains can be finite, such as the 52 cards of a deck of cards; countably infinite, such as the integers; or uncountably infinite, such as the reals. But all domains are nonempty.

The **assignment** α_I of interpretation I maps constant, function, and predicate symbols to elements, functions, and predicates over D_I. It also maps variables to elements of D_I:

- each variable symbol x is assigned a value x_I from D_I;
- each n-ary function symbol f is assigned an n-ary function

$$f_I : D_I^n \to D_I$$

  that maps n elements of D_I to an element of D_I;
- each n-ary predicate symbol p is assigned an n-ary predicate

$$p_I : D_I^n \to \{\text{true, false}\}$$

  that maps n elements of D_I to a truth value.

In particular, each constant (0-ary function symbol) is assigned a value from D_I, and each propositional variable (0-ary predicate symbol) is assigned a truth value.

An interpretation $I : (D_I, \alpha_I)$ is thus a pair consisting of a domain and an assignment.

Example 2.7. The formula

$$F : \ x + y > z \ \to \ y > z - x$$

contains the binary function symbols $+$ and $-$, the binary predicate symbol $>$, and the variables x, y, and z. Again, $+$, $-$, and $>$ are just symbols: we choose these names to provide intuition for the intended meaning of the formulae. We could just as easily have written

$$F' : \ p(f(x, y), z) \ \to \ p(y, g(z, x)) \ .$$

We construct a "standard" interpretation. The domain is the integers, $\mathbb{Z}$:

$$D_I = \mathbb{Z} = \{\ldots, -2, -1, 0, 1, 2, \ldots\} \ .$$

To $+$ and $-$ we assign standard addition $+_\mathbb{Z}$ and subtraction $-_\mathbb{Z}$ of integers, respectively. To $>$ we assign the standard greater-than relation $>_\mathbb{Z}$ of integers. Finally, to x, y, and z, we assign the values 13, 42, and 1, respectively. We ignore the countably infinitely many other constant, function, and predicate symbols that do not appear in F. We thus have interpretation $I : (\mathbb{Z}, \alpha_I)$, where

$$\alpha_I : \{+ \mapsto +_\mathbb{Z}, \ - \mapsto -_\mathbb{Z}, \ > \mapsto >_\mathbb{Z}, \ x \mapsto 13, \ y \mapsto 42, \ z \mapsto 1, \ \ldots\} \ .$$

The elision reminds us that, as always, α_I provides values for the countably infinitely many other constant, function, and predicate symbols. Usually, we do not write the elision.   ∎

Given a FOL formula F and interpretation $I : (D_I, \alpha_I)$, we want to compute if F evaluates to true under interpretation I, $I \models F$, or if F evaluates to false under interpretation I, $I \not\models F$. We define the semantics inductively as in PL. To start, define the meaning of truth symbols:

$$I \models \top$$
$$I \not\models \bot$$

Next, consider more complicated atoms. α_I gives meaning $\alpha_I[x]$, $\alpha_I[c]$, and $\alpha_I[f]$ to variables x, constants c, and functions f. Evaluate arbitrary terms recursively:

$$\alpha_I[f(t_1, \ldots, t_n)] \ = \ \alpha_I[f](\alpha_I[t_1], \ldots, \alpha_I[t_n]) \ ,$$

for terms $t_1, \ldots, t_n$. That is, define the value of $f(t_1, \ldots, t_n)$ under α_I by evaluating the function $\alpha_I[f]$ over the terms $\alpha_I[t_1]$, $\ldots$, $\alpha_I[t_n]$. Similarly, evaluate arbitrary atoms recursively:

$$\alpha_I[p(t_1, \ldots, t_n)] \ = \ \alpha_I[p](\alpha_I[t_1], \ldots, \alpha_I[t_n]) \ .$$

Then

$$I \models p(t_1, \ldots, t_n) \qquad \text{iff } \alpha_I[p(t_1, \ldots, t_n)] = \text{true}$$

Having completed the base cases of our inductive definition, we turn to the inductive step. Assume that formulae F_1 and F_2 have fixed truth values. From these formulae, evaluate the semantics of more complex formulae. The logical connectives are handled in FOL in precisely the same way as in PL:

$$
\begin{aligned}
&I \models \neg F && \text{iff } I \not\models F \\
&I \models F_1 \wedge F_2 && \text{iff } I \models F_1 \text{ and } I \models F_2 \\
&I \models F_1 \vee F_2 && \text{iff } I \models F_1 \text{ or } I \models F_2 \\
&I \models F_1 \rightarrow F_2 && \text{iff, if } I \models F_1 \text{ then } I \models F_2 \\
&I \models F_1 \leftrightarrow F_2 && \text{iff } I \models F_1 \text{ and } I \models F_2, \text{ or } I \not\models F_1 \text{ and } I \not\models F_2
\end{aligned}
$$

Example 2.8. Recall the formula

$$F: \ x + y > z \ \rightarrow \ y > z - x$$

of Example 2.7 and the interpretation $I : (\mathbb{Z}, \alpha_I)$, where

$$\alpha_I : \ \{+ \mapsto +_{\mathbb{Z}}, \ - \mapsto -_{\mathbb{Z}}, \ > \mapsto >_{\mathbb{Z}}, \ x \mapsto 13_{\mathbb{Z}}, \ y \mapsto 42_{\mathbb{Z}}, \ z \mapsto 1_{\mathbb{Z}}\} .$$

Compute the truth value of F under I as follows:

1. $I \models x + y > z$ since $\alpha_I[x + y > z] = 13_{\mathbb{Z}} +_{\mathbb{Z}} 42 >_{\mathbb{Z}} 1_{\mathbb{Z}}$
2. $I \models y > z - x$ since $\alpha_I[y > z - x] = 42_{\mathbb{Z}} >_{\mathbb{Z}} 1_{\mathbb{Z}} -_{\mathbb{Z}} 13_{\mathbb{Z}}$
3. $I \models F$ by 1, 2, and the semantics of $\rightarrow$

■

For the quantifiers, let x be a variable. Define an x-**variant** of an interpretation $I : (D_I, \alpha_I)$ as an interpretation $J : (D_J, \alpha_J)$ such that

- $D_I = D_J$;
- and $\alpha_I[y] = \alpha_J[y]$ for all constant, free variable, function, and predicate symbols y, except possibly x.

That is, I and J agree on everything except possibly the value of variable x. Denote by $J : \ I \triangleleft \{x \mapsto v\}$ the x-variant of I in which $\alpha_J[x] = v$ for some $v \in D_I$. Then

$$I \models \forall x. \ F \quad \text{iff for all } v \in D_I, \ I \triangleleft \{x \mapsto v\} \models F$$
$$I \models \exists x. \ F \quad \text{iff there exists } v \in D_I \text{ such that } I \triangleleft \{x \mapsto v\} \models F$$

In words, I is an interpretation of $\forall x. \ F$ iff all x-variants of I are interpretations of F. I is an interpretation of $\exists x. \ F$ iff some x-variant of I is an interpretation of F.

Example 2.9. Consider the formula

$$F: \ \exists x. \ f(x) = g(x)$$

and the interpretation $I : (D : \{\circ, \bullet\}, \ \alpha_I)$ in which

$$\alpha_I : \ \{f(\circ) \mapsto \circ, \ f(\bullet) \mapsto \bullet, \ g(\circ) \mapsto \bullet, \ g(\bullet) \mapsto \circ\} .$$

Compute the truth value of F under I as follows:

1. $I \triangleleft \{x \mapsto v\} \not\models f(x) = g(x)$ for $v \in D$
2. $\qquad\qquad I \not\models \exists x. \ f(x) = g(x)$ since $v \in D$ is arbitrary

In the first line, basic reasoning about the interpretation I reveals that f and g always disagree. The second line follows from the first by the semantics of existential quantification. ■

2.3 Satisfiability and Validity

A formula F is said to be **satisfiable** iff there exists an interpretation I such that $I \models F$. A formula F is said to be **valid** iff for all interpretations I, $I \models F$. Determining satisfiability and validity of formulae are important tasks in FOL. Recall that satisfiability and validity are dual: F is valid iff $\neg F$ is unsatisfiable.

Technically, satisfiability and validity only apply to closed FOL formulae, which do not have free variables. However, let us agree on a convention: if we say that a formula F such that $\mathsf{free}(F) \neq \emptyset$ is valid, we mean that its universal closure $\forall *. F$ is valid; and if we say that it is satisfiable, we mean that its existential closure $\exists *. F$ is satisfiable. Duality still holds: a formula F with free variables is valid ($\forall *. F$ is valid) iff its negation is unsatisfiable ($\exists *. \neg F$ is unsatisfiable). Henceforth, we freely discuss the validity and satisfiability of formulae with free variables.

For arguing the validity of FOL formulae, we extend the semantic argument method from PL to FOL. Most of the concepts carry over to the FOL case without change. In addition to the rules for the logical connectives of PL (see Section 1.3), we have the following rules for the quantifiers.

- According to the semantics of universal quantification, from $I \models \forall x.\ F$, deduce $I \triangleleft \{x \mapsto \mathsf{v}\} \models F$ for any $\mathsf{v} \in D_I$.

$$\frac{I \models \forall x.\ F}{I \triangleleft \{x \mapsto \mathsf{v}\} \models F} \qquad \text{for any } \mathsf{v} \in D_I$$

  In practice, we usually apply this rule using a domain element v that was introduced earlier in the proof.

- Similarly, from the semantics of existential quantification, from $I \not\models \exists x.\ F$, deduce $I \triangleleft \{x \mapsto \mathsf{v}\} \not\models F$ for any $\mathsf{v} \in D_I$.

$$\frac{I \not\models \exists x.\ F}{I \triangleleft \{x \mapsto \mathsf{v}\} \not\models F} \qquad \text{for any } \mathsf{v} \in D_I$$

  Again, we usually apply this rule using a domain element v that was introduced earlier in the proof.

- According to the semantics of existential quantification, from $I \models \exists x.\ F$, deduce $I \triangleleft \{x \mapsto \mathsf{v}\} \models F$ for some $\mathsf{v} \in D_I$ that has *not* been previously used in the proof.

$$\frac{I \models \exists x.\ F}{I \triangleleft \{x \mapsto \mathsf{v}\} \models F} \qquad \text{for a } \textit{fresh } \mathsf{v} \in D_I$$

- Similarly, from the semantics of universal quantification, from $I \not\models \forall x.\ F$, deduce $I \triangleleft \{x \mapsto \mathsf{v}\} \not\models F$ for some $\mathsf{v} \in D_I$ that has *not* been previously used in the proof.

$$\frac{I \not\models \forall x.\ F}{I \triangleleft \{x \mapsto \mathsf{v}\} \not\models F} \qquad \text{for a } \textit{fresh } \mathsf{v} \in D_I$$

The restriction in the latter two rules corresponds to our intuition: if all we know is that $\exists x.\ F$, then we certainly do not know which value in particular satisfies F. Hence, we choose a new value v that does not appear previously in the proof: it was never introduced before by a quantification rule. Moreover, α_I does not already assign it to some constant, $\alpha_I[a]$, or to some function application, $\alpha_I[f(t_1, \ldots, t_n)]$.

Notice the similarity between the first two and between the final two rules. The first two rules handle a case that is universal in character. Consider the second rule: if there does not exist an x such that F, then for all values, F does not hold. The final two rules are existential in character.

Lastly, the contradiction rule is modified for the FOL case.

- A contradiction exists if two variants of the original interpretation I disagree on the truth value of an n-ary predicate p for a given tuple of domain values.

$$\frac{J : I \lhd \cdots \models p(s_1, \ldots, s_n) \qquad K : I \lhd \cdots \not\models p(t_1, \ldots, t_n)}{I \models \bot} \quad \text{for } i \in \{1, \ldots, n\},\ \alpha_J[s_i] = \alpha_K[t_i]$$

The intuition behind the contradiction rule is the following. The variants J and K are constructed only through the rules for quantification. Hence, the truth value of p on the given tuple of domain values is already established by I. Therefore, the disagreement between J and K on the truth value of p indicates a problem with I.

None of these rules cause branching, but several of the rules for the logical connectives do. Thus, a proof in general is a tree. A branch is closed if it contains a contradiction according to the (first-order) contradiction rule; it is open otherwise. All branches are closed in a finished proof of a valid formula. We exhibit the proof method through several examples.

Example 2.10. We prove that

$$F : (\forall x.\ p(x)) \rightarrow (\forall y.\ p(y))$$

is valid. Suppose not; then there is an interpretation I such that $I \not\models F$:

1.	$I \not\models F$	assumption
2.	$I \models \forall x.\ p(x)$	1 and semantics of $\rightarrow$
3.	$I \not\models \forall y.\ p(y)$	1 and semantics of $\rightarrow$
4.	$I \lhd \{y \mapsto v\} \not\models p(y)$	3 and semantics of $\forall$, for some $v \in D_I$
5.	$I \lhd \{x \mapsto v\} \models p(x)$	2 and semantics of $\forall$

Lines 2 and 3 state the case in which line 1 holds: the antecedent and consequent of F are respectively true and false under I. Line 4 states that because of 3, there must be a value $v \in D_I$ such that $I \lhd \{y \mapsto v\} \not\models p(y)$. Line 5 uses this same value v and the semantics of $\forall$ with 2 to derive a contradiction: under I, $p(v)$ is false by 4 and true by 5. Thus, F is valid. ∎

For concision we shorten, for example, "semantics of $\forall$" to "$\forall$" in the explanation column of our arguments.

Example 2.11. Consider the following relation between universal and existential quantification:

$$F : (\forall x.\ p(x)) \ \leftrightarrow \ (\neg \exists x.\ \neg p(x)) \ .$$

Is it valid? Suppose not. Then there is an interpretation I such that $I \not\models F$. Consider the forward ($\rightarrow$) and backward ($\leftarrow$) directions of $\leftrightarrow$ as separate cases. In the first case,

1.	$I \models \forall x.\ p(x)$	assumption
2.	$I \not\models \neg \exists x.\ \neg p(x)$	assumption
3.	$I \models \exists x.\ \neg p(x)$	2 and $\neg$
4.	$I \lhd \{x \mapsto \mathsf{v}\} \models \neg p(x)$	3 and $\exists$, for some $\mathsf{v} \in D_I$
5.	$I \lhd \{x \mapsto \mathsf{v}\} \models p(x)$	1 and $\forall$

Lines 4 and 5 are contradictory. In line 5, we use the value introduced in line 4 with the semantics of $\forall$ and line 1. We are allowed to choose this same value v precisely because line 1 states that *for all* x, $p(x)$.

For the second case,

1.	$I \not\models \forall x.\ p(x)$	assumption
2.	$I \models \neg \exists x.\ \neg p(x)$	assumption
3.	$I \lhd \{x \mapsto \mathsf{v}\} \not\models p(x)$	1 and $\forall$, for some $\mathsf{v} \in D_I$
4.	$I \not\models \exists x.\ \neg p(x)$	2 and $\neg$
5.	$I \lhd \{x \mapsto \mathsf{v}\} \not\models \neg p(x)$	4 and $\exists$
6.	$I \lhd \{x \mapsto \mathsf{v}\} \models p(x)$	5 and $\neg$

Lines 3 and 6 are contradictory. Line 4 says that $\exists x.\ \neg p(x)$ is false under I. Thus, by the semantics of $\exists$, no value w from D_I is such that $p(\mathsf{w})$ is true. In particular, line 5 identifies v, introduced in line 3.

As both cases end in contradictions for arbitrary interpretation I, F is valid. ■

It is sometimes useful to reference known values, as the following simple example illustrates.

Example 2.12. To prove that

$$F : p(a) \ \rightarrow \ \exists x.\ p(x)$$

is valid, assume otherwise and derive a contradiction.

1.	$I \not\models F$	assumption
2.	$I \models p(a)$	1 and $\rightarrow$
3.	$I \not\models \exists x.\ p(x)$	1 and $\rightarrow$
4.	$I \lhd \{x \mapsto \alpha_I[a]\} \not\models p(x)$	3 and $\exists$
5.	$I \models \bot$	2, 4

In line 4, we used the value assigned to a to instantiate the quantified variable of line 3, which has universal character. Because lines 2 and 4 are contradictory, F is valid. ∎

To show that a formula F is invalid, it suffices to find an interpretation I such that $I \models \neg F$.

Example 2.13. Consider the formula

$$F : (\forall x.\ p(x,x)) \rightarrow (\exists x.\ \forall y.\ p(x,y)) .$$

To show that it is invalid, we find an interpretation I such that

$$I \models \neg((\forall x.\ p(x,x)) \rightarrow (\exists x.\ \forall y.\ p(x,y))) ,$$

or, according to the semantics of $\rightarrow$,

$$I \models (\forall x.\ p(x,x)) \land \neg(\exists x.\ \forall y.\ p(x,y)) .$$

Choose

$$D_I = \{0,1\}$$

and

$$p_I = \{(0,0),\ (1,1)\} .$$

We use a common notation for defining relations: $p_I(a,b)$ is true iff $(a,b) \in p_I$. Here, $p_I(0,0)$ is true, and $p_I(1,0)$ is false.

Both $\forall x.\ p(x,x)$ and $\neg(\exists x.\ \forall y.\ p(x,y))$ evaluate to true under I, so

$$I \models (\forall x.\ p(x,x)) \land \neg(\exists x.\ \forall y.\ p(x,y)) ,$$

which shows that F is invalid. Interpretation I is a falsifying interpretation of F. ∎

We apply the semantic argument method to more examples in Section 3.1.

Equivalence $(F_1 \Leftrightarrow F_2)$ and implication $(F_1 \Rightarrow F_2)$ extend directly from PL to FOL. Equivalence of and implication between two formulae can be argued using the semantic argument method. See, for example, Example 2.11.

2.4 Substitution

Substitution for FOL is more complex than substitution for PL because of quantification. We introduce two types of substitution in this section with the goal of generalizing Propositions 1.15 and 1.17 to the FOL setting. As in PL, substitution allows us to consider the validity of entire sets of formulae simultaneously.

First, we define the **renaming** of a quantified variable. If variable x is quantified in F so that F has the form $F[\forall x.\ G[x]]$, then the renaming of x to fresh variable x' produces the formula $F[\forall x'.\ G[x']]$. A "fresh variable" is any variable that does not occur in F. By the semantics of universal quantification, the original and final formulae are equivalent. The case is similar for existential quantification. Often, we simply say that a variable is renamed to mean that its bound occurrences are renamed to a fresh variable. Free occurrences of variables are never renamed.

Example 2.14. Renaming the bound variable x to fresh variable x' in

$$F:\ p(x)\ \wedge\ \forall x.\ q(x,y)$$

produces

$$F':\ p(x)\ \wedge\ \forall x'.\ q(x',y)\ .$$

Renaming y does not cause any change because y does not occur bound. ∎

A **substitution** is a map from FOL formulae to FOL formulae:

$$\sigma:\ \{F_1 \mapsto G_1,\ \ldots,\ F_n \mapsto G_n\}\ .$$

As in PL, $\mathsf{domain}(\sigma) = \{F_1,\ldots,F_n\}$ and $\mathsf{range}(\sigma) = \{G_1,\ldots,G_n\}$. To compute the application of σ to F, $F\sigma$, replace each occurrence of F_i in F by G_i simultaneously. When both subformulae F_j and F_k are in the domain of σ and F_k is a strict subformula of F_j, replace occurrences of F_j by G_j.

Example 2.15. Consider formula

$$F:\ (\forall x.\ p(x,y))\ \rightarrow\ q(f(y),x)$$

and substitution

$$\sigma:\ \{x \mapsto g(x),\ y \mapsto f(x),\ q(f(y),x) \mapsto \exists x.\ h(x,y)\}\ .$$

Then

$$F\sigma:\ (\forall x.\ p(g(x),f(x)))\ \rightarrow\ \exists x.\ h(x,y)\ .$$

Notice how there are more bound occurrences of x in $F\sigma$ than in F. ∎

Use care when substitutions include quantifiers in the domain. Substituting for a quantified subformula $\forall x.\ F$ requires that all of $\forall x.\ F$ be replaced.

Example 2.16. Consider formula

$$F:\ \exists y.\ p(x,y)\ \wedge\ p(y,x)$$

and substitution

$$\sigma:\ \{\exists y.\ p(x,y) \mapsto p(x,a)\}\ ,$$

where a is a constant. $F\sigma = F$ because the scope of the quantifier $\exists y$ in F is $p(x,y) \wedge p(y,x)$, not just $p(x,y)$. ∎

2.4.1 Safe Substitution

A restricted application of substitution has a useful semantic property.
Define for a substitution σ its set of free variables:

$$V_\sigma = \bigcup_i (\text{free}(F_i) \cup \text{free}(G_i)) \ .$$

V_σ consists of the free variables of all formulae F_i and G_i of the domain and
range of σ. Compute the **safe substitution** $F\sigma$ of formula F as follows:

1. For each quantified variable x in F such that $x \in V_\sigma$, rename x to a fresh
   variable to produce F'.
2. Compute $F'\sigma$.

Example 2.17. Consider again formula

$$F : (\forall x. \, p(x, y)) \ \rightarrow \ q(f(y), x)$$

and substitution

$$\sigma : \{x \mapsto g(x), \ y \mapsto f(x), \ q(f(y), x) \mapsto \exists x. \, h(x, y)\} \ .$$

To compute the safe substitution $F\sigma$, first compute

$$
\begin{aligned}
V_\sigma &= \text{free}(x) \ \cup \ \text{free}(g(x)) \ \cup \ \text{free}(y) \ \cup \ \text{free}(f(x)) \\
&\quad \cup \ \text{free}(q(f(y), x)) \ \cup \ \text{free}(\exists x. h(x, y)) \\
&= \{x\} \cup \{x\} \cup \{y\} \cup \{x\} \cup \{x, y\} \cup \{y\} \\
&= \{x, y\}
\end{aligned}
$$

Then

1. $x \in V_\sigma$, so rename bound occurrences in F:

   $$F' : (\forall x'. \, p(x', y)) \ \rightarrow \ q(f(y), x) \ .$$

   x also occurs free in F.
2. $F'\sigma : (\forall x'. \, p(x', f(x))) \ \rightarrow \ \exists x. \, h(x, y).$

The first step of computing a safe substitution becomes trivial if each
quantified variable has a unique name.

Example 2.18. Consider formula

$$F : (\forall z. \, p(z, y)) \ \rightarrow \ q(f(y), x) \ ,$$

in which the quantified variable has a different name than any free variable
of F or the substitution

$$\sigma : \{x \mapsto g(x), \ y \mapsto f(y), \ q(f(y), x) \mapsto \exists w. \ h(w, y)\} \ .$$

Compared to Example 2.17, the quantified variable z in F and the quantified variable w of σ have different names than any other variable of F or σ. The safe substitution is the unrestricted substitution

$$F\sigma : \ (\forall z. \ p(z, f(y))) \ \rightarrow \ \exists w. \ h(w, y) \ .$$

■

Proposition 2.19 (Substitution of Equivalent Formulae). *Consider substitution*

$$\sigma : \ \{F_1 \mapsto G_1, \ \ldots, \ F_n \mapsto G_n\}$$

such that for each i, $F_i \Leftrightarrow G_i$. Then $F \Leftrightarrow F\sigma$ when $F\sigma$ is computed as a safe substitution.

The language of Propositions 2.19 and 1.15 are almost identical.

2.4.2 Schema Substitution

Example 2.11 proves an interesting relation between universal and existential quantification $(\forall x. \ p(x) \Leftrightarrow \neg \exists x. \ \neg p(x))$, but the result is not general. We would like to prove that for any FOL formula F,

$$H : \ (\forall x. \ F) \ \leftrightarrow \ (\neg \exists x. \ \neg F)$$

is valid. H is a **formula schema** (plural: **schemata**). Formula schema and **schema substitutions** provide the desired generality.

A **formula schema** H contains at least one **placeholder** $F_1, F_2, \ldots$. For example, F is a placeholder in the formula schema H above. A formula schema can also have **side conditions** that specify that certain variables do not occur free in the placeholders.

Consider a substitution σ mapping placeholders to FOL formulae. A **schema substitution** is an (unrestricted) application of σ to a formula schema. It is legal only if σ obeys the side conditions of the formula schema.

Example 2.20. Recall from Example 2.11 that

$$(\forall x. \ p(x)) \ \leftrightarrow \ (\neg \exists x. \ \neg p(x))$$

is valid. It can act as a formula schema. First, rewrite the formula using placeholders:

$$H : \ (\forall x. \ F) \ \leftrightarrow \ (\neg \exists x. \ \neg F) \ .$$

H does not have any side conditions. Next, to prove the validity of

$$G : \ (\forall x. \ \exists y. \ q(x,y)) \ \leftrightarrow \ (\neg \exists x. \ \neg \exists y. \ q(x,y)) \ ,$$

show that G is derivable from H via a schema substitution:

$$\sigma : \ \{F \mapsto \exists y. \ q(x,y)\} \ .$$

Then $H\sigma = G$ ($H\sigma$ is syntactically identical to G), so that by Proposition 2.25 below, G is valid. ∎

A formula schema H is **valid** if $H\sigma$ is valid for every schema substitution σ that obeys the side conditions of H. Apply the semantic method to prove the validity of a formula schema.

Example 2.21. To prove the validity of the formula schema

$$H : \ (\forall x. \ F_1 \wedge F_2) \ \leftrightarrow \ (\forall x. \ F_1) \ \wedge \ (\forall x. \ F_2) \ ,$$

consider the two directions. First, assume that $I \not\models (\forall x. \ F_1 \wedge F_2) \rightarrow (\forall x. \ F_1) \wedge (\forall x. \ F_2)$:

1.	$I \models \forall x. \ F_1 \wedge F_2$	assumption
2.	$I \not\models (\forall x. \ F_1) \wedge (\forall x. \ F_2)$	assumption
3.	$I \models (\exists x. \ \neg F_1) \vee (\exists x. \ \neg F_2)$	2, $\neg$

There are two cases to consider:

4a.	$I \models \exists x. \ \neg F_1$	3, $\vee$
5a.	$I \triangleleft \{x \mapsto v\} \models \neg F_1$	4a, $\exists$, for some $v \in D_I$
6a.	$I \triangleleft \{x \mapsto v\} \models F_1 \wedge F_2$	1, $\forall$
7a.	$I \triangleleft \{x \mapsto v\} \models F_1$	6a, $\wedge$

ending in a contradiction. The second disjunctive case is similar.

For the second main case, assume that $I \not\models (\forall x. \ F_1) \wedge (\forall x. \ F_2) \rightarrow (\forall x. \ F_1 \wedge F_2)$:

1.	$I \not\models \forall x. \ F_1 \wedge F_2$	assumption
2.	$I \models (\forall x. \ F_1) \wedge (\forall x. \ F_2)$	assumption
3.	$I \models \exists x. \ \neg F_1 \vee \neg F_2$	1, $\neg$
4.	$I \triangleleft \{x \mapsto v\} \models \neg F_1 \vee \neg F_2$	3, $\exists$, for some $v \in D_I$
5.	$I \models \forall x. \ F_1$	2, $\wedge$
6.	$I \models \forall x. \ F_2$	2, $\wedge$
7.	$I \triangleleft \{x \mapsto v\} \models F_1$	5, $\forall$
8.	$I \triangleleft \{x \mapsto v\} \models F_2$	6, $\forall$

Again, there are two cases to consider:

9a.	$I \triangleleft \{x \mapsto v\} \models \neg F_1$	4, $\vee$

ending in a contradiction. The second disjunctive case is similar. Thus, H is a valid formula schema. ∎

We now consider formula schemata with side conditions.

Example 2.22. Consider the formula schema with side condition

$$H: (\forall x.\ F) \leftrightarrow F \quad \text{provided } x \notin \text{free}(F)\ .$$

If we disregard the side condition, then H is an invalid formula schema as, for example,

$$G_1: (\forall x.\ p(x)) \leftrightarrow p(x)\ ,$$

obtained from H by schema substitution

$$\sigma: \{F \mapsto p(x)\}\ ,$$

is invalid. However, σ is disallowed by the side condition that x should not occur free in F.

H (with the side condition) is a valid formula schema. Thus, the formula

$$G_2: (\forall x.\ \exists y.\ p(z,y)) \leftrightarrow \exists y.\ p(z,y)$$

is valid: obtain it via the schema substitution

$$\sigma: \{F \mapsto \exists y.\ p(z,y)\}\ ,$$

which obeys H's side condition.   ■

Reasoning about the validity of a formula schema with side conditions usually requires invoking its side conditions during a semantic argument.

Example 2.23. To prove the validity of

$$H: (\forall x.\ F) \leftrightarrow F \quad \text{provided } x \notin \text{free}(F)\ ,$$

consider the two directions of $\leftrightarrow$. First,

1. $I \models \forall x.\ F$ assumption
2. $I \not\models F$ assumption
3. $I \models F$ 1, $\forall$, since $x \notin \text{free}(F)$
4. $I \models \bot$ 2, 3

Second,

1. $I \not\models \forall x.\ F$ assumption
2. $I \models F$ assumption
3. $I \models \exists x.\ \neg F$ 1 and $\neg$
4. $I \models \neg F$ 3, $\exists$, since $x \notin \text{free}(F)$
5. $I \models \bot$ 2, 4

Thus, H is a valid formula schema.   ■

Example 2.24. To prove the validity of

$$H : (\forall x.\ F_1 \wedge F_2) \ \leftrightarrow\ (\forall x.\ F_1)\ \wedge\ F_2 \quad \text{provided } x \notin \text{free}(F_2)\ ,$$

consider two cases. First,

1.	$I \models \forall x.\ F_1\ \wedge\ F_2$	assumption
2.	$I \not\models (\forall x.\ F_1)\ \wedge\ F_2$	assumption
3.	$I \models (\forall x.\ F_1)\ \wedge\ (\forall x.\ F_2)$	1, valid schema from Example 2.21
4.	$I \models (\forall x.\ F_1)\ \wedge\ F_2$	3, Example 2.23, since $x \notin \text{free}(F_2)$
5.	$I \models \perp$	2, 4

Observe the application of valid formula schemata from previous examples in lines 3 and 4. Second,

1.	$I \not\models \forall x.\ F_1\ \wedge\ F_2$	assumption
2.	$I \models (\forall x.\ F_1)\ \wedge\ F_2$	assumption
3.	$I \models (\forall x.\ F_1)\ \wedge\ (\forall x.\ F_2)$	2, Example 2.23, since $x \notin \text{free}(F_2)$
4.	$I \models \forall x.\ F_1\ \wedge\ F_2$	3, Example 2.21
5.	$I \models \perp$	1, 4

Thus, H is a valid formula schema.   ∎

Proposition 2.25 (Formula Schema). *If H is a valid formula schema and σ is a substitution obeying H's side conditions, then $H\sigma$ is also valid.*

The valid PL formula

$$(P \rightarrow Q)\ \leftrightarrow\ (\neg P \vee Q)$$

can be treated as a valid formula schema:

$$(F_1 \rightarrow F_2)\ \leftrightarrow\ (\neg F_1 \vee F_2)\ .$$

In general, valid propositional templates are valid formulae schemata, so that Proposition 2.25 generalizes Proposition 1.17.

2.5 Normal Forms

The normal forms of PL extend to FOL. A FOL formula F can be transformed into negation normal form (NNF) by using the procedure of Section 1.6 augmented with these two (schema) equivalences:

$$\neg \forall x.\ F[x] \ \Leftrightarrow\ \exists x.\ \neg F[x] \qquad \neg \exists x.\ F[x] \ \Leftrightarrow\ \forall x.\ \neg F[x]\ .$$

Example 2.26. We apply the procedure to find a formula in NNF that is equivalent to

$$G : \forall x.\ (\exists y.\ p(x,y)\ \wedge\ p(x,z))\ \rightarrow\ \exists w.p(x,w)\ .$$

Each formula below is equivalent to G and is obtained from the previous one through an application of an equivalence.

1. $\forall x.\ (\exists y.\ p(x,y)\ \wedge\ p(x,z))\ \rightarrow\ \exists w.\ p(x,w)$
2. $\forall x.\ \neg(\exists y.\ p(x,y)\ \wedge\ p(x,z))\ \vee\ \exists w.\ p(x,w)$
3. $\forall x.\ (\forall y.\ \neg(p(x,y)\ \wedge\ p(x,z)))\ \vee\ \exists w.\ p(x,w)$
4. $\forall x.\ (\forall y.\ \neg p(x,y)\ \vee\ \neg p(x,z))\ \vee\ \exists w.\ p(x,w)$

Formula 2 follows from the equivalence

$$F_1 \rightarrow F_2 \ \Leftrightarrow\ \neg F_1 \vee F_2 \ .$$

Formula 3 arises from an application of

$$\neg\exists x.\ F[x] \ \Leftrightarrow\ \forall x.\ \neg F[x] \ ,$$

and the final formula, which is in NNF, follows from De Morgan's Law. ∎

A formula is in **prenex normal form** (**PNF**) if all of its quantifiers appear at the beginning of the formula:

$$Q_1 x_1.\ \ldots Q_n x_n.\ F[x_1,\ldots,x_n] \ ,$$

where $Q_i \in \{\forall, \exists\}$ and F is quantifier-free. Every FOL formula F can be transformed into an equivalent formula F' in PNF. To compute an equivalent PNF F' of F,

1. Convert F into NNF formula F_1.
2. When multiple quantified variables have the same name, rename them to fresh variables, resulting in F_2.
3. Remove all quantifiers from F_2 to produce quantifier-free formula F_3.
4. Add the quantifiers before F_3,

    $$F_4 :\ Q_1 x_1.\ \ldots Q_n x_n.\ F_3 \ ,$$

    where the Q_i are the quantifiers such that if Q_j is in the scope of Q_i in F_1, then $i < j$.

F_4 is equivalent to F.

Example 2.27. We apply the procedure to find a PNF equivalent of

$$F :\ \forall x.\ \neg(\exists y.\ p(x,y)\ \wedge\ p(x,z))\ \vee\ \exists y.\ p(x,y) \ .$$

1. Write F in NNF:

    $$F_1 :\ \forall x.\ (\forall y.\ \neg p(x,y)\ \vee\ \neg p(x,z))\ \vee\ \exists y.\ p(x,y) \ .$$

2. Rename quantified variables:

    $$F_2 :\ \forall x.\ (\forall y.\ \neg p(x,y)\ \vee\ \neg p(x,z))\ \vee\ \exists w.\ p(x,w) \ .$$

3. Remove all quantifiers to produce quantifier-free formula

$$F_3 : \quad \neg p(x, y) \ \lor \ \neg p(x, z) \ \lor \ p(x, w) \ .$$

4. Add the quantifiers before F_3:

$$F_4 : \quad \forall x. \ \forall y. \ \exists w. \ \neg p(x, y) \ \lor \ \neg p(x, z) \ \lor \ p(x, w) \ .$$

Alternately, choose order

$$F_4' : \quad \forall x. \ \exists w. \ \forall y. \ \neg p(x, y) \ \lor \ \neg p(x, z) \ \lor \ p(x, w) \ .$$

Both F_4 and F_4' are equivalent to F. However,

$$G : \quad \forall y. \ \exists w. \ \forall x. \ \neg p(x, y) \ \lor \ \neg p(x, z) \ \lor \ p(x, w)$$

is not equivalent to F.

■

A FOL formula is in CNF (DNF) if it is in PNF and its main quantifier-free subformula is in CNF (DNF). CNF and DNF equivalents are obtained by transforming formula F into PNF formula F' and then applying the relevant procedure of Section 1.6 to the main quantifier-free subformula of F'.

2.6 Decidability and Complexity

We review the main concepts from decidability and complexity theory. **Bibliographic Remarks** refers the interested reader to other texts that focus on these topics.

2.6.1 Satisfiability as a Formal Language

Satisfiability of formulae is the primary decision problem in logic. We can formalize satisfiability as a formal language decision problem. Consider PL. Let L_{PL} be the set of all satisfiable formulae. That is, the word $w \in L_{\mathsf{PL}}$ iff

1. w is a syntactically well-formed formulae: it parses according to the definition of Section 1.1;
2. and when w is viewed as a PL formula F, F is satisfiable.

Then the formal decision problem is the following: given a word w, is $w \in L_{\mathsf{PL}}$?

Satisfiability of FOL formulae can be similarly formalized as a language question. Let L_{FOL} be the set of all FOL formulae (words that parse according to Section 2.1) that are satisfiable. Then the formal decision problem is the following: given a word w, is $w \in L_{\mathsf{FOL}}$? In other words, is it a well-formed FOL formula, and if so, is it satisfiable? Dually, we can define the validity problem for PL and FOL.

2.6.2 Decidability

A formal language L is **decidable** if there exists a procedure that, given a word w, (1) eventually halts and (2) answers *yes* if $w \in L$ and *no* if $w \notin L$. Other terms for "decidable" are **recursive** and **Turing-decidable**. A procedure for a decidable language is called an **algorithm**. Satisfiability of PL formulae is decidable: the truth-table method is a decision procedure.

A formal language is **undecidable** if it is not decidable.

A formal language L is **semi-decidable** if there exists a procedure that, given a word w, (1) halts and answers *yes* iff $w \in L$, (2) halts and answers *no* if $w \notin L$, or (3) does not halt if $w \notin L$. The possible outcomes (2) and (3) for the case $w \notin L$ mean that the procedure may or may not halt. Unlike a decidable language, the procedure is only guaranteed to halt if $w \in L$. Other terms for "semi-decidable" are **partially decidable**, **recursively enumerable**, and **Turing-recognizable**.

The terms "Turing-decidable" and "Turing-recognizable" arise from Alan Turing's classic formalization of procedures as **Turing machines**. A Turing machine consists of a finite automaton coupled with an infinite tape and tape head. Each cell of the tape can hold one character from a finite alphabet. The state of the automaton changes based on its control structure and the character currently under the tape head. During a state change, the automaton instructs the tape head to write a new character to the current cell and to move one position left or right.

Church and Turing showed that L_{FOL} is undecidable: there does not exist an algorithm for deciding if a FOL formula F is satisfiable (and similarly for validity). However, there is a procedure that halts and says *yes* if F is valid, so validity is semi-decidable. We describe such a procedure based on the semantic argument method in Section 2.7.

2.6.3 ⋆Complexity

If a language is decidable, then one considers the complexity of the decision problem. We define several of the main complexity classes here. A language L is **polynomial-time decidable**, or in PTIME (also, in P), if there exists a procedure that, given w, answers *yes* when $w \in L$, answers *no* when $w \notin L$, and halts with the answer in a number of steps that is at most proportionate to some polynomial of the size of w. For example, determining if the word w is a well-formed FOL formula is polynomial-time decidable and can be implemented using standard parsing methods.

A language L is **nondeterministic-polynomial-time decidable**, or in NPTIME (also, in NP), if there exists a nondeterministic procedure that, given w,

1. guesses a **witness** W to the fact that $w \in L$ that is at most proportionate in size to some polynomial of the size of w;

2. checks in time at most proportionate to some polynomial of the size of w that W really is a witness to $w \in L$;
3. and answers *yes* if the check succeeds and *no* otherwise.

For example, L_{PL} is in NP, as exhibited by the following nondeterministic procedure for deciding if a PL formula is satisfiable:

1. parse the input w as formula F (return *no* if w is not a well-formed PL formula);
2. guess an interpretation I, which is linear in the size of w;
3. check that $I \models F$.

I is the witness to the satisfiability of F.

A language L is in **co-NP** if its complement language $\overline{L}$ is in NP. For example, unsatisfiability of PL formulae is in co-NP because satisfiability is in NP. It is not known if unsatisfiability of PL formulae is in NP. While a satisfiable PL formula has a polynomial size witness of its satisfiability (a satisfying interpretation I), there is no known polynomial size witness of unsatisfiability.

A language L is **NP-hard** if every instance $v \in L'$ of every other NP decidable language L' can be reduced to deciding an instance $w_{L'}^v \in L$. Moreover, the size of $w_{L'}^v$ must be at most proportionate to some polynomial of the size of v. That is, L is NP-hard if every query $v \in L'$ of every NP language L' can be encoded into a query $w \in L$, where w is not much larger than v. L is **NP-complete** if it is in NP and is NP-hard.

L_{PL} is NP-complete. Indeed, L_{PL}, also called SAT, was the first language shown to be NP-complete. We proved that L_{PL} is in NP above by describing a nondeterministic polynomial time procedure. The Cook-Levin theorem shows that all NP-languages L can be reduced to L_{PL}, so that L_{PL} is NP-hard. They exhibited a polynomial time algorithm that, given L and input w, constructs an encoding into PL of a simulation of a run of a nondeterministic Turing machine for L on w. The encoding as PL formula F has length that is polynomial in the length of w. F is satisfiable iff the Turing machine decides that $w \in L$.

For discussing the complexity of decision problems and algorithms, we use the standard notation. Consider a function $f(n)$ over integers. For example, $f(n) = \log n$, $f(n) = n^2$, $f(n) = 2^n$, or $f(n) = 2^{2^n}$. A function $g(n)$ is of at most **order** $f(n)$ if there exist a scalar $c \geq 0$ and an integer $n_0 \geq 0$ such that

$$\forall n \geq n_0.\; g(n) \leq cf(n) .$$

$O(f(n))$ denotes the set of all functions of at most order $f(n)$. Similarly, $\Omega(f(n))$ denotes the set of all function of at least order $f(n)$: a function $g(n)$ is of at least order $f(n)$ if there exist a scalar $c \geq 0$ and an an integer $n_0 \geq 0$ such that

$$\forall n \geq n_0.\; g(n) \geq cf(n) .$$

Finally, $\Theta(f(n)) = \Omega(f(n)) \cap O(f(n))$ denotes the set of all functions of precisely order $f(n)$.

Example 2.28.

- $3n^2 + n \in O(n^2)$
- $3n^2 + n \in \Omega(n^2)$
- $3n^2 + n \in \Theta(n^2)$
- $\frac{1}{99}n^2 + n \in \Omega(n^2)$
- $3n^2 + n \in O(2^n)$
- $3n^2 + n \in \Omega(n)$
- $3n^2 + n \notin \Omega(2^n)$
- $3n^2 + n \notin \Theta(2^n)$
- $2^n \in \Omega(n^3)$
- $2^n \notin O(n^3)$

■

A decision problem has time complexity $O(f(n))$ if there exists a decision algorithm P for the problem and a function $g(n) \in O(f(n))$ such that P runs in time at most $g(n)$ on input of size n. A decision problem has time complexity $\Omega(f(n))$ if there exists a function $g(n) \in \Omega(f(n))$ such that all decision algorithms P for the problem run in time at least $g(n)$ on input of size n. Finally, a decision problem has time complexity $\Theta(f(n))$ if it has time complexities $\Omega(f(n))$ and $O(f(n))$.

Example 2.29. The algorithm SAT for deciding PL satisfiability runs in time $\Theta(2^n)$, where n is the number of variables in the input formula, because each level of recursion branches. Hence, the problem of PL satisfiability has time complexity $O(2^n)$. ■

2.7 *Meta-Theorems of First-Order Logic

We prove that the semantic argument method for FOL is sound and, given a proper strategy of applying the proof rules, complete. A proof method is **sound** if every formula that has a proof according to the method is valid. A proof method is **complete** if every formula that is valid has a proof according to the method. That the semantic argument method is sound means that a closed semantic argument for $I \not\models F$ proves the validity of F; and that the semantic argument method is complete means that every valid formula F of FOL has a closed semantic argument proving its validity. Because there exists a complete proof method for FOL, FOL is a complete logic: every valid formula of FOL has a proof of its validity.

The second half of this section is devoted to proving two classic theorems that we apply in Chapter 10.

2.7.1 Simplifying the Language of FOL

In preparation for the proofs, we simplify the language of FOL without losing expressiveness. Exercises 1.3 and 4.6 show that we have many redundant logical connectives. We choose to use only the logical constant $\top$ and the connectives $\neg$ and $\wedge$, from which the others can be constructed. Additionally, we need only one quantifier since $\exists x.\ F$ is equivalent to $\neg \forall x.\ \neg F$. We choose $\forall$.

A second simplification is more involved. The goal is to remove constant and function symbols from the language by using predicate symbols instead. Given a formula F, let S be the set of function symbols appearing in it. Associate with each n-ary function symbol f of S a new $(n+1)$-ary predicate p_f. Then for each occurrence of a function f in a literal L of F

$$L[f(t_1, \ldots, t_n)] ,$$

replace L in F with the new formula

$$\exists x.\ p_f(t_1, \ldots, t_n, x)\ \wedge\ L[x] .$$

After all replacements, the resulting formula G does not contain any function symbols.

The next step ensures that the new predicate p_f describes a function f: it associates with each tuple of domain values $v_1, \ldots, v_n$ precisely one value v. For each introduced predicate p_f, construct the formula

$$I_f :\ \forall \overline{x}.\ \exists y.\ p_f(\overline{x}, y)\ \wedge\ (\forall z.\ p_f(\overline{x}, z)\ \rightarrow\ y = z) .$$

Then construct the formula

$$H :\ \left(\bigwedge_{f \in S} I_f \right)\ \rightarrow\ G .$$

The equality predicate $=$ is not yet defined. To make $=$ an equivalence relation, assert that it is reflexive, symmetric, and transitive:

$$E :\quad \begin{array}{l} (\forall x.\ x = x) \\ \wedge\ (\forall x, y.\ x = y\ \rightarrow\ y = x) \\ \wedge\ (\forall x, y, z.\ x = y\ \wedge\ y = z\ \rightarrow\ x = z) \end{array}$$

Additionally, every predicate symbol p appearing in G should obey $=$:

$$E_p :\ \forall \overline{x}, \overline{y}.\ \overline{x} = \overline{y}\ \rightarrow\ (p(\overline{x}) \leftrightarrow p(\overline{y}))$$

Let T be the set of predicate symbols of G. Construct the final formula

$$F' :\ \left(E\ \wedge\ \bigwedge_{p \in T} E_p \right)\ \rightarrow\ H .$$

F' is valid iff F is valid. Moreover, F' does not contain any function symbols.

For the special case of constant symbols, it is simpler to replace $F[a]$ with $F' : \forall x.\ F[x]$.

For the remainder of this section, we consider a version of FOL with only the logical constant $\top$, the connectives $\neg$ and $\wedge$, the quantifier $\forall$, and predicate symbols. It is equivalent in expressive power to the richer language studied earlier in the chapter.

2.7.2 Semantic Argument Proof Rules

In this simplified form of FOL, we need only the following seven proof rules.

- For handling negation:

$$\frac{I \models \neg F}{I \not\models F} \qquad \frac{I \not\models \neg F}{I \models F}$$

- For handling conjunction:

$$\frac{I \models F \wedge G}{\begin{array}{c} I \models F \\ I \models G \end{array}} \qquad \frac{I \not\models F \wedge G}{I \not\models F \ \mid \ I \not\models G}$$

- For handling universal quantification:

$$\frac{I \models \forall x.\ F}{I \triangleleft \{x \mapsto v\} \models F} \qquad \text{for any } v \in D_I$$

and

$$\frac{I \not\models \forall x.\ F}{I \triangleleft \{x \mapsto v\} \not\models F} \qquad \text{for a } \textit{fresh } v \in D_I$$

- For deriving a contradiction:

$$\frac{\begin{array}{l} J : I \triangleleft \cdots \ \models \ p(x_1, \ldots, x_n) \\ K : I \triangleleft \cdots \ \not\models \ p(y_1, \ldots, y_n) \end{array}}{I \models \bot} \qquad \text{for } i \in \{1, \ldots, n\},\ \alpha_J[x_i] = \alpha_K[y_i]$$

Only the second rule for conjunction requires a case analysis.

2.7.3 Soundness and Completeness

That the semantic argument method is sound is fairly obvious for the first six rules: each follows almost directly from the semantics of FOL. The final rule for deriving a contradiction requires some explanation. The variants J and K are constructed only through the rules for handling quantification so that they simply assign values to the arguments of p. Hence, the truth value of p on the given tuple of domain values is already established by I. Furthermore, the disagreement between J and K on the truth value of p indicates that I is not in fact an interpretation. Therefore, we have the following theorem.

Theorem 2.30 (Sound). *If every branch of a semantic argument proof of* $I \not\models F$ *closes, then* F *is valid.*

Completeness is more complicated. We want to show that there exists a closed semantic argument proof of $I \not\models F$ when F is valid. Our strategy is as follows. We define a procedure for applying the proof rules. When applying the quantification rules, the procedure selects values from a predetermined countably infinite domain. We then show that when some falsifying interpretation I exists (such that $I \not\models F$) our procedure constructs, *at the limit*, a falsifying interpretation. Therefore, F must be valid if the procedures actually discovers an argument in which all branches are closed. We now proceed according to this proof plan.

Let D be a countably infinite domain of values $v_1, v_2, v_3, \ldots$ which we can enumerate in some fixed order. Start the semantic argument by placing $I \not\models F$ at the root and marking it as *unused*. Now assume that the procedure has constructed a partial semantic argument and that each line is marked as either *used* or *unused*. We describe the next iteration.

Select the earliest line $L : I \models G$ or $L : I \not\models G$ in the argument that is marked *unused*, and choose the appropriate proof rule to apply according to the root symbol of G's parse tree. To apply a rule, add the appropriate deductions at the end of every open branch that passes through line L; mark each new deduction as *unused*; and mark L as *used*. The application of the negation rules and the first conjunction rule is then straightforward. Applying the second (branching) conjunction rule introduces a fork at the end of every open branch, doubling the number of open branches. In applying the second quantification rule, choose the next domain element v_i that does not appear in the semantic argument so far. For the first quantification rule, assume that G has the form $\forall x. H$. Choose the first value v_i on which $\forall x. H$ has not been instantiated in any ancestor of L. Additionally, consider $I \models G$ as a second "deduction" of this rule (so that both $I \triangleleft \{x \mapsto v_i\} \models H$ and $I \models G$ are added to every branch passing through L and marked as *unused*). This trick guarantees that x of $\forall x. H$ is instantiated on every domain element without preventing the rest of the proof from progressing. Finally, close any branch that has a contradiction resulting from a deduction in this iteration.

Recall that a semantic argument is finished if no further applications of rules are possible. In our proof procedure, this situation occurs when all lines are marked as *used*. Although we can never construct a finished semantic argument with infinitely many lines in practice, we can reason about such arguments. For example, such an argument has an infinitely long branch. For suppose not: then every branch has finite length, so there must be an infinite number of these finite branches. But such a situation requires a deduction step that results in an infinite number of branches, whereas each proof rule produces at most two branches. This result is known as **König's Lemma**. We next prove that each open branch of a finished semantic argument describes a falsifying interpretation.

Lemma 2.31. *Each open branch of a finished semantic argument for $I \not\models F$ defines a falsifying interpretation of F.*

Proof. We apply structural induction on the formulae appearing in the branch to conclude that each line $L : I \models G$ or $L : I \not\models G$ holds, including $I \not\models F$. In that case, I is a falsifying interpretation of F. The technique of **structural induction** is defined in Section 4.4.

For the base case, consider lines in which G is an atom. As the contradiction rule is never applied (otherwise, the branch would be closed) no contradiction exists. Therefore, each instance $I \triangleleft \cdots \models p(x_1, \ldots, x_n)$ or $I \triangleleft \cdots \not\models p(x_1, \ldots, x_n)$ defines the truth value of p on one tuple of domain elements without contradicting any other definition on the branch. (For tuples of domain elements on which p is not explicitly defined on the branch, p may take any value, say false.)

Consider when G is formed by applying a logical connective to one or two formulae. As the procedure applied the appropriate proof rule, the inductive hypothesis and the semantics of the logical connectives tell us that L holds. For example, consider the case $L : I \models F_1 \wedge F_2$. Then $I \models F_1$ and $I \models F_2$ appear on the branch, and both lines hold by the inductive hypothesis. The reader may verify the other logical connectives with similar reasoning.

Consider the case $L : I \not\models \forall x. F$. For L to hold, it must be the case that for some fresh domain value v, $M : I \triangleleft \{x \mapsto \mathsf{v}\} \not\models F$. But the procedure guarantees that M is a descendant of L. Moreover, F is a subformula of $\forall x. F$, so the inductive hypothesis asserts that M holds. Then so does L.

Consider the case $L : I \models \forall x. F$. For L to hold, it must be the case that for all domain values v, $M : I \triangleleft \{x \mapsto \mathsf{v}\} \models F$. But the procedure guarantees that such a line exists for every v. Moreover, F is a subformula of $\forall x. F$, so the inductive hypothesis asserts that each such lines holds. Hence, so does L, finishing the proof. ∎

Remark 2.32. The formulae that appear on an open branch of a finished semantic proof comprise a **Hintikka set**. The proof strategy that we employed is essentially that used in proving **Hintikka's Lemma**, which asserts that a Hintikka set is satisfiable.

Remark 2.33. We defined the procedure with a fixed countably infinite domain in mind and then proved that an open branch of a finished semantic argument corresponds to at least one falsifying interpretation. Therefore, we have proved an additional fact: every satisfiable FOL formula is satisfied by an interpretation with a countable domain. This result is **Löwenheim's Theorem**.

Theorem 2.34 (Complete). *The semantic argument method is complete: each valid formula F has a semantic argument proof (in which every branch is closed).*

Proof. Suppose that F is valid, yet no semantic argument proof exists. Then a finished semantic argument constructed according to our procedure has an open branch. By Lemma 2.31, this branch describes a falsifying interpretation of F, a contradiction. Hence, all branches of a finished semantic argument must in fact be closed (and thus finite). By König's Lemma, the semantic argument itself has finite size.   ∎

2.7.4 Additional Theorems

Is a countable (but possibly infinite) set S of satisfiable formulae **simultaneously satisfiable**? That is, does there exist a single interpretation I that satisfies every member of S? The **Compactness Theorem** relates simultaneous satisfiability of S to satisfiability of the conjunction of each finite subset of S. Dually, we might consider whether the disjunction of a countable set of formulae is valid.

Theorem 2.35 (Compactness Theorem). *A countable set of first-order formulae S is simultaneously satisfiable iff the conjunction of every finite subset is satisfiable.*

Proof. The forward direction is clear: if I simultaneously satisfies the members of S, then it satisfies each finite conjunction.

For the other direction, extend the proof procedure of the previous section as follows. Arrange the members of S in some order $F_1, F_2, F_3, \ldots$, which is possible because S is countable. Start the procedure with $I \not\models \neg F_1$. At the end of each iteration of the procedure, choose the next formula F_i in the sequence and append $I \not\models \neg F_i$ to every open branch, marking it as *unused*. Since each finite subset of S is satisfiable, at least one branch remains open and the procedure does not terminate.

A finished semantic argument constructed in this manner enumerates an interpretation that falsifies every $\neg F_i$ and thus satisfies every F_i. Hence, S is simultaneously satisfiable.   ∎

Remark 2.36. This proof proves an additional fact that extends Löwenheim's Theorem: every simultaneously satisfiable countable set of FOL formulae is simultaneously satisfied by an interpretation with a countable domain. This result is the **Löwenheim-Skolem Theorem**.

We apply the next theorem, the **Craig Interpolation Lemma**, in Chapter 10. It asserts that if $F \to G$ is valid, then there is a formula H (called an **interpolant**) such that $F \to H$ and $H \to G$ are valid and whose predicates and free variables occur in both F and G. The proof is constructive: it describes a procedure for extracting the interpolant from a proof of the validity of $F \to G$. However, proofs constructed via the proof rules of Section 2.7.2 are not directly amenable to the interpolation procedure. We describe an alternate set of proof rules instead and show that any proof constructed from the rules of 2.7.2 can be translated into a proof using the new rules. Then we prove the Craig Interpolation Lemma using these new proof rules.

One trick that will prove convenient is the following. Associate a fresh variable x_i with each domain value v_i introduced during the proof. Whenever a variant $I \triangleleft \{x \mapsto v_i\}$ is used, rename x to the variable x_i corresponding to the value v_i in both the variant interpretation and the formula. This renaming does not affect the soundness of the proof, but it makes contradictions more obvious.

The new rules are the following:

- For handling double negation:

$$\frac{I \models \neg\neg F}{I \models F} \qquad \frac{I \not\models \neg\neg F}{I \not\models F}$$

- For handling conjunction:

$$\frac{I \models F \wedge G}{\begin{array}{c} I \models F \\ I \models G \end{array}} \qquad \frac{I \not\models F \wedge G}{I \not\models F \mid I \not\models G}$$

and

$$\frac{I \models \neg(F \wedge G)}{I \models \neg F \mid I \models \neg G} \qquad \frac{I \not\models \neg(F \wedge G)}{\begin{array}{c} I \not\models \neg F \\ I \not\models \neg G \end{array}}$$

- For handling universal quantification:

$$\frac{I \models \forall x.\ F}{I \triangleleft \{x \mapsto v\} \models F} \qquad \frac{I \not\models \neg\forall x.\ F}{I \triangleleft \{x \mapsto v\} \not\models \neg F} \qquad \text{for any } v \in D_I$$

and

$$\frac{I \not\models \forall x.\ F}{I \triangleleft \{x \mapsto v\} \not\models F} \qquad \frac{I \models \neg\forall x.\ F}{I \triangleleft \{x \mapsto v\} \models \neg F} \qquad \text{for a } \textit{fresh } v \in D_I$$

- For deriving a contradiction (recall our trick of renaming variables to correspond uniquely to domain values):

$$\frac{\begin{array}{l} J : I \triangleleft \cdots \models p(x_1, \ldots, x_n) \\ K : I \triangleleft \cdots \not\models p(x_1, \ldots, x_n) \end{array}}{I \models \bot}$$

and

$$\frac{\begin{array}{l} J : I \triangleleft \cdots \models p(x_1, \ldots, x_n) \\ K : I \triangleleft \cdots \models \neg p(x_1, \ldots, x_n) \end{array}}{I \models \bot} \qquad \frac{\begin{array}{l} J : I \triangleleft \cdots \not\models p(x_1, \ldots, x_n) \\ K : I \triangleleft \cdots \not\models \neg p(x_1, \ldots, x_n) \end{array}}{I \models \bot}$$

The important characteristic (for proving the interpolation lemma) of this set of proof rules is that premises and deductions agree on the use of $\models$ or $\not\models$, except in the contradiction rules. In contrast, the negation rules of Section 2.7.2 do not have this property. We obtained this property by folding each negation rule into every other rule.

Before proving the interpolation lemma, let us prove that the new semantic argument proof system based on these rules is sound and complete. Soundness is fairly obvious; for completeness, we briefly describe how to map a proof from the system of Section 2.7.2 to a proof using these rules.

Lemma 2.37. *Every proof in the proof system of Section 2.7.2 has a corresponding proof in the new proof system.*

Proof. In constructing the new proof, ignore any use of the negation rules of Section 2.7.2, instead choosing from the (doubled) set of conjunction and quantification rules depending on whether a $\neg$ is at the root of the parse tree of a formula. Use the new negation rules to remove double negations when necessary. For deriving a contradiction, one of the three cases represented by the contradiction rules must occur when a contradiction occurs in the original proof. ∎

We can now prove the theorem.

Theorem 2.38 (Craig Interpolation Lemma). *If $F \to G$ is valid, then there exists a formula H such that $F \to H$ and $H \to G$ are valid and whose predicates and free variables occur in both F and G.*

Proof. We prove the result by describing a procedure that extracts from a (closed) semantic argument proof of the validity of $F \to G$ the interpolant H. For convenience, let the proof itself begin with the lines

1. $I \models F$ assumption
2. $I \not\models G$ assumption

Notice that with the new set of proof rules, only $\models$ rules will be applied to deductions stemming from line 1, while only $\not\models$ rules will be applied to those stemming from line 2. The three contradiction rules correspond to three possible situations: a contradiction between $I \models F$ and $I \not\models G$ ($F \to G$ is valid), within $I \models F$ itself (F is unsatisfiable), and within $I \not\models G$ itself (G is valid).

The procedure runs backwards through a proof. It associates with each line L of the proof a set of *positive* formulae U and a set of *negative* formulae V. U consists of formulae on lines from which L descends (including itself) that are satisfied by their interpretation (lines of the form $K \models F_1$). V consists of formulae on lines from which L descends (including itself) that are falsified by their interpretation (lines of the form $K \not\models F_2$). Define L's **characteristic formula** as

$$\bigwedge U \rightarrow \bigvee V \;,$$

written as $\{U\} \rightarrow \{V\}$ for concision. That the branch on which L lies ends in a contradiction implies that $\{U\} \rightarrow \{V\}$ is valid. The procedure constructs for each line an interpolant X of $\{U\} \rightarrow \{V\}$; that is, X is such that

$$\bigwedge U \Rightarrow X \quad \text{and} \quad X \Rightarrow \bigvee V$$

and the predicates and free variables of X appear in both U and V. The interpolant of line 2 of the proof is the interpolant H that we seek.

Let us begin with the end of a branch, $L : I \models \perp$. It must have been deduced via a contradiction. If the first contradiction rule produced L, then its characteristic formula is of the form

$$\{U, p(x_1, \ldots, x_n), \perp\} \rightarrow \{V, p(x_1, \ldots, x_n)\} \;,$$

where the variable renaming trick ensures that the arguments to p are syntactically the same. Its parent has characteristic formula

$$\{U, p(x_1, \ldots, x_n)\} \rightarrow \{V, p(x_1, \ldots, x_n)\} \;,$$

and both have interpolant $p(x_1, \ldots, x_n)$. If the second contradiction rule produced L, then its characteristic formula is of the form

$$\{U, p(x_1, \ldots, x_n), \neg p(x_1, \ldots, x_n), \perp\} \rightarrow \{V\} \;,$$

and its parent's is of the form

$$\{U, p(x_1, \ldots, x_n), \neg p(x_1, \ldots, x_n)\} \rightarrow \{V\} \;.$$

Both have interpolant $\perp$ ($\neg\top$ in the restricted language). Similarly, if the third contradiction rule produced L, then the interpolant is $\top$.

Consider lines derived via the conjunction rules. Suppose $L : I \models F$ is deduced from $I \models F \wedge G$. Then the characteristic formulae of L and its parent are

$$\{U, F \wedge G, F\} \rightarrow \{V\} \quad \text{and} \quad \{U, F \wedge G\} \rightarrow \{V\} \;,$$

respectively. If L has interpolant X, then so does its parent. The case is similar for a line $L : I \not\models \neg F$ deduced from $I \not\models \neg(F \wedge G)$.

For the next conjunction rule, suppose that $L : I \not\models F$ is deduced on one branch from $I \not\models F \wedge G$. Then L is at a fork in the proof and has sibling line $L' : I \not\models G$. The characteristic formulae of L, L', and their parent are

$$\{U\} \rightarrow \{V, F \wedge G, F\} \;, \quad \{U\} \rightarrow \{V, F \wedge G, G\} \;, \quad \text{and} \quad \{U\} \rightarrow \{V, F \wedge G\} \;,$$

respectively. If L and L' have interpolants X and Y, respectively, then their parent has interpolant $X \wedge Y$.

Similarly, suppose $L : I \models \neg F$ is deduced on one branch from $I \models \neg(F \wedge G)$ (so that its sibling is $L' : I \models \neg G$). If L and L' have interpolants X and Y, respectively, then their parent has interpolant $X \vee Y$ ($\neg(\neg X \wedge \neg Y)$) in the restricted language.

The interpolant X of a line L derived via a double-negation rule passes directly to its parent, for the characteristic formula of L simply has a repetition $\neg\neg F$ of a formula F that the parent's characteristic formula does not have.

We turn to the quantification rules. Consider a line $L : I \triangleleft \{z \mapsto v\} \not\models F$ derived from $I \not\models \forall x.\ F$. L and its parent M have characteristic formulae

$$\{U\} \to \{V, \forall x.\ F, F\} \quad \text{and} \quad \{U\} \to \{V, \forall x.\ F\}\ ,$$

respectively. Moreover, v is fresh, and thus z does not appear in either U or V according to our trick. Hence, z cannot occur free in L's interpolant X. It thus follows that

$$\forall *.\ \forall z.\ X \ \to\ V \vee \forall x.F \vee F$$

is equivalent to

$$\forall *.\ X \ \to\ V \vee \forall x.F \vee \forall z.\ F$$

and thus to

$$\forall *.\ X \ \to\ V \vee \forall x.F\ .$$

Therefore, X is an interpolant of M. Similarly, X is an interpolant of the parent of $L : I \triangleleft \{z \mapsto v\} \models \neg F$ deduced from $I \models \neg\forall x.\ F$.

Consider $L : I \triangleleft \{z \mapsto v\} \models F$ with interpolant X derived from $I \models \forall x.\ F$, where z is not necessarily fresh. The characteristic formulae of L and its parent M are

$$\{U, \forall x.\ F, F\} \to \{V\} \quad \text{and} \quad \{U, \forall x.\ F\} \to \{V\}\ ,$$

respectively. Clearly,

$$U \wedge \forall x.\ F \wedge F \Rightarrow X$$

implies that

$$U \wedge \forall x.\ F \Rightarrow X\ .$$

Hence, X is an interpolant of M when z is not free in U or V (so that z is not free in X) and when it is free in both. However, if z is free in V but not in U, then X is not an interpolant of M. But $\forall z.\ X$ is an interpolant. In particular, we have

$$U \wedge \forall x.\ F \Rightarrow \forall z.\ X$$

and

$$\forall z.\ X \ \Rightarrow\ V \quad \text{because} \quad \forall z.\ X \ \Rightarrow\ X \quad \text{and} \quad X \ \Rightarrow\ V\ .$$

For the final case, suppose that $L : I \lhd \{z \mapsto \mathsf{v}\} \not\models \neg F$ is deduced from $I \not\models \neg \forall x.\ F$. The characteristic formula of L is

$$\{U\} \to \{V, \neg\forall x.\ F, F\}\ .$$

Then X is the interpolant of the parent M unless z is free in U but not free in V. In the latter case, the interpolant is $\exists z.\ X$ ($\neg\forall z.\ \neg X$ in the restricted language). The reasoning is similar to the previous case, completing the proof. ∎

2.8 Summary

Building on the presentation of PL in Chapter 1, this chapter introduces first-order logic (FOL). It covers:

- Its *syntax*. How one constructs a FOL formula. Variables, terms, function symbols, predicate symbols, atoms, literals, logical connectives, quantifiers.
- Its *semantics*. What a FOL formula means. Truth values true and false. Interpretations: domain and assignments. Difference between a function (predicate) symbol and a function (predicate) over a domain.
- *Satisfiability* and *validity*. Whether a FOL formula evaluates to true under any or all interpretations. Semantic argument method.
- *Substitution*, which is a tool for manipulating formulae and making general claims. Safe and schema substitutions. Substitution of equivalent formulae. Valid schemata.
- *Normal forms*. A normal form is a set of syntactically restricted formulae such that every FOL formula is equivalent to some member of the set.
- A review of *decidability and complexity theory*, which provides the concepts necessary for discussing decidability and complexity questions in logic.
- *Meta-theorems*. Semantic argument method is sound and complete. Compactness Theorem. Craig Interpolation Lemma.

The results of Section 2.7 are the groundwork for our theoretical treatment of the Nelson-Oppen combination method in Chapter 10.

FOL is the most general logic that is discussed in this book. Its applications include software and hardware design and analysis, knowledge representation, and complexity and decidability theory.

FOL is a complete logic: every valid FOL formula has a proof in the semantic argument method. However, validity is undecidable. Many applications benefit from complete automation, which is impossible when considering all of FOL. Therefore, Chapter 3 introduces first-order theories, which formalize interesting structures, such as integers, rationals, lists, stacks, and arrays. Part II of this book explores algorithms for reasoning within these theories.

Bibliographic Remarks

For a complete and concise presentation of propositional and first-order logic, see Smullyan's text *First-Order Logic* [87]. The semantic argument method is similar to Smullyan's tableau method. Also, the proofs of completeness of the semantic argument method, the Compactness Theorem, and the Craig Interpolation Lemma are inspired by Smullyan's presentation.

The history of the development of mathematical logic is rich. For an overview, see [98] and related articles in *The Stanford Encyclopedia of Philosophy*. We mention in particular *Hilbert's program* of the 1920s — see, for example, [38] — to find a consistent and complete axiomatization of arithmetic. Gödels two *incompleteness theorems* proved that such a goal is impossible. The first incompleteness theorem, which Gödel presented in a lecture in September, 1930, and then in [36], states that any axiomatization of arithmetic contains theorems that are not provable within the theory. The second, which Gödel had proved by October, 1930, states that a theory such as Peano arithmetic cannot prove its own consistency unless it is itself inconsistent. Earlier, Gödel proved that first-order logic is complete [35]: every theorem has a proof. However, Church — and, independently, Turing — proved that satisfiability in first-order logic is undecidable [13]. Thus, while every theorem of first-order logic has a finite proof, invalid formulae need not have a finite proof of their invalidity.

For an introduction to formal languages, decidability, and complexity theory, see [85, 72, 41].

Exercises

2.1 (English and FOL). Encode the following English sentences into FOL.

(a) Some days are longer than others.
(b) In all the world, there is but one place that I call home.
(c) My mother's mother is my grandmother.
(d) The intersection of two convex sets is convex.

2.2 (FOL validity & satisfiability). For each of the following FOL formulae, identify whether it is valid or not. If it is valid, prove it with a semantic argument; otherwise, identify a falsifying interpretation.

(a) $(\forall x, y.\ p(x, y) \rightarrow p(y, x)) \rightarrow \forall z.\ p(z, z)$
(b) $\forall x, y.\ p(x, y) \rightarrow p(y, x) \rightarrow \forall z.\ p(z, z)$
(c) $(\exists x.\ p(x)) \rightarrow \forall y.\ p(y)$
(d) $(\forall x.\ p(x)) \rightarrow \exists y.\ p(y)$
(e) $\exists x, y.\ (p(x, y) \rightarrow (p(y, x) \rightarrow \forall z.\ p(z, z)))$

2.3 (Semantic argument). Use the semantic argument method to prove the following formula schemata.

(a) $\neg(\forall x.\ F) \Leftrightarrow \exists x.\ \neg F$

(b) $\neg(\exists x.\ F) \Leftrightarrow \forall x.\ \neg F$

(c) $\forall x, y.\ F \Leftrightarrow \forall y, x.\ F$

(d) $\exists y.\ \forall x.\ F \Rightarrow \forall x.\ \exists y.\ F$

(e) $\exists x.\ F \vee G \Leftrightarrow (\exists x.\ F) \vee (\exists y.\ G)$

(f) $\exists x.\ F \rightarrow G \Leftrightarrow (\forall x.\ F) \rightarrow (\exists x.\ G)$

(g) $\exists x.\ F \vee G \Leftrightarrow (\exists x.\ F) \vee G$, provided $x \notin \text{free}(G)$

(h) $\forall x.\ F \vee G \Leftrightarrow (\forall x.\ F) \vee G$, provided $x \notin \text{free}(G)$

(i) $\exists x.\ F \wedge G \Leftrightarrow (\exists x.\ F) \wedge G$, provided $x \notin \text{free}(G)$

(j) $\forall x.\ F \rightarrow G \Leftrightarrow (\exists x.\ F) \rightarrow G$, provided $x \notin \text{free}(G)$

2.4 (Normal forms). Put the following formulae into prenex normal form.

(a) $(\forall x.\ \exists y.\ p(x, y)) \rightarrow \forall x.\ p(x, x)$

(b) $\exists z.\ (\forall x.\ \exists y.\ p(x, y)) \rightarrow \forall x.\ p(x, z)$

(c) $\forall w.\ \neg(\exists x, y.\ \forall z.\ p(x, z) \rightarrow q(y, z)) \wedge \exists z.\ p(w, z)$

2.5 (★Characteristic formula). Why is the characteristic formula of a line on a closed branch of a semantic argument valid?

3

First-Order Theories

Formalization works as "an early-warning system" when things are getting contorted.

— Edsger W. Dijkstra
EWD764: Repaying Our Debts, 1980

When reasoning in particular application domains such as software or hardware, one often has particular structures in mind. For example, programs manipulate numbers, lists, and arrays. **First-order theories** formalize these structures to enable reasoning about them. This chapter introduces first-order theories in general and then focuses on theories useful in verification and related tasks. These theories include a theory of equality, of integers, of rationals and reals, of recursive data structures, and of arrays.

There is another reason to study first-order theories. While validity in FOL is undecidable, validity in particular theories or fragments of theories is sometimes decidable. Many of the theories studied in this chapter have important fragments for which validity is efficiently decidable. For each theory, we identify the decidable and efficiently decidable fragments, which we summarize in Section 3.7. Part II studies decision procedures for the decidable fragments.

3.1 First-Order Theories

A first-order **theory** T is defined by the following components.

1. Its **signature** Σ is a set of constant, function, and predicate symbols.
2. Its set of **axioms** $\mathcal{A}$ is a set of closed FOL formulae in which only constant, function, and predicate symbols of Σ appear.

A Σ-**formula** is constructed from constant, function, and predicate symbols of Σ, as well as variables, logical connectives, and quantifiers. As usual, the symbols of Σ are just symbols without prior meaning. The axioms $\mathcal{A}$ provide their meaning.

A Σ-formula F is **valid in the theory** T, or T**-valid**, if every interpretation I that satisfies the axioms of T,

$$I \models A \quad \text{for every } A \in \mathcal{A} , \tag{3.1}$$

also satisfies F: $I \models F$. For this reason, we write

$$T \models F$$

to mean that F is T-valid. Formally, the theory T consists of all (closed) formulae that are T-valid. We call an interpretation satisfying (3.1) a T-**interpretation**.

A Σ-formula F is **satisfiable in** T, or T**-satisfiable**, if there is a T-interpretation I that satisfies F.

A theory T is **complete** if for every closed Σ-formula F, $T \models F$ or $T \models \neg F$. A theory is **consistent** if there is at least one T-interpretation. In particular, in a consistent theory T, there does not exist a Σ-formula F such that both $T \models F$ and $T \models \neg F$. (Otherwise, by the semantics of conjunction, $T \models F \wedge \neg F$ and thus $T \models \bot$; but $\bot$ is not satisfied by any interpretation.)

Concepts from general FOL validity carry over to first-order theories in the natural way. For example, two formulae F_1 and F_2 are **equivalent in** T, or T**-equivalent**, if $T \models F_1 \leftrightarrow F_2$: for every T-interpretation I, $I \models F_1$ iff $I \models F_2$.

A **fragment** of a theory is a syntactically-restricted subset of formulae of the theory. For example, the **quantifier-free fragment** of a theory T is the set of formulae without quantifiers that are valid in T. Recall our convention that non-closed formula F is valid iff its universal closure is valid. Technically, the "quantifier-free fragment" of T actually consists of valid formulae in which all variables are universally quantified. However, the term "quantifier-free fragment" is the common and accepted name for this fragment. Subsequent chapters show that the quantifier-free fragments of theories are of great practical and theoretical importance.

A theory T is **decidable** if $T \models F$ is decidable for every Σ-formula F. That is, there is an algorithm that always terminates with "yes" if F is T-valid or with "no" if F is T-invalid. A fragment of T is decidable if $T \models F$ is decidable for every Σ-formula F that obeys the fragment's syntactic restrictions.

The union $T_1 \cup T_2$ of two theories T_1 and T_2 has signature $\Sigma_1 \cup \Sigma_2$ and axioms $\mathcal{A}_1 \cup \mathcal{A}_2$. Clearly, a $(T_1 \cup T_2)$-interpretation is both a T_1-interpretation and a T_2-interpretation since it satisfies the axioms of both T_1 and T_2. Hence, a formula that is T_1-valid or T_2-valid is $(T_1 \cup T_2)$-valid, while a formula that is $(T_1 \cup T_2)$-satisfiable is both T_1-satisfiable and T_2-satisfiable.

Because FOL (the "empty" theory, or the theory without axioms) is undecidable in general, we must turn to theories and fragments of theories for the possibility of fully automated reasoning. While many interesting theories are undecidable, there are several important theories and fragments of theories that are decidable. These theories and fragments are the main subject of Part

II of this book. We introduce them in the following sections. In Section 3.7, we summarize the decidability and complexity results for these theories and fragments.

3.2 Equality

The theory of equality T_E is the simplest first-order theory. Its signature

$$\Sigma_E : \{=, a, b, c, \ldots, f, g, h, \ldots, p, q, r, \ldots\}$$

consists of

- $=$ (equality), a binary predicate;
- and all constant, function, and predicate symbols.

Equality $=$ is an **interpreted** predicate symbol: its meaning is defined via the axioms of T_E. The other constant, function, and predicate symbols are uninterpreted except as they relate to equality. The axioms of T_E are the following:

1. $\forall x.\ x = x$ (reflexivity)
2. $\forall x, y.\ x = y\ \rightarrow\ y = x$ (symmetry)
3. $\forall x, y, z.\ x = y\ \wedge\ y = z\ \rightarrow\ x = z$ (transitivity)
4. for each positive integer n and n-ary function symbol f,

$$\forall \overline{x}, \overline{y}.\ \left(\bigwedge_{i=1}^{n} x_i = y_i \right)\ \rightarrow\ f(\overline{x}) = f(\overline{y}) \qquad \text{(function congruence)}$$

5. for each positive integer n and n-ary predicate symbol p,

$$\forall \overline{x}, \overline{y}.\ \left(\bigwedge_{i=1}^{n} x_i = y_i \right)\ \rightarrow\ (p(\overline{x}) \leftrightarrow p(\overline{y})) \qquad \text{(predicate congruence)}$$

The notation $\overline{x}$ stands for the list of variables $x_1, \ldots, x_n$. Axioms (function congruence) and (predicate congruence) are actually axiom schemata. An **axiom schema** stands for a set of axioms, each an instantiation of the parameters (f and p in (function congruence) and (predicate congruence), respectively). For example, for binary function symbol f_2, (function congruence) instantiates to the following axiom:

$$\forall x_1, x_2, y_1, y_2.\ x_1 = y_1\ \wedge\ x_2 = y_2\ \rightarrow\ f_2(x_1, x_2) = f_2(y_1, y_2)\ .$$

The first three axioms state that $=$ is an **equivalence relation**: it is a binary predicate that obeys reflexivity, symmetry, and transitivity. The final two axiom schemata formalize our intuition for the behavior of functions and predicates under equality. A function (predicate) always evaluates to the same value (truth value) for a given set of argument values. They assert that $=$ is a **congruence relation**.

T_E is just as undecidable as full FOL because it allows all constant, function, and predicate symbols. In particular, any FOL formula F can be encoded as a Σ_E-formula F' simply by replacing occurrences of the symbol $=$ with a fresh symbol. Since $=$ does not occur in this transformed formula F', the axioms of T_E are irrelevant; hence, F' is T_E-satisfiable iff F' is first-order satisfiable.

However, the quantifier-free fragment of T_E is both interesting and efficiently decidable, as we show in Chapter 9.

Example 3.1. Without quantifiers, free variables and constants play the same role. In the formula

$$F : a = b \land b = c \rightarrow g(f(a), b) = g(f(c), a) ,$$

a, b, and c are constants, while in

$$F' : x = y \land y = z \rightarrow g(f(x), y) = g(f(z), x) ,$$

x, y, and z are free variables. F is T_E-valid iff F' is T_E-valid; F is T_E-satisfiable iff F' is T_E-satisfiable. ∎

It is often useful to reason about the T-satisfiability or T-validity of a Σ-formula F in a structured but informal way. We show how to use the semantic argument method with T_E.

Example 3.2. To prove that

$$F : a = b \land b = c \rightarrow g(f(a), b) = g(f(c), a)$$

is T_E-valid, assume otherwise: there exists a T_E-interpretation I such that $I \not\models F$:

1. $I \not\models F$ assumption
2. $I \models a = b \land b = c$ $1, \rightarrow$
3. $I \not\models g(f(a), b) = g(f(c), a)$ $1, \rightarrow$
4. $I \models a = b$ $2, \land$
5. $I \models b = c$ $2, \land$
6. $I \models a = c$ 4, 5, (transitivity)
7. $I \models f(a) = f(c)$ 6, (function congruence)
8. $I \models b = a$ 4, (symmetry)
9. $I \models g(f(a), b) = g(f(c), a)$ 7, 8 (function congruence)
10. $I \models \bot$ 3, 9

Our assumption is apparently false: F is T_E-valid. ∎

3.3 Natural Numbers and Integers

Arithmetic involving the addition and multiplication of the natural numbers $\mathbb{N} = \{0, 1, 2, \ldots\}$ is perhaps the oldest of mathematical theories. In this section we describe three theories of arithmetic. **Peano arithmetic** allows addition and multiplication over natural numbers, while **Presburger arithmetic** is restricted to addition over natural numbers. The final theory, the **theory of integers**, is convenient for automated reasoning but is no more expressive than Presburger arithmetic.

3.3.1 Peano Arithmetic

The **theory of Peano arithmetic** T_{PA}, or **first-order arithmetic**, has signature

$$\Sigma_{PA} : \{0, \ 1, \ +, \ \cdot, \ =\} \ ,$$

where

- 0 and 1 are constants;
- $+$ (addition) and $\cdot$ (multiplication) are binary functions;
- and $=$ (equality) is a binary predicate.

Its axioms are the following:

1. $\forall x. \ \neg(x + 1 = 0)$ (zero)
2. $\forall x, y. \ x + 1 = y + 1 \ \rightarrow \ x = y$ (successor)
3. $F[0] \ \wedge \ (\forall x. \ F[x] \rightarrow F[x + 1]) \ \rightarrow \ \forall x. \ F[x]$ (induction)
4. $\forall x. \ x + 0 = x$ (plus zero)
5. $\forall x, y. \ x + (y + 1) = (x + y) + 1$ (plus successor)
6. $\forall x. \ x \cdot 0 = 0$ (times zero)
7. $\forall x, y. \ x \cdot (y + 1) = x \cdot y + x$ (times successor)

These axioms concisely define addition, multiplication, and equality over natural numbers. Informally, axioms (zero), (plus zero), and (times zero) define 0 as we understand it: it is the minimal element of the natural numbers; it is the identity for addition ($x + 0 = x$); and under multiplication, it maps any number to 0 ($x \cdot 0 = 0$). Axioms (zero), (successor), (plus zero), and (plus successor) define addition. Axioms (times zero) and (times successor) define multiplication: in particular, (times successor) defines multiplication in terms of addition.

(induction) is an axiom schema: it stands for the set of axioms obtained by substituting for F each Σ_{PA}-formula that has precisely one free variable. It asserts that every T_{PA}-interpretation I obeys induction: if I satisfies $F[0]$ and $\forall x. \ F[x] \rightarrow F[x + 1]$, then I also satisfies $\forall x. \ F[x]$.

For convenience, we usually do not write the "$\cdot$" for multiplication. For example, we write xy rather than $x \cdot y$.

The **intended interpretations** of T_{PA} have domain $\mathbb{N}$ and assignments α_I defining 0, 1, +, ·, and = as we understand them in everyday arithmetic. In particular,

- $\alpha_I[0]$ is $0_{\mathbb{N}}$: α_I maps the symbols "0" to $0_{\mathbb{N}} \in \mathbb{N}$;
- $\alpha_I[1]$ is $1_{\mathbb{N}}$: α_I maps the symbols "1" to $1_{\mathbb{N}} \in \mathbb{N}$;
- $\alpha_I[+]$ is $+_{\mathbb{N}}$, addition over $\mathbb{N}$;
- $\alpha_I[\cdot]$ is $\cdot_{\mathbb{N}}$, multiplication over $\mathbb{N}$;
- $\alpha_I[=]$ is $=_{\mathbb{N}}$, equality over $\mathbb{N}$.

Example 3.3. The formula $3x + 5 = 2y$ can be written using the signature Σ_{PA} as

$$x + x + x + 1 + 1 + 1 + 1 + 1 = y + y$$

or as

$$(1 + 1 + 1) \cdot x + 1 + 1 + 1 + 1 + 1 = (1 + 1) \cdot y \, .$$

In practice, we use the abbreviated notation $3x + 5 = 2y$. ∎

Example 3.4. Rather than augmenting T_{PA} with axioms defining inequality $>$, we can transform formulae with inequality into formulae over the restricted signature Σ_{PA}. Write

$$3x + 5 > 2y \quad \text{as} \quad \exists z.\, z \neq 0 \,\wedge\, 3x + 5 = 2y + z \, ,$$

where $z \neq 0$ abbreviates $\neg(z = 0)$. The latter formula is a Σ_{PA}-formula. Weak inequality can be similarly transformed. Write

$$3x + 5 \geq 2y \quad \text{as} \quad \exists z.\, 3x + 5 = 2y + z \, .$$

∎

Example 3.5. The Σ_{PA}-formula

$$\exists x, y, z.\, x \neq 0 \,\wedge\, y \neq 0 \,\wedge\, z \neq 0 \,\wedge\, xx + yy = zz$$

is T_{PA}-valid. It asserts that there exists a triple of positive integers fulfilling the Pythagorean Theorem. The formula

$$\exists x, y, z.\, x \neq 0 \,\wedge\, y \neq 0 \,\wedge\, z \neq 0 \,\wedge\, xxx + yyy = zzz$$

is the cubic analogue. For constant n, let x^n represent n multiplications of x; then every formula of the set

$$\{\forall x, y, z.\, x \neq 0 \,\wedge\, y \neq 0 \,\wedge\, z \neq 0 \,\rightarrow\, x^n + y^n \neq z^n \; : \; n > 2 \,\wedge\, n \in \mathbb{Z}\}$$

is T_{PA}-valid, as claimed by Fermat's Last Theorem and proved by Andrew Wiles in 1994. ∎

Remark 3.6. Gödel's first incompleteness theorem (see **Bibliographic Remarks** of Chapter 2) implies that Peano arithmetic T_{PA} does not capture true arithmetic: there exist closed Σ_{PA}-formulae representing valid propositions of number theory that are T_{PA}-invalid. Gödel's proof constructs such a formula: it encodes the assertion that the formula itself cannot be proved. Now, either this formula can be proved from the axioms of T_{PA} (contradicting itself so that T_{PA} is inconsistent) or it cannot be proved (so that T_{PA} is incomplete).

Satisfiability and validity in T_{PA} is undecidable. Therefore, we turn to a more restricted theory of arithmetic that does not allow multiplication.

3.3.2 Presburger Arithmetic

The **theory of Presburger arithmetic** $T_{\mathbb{N}}$ has signature

$$\Sigma_{\mathbb{N}} : \{0,\ 1,\ +,\ =\}\ ,$$

where

- 0 and 1 are constants;
- + (addition) is a binary function;
- and = (equality) is a binary predicate.

Its axioms are a subset of the axioms of T_{PA}:

1. $\forall x.\ \neg(x+1=0)$ (zero)
2. $\forall x, y.\ x+1=y+1\ \rightarrow\ x=y$ (successor)
3. $F[0]\ \wedge\ (\forall x.\ F[x] \rightarrow F[x+1])\ \rightarrow\ \forall x.\ F[x]$ (induction)
4. $\forall x.\ x+0=x$ (plus zero)
5. $\forall x, y.\ x+(y+1)=(x+y)+1$ (plus successor)

Again, (induction) is an axiom schema standing for the set of axioms obtained by replacing F with each $\Sigma_{\mathbb{N}}$-formula that has precisely one free variable.

The intended interpretations of $T_{\mathbb{N}}$ have domain $\mathbb{N}$ and are such that

- $\alpha_I[0]$ is $0_{\mathbb{N}} \in \mathbb{N}$;
- $\alpha_I[1]$ is $1_{\mathbb{N}} \in \mathbb{N}$;
- $\alpha_I[+]$ is $+_{\mathbb{N}}$, addition over $\mathbb{N}$;
- $\alpha_I[=]$ is $=_{\mathbb{N}}$, equality over $\mathbb{N}$.

How does one reason about all integers, $\mathbb{Z} = \{\ldots, -2, -1, 0, 1, 2, \ldots\}$? Such formulae can be encoded as $\Sigma_{\mathbb{N}}$-formulae.

Example 3.7. Consider the formula

$$F_0 :\ \forall w, x.\ \exists y, z.\ x+2y-z-13 > -3w+5\ ,$$

where $-$ is meant to be interpreted as standard subtraction, and w, x, y, and z are intended to range over $\mathbb{Z}$. The formula

$$F_1 : \begin{array}{l} \forall w_p, w_n, x_p, x_n. \ \exists y_p, y_n, z_p, z_n. \\ \quad (x_p - x_n) + 2(y_p - y_n) - (z_p - z_n) - 13 > -3(w_p - w_n) + 5 \end{array}$$

introduces two variables, v_p and v_n, for each variable v of F_0. While each of v_p and v_n can only range over $\mathbb{N}$, $v_p - v_n$ should range over the integers. But how is $-$ interpreted? Moving negated terms to the other side of the inequality eliminates $-$:

$$F_2 : \begin{array}{l} \forall w_p, w_n, x_p, x_n. \ \exists y_p, y_n, z_p, z_n. \\ \quad x_p + 2y_p + z_n + 3w_p > x_n + 2y_n + z_p + 13 + 3w_n + 5 \ . \end{array}$$

The final transformation eliminates constant coefficients and strict inequality:

$$F_3 : \begin{array}{l} \forall w_p, w_n, x_p, x_n. \ \exists y_p, y_n, z_p, z_n. \ \exists u. \\ \quad \neg(u = 0) \ \wedge \\ \quad x_p + y_p + y_p + z_n + w_p + w_p + w_p \\ \quad = x_n + y_n + y_n + z_p + w_n + w_n + w_n + u \\ \quad + 1 + 1 + 1 + 1 + 1 + 1 + 1 + 1 + 1 \\ \quad + 1 + 1 + 1 + 1 + 1 + 1 + 1 + 1 + 1 \ . \end{array}$$

■

Presburger showed in 1929 that $T_\mathbb{N}$ is decidable. Therefore, the "theory of (negative and positive) integers" that we loosely constructed above is also decidable via the syntactic rewriting of formulae into $\Sigma_\mathbb{N}$-formulae. Rather than using this cumbersome rewriting, however, we next study a theory of integers.

3.3.3 Theory of Integers

The **theory of integers** $T_\mathbb{Z}$ has signature

$$\Sigma_\mathbb{Z} : \ \{\ldots, -2, -1, 0, \ 1, \ 2, \ \ldots, -3\cdot, -2\cdot, \ 2\cdot, \ 3\cdot, \ \ldots, \ +, \ -, \ =, \ >\} \ ,$$

where

- $\ldots, -2, -1, 0, 1, 2, \ldots$ are constants, intended to be assigned the obvious corresponding values in the intended domain of integers $\mathbb{Z}$;
- $\ldots, -3\cdot, -2\cdot, 2\cdot, 3\cdot, \ldots$ are unary functions, intended to represent constant coefficients (*e.g.*, $2 \cdot x$, abbreviated $2x$);
- $+$ and $-$ are binary functions, intended to represent the obvious corresponding functions over $\mathbb{Z}$;
- $=$ and $>$ are binary predicates, intended to represent the obvious corresponding predicates over $\mathbb{Z}$.

Since Example 3.7 shows that $\Sigma_\mathbb{Z}$-formulae can be reduced to $\Sigma_\mathbb{N}$-formulae, we do not axiomatize $T_\mathbb{Z}$. $T_\mathbb{Z}$ is merely a convenient representation for reasoning about addition over all integers.

The intended interpretations of $T_\mathbb{Z}$ have domain $\mathbb{Z}$ and are such that α_I assigns the obvious values, functions, and predicates to the constant, function, and predicate symbols of $\Sigma_\mathbb{Z}$.

In Chapter 7, we discuss Cooper's decision procedure for deciding $T_\mathbb{Z}$-validity, while in Chapter 8, we discuss decision procedures for the quantifier-free fragment of $T_\mathbb{Z}$. These procedures decide $T_\mathbb{N}$-validity as well: the following example illustrates that $\Sigma_\mathbb{N}$-formulae can be reduced to $\Sigma_\mathbb{Z}$-formulae.

Example 3.8. To decide the $T_\mathbb{N}$-validity of

$$\forall x.\, \exists y.\, x = y + 1\ ,$$

decide the $T_\mathbb{Z}$-validity of

$$\forall x.\, x \geq 0 \;\rightarrow\; \exists y.\, y \geq 0 \,\wedge\, x = y + 1\ ,$$

where $t_1 \geq t_2$ expands to $t_1 = t_2 \,\vee\, t_1 > t_2$. ∎

We prove the validity of several $\Sigma_\mathbb{Z}$-formulae using the semantic argument method. Our application of the semantic argument method in this context is informal; it is intended to allow us to argue intuitively about validity until Chapter 7.

Example 3.9. To prove that the $\Sigma_\mathbb{Z}$-formula

$$F: \;\forall x, y, z.\, x > z \,\wedge\, y \geq 0 \;\rightarrow\; x + y > z\ .$$

is $T_\mathbb{Z}$-valid, assume otherwise: there is a $T_\mathbb{Z}$-interpretation I such that $I \not\models F$:

1. $\quad I \not\models F$ $\hfill$ assumption
2. $\quad I_1 : \; I \lhd \{x \mapsto v_1\} \lhd \{y \mapsto v_2\} \lhd \{z \mapsto v_3\}$
   $\qquad \not\models x > z \,\wedge\, y \geq 0 \;\rightarrow\; x + y > z \quad$ 1, $\forall$
3. $\quad I_1 \models x > z \,\wedge\, y \geq 0$ $\hfill$ 2, $\rightarrow$
4. $\quad I_1 \not\models x + y > z$ $\hfill$ 2, $\rightarrow$
5. $\quad I_1 \models \neg(x + y > z)$ $\hfill$ 4, $\neg$

We derive a contradiction by collecting formulae from lines 3 and 5, applying the variant interpretation I_1, and querying the theory $T_\mathbb{Z}$: are there integers v_1, v_2, v_3 such that

$$v_1 > v_3 \,\wedge\, v_2 \geq 0 \,\wedge\, \neg(v_1 + v_2 > v_3)\ ?$$

No, for $v_1 > v_3 \,\wedge\, v_2 \geq 0$ implies $v_1 + v_2 > v_3$. We summarize this reasoning in $T_\mathbb{Z}$ with the line

6. $\quad I_1 \models \bot \quad$ 3, 5, $T_\mathbb{Z}$

Therefore, F is $T_\mathbb{Z}$-valid. ∎

Arguing the validity of arithmetic formulae at the level of axioms is tedious. Therefore, unlike in Example 3.2 in which the theory-specific reasoning is incorporated into the semantic argument method by applying and stating specific axioms of T_E, the semantic argument method for T_Z handles the "logical" aspects of the structured reasoning, while a separate informal argument reasons about the theory-specific elements.

Example 3.10. To prove that the Σ_Z-formula

$$F: \ \forall x, y. \ x > 0 \ \wedge \ (x = 2y \ \vee \ x = 2y + 1) \ \rightarrow \ x - y > 0$$

is T_Z-valid, assume otherwise: there is a T_Z-interpretation I such that $I \not\models F$:

1.	$I \not\models F$	assumption
2.	$I_1 : \ I \lhd \{x \mapsto v_1\} \lhd \{y \mapsto v_2\}$	
	$\not\models \ x > 0 \ \wedge \ (x = 2y \ \vee \ x = 2y + 1) \ \rightarrow \ x - y > 0$	
		1, $\forall$
3.	$I_1 \models x > 0 \ \wedge \ (x = 2y \ \vee \ x = 2y + 1)$	2, $\rightarrow$
4.	$I_1 \models x > 0$	3, $\wedge$
5.	$I_1 \models x = 2y \ \vee \ x = 2y + 1$	3, $\wedge$
6.	$I_1 \not\models x - y > 0$	2, $\rightarrow$
7.	$I_1 \models \neg(x - y > 0)$	6, $\neg$

There are two cases to consider. In the first case,

8a.	$I_1 \models x = 2y$	5, $\vee$

We collect the formulae of lines 4, 7, and 8a, apply the variant interpretation I_1, and query the theory T_Z: are there integers v_1, v_2 such that

$$v_1 > 0 \ \wedge \ v_1 = 2v_2 \ \wedge \ \neg(v_1 - v_2 > 0) \ ?$$

No, for substituting $v_1 = 2v_2$ throughout produces

$$2v_2 > 0 \ \wedge \ \neg(2v_2 - v_2 > 0) \ ,$$

which simplifies to

$$v_2 > 0 \ \wedge \ \neg(v_2 > 0) \ ,$$

a contradiction. This reasoning is summarized by

9a.	$I_1 \models \ \bot$	4, 7, 8a, T_Z

In the second case,

8b.	$I_1 \models x = 2y + 1$	5, $\vee$

Considering lines 4, 7, and 8b, are there integers v_1, v_2 such that

$$v_1 > 0 \ \wedge \ v_1 = 2v_2 + 1 \ \wedge \ \neg(v_1 - v_2 > 0) \ ?$$

No, for substituting $v_1 = 2v_2 + 1$ throughout produces

$$2v_2 + 1 > 0 \ \wedge \ \neg(2v_2 + 1 - v_2 > 0) \ ,$$

which simplifies to

$$2v_2 + 1 > 0 \ \wedge \ \neg(v_2 + 1 > 0) \ .$$

The first literal holds only when $v_2 > -1$, while the second holds only when $v_2 \leq -1$, a contradiction. This reasoning is summarized by

9b. $I_1 \models \bot$ 4, 7, 8b, $T_{\mathbb{Z}}$

Thus, F is $T_{\mathbb{Z}}$-valid.   ∎

3.4 Rationals and Reals

Almost as old as arithmetic on integers is arithmetic on the rational numbers $\mathbb{Q}$ and (not quite as old) on the real numbers $\mathbb{R}$. In this section, we describe two theories of real arithmetic. The latter theory can also be seen as a theory of rational arithmetic.

The first theory is the **theory of reals**, involving addition and multiplication over $\mathbb{R}$; it is also known as **elementary algebra**. The term "elementary" refers to the restriction that variables range only over domain elements (as in all first-order theories), not over sets or functions of domain elements. Most junior high students are familiar with elementary algebra. As a first-order theory, elementary algebra is of course more complex since formulae are constructed with logical connectives and quantifiers.

The second theory is the theory of addition over $\mathbb{R}$ or $\mathbb{Q}$. Interpretations with domains of $\mathbb{R}$ are indistinguishable from interpretations with domains of $\mathbb{Q}$, as we discuss below. For this reason, we call this second theory the **theory of rationals**.

Example 3.11. Let us distinguish informally between the theories of integers (with only addition), reals (with addition and multiplication), and rationals (with only addition).

In the theory of integers,

$$F : \ \exists x. \ 2x = 7$$

is $T_{\mathbb{Z}}$-invalid. However, assigning to x the rational number $\frac{7}{2}$ satisfies $2x = 7$, so F should be satisfiable in the theory of rationals. Moreover, $\frac{7}{2}$ is also a real number, so F should also be satisfiable in the theory of reals.

The theory of reals includes multiplication, allowing a formula like

$$G: \exists x.\ x^2 = 2$$

to be expressed, where x^2 abbreviates $x \cdot x$. G should be valid in the theory of reals because assigning to x the real number $\sqrt{2}$ satisfies $x^2 = 2$. $\sqrt{2}$ is irrational.   ∎

3.4.1 Theory of Reals

The **theory of reals** $T_{\mathbb{R}}$, or **elementary algebra**, has signature

$$\Sigma_{\mathbb{R}}: \{0,\ 1,\ +,\ -,\ \cdot,\ =,\ \geq\}\,,$$

where

- 0 and 1 are constants;
- $+$ (addition) and $\cdot$ (multiplication) are binary functions;
- $-$ (negation) is a unary function;
- and $=$ (equality) and $\geq$ (weak inequality) are binary predicates.

$T_{\mathbb{R}}$ has the most complex axiomatization of the theories that we study. We group axioms by their mathematical content.

First are the axioms of an **abelian group**. An abelian group is a structure with additive identity 0, associative and commutative addition $+$, additive inverse $-$, and equality $=$. The qualifier "abelian" simply means that addition is commutative. The axioms are the following:

1. $\forall x, y, z.\ (x+y)+z = x+(y+z)$	($+$ associativity)
2. $\forall x.\ x+0 = x$	($+$ identity)
3. $\forall x.\ x+(-x) = 0$	($+$ inverse)
4. $\forall x, y.\ x+y = y+x$	($+$ commutativity)

The first three axioms are the axioms of a **group**.

Second are the additional axioms of a **ring**. A ring is an abelian group with a multiplicative identity 1 and associative multiplication $\cdot$ that distributes over addition. For convenience, we usually shorten $x \cdot y$ to xy.

1. $\forall x, y, z.\ (xy)z = x(yz)$	($\cdot$ associativity)
2. $\forall x.\ x1 = x$	($\cdot$ left identity)
3. $\forall x.\ 1x = x$	($\cdot$ right identity)
4. $\forall x, y, z.\ x(y+z) = xy + xz$	(left distributivity)
5. $\forall x, y, z.\ (x+y)z = xz + yz$	(right distributivity)

Both left and right identity and distributivity axioms are required since $\cdot$ is not commutative (yet). It is made so in the next set of axioms.

Third are the additional axioms of a **field**. In a field, $\cdot$ is commutative; the additive and multiplicative identities are different; and the multiplicative inverse of a non-0 value exists (*e.g.*, $\frac{1}{2}$ is the multiplicative inverse of 2).

1. $\forall x, y.\ xy = yx$	($\cdot$ commutativity)

2. $0 \neq 1$ (separate identities)

3. $\forall x.\ x \neq 0\ \rightarrow\ \exists y.\ xy = 1$ ($\cdot$ inverse)

The axiom ($\cdot$ commutativity) makes the ($\cdot$ right identity) and (right distributivity) axioms redundant.

Fourth are the additional axioms characterizing $\geq$ as a **total order**.

1. $\forall x, y.\ x \geq y\ \wedge\ y \geq x\ \rightarrow\ x = y$ (antisymmetry)

2. $\forall x, y, z.\ x \geq y\ \wedge\ y \geq z\ \rightarrow\ x \geq z$ (transitivity)

3. $\forall x, y.\ x \geq y\ \vee\ y \geq x$ (totality)

Finally are the additional axioms of a **real closed field**.

1. $\forall x, y, z.\ x \geq y\ \rightarrow\ x + z \geq y + z$ (+ ordered)

2. $\forall x, y.\ x \geq 0\ \wedge\ y \geq 0\ \rightarrow\ xy \geq 0$ ($\cdot$ ordered)

3. $\forall x.\ \exists y.\ x = y^2\ \vee\ x = -y^2$ (square-root)

4. for each odd integer n,

$$\forall \bar{x}.\ \exists y.\ y^n + x_1 y^{n-1} + \cdots + x_{n-1} y + x_n = 0 \qquad \text{(at least one root)}$$

We again abbreviate $x_1, \ldots, x_n$ by $\bar{x}$. By y^n, we mean y multiplied by itself n times: $y \cdots y$. The axioms (+ ordered) and ($\cdot$ ordered) assert that every $T_{\mathbb{R}}$-interpretation is an **ordered field**. The axiom (square-root) asserts the existence of the square-root of every value. The final axiom schema states that polynomials of odd degree have at least one root.

Putting all axioms together and pruning redundant axioms, we have:

1. $\forall x, y.\ x \geq y\ \wedge\ y \geq x\ \rightarrow\ x = y$ (antisymmetry)

2. $\forall x, y, z.\ x \geq y\ \wedge\ y \geq z\ \rightarrow\ x \geq z$ (transitivity)

3. $\forall x, y.\ x \geq y\ \vee\ y \geq x$ (totality)

4. $\forall x, y, z.\ (x + y) + z = x + (y + z)$ (+ associativity)

5. $\forall x.\ x + 0 = x$ (+ identity)

6. $\forall x.\ x + (-x) = 0$ (+ inverse)

7. $\forall x, y.\ x + y = y + x$ (+ commutativity)

8. $\forall x, y, z.\ x \geq y\ \rightarrow\ x + z \geq y + z$ (+ ordered)

9. $\forall x, y, z.\ (xy)z = x(yz)$ ($\cdot$ associativity)

10. $\forall x.\ 1x = x$ ($\cdot$ identity)

11. $\forall x.\ x \neq 0\ \rightarrow\ \exists y.\ xy = 1$ ($\cdot$ inverse)

12. $\forall x, y.\ xy = yx$ ($\cdot$ commutativity)

13. $\forall x, y.\ x \geq 0\ \wedge\ y \geq 0\ \rightarrow\ xy \geq 0$ ($\cdot$ ordered)

14. $\forall x, y, z.\ x(y + z) = xy + xz$ (distributivity)

15. $0 \neq 1$ (separate identities)

16. $\forall x.\ \exists y.\ x = y^2\ \vee\ -x = y^2$ (square-root)

17. for each odd integer n,

$$\forall \overline{x}.\ \exists y.\ y^n + x_1 y^{n-1} + \cdots + x_{n-1} y + x_n = 0 \qquad \text{(at least one root)}$$

Example 3.12. The method of **quantifier elimination**, which we study in Chapter 7, eliminates quantifiers from a formula to produce an equivalent quantifier-free formula. If a formula F contains free variables, then a quantifier elimination procedure produces an equivalent quantifier-free formula F' such that $\mathrm{free}(F') \subseteq \mathrm{free}(F)$. For example, when is the formula

$$F:\ \exists x.\ ax^2 + bx + c = 0$$

satisfiable? That is, what are the conditions on a, b, and c such that a quadratic polynomial has a real root? Recall that the discriminant must be nonnegative:

$$F':\ b^2 - 4ac \geq 0 \ .$$

F' is the quantifier-free formula that is $T_{\mathbb{R}}$-equivalent to F.   ∎

Tarski proved that $T_{\mathbb{R}}$ was decidable in the 1930s, although the Second World War prevented his publishing the result until 1956. Collins proposed the more efficient technique of **cylindrical algebraic decomposition** (CAD) in 1975. Unfortunately, even the most efficient decision procedures for $T_{\mathbb{R}}$ have prohibitively high time complexity: CAD runs in time proportionate to $2^{2^{k|F|}}$, for some constant k and for $|F|$ the length of $\Sigma_{\mathbb{R}}$-formula F.

3.4.2 Theory of Rationals

Given the high complexity of deciding $T_{\mathbb{R}}$-validity (and the high intellectual complexity of Tarski's and subsequent decision procedures for $T_{\mathbb{R}}$), we turn to a simpler theory without multiplication, the **theory of rationals** $T_{\mathbb{Q}}$. It has signature

$$\Sigma_{\mathbb{Q}}:\ \{0,\ 1,\ +,\ -,\ =,\ \geq\}\ ,$$

where

- 0 and 1 are constants;
- + (addition) is a binary function;
- − (negation) is a unary function;
- and = (equality) and ≥ (weak inequality) are binary predicates.

Its axioms are the following:

1. $\forall x, y.\ x \geq y\ \wedge\ y \geq x\ \rightarrow\ x = y$ (antisymmetry)
2. $\forall x, y, z.\ x \geq y\ \wedge\ y \geq z\ \rightarrow\ x \geq z$ (transitivity)
3. $\forall x, y.\ x \geq y\ \vee\ y \geq x$ (totality)

4. $\forall x, y, z.\ (x + y) + z = x + (y + z)$ (+ associativity)
5. $\forall x.\ x + 0 = x$ (+ identity)
6. $\forall x.\ x + (-x) = 0$ (+ inverse)
7. $\forall x, y.\ x + y = y + x$ (+ commutativity)
8. $\forall x, y, z.\ x \geq y\ \rightarrow\ x + z \geq y + z$ (+ ordered)

9. for each positive integer n,

$$\forall x.\ nx = 0\ \rightarrow\ x = 0 \qquad \text{(torsion-free)}$$

10. for each positive integer n,

$$\forall x.\ \exists y.\ x = ny \qquad \text{(divisible)}$$

By nx we mean x added to itself n times: $x + \cdots + x$. The first eight axioms are a subset of the axioms of $T_{\mathbb{R}}$. They state that every $T_{\mathbb{Q}}$-interpretation is an ordered abelian group. $\geq$ is a total order by the first three axioms. Identity 0, addition $+$, additive inverse $-$, and equality $=$ comprise an abelian group by the next four axioms. The eighth axiom asserts that the abelian group is ordered.

The axiom schema (torsion-free) states that only 0 can be added to itself to produce 0. The name "torsion-free" comes from the following mathematical context. In a group, the **order** of an element v is the integer n such that nv is the identity element 0: nv $= 0$. If no such n exists, then the element v has infinite order. A group is **torsion-free** if the only element with finite order is the identity 0.

Finally, the axiom schema (divisible) asserts that all elements of the domain D_I of a $T_{\mathbb{Q}}$-interpretation I are divisible. That is, for every positive integer n, every element v $\in D_I$ is the sum of n of some other element w $\in D_I$.

Thus, every $T_{\mathbb{Q}}$-interpretation is a divisible torsion-free abelian group. In particular, the rationals and reals with $+$, $-$, $=$, and $\geq$ are divisible torsion-free abelian groups. As $T_{\mathbb{Q}}$-interpretations, the rationals and reals are **elementarily equivalent**: there does not exist a $\Sigma_{\mathbb{Q}}$-formula that distinguishes between a real $T_{\mathbb{Q}}$-interpretation (an interpretation with domain $\mathbb{R}$) and a rational $T_{\mathbb{Q}}$-interpretation (an interpretation with domain $\mathbb{Q}$).

This characteristic makes sense, intuitively: no linear expression with only integer coefficients can capture, say, $\sqrt{2}$ without also being satisfied by some rational values. When junior high students solve linear algebra problems, they apply addition, subtraction, multiplication, and division; but they do not take roots.

In contrast, $T_{\mathbb{R}}$ is a theory of reals: the $\Sigma_{\mathbb{R}}$-formula $x \cdot x = 2$ is only satisfied by $T_{\mathbb{R}}$-interpretations I in which $\alpha_I[x] = -\sqrt{2}$ or $\alpha_I[x] = \sqrt{2}$.

Example 3.13. Strict inequality is simple to express in $T_{\mathbb{Q}}$. Write

$$\forall x, y.\ \exists z.\ x + y > z$$

as the $\Sigma_{\mathbb{Q}}$-formula

$$\forall x, y. \ \exists z. \ \neg(x + y = z) \ \wedge \ x + y \geq z \ .$$

The situation is similar for $T_{\mathbb{R}}$.   ∎

Example 3.14. Rational coefficients are simple to express in $T_{\mathbb{Q}}$. Write

$$\frac{1}{2}x + \frac{2}{3}y \geq 4$$

as the $\Sigma_{\mathbb{Q}}$-formula $3x + 4y \geq 24$.   ∎

For convenience, we sometimes write $x \leq y$ for $y \geq x$.

In Chapter 7, we study a procedure for eliminating quantifiers in the theory $T_{\mathbb{Q}}$. On closed formulae, this procedure decides validity. In Chapter 8, we study a decision procedure for the quantifier-free fragment of $T_{\mathbb{Q}}$, which is efficiently decidable.

3.5 Recursive Data Structures

The **theory of recursive data structures (RDS)** describes a set of data structures that are ubiquitous in programming. The most basic RDS is a non-recursive structure, like C's `struct`, in which a single variable has multiple fields. Truly recursive RDSs include lists, stacks, and binary trees.

The theory of recursive data structures T_{RDS} formalizes the reasoning about such structures. It builds on the theory of equality T_{E}.

Theory of Lists

We first focus on the theory of LISP-like lists, T_{cons}, which has signature

$$\Sigma_{\mathsf{cons}} : \ \{\mathsf{cons}, \ \mathsf{car}, \ \mathsf{cdr}, \ \mathsf{atom}, \ =\} \ ,$$

where

- `cons` is a binary function, called the constructor: $\mathsf{cons}(a, b)$ represents the list constructed by concatenating a to b;
- `car` is a unary function, called the left projector: $\mathsf{car}(\mathsf{cons}(a, b)) = a$;
- `cdr` is a unary function, called the right projector: $\mathsf{cdr}(\mathsf{cons}(a, b)) = b$;
- `atom` is a unary predicate: $\mathsf{atom}(x)$ is true iff x is a single-element list;
- and $=$ (equality) is a binary predicate.

`car` and `cdr` are historical names abbreviating "contents of address register" and "contents of decrement register", respectively. In the intended interpretations, atoms are individual elements, while lists are multiple elements assembled together via cons. For example, $\mathsf{cons}(a, \mathsf{cons}(b, c))$ is a list of three elements, while a for which atom(a) holds is an atom. car and cdr are functions for accessing parts of lists. For example, car(cons(a, cons(b, c))) returns the head a of the list; cdr(cons(a, cons(b, c))) returns the tail cons(b, c) of the list; and cdr(cdr(cons(a, cons(b, c)))) returns c.

The axioms of T_{cons} are the following:

1. the axioms of (reflexivity), (symmetry), and (transitivity) of T_E
2. instantiations of the (function congruence) axiom schema for cons, car, and cdr:

$$\forall x_1, x_2, y_1, y_2.\ x_1 = x_2 \ \wedge \ y_1 = y_2 \ \rightarrow \ \text{cons}(x_1, y_1) = \text{cons}(x_2, y_2)$$

$$\forall x, y.\ x = y \ \rightarrow \ \text{car}(x) = \text{car}(y)$$

$$\forall x, y.\ x = y \ \rightarrow \ \text{cdr}(x) = \text{cdr}(y)$$

3. an instantiation of the (predicate congruence) axiom schema for atom:

$$\forall x, y.\ x = y \ \rightarrow \ (\text{atom}(x) \leftrightarrow \text{atom}(y))$$

4. $\forall x, y.\ \text{car}(\text{cons}(x, y)) = x$ (left projection)
5. $\forall x, y.\ \text{cdr}(\text{cons}(x, y)) = y$ (right projection)
6. $\forall x.\ \neg\text{atom}(x) \ \rightarrow \ \text{cons}(\text{car}(x), \text{cdr}(x)) = x$ (construction)
7. $\forall x, y.\ \neg\text{atom}(\text{cons}(x, y))$ (atom)

The first three sets of axioms define $=$ to be a congruence relation for cons, car, cdr, and atom. The axioms (left projection) and (right projection) define the behavior of car and cdr on non-atom lists: car returns the first element of a cons structure, and cdr returns the second element. However, they do not specify the behavior of car and cdr on atoms. The (construction) axiom states that the cons of car(x) and cdr(x) is x itself, unless x is an atom. In other words, cons constructs structures, and car and cdr deconstruct them. Finally, the axiom (atom) asserts that a term with root function symbol cons is not an atom; it is a non-atomic list.

The congruence axioms for cons, car, and cdr assert an important property about lists: two lists are equal iff their components are equal. The forward direction — if two lists are equal, then their components are equal — is a consequence of the (function congruence) axioms for car and cdr. The backward direction is a consequence of the (function congruence) axiom for cons. This relationship between two structures and their components is sometimes called **extensionality**. We see it in arrays as well.

General Theory of RDS

T_{cons} is an instance of the general theory of recursive data structures T_{RDS}. Each RDS contributes the following to the signature:

- an n-ary constructor C;

- n projection functions $\pi_1^C, \ldots, \pi_n^C$;
- and one atom predicate atom_C.

Associated with each RDS is an instantiation of the following axiom schema:

1. the axioms of (reflexivity), (symmetry), and (transitivity) of T_E;
2. instantiations of the (function congruence) axiom schema for constructor C and set of projectors $\pi_1^C, \ldots, \pi_n^C$;
3. an instantiation of the (predicate congruence) axiom schema for atom_C;
4. for each $i \in \{1, \ldots, n\}$,

$$\forall x_1, \ldots, x_n. \ \pi_i^C(C(x_1, \ldots, x_n)) = x_i \qquad \text{(projection)}$$

5. $\forall x. \ \neg\mathsf{atom}_C(x) \ \rightarrow \ C(\pi_1^C(x), \ldots, \pi_n^C(x)) = x \qquad \text{(construction)}$
6. $\forall x_1, \ldots, x_n. \ \neg\mathsf{atom}_C(C(x_1, \ldots, x_n)) \qquad \text{(atom)}$

The axioms of T_{cons} are an instantiation of this schema. We subsequently focus on T_{cons} for concreteness.

Theory of Acyclic Lists

A variation on this theory in which data structures are acyclic has been studied. Acyclicity makes sense for stacks, but not necessarily for lists and other data structures. Consider the theory of acyclic LISP-like lists, T_{cons}^+. Its axioms include those of T_{cons} and the following axiom schema:

$\forall x. \ \mathsf{car}(x) \neq x$
$\forall x. \ \mathsf{cdr}(x) \neq x$
$\forall x. \ \mathsf{car}(\mathsf{car}(x)) \neq x$
$\forall x. \ \mathsf{car}(\mathsf{cdr}(x)) \neq x$
$\forall x. \ \mathsf{cdr}(\mathsf{car}(x)) \neq x$
$\cdots$

T_{cons}^+ is decidable, but T_{cons} is not. However, the quantifier-free fragments of these theories are efficiently decidable.

Theory of Lists with Specified Atoms

The axioms of T_{cons} leave the behavior of car and cdr on atoms unspecified. Adding the axiom

$$\forall x. \ \mathsf{atom}(x) \ \rightarrow \ \mathsf{atom}(\mathsf{car}(x)) \ \wedge \ \mathsf{atom}(\mathsf{cdr}(x))$$

to those of T_{cons} makes decidability of the resulting theory $T_{\mathrm{cons}}^{\mathrm{atom}}$ NP-complete.

Theory of Lists with Equality

In Chapter 9, we describe a decision procedure for satisfiability in the quantifier-free fragment of T_{cons}. The decision procedure is actually applicable to the quantifier-free fragment of a more expressive theory, $T^{=}_{\text{cons}}$, which is the combination of T_{E} and T_{cons} and thus includes uninterpreted constants, functions, and predicates. Thus, its signature is $\Sigma_{\text{E}} \cup \Sigma_{\text{cons}}$, and its axioms are the union of the axioms of T_{E} and T_{cons}. In Section 3.8 and Chapter 10, we discuss more general combinations of theories.

Example 3.15. To prove that the $\Sigma^{=}_{\text{cons}}$-formula

$$F : \quad \begin{array}{l} \mathsf{car}(a) = \mathsf{car}(b) \ \wedge \ \mathsf{cdr}(a) = \mathsf{cdr}(b) \ \wedge \ \neg\mathsf{atom}(a) \ \wedge \ \neg\mathsf{atom}(b) \\ \rightarrow \ f(a) = f(b) \end{array}$$

is $T^{=}_{\text{cons}}$-valid, assume otherwise: there exists a $T^{=}_{\text{cons}}$-interpretation I such that $I \not\models F$:

1.	$I \not\models F$	assumption
2.	$I \models \mathsf{car}(a) = \mathsf{car}(b)$	$1, \rightarrow, \wedge$
3.	$I \models \mathsf{cdr}(a) = \mathsf{cdr}(b)$	$1, \rightarrow, \wedge$
4.	$I \models \neg\mathsf{atom}(a)$	$1, \rightarrow, \wedge$
5.	$I \models \neg\mathsf{atom}(b)$	$1, \rightarrow, \wedge$
6.	$I \not\models f(a) = f(b)$	$1, \rightarrow$
7.	$I \models \mathsf{cons}(\mathsf{car}(a), \mathsf{cdr}(a)) = \mathsf{cons}(\mathsf{car}(b), \mathsf{cdr}(b))$	
		$2, 3,$ (function congruence)
8.	$I \models \mathsf{cons}(\mathsf{car}(a), \mathsf{cdr}(a)) = a$	$4,$ (construction)
9.	$I \models \mathsf{cons}(\mathsf{car}(b), \mathsf{cdr}(b)) = b$	$5,$ (construction)
10.	$I \models a = b$	$7, 8, 9,$ (transitivity)
11.	$I \models f(a) = f(b)$	$10,$ (function congruence)
12.	$I \models \bot$	$6, 11$

Therefore, F is $T^{=}_{\text{cons}}$-valid. ∎

3.6 Arrays

Arrays are another common data structure in programming. They are similar to the uninterpreted functions of T_{E} except that they can be modified. The **theory of arrays** T_{A} describes the basic characteristic of an array: if value v is written to position i of array a, then subsequently reading from position i of a should return v. Because logic is static, modified arrays are represented functionally, as in functional programming.

The theory of arrays T_{A} has signature

$$\Sigma_{\text{A}} : \ \{ \cdot[\cdot], \ \cdot\langle\cdot \triangleleft \cdot\rangle, \ = \} \ ,$$

where

- $a[i]$ (read) is a binary function: $a[i]$ represents the value of array a at position i;
- $a\langle i \triangleleft v\rangle$ (write) is a ternary function: $a\langle i \triangleleft v\rangle$ represents the modified array a in which position i has value v;
- and $=$ (equality) is a binary predicate.

$\cdot[\cdot]$ and $\cdot\langle\cdot\triangleleft\cdot\rangle$ really are binary and ternary functions, respectively, even though we write them using a convenient notation. Writing $a[i]$ as $\mathsf{read}(a, i)$ and $a\langle i \triangleleft e\rangle$ as $\mathsf{write}(a, i, e)$ emphasizes that they are functions.

Arrays are represented functionally. The term $a\langle i \triangleleft v\rangle$ is an array that is like a except that it has value v at position i. The term $a\langle i \triangleleft v\rangle[j]$ (which abbreviates $(a\langle i \triangleleft v\rangle)[j])$ is equal to the value of array $a\langle i \triangleleft v\rangle$ at position j: it is v if $j = i$ and $a[j]$ otherwise. $a\langle i \triangleleft v\rangle\langle j \triangleleft w\rangle$ (which abbreviates $(a\langle i \triangleleft v\rangle)\langle j \triangleleft w\rangle)$ is an array that is like a except that it differs at the positions i, where it has value v, and j, where is has value w. Finally, the term $a\langle i \triangleleft v\rangle\langle j \triangleleft w\rangle[k]$ (which abbreviates $((a\langle i \triangleleft v\rangle)\langle j \triangleleft w\rangle)[k])$ has value w if $k = j$ (even if $k = i$ also), value v if $k = i$ and $k \neq j$, and value $a[k]$ otherwise.

The axioms of T_A are the following:

1. the axioms of (reflexivity), (symmetry), and (transitivity) of T_E;
2. $\forall a, i, j.\ i = j \;\rightarrow\; a[i] = a[j]$ (array congruence)
3. $\forall a, v, i, j.\ i = j \;\rightarrow\; a\langle i \triangleleft v\rangle[j] = v$ (read-over-write 1)
4. $\forall a, v, i, j.\ i \neq j \;\rightarrow\; a\langle i \triangleleft v\rangle[j] = a[j]$ (read-over-write 2)

The first set of axioms defines $=$ as an equivalence relation. The next axiom asserts that accessing an array with two equal expressions produces the same element. The final two axioms capture the basic characteristic of arrays: reading at an index that has been written produces the most recently written value.

The equality predicate $=$ is only defined for array "elements". For example,

$$F:\ a[i] = e \;\rightarrow\; a\langle i \triangleleft e\rangle = a$$

is not T_A-valid, although our intuition suggests that it should be. The problem is that the interaction between $=$ and the read and write functions is not captured in the axioms of T_A. In other words, equality between arrays, not just between elements, is undefined.

Instead of F, we write

$$F':\ a[i] = e \;\rightarrow\; \forall j.\ a\langle i \triangleleft e\rangle[j] = a[j]\ ,$$

which is T_A-valid.

Example 3.16. To prove that

$$F':\ a[i] = e \;\rightarrow\; \forall j.\ a\langle i \triangleleft e\rangle[j] = a[j]\ ,$$

is T_A-valid, assume otherwise: there is a T_A-interpretation I such that $I \not\models F'$:

1.	$I \not\models F'$	assumption
2.	$I \models a[i] = e$	$1, \rightarrow$
3.	$I \not\models \forall j.\ a\langle i \triangleleft e\rangle[j] = a[j]$	$1, \rightarrow$
4.	$I_1 : I \triangleleft \{j \mapsto j\} \not\models a\langle i \triangleleft e\rangle[j] = a[j]$	$3, \forall,$ for some $j \in D_I$
5.	$I_1 \models a\langle i \triangleleft e\rangle[j] \neq a[j]$	$4, \neg$
6.	$I_1 \models i = j$	$5,$ (read-over-write 2)
7.	$I_1 \models a[i] = a[j]$	$6,$ (array congruence)
8.	$I_1 \models a\langle i \triangleleft e\rangle[j] = e$	$6,$ (read-over-write 1)
9.	$I_1 \models a\langle i \triangleleft e\rangle[j] = a[j]$	$2, 7, 8,$ (transitivity)
10.	$I_1 \models \bot$	$4, 9$

We derive line 6 from line 5 by using the **contrapositive** of (read-over-write 2). The contrapositive of $F_1 \rightarrow F_2$ is $\neg F_2 \rightarrow \neg F_1$, and

$$F_1 \rightarrow F_2 \iff \neg F_2 \rightarrow \neg F_1 \ .$$

Lines 4 and 9 are contradictory, so that actually $I \models F'$. Thus, F' is T_A-valid. ∎

Unfortunately, T_A-validity is undecidable. It is straightforward to encode arbitrary formulae of FOL in T_A by viewing functions as multi-dimensional arrays (arrays whose elements are arrays). Therefore, a theory $T_\mathsf{A}^=$ in which the behavior of $=$ on arrays is axiomatized has been studied. Its quantifier-free fragment is decidable. The signature of $T_\mathsf{A}^=$ is the same as that of T_A. Its axioms consists of those of T_A and the following axiom:

$$\forall a, b.\ (\forall i.\ a[i] = b[i]) \ \leftrightarrow \ a = b \qquad \text{(extensionality)}$$

Example 3.17. To prove that

$$F :\ a[i] = e \ \rightarrow \ a\langle i \triangleleft e\rangle = a$$

is $T_\mathsf{A}^=$-valid, assume otherwise: there is a $T_\mathsf{A}^=$-interpretation I such that $I \not\models F$:

1.	$I \not\models F$	assumption
2.	$I \models a[i] = e$	$1, \rightarrow$
3.	$I \not\models a\langle i \triangleleft e\rangle = a$	$1, \rightarrow$
4.	$I \models a\langle i \triangleleft e\rangle \neq a$	$3, \neg$
5.	$I \models \neg(\forall j.\ a\langle i \triangleleft e\rangle[j] = a[j])$	$4,$ (extensionality)
6.	$I \not\models \forall j.\ a\langle i \triangleleft e\rangle[j] = a[j]$	$5, \neg$

The rest of the proof then proceeds as in Example 3.16. ∎

We present a decision procedure for the quantifier-free fragment of T_A in Chapter 9. In Chapter 11, we present a decision procedure for satisfiability in a fragment of T_A that is more expressive than even the quantifier-free fragment of $T_\mathsf{A}^=$.

Table 3.1. Decidability of theories and quantifier-free fragments

Theory	Description	Full	QFF
T_{E}	equality	no	yes
T_{PA}	Peano arithmetic	no	no
$T_{\mathbb{N}}$	Presburger arithmetic	yes	yes
$T_{\mathbb{Z}}$	linear integers	yes	yes
$T_{\mathbb{R}}$	reals (with $\cdot$)	yes	yes
$T_{\mathbb{Q}}$	rationals (without $\cdot$)	yes	yes
T_{RDS}	recursive data structures	no	yes
T_{RDS}^{+}	acyclic recursive data structures	yes	yes
T_{A}	arrays	no	yes
$T_{\mathsf{A}}^{=}$	arrays with extensionality	no	yes

Table 3.2. Complexities for decidable theories

Theory	Complexity
PL	NP-complete
$T_{\mathbb{N}}, T_{\mathbb{Z}}$	$\Omega\left(2^{2^{n}}\right),\, O\left(2^{2^{2^{kn}}}\right)$
$T_{\mathbb{R}}$	$O\left(2^{2^{kn}}\right)$
$T_{\mathbb{Q}}$	$\Omega\left(2^{n}\right),\, O\left(2^{2^{kn}}\right)$
T_{RDS}^{+}	not elementary recursive

3.7 ⋆Survey of Decidability and Complexity

We survey the known decidability and complexity results of the theories of this chapter.

Table 3.1 summarizes the decidability results for the first-order theories. The quantifier-free fragment of each theory that we study in Part II of this book is decidable.

Table 3.2 summarizes the complexity results for satisfiability in PL and the decidable first-order theories. For all complexities, n is the size of the input formula, and k is some positive integer. A decision problem is not **elementary recursive** if its running time cannot be bounded by a fixed-height stack of exponentials. Only decision procedures for satisfiability in PL scale well to large problems.

Table 3.3 summarizes the complexity results for the quantifier-free fragments. As satisfiability in PL is already NP-complete, we consider only **conjunctive** formulae, which are just conjunctions of literals. For example, satisfiability of propositional conjunctive formulae is decidable in linear time: if both P and $\neg P$ appear in F, for some propositional variable P, then F is unsatisfiable; otherwise, F is satisfiable. For quantifier-free (but not conjunctive) formulae, all complexities except that for $T_{\mathbb{R}}$ are NP-complete. Satisfiability in the quantifier-free fragments of T_{E}, $T_{\mathbb{Q}}$, T_{RDS}, and T_{RDS}^{+} is efficiently decidable.

Table 3.3. Complexities for quantifier-free, conjunctive fragments of theories

Theory	Complexity	Theory	Complexity
PL	$\Theta(n)$	T_{E}	$O(n \log n)$
$T_{\mathsf{N}}, T_{\mathbb{Z}}$	NP-complete	$T_{\mathbb{R}}$	$O\left(2^{2^{kn}}\right)$
$T_{\mathbb{Q}}$	PTIME	T_{RDS}^{+}	$\Theta(n)$
T_{RDS}	$O(n \log n)$	T_{A}	NP-complete

3.8 Combination Theories

In practice, the formulae that we want to check for satisfiability or validity span multiple theories. For example, in program verification, one might want to prove a property about an array of integers or a list of reals. We will see many such examples in Chapter 5. Thus, decision procedures for fragments of first-order theories are essentially useless unless they can be combined.

What does every signature of every theory presented so far have in common? They all have equality, =. Nelson and Oppen made equality the focal predicate in their general method for combining quantifier-free fragments of first-order theories (with some restrictions). Given two theories T_1 and T_2 such that $\Sigma_1 \cap \Sigma_2 = \{=\}$ — only = is shared — the combined theory $T_1 \cup T_2$ has signature $\Sigma_1 \cup \Sigma_2$ and axioms $A_1 \cup A_2$. Nelson and Oppen showed that if

- satisfiability in the quantifier-free fragment of T_1 is decidable;
- satisfiability in the quantifier-free fragment of T_2 is decidable;
- and certain technical requirements are met,

then satisfiability in the quantifier-free fragment of $T_1 \cup T_2$ is decidable. Furthermore, if the decision procedures for T_1 and T_2 are in P (in NP), then the combined decision procedure for $T_1 \cup T_2$ is in P (in NP).

Chapter 10 studies the Nelson-Oppen combination of decision procedures.

Example 3.18. To prove that the $(\Sigma_{\mathsf{A}}^{=} \cup \Sigma_{\mathbb{Z}})$-formula

$$F : \quad a = b \;\rightarrow\; a[i] \geq b[i]$$

is $(T_{\mathsf{A}}^{=} \cup T_{\mathbb{Z}})$-valid we assume otherwise: there is a $(T_{\mathsf{A}}^{=} \cup T_{\mathbb{Z}})$-interpretation I such that $I \not\models F$:

1. $I \not\models F$ assumption
2. $I \models a = b$ $1, \rightarrow$
3. $I \not\models a[i] \geq b[i]$ $1, \rightarrow$
4. $I \models \neg(a[i] \geq b[i])$ $3, \neg$
5. $I \models a[i] = b[i]$ $2, T_{\mathsf{A}}^{=}$ (extensionality)
6. $I \models \bot$ $4, 5, T_{\mathsf{A}}^{=} \cup T_{\mathbb{Z}}$

Line 6 summarizes the argument that it is impossible for a $T_{\mathbb{Z}}$-interpretation to satisfy both $a[i] = b[i]$ and $\neg(a[i] \geq b[i])$. ∎

Example 3.19. The $(\Sigma_\mathsf{E} \cup \Sigma_\mathbb{Z})$-formula

$$1 \leq x \ \wedge \ x \leq 2 \ \wedge \ f(x) \neq f(1) \ \wedge \ f(x) \neq f(2)$$

is $(T_\mathsf{E} \cup T_\mathbb{Z})$-unsatisfiable, for x cannot be either 1 or 2 without violating (function congruence). Seen as a $(\Sigma_\mathsf{E} \cup \Sigma_\mathbb{Q})$-formula, it is $(T_\mathsf{E} \cup T_\mathbb{Q})$-satisfiable: choose $x = \frac{3}{2}$.

The $(\Sigma_\mathsf{E} \cup \Sigma_\mathbb{Q})$-formula

$$f(f(x) - f(y)) \neq f(z) \ \wedge \ x \leq y \ \wedge \ y + z \leq x \ \wedge \ 0 \leq z$$

is $(T_\mathsf{E} \cup T_\mathbb{Q})$-unsatisfiable. In particular, the final three literals imply that $z = 0$ and $x = y$, so that $f(x) = f(y)$. But then from the first literal, $f(0) \neq f(0)$ since both $f(x) - f(y)$ and z equal 0.

Finally, the $(\Sigma_\mathsf{E} \cup \Sigma_\mathbb{Z})$-formula

$$1 \leq x \ \wedge \ x \leq 3 \ \wedge \ f(x) \neq f(1) \ \wedge \ f(x) \neq f(3) \ \wedge \ f(1) \neq f(2)$$

is $(T_\mathsf{E} \cup T_\mathbb{Z})$-satisfiable since x can be 2 without violating (function congruence). ■

3.9 Summary

Important data types in software and hardware models include integers; rationals; recursive data structures like records, lists, stacks, and trees; and arrays. This chapter introduces first-order theories that formalize these data types. It covers:

- *First-order theories.* Formalizations of structures and operations into first-order logic: signatures, axioms. Fragments of theories, in particular quantifier-free fragments. Interpretations, satisfiability, validity.
- Specific theories:
  - *Equality* defines the binary predicate $=$ as a congruence relation. Satisfiability in the quantifier-free fragment is efficiently decidable, and the decision procedure is the basis for decision procedures for data structures (see Chapter 9).
  - *Integer arithmetic.* Satisfiability in integer arithmetic without multiplication is decidable.
  - *Rational* and *real arithmetic*. Satisfiability in real arithmetic with multiplication is decidable with high complexity. Satisfiability in rational arithmetic without multiplication is efficiently decidable. Rational arithmetic without multiplication is indistinguishable from real arithmetic without multiplication.
  - *Recursive data structures* include records, lists, stacks, and queues. Satisfiability in the quantifier-free fragment is efficiently decidable.

- *Arrays* can be read and written. Satisfiability in the quantifier-free fragment is decidable. Chapter 11 studies a larger fragment in which satisfiability is still decidable.
- *Combination theories.* How can decision procedures for multiple theories be combined to decide satisfiability in combination theories?

Studying first-order theories is important for two reasons. First, theories formalize into FOL interesting structures and operations on the structures. Second, satisfiability in some theories or fragments of theories is decidable and thus can be reasoned about algorithmically, whereas satisfiability in general FOL is undecidable. Part II of this book focuses on such theories and fragments that are useful for program analysis. Chapters 5 and 6 provide many examples of formulae from combinations of these theories in the context of program verification.

Bibliographic Remarks

The undecidability of validity in FOL [13] motivated the subsequent study of first-order theories and fragments. In 1929, Presburger proved that satisfiability in arithmetic without multiplication is decidable [73]. Tarski showed in the 1930s that real arithmetic is decidable even with multiplication, although the Second World War delayed the publication of this result [90]. The axiomatization of recursive data structures that we study is from work by Nelson and Oppen [66]. Oppen studied a variation in which structures are acyclic [69]. The axiomatization of arrays, in particular the read-over-write axioms, is due to McCarthy [59]. The Nelson-Oppen combination method is based on work by Nelson and Oppen in the late 1970s and early 1980s [65].

Exercises

3.1 (Semantic argument in T_E). Use the semantic method to argue the validity of the following Σ_E-formulae, or identify a counterexample (a falsifying T_E-interpretation).

(a) $f(x, y) = f(y, x) \rightarrow f(a, y) = f(y, a)$
(b) $f(g(x)) = g(f(x)) \land f(g(g(f(y)))) = x \land f(y) = x \rightarrow g(f(x)) = x$
(c) $f(f(f(a))) = f(f(a)) \land f(f(f(f(a)))) = a \rightarrow f(a) = a$
(d) $f(f(f(a))) = f(a) \land f(f(a)) = a \rightarrow f(a) = a$
(e) $p(x) \land f(f(x)) = x \land f(f(f(x))) = x \rightarrow p(f(x))$

3.2 (Semantic argument in $T_{\mathbb{Z}}$). Use the semantic method to argue the validity of the following $\Sigma_{\mathbb{Z}}$-formulae, or identify a counterexample (a falsifying $T_{\mathbb{Z}}$-interpretation).

(a) $x \leq y \land z = x + 1 \rightarrow z \leq y$

(b) $x \le y \ \wedge \ z = x - 1 \ \rightarrow \ z \le y$
(c) $3x = 2 \ \rightarrow \ x \le 0$
(d) $1 \le x \ \wedge \ x \le 2 \ \rightarrow \ x = 1 \ \vee \ x = 2$
(e) $1 \le x \ \wedge \ x + y \le 3 \ \wedge \ 1 \le y \ \rightarrow \ x = 1 \ \vee \ x = 2$
(f) $0 \le x \ \wedge \ 0 \le x + y \ \wedge \ x + y \le 1 \ \wedge \ (y \le -2 \ \vee \ 2 \le y) \ \rightarrow \ 0 \le -1$

3.3 (Semantic argument in $T_\mathbb{Q}$). Use the semantic method to argue the validity of the following $\Sigma_\mathbb{Q}$-formulae, or identify a counterexample (a falsifying $T_\mathbb{Q}$-interpretation).

(a) $3x = 2 \ \rightarrow \ x \le 0$
(b) $0 \le x + 2y \ \wedge \ 2x + y \le 1$
(c) $1 \le x \ \wedge \ x \le 2 \ \rightarrow \ x = 1 \ \vee \ x = 2$

3.4 (Semantic argument in T_{cons}). Use the semantic method to argue the validity of the following Σ_{cons}-formulae, or identify a counterexample (a falsifying T_{cons}-interpretation).

(a) $\text{car}(x) = y \ \wedge \ \text{cdr}(x) = z \ \rightarrow \ x = \text{cons}(y, z)$
(b) $\neg\text{atom}(x) \ \wedge \ \text{car}(x) = y \ \wedge \ \text{cdr}(x) = z \ \rightarrow \ x = \text{cons}(y, z)$

3.5 (Semantic argument in T_A). Use the semantic method to argue the validity of the following Σ_A-formulae, or identify a counterexample (a falsifying T_A-interpretation).

(a) $a\langle i \lhd e\rangle[j] = e \ \rightarrow \ i = j$
(b) $a\langle i \lhd e\rangle[j] = e \ \rightarrow \ a[j] = e$
(c) $a\langle i \lhd e\rangle[j] = e \ \rightarrow \ i = j \ \vee \ a[j] = e$
(d) $a\langle i \lhd e\rangle\langle j \lhd f\rangle[k] = g \ \wedge \ j \ne k \ \wedge \ i = j \ \rightarrow \ a[k] = g$

3.6 (Semantic argument in combinations). For each of the following formulae, identify the combination of theories in which it lies. To avoid ambiguity, prefer $T_\mathbb{Z}$ to $T_\mathbb{Q}$. Then argue its validity in that combination of theories using the semantic method, or identify a counterexample.

(a) $1 \le x \ \wedge \ x \le 2 \ \wedge \ \text{cons}(1, y) \ne \text{cons}(x, y) \ \rightarrow \ \text{cons}(2, y) = \text{cons}(x, y)$
(b) $a[i] \ge 1 \ \wedge \ a[i] + x \le 2 \ \wedge \ x > 0 \ \wedge \ x = i \ \rightarrow \ a\langle x \lhd 2\rangle[i] = 1$
(c) $1 \le x \ \wedge \ x \le 2 \ \wedge \ \text{cons}(1, y) \ne \text{cons}(x, y) \ \rightarrow \ \text{cons}(2, y) = \text{cons}(x, y)$
(d) $x + y = z \ \wedge \ f(z) = z \ \rightarrow \ f(x + y) = z$
(e) $g(x + y, z) = f(g(x, y)) \ \wedge \ x + z = y \ \wedge \ z \ge 0 \ \wedge \ x \ge y \ \wedge \ g(x, x) = z$
     $\rightarrow \ f(z) = g(2x, 0)$

3.7 (Semantic argument in combinations). Redo Exercise 3.6, preferring $T_\mathbb{Q}$ to $T_\mathbb{Z}$.

4

Induction

Even though this proposition may have an infinite number of cases, I shall give a very short proof of it assuming two lemmas. The first, which is self evident, is that the proposition is valid for the second row. The second is that if the proposition is valid for any row then it must necessarily be valid for the following row.

— Blaise Pascal
Traité du Triangle Arithmetique, c. 1654

This chapter discusses **induction**, a classic proof technique for proving first-order theorems with universal quantifiers. Section 4.1 begins with **stepwise induction**, which may be familiar to the reader from earlier education. Section 4.2 then introduces **complete induction** in the context of arithmetic. Complete induction is theoretically equivalent in power to stepwise induction but sometimes produces more concise proofs. Section 4.3 generalizes complete induction to **well-founded induction** in the context of arithmetic and recursive data structures. Finally, Section 4.4 covers a form of well-founded induction over logical formulae called **structural induction**. It is useful for reasoning about correctness of decision procedures and properties of logical theories and their interpretations.

We apply induction in various ways throughout the book. Structural induction is applied in proofs. Additionally, induction is the basis for the program verification methods of Chapter 5.

4.1 Stepwise Induction

We review stepwise induction for arithmetic and then show that it extends naturally to other theories, such as the theory of lists T_{cons}.

Arithmetic

Recall from Chapter 3 that the theory of Peano arithmetic T_{PA} formalizes arithmetic over the natural numbers. Its axioms include an instance of the (induction) axiom schema

$$F[0] \wedge (\forall n.\ F[n] \rightarrow F[n+1]) \rightarrow \forall x.\ F[x]$$

for each Σ_{PA}-formula $F[x]$ with only one free variable x. This axiom schema says that to prove $\forall x.\ F[x]$ — that is, $F[x]$ is T_{PA}-valid for all natural numbers x — it is sufficient to do the following:

- For the **base case**, prove that $F[0]$ is T_{PA}-valid.
- For the **inductive step**, assume as the **inductive hypothesis** that for some arbitrary natural number n, $F[n]$ is T_{PA}-valid. Then prove that $F[n+1]$ is T_{PA}-valid under this assumption.

These two steps comprise the **stepwise induction principle** for Peano (and Presburger) arithmetic.

Example 4.1. Consider the theory T_{PA}^+ obtained from augmenting T_{PA} with the following axioms:

- $\forall x.\ x^0 = 1$ (exp. zero)
- $\forall x, y.\ x^{y+1} = x^y \cdot x$ (exp. successor)
- $\forall x, z.\ exp_3(x, 0, z) = z$ (exp_3 zero)
- $\forall x, y, z.\ exp_3(x, y+1, z) = exp_3(x, y, x \cdot z)$ (exp_3 successor)

The first two axioms define exponentiation x^y, while the latter two axioms define a ternary function $exp_3(x, y, z)$.

Let us prove that the following formula is T_{PA}^+-valid:

$$\forall x, y.\ exp_3(x, y, 1) = x^y\ . \tag{4.1}$$

We need to choose either x or y as the induction variable. Considering the exp_3 axioms, it appears that y is the smarter choice: (exp_3 successor) defines exp_3 recursively by considering the predecessor of $y + 1$.

Therefore, we prove by stepwise induction on y that

$$F[y] :\ \forall x.\ exp_3(x, y, 1) = x^y\ .$$

For the **base case**, we prove

$$F[0] :\ \forall x.\ exp_3(x, 0, 1) = x^0\ .$$

But $x^0 = 1$ by (exp. zero), and $exp_3(x, 0, 1) = 1$ by (exp_3 zero).
Assume as the inductive hypothesis that for arbitrary natural number n,

$$F[n] :\ \forall x.\ exp_3(x, n, 1) = x^n\ . \tag{4.2}$$

We want to prove that

$$F[n+1]: \quad \forall x. \ exp_3(x, n+1, 1) = x^{n+1} \ . \tag{4.3}$$

By $(exp_3 \ \mathsf{successor})$, we have

$$exp_3(x, n+1, 1) = exp_3(x, n, x \cdot 1) \ .$$

Unfortunately, the inductive hypothesis (4.2) does not apply to the left side of the equation since $n \neq n+1$, and it does not apply to the right side of the equation because the third argument is $x \cdot 1$ rather than 1. Continuing to apply axioms is unlikely to bring us closer to the proof. Thus, we have failed to prove the property.

What went wrong in the proof? Did we choose the wrong induction variable? Would x have worked better? In fact, it is often the case that the property must be **strengthened** to allow the induction to go through. A stronger theorem provides a stronger inductive hypothesis.

Let us strengthen the property to be proved to

$$\forall x, y, z. \ exp_3(x, y, z) = x^y \cdot z \ . \tag{4.4}$$

It clearly implies the desired property (4.1): just choose $z = 1$.

Again, we must choose the induction variable. Based on $(exp_3 \ \mathsf{successor})$, we use y again. Thus, we prove by stepwise induction on y that

$$F[y]: \quad \forall x, z. \ exp_3(x, y, z) = x^y \cdot z \ .$$

For the base case, we prove

$$F[0]: \quad \forall x, z. \ exp_3(x, 0, z) = x^0 \cdot z \ .$$

From $(exp_3 \ \mathsf{zero})$, we have $exp_3(x, 0, z) = z$, while from $(\mathsf{exp. \ zero})$, we have $x^0 \cdot z = 1 \cdot z = z$.

Assume as the inductive hypothesis that

$$F[n]: \quad \forall x, z. \ exp_3(x, n, z) = x^n \cdot z \tag{4.5}$$

for arbitrary natural number n. We want to prove that

$$F[n+1]: \quad \forall x, z'. \ exp_3(x, n+1, z') = x^{n+1} \cdot z' \ , \tag{4.6}$$

where we have renamed z to z' for convenience. We have

$$
\begin{aligned}
exp_3(x, n+1, z') &= exp_3(x, n, x \cdot z') && (exp_3 \ \mathsf{successor}) \\
&= x^n \cdot (x \cdot z') && \text{IH (4.5)}, \ z \mapsto x \cdot z' \\
&= x^{n+1} \cdot z' && (\mathsf{exp. \ successor})
\end{aligned}
$$

finishing the proof. The annotation $z \mapsto x \cdot z'$ indicates that $x \cdot z'$ is substituted for z when applying the inductive hypothesis (4.5). This substitution is justified because z is universally quantified. Renaming z to z' avoids confusion during the application of the inductive hypothesis in the second line. ∎

Lists

We can define stepwise induction over recursive data structures such as lists (see Chapters 3 and 9). Consider the theory of lists T_{cons}. **Stepwise induction** in T_{cons} is defined according to the following schema

$$(\forall\ \text{atom}\ u.\ F[u]) \ \wedge\ (\forall u, v.\ F[v] \rightarrow F[\text{cons}(u, v)]) \ \rightarrow\ \forall x.\ F[x]$$

for Σ_{cons}-formulae $F[x]$ with only one free variable x. The notation $\forall$ atom $u.\ F[u]$ abbreviates $\forall u.\ \text{atom}(u) \rightarrow F[u]$. In other words, to prove $\forall x.\ F[x]$ — that is, $F[x]$ is T_{cons}-valid for all lists x — it is sufficient to do the following:

- For the **base case**, prove that $F[u]$ is T_{cons}-valid for an arbitrary atom u.
- For the **inductive step**, assume as the **inductive hypothesis** that for some arbitrary list v, $F[v]$ is valid. Then prove that for arbitrary list u, $F[\text{cons}(u, v)]$ is T_{cons}-valid under this assumption.

These steps comprise the **stepwise induction principle** for lists.

Example 4.2. Consider the theory T_{cons}^+ obtained from augmenting T_{cons} with the following axioms:

- $\forall$ atom $u.\ \forall v.\ concat(u, v) = \text{cons}(u, v)$ (concat. atom)
- $\forall u, v, x.\ concat(\text{cons}(u, v), x) = \text{cons}(u, concat(v, x))$ (concat. list)
- $\forall$ atom $u.\ rvs(u) = u$ (reverse atom)
- $\forall x, y.\ rvs(concat(x, y)) = concat(rvs(y), rvs(x))$ (reverse list)
- $\forall$ atom $u.\ flat(u)$ (flat atom)
- $\forall u, v.\ flat(\text{cons}(u, v)) \leftrightarrow \text{atom}(u) \wedge flat(v)$ (flat list)

The first two axioms define the *concat* function, which concatenates two lists together. For example,

$$concat(\text{cons}(a, b), \text{cons}(b, \text{cons}(c, d)))$$
$$= \text{cons}(a, \text{cons}(b, \text{cons}(b, \text{cons}(c, \text{cons}(d))))) \ .$$

The next two axioms define the *rvs* function, which reverses a list. For example,

$$rvs(\text{cons}(a, \text{cons}(b, c))) = \text{cons}(c, \text{cons}(b, a)) \ .$$

Note, however, that *rvs* is undefined on lists like $\text{cons}(\text{cons}(a, b), c)$, for $\text{cons}(\text{cons}(a, b), c)$ cannot result from concatenating two lists together. Therefore, the final two axioms define the *flat* predicate, which evaluates to $\top$ on a list iff every element is an atom. For example, $\text{cons}(a, \text{cons}(b, c))$ is *flat*, but $\text{cons}(\text{cons}(a, b), c)$ is not because the first element of the list is itself a list.

Let us prove that the following formula is T_{cons}^+-valid:

$$\forall x.\ flat(x) \ \rightarrow\ rvs(rvs(x)) = x \ . \tag{4.7}$$

For example,

$$rvs(rvs(\text{cons}(a, \text{cons}(b, c)))) = rvs(\text{cons}(c, \text{cons}(b, a)))$$
$$= \text{cons}(a, \text{cons}(b, c))$$

We prove by stepwise induction on x that

$$F[x]: \; flat(x) \; \rightarrow \; rvs(rvs(x)) = x \; .$$

For the base case, we consider arbitrary atom u and prove

$$F[u]: \; flat(u) \; \rightarrow \; rvs(rvs(u)) = u \; .$$

But $rvs(rvs(u)) = u$ follows from two applications of (reverse atom).
Assume as the inductive hypothesis that for arbitrary list v,

$$F[v]: \; flat(v) \; \rightarrow \; rvs(rvs(v)) = v \; . \tag{4.8}$$

We want to prove that for arbitrary list u,

$$F[\text{cons}(u, v)]: \; flat(\text{cons}(u, v)) \; \rightarrow \; rvs(rvs(\text{cons}(u, v))) = \text{cons}(u, v) \; . \tag{4.9}$$

Consider two cases: either atom(u) or $\neg$atom(u).
If $\neg$atom(u), then

$$flat(\text{cons}(u, v)) \; \Leftrightarrow \; \text{atom}(u) \wedge flat(v) \; \Leftrightarrow \; \bot \; ,$$

by (flat list) and assumption. Therefore, (4.9) holds since its antecedent is $\bot$.
If atom(u), then we have that

$$flat(\text{cons}(u, v)) \; \Leftrightarrow \; \text{atom}(u) \wedge flat(v) \; \Leftrightarrow \; flat(v)$$

by (flat list). Furthermore,

$$
\begin{aligned}
rvs(rvs(\text{cons}(u, v))) & \\
&= rvs(rvs(concat(u, v))) && \text{(concat. atom)} \\
&= rvs(concat(rvs(v), rvs(u))) && \text{(reverse list)} \\
&= concat(rvs(rvs(u)), rvs(rvs(v))) && \text{(reverse list)} \\
&= concat(u, rvs(rvs(v))) && \text{(reverse atom)} \\
&= concat(u, v) && \text{IH (4.8), since } flat(v) \\
&= \text{cons}(u, v) && \text{(concat. atom)}
\end{aligned}
$$

which finishes the proof. ∎

4.2 Complete Induction

Complete induction is a form of induction that sometimes yields more concise proofs. For the theory of arithmetic T_{PA} it is defined according to the following schema

$$(\forall n.\ (\forall n'.\ n' < n \to F[n']) \to F[n]) \quad\to\quad \forall x.\ F[x]$$

for Σ_{PA}-formulae $F[x]$ with only one free variable x. In other words, to prove $\forall x.\ F[x]$ — that is, $F[x]$ is T_{PA}-valid for all natural numbers x — it is sufficient to follow the **complete induction principle**:

- Assume as the **inductive hypothesis** that for arbitrary natural number n and for every natural number n' such that $n' < n$, $F[n']$ is T_{PA}-valid. Then prove that $F[n]$ is T_{PA}-valid.

It appears that we are missing a base case. In practice, a case analysis usually requires at least one base case. In other words, the base case is implicit in the structure of complete induction. For example, for $n = 0$, the inductive hypothesis does not provide any information — there does not exist a natural number $n' < 0$. Hence, $F[0]$ must be shown separately without assistance from the inductive hypothesis.

Example 4.3. Consider another augmented version of Peano arithmetic, T^*_{PA}, that defines integer division. It has the usual axioms of T_{PA} plus the following:

- $\forall x, y.\ x < y \ \to\ quot(x, y) = 0$ (quotient less)
- $\forall x, y.\ y > 0 \ \to\ quot(x + y, y) = quot(x, y) + 1$ (quotient successor)
- $\forall x, y.\ x < y \ \to\ rem(x, y) = x$ (remainder less)
- $\forall x, y.\ y > 0 \ \to\ rem(x + y, y) = rem(x, y)$ (remainder successor)

These axioms define functions for computing integer quotients $quot(x, y)$ and remainders $rem(x, y)$. For example, $quot(5, 3) = 1$ and $rem(5, 3) = 2$. We prove two properties, which the reader may recall from grade school, about these functions. First, we prove that the remainder is always less than the divisor:

$$\forall x, y.\ y > 0 \ \to\ rem(x, y) < y\ . \tag{4.10}$$

Then we prove that

$$\forall x, y.\ y > 0 \ \to\ x = y \cdot quot(x, y) + rem(x, y)\ . \tag{4.11}$$

For property (4.10), (remainder successor) suggests that we apply complete induction on x to prove

$$F[x]:\ \forall y.\ y > 0 \ \to\ rem(x, y) < y\ . \tag{4.12}$$

Thus, for the inductive hypothesis, assume that for arbitrary natural number x,

$$\forall x'.\ x' < x \ \to\ \underbrace{\forall y.\ y > 0 \ \to\ rem(x', y) < y}_{F[x']}\ . \tag{4.13}$$

Let y be an arbitrary positive natural number. Consider two cases: either $x < y$ or $\neg(x < y)$.

If $x < y$, then

$$rem(x, y) = x \qquad\qquad \text{(remainder less)}$$
$$< y \qquad\qquad \text{by assumption } x < y$$

as desired.

If $\neg(x < y)$, then there is a natural number n, $n < x$, such that $x = n + y$. Compute

$$rem(x, y) = rem(n + y, y) \qquad\qquad x = n + y$$
$$= rem(n, y) \qquad\qquad \text{(remainder successor)}$$
$$< y \qquad\qquad \text{IH (4.13), } x' \mapsto n, \text{ since } n < x$$

finishing the proof of this property.

For property (4.11), (remainder successor) again suggests that we apply complete induction on x to prove

$$G[x] : \quad \forall y.\ y > 0 \ \rightarrow\ x = y \cdot quot(x, y) + rem(x, y) \ . \tag{4.14}$$

Thus, for the inductive hypothesis, assume that for arbitrary natural number x,

$$\forall x'.\ x' < x \ \rightarrow\ \underbrace{\forall y.\ y > 0 \ \rightarrow\ x' = y \cdot quot(x', y) + rem(x', y)}_{G[x']} \ . \tag{4.15}$$

Let y be an arbitrary positive natural number. Consider two cases: either $x < y$ or $\neg(x < y)$.

If $x < y$, then

$$y \cdot quot(x, y) + rem(x, y)$$
$$= y \cdot 0 + rem(x, y) \qquad\qquad \text{(quotient less)}$$
$$= x \qquad\qquad \text{(remainder less)}$$

as desired.

If $\neg(x < y)$, then there is a natural number $n < x$ such that $x = n + y$. Compute

$$y \cdot quot(x, y) + rem(x, y)$$
$$= y \cdot quot(n + y, y) + rem(n + y, y) \qquad\qquad x = n + y$$
$$= y \cdot (quot(n, y) + 1) + rem(n + y, y) \qquad\qquad \text{(quotient successor)}$$
$$= y \cdot (quot(n, y) + 1) + rem(n, y) \qquad\qquad \text{(remainder successor)}$$
$$= (y \cdot quot(n, y) + rem(n, y)) + y$$
$$= n + y \qquad\qquad \text{IH (4.15), } x' \mapsto n, \text{ since } n < x$$
$$= x \qquad\qquad x = n + y$$

finishing the proof of this property. ∎

In the next section, we generalize complete induction so that we can apply it in other theories.

4.3 Well-Founded Induction

A binary predicate $\prec$ over a set S is a **well-founded relation** iff there does not exist an infinite sequence $s_1, s_2, s_3, \ldots$ of elements of S such that each successive element is less than its predecessor:

$$s_1 \succ s_2 \succ s_3 \succ \cdots ,$$

where $s \prec t$ iff $t \succ s$. In other words, each sequence of elements of S that decreases according to $\prec$ is finite.

Example 4.4. The relation $<$ is well-founded over the natural numbers. Any sequence of natural numbers decreasing according to $<$ is finite:

$$1023 > 39 > 30 > 29 > 8 > 3 > 0 .$$

However, the relation $<$ is not well-founded over the rationals. Consider the infinite decreasing sequence

$$1 > \frac{1}{2} > \frac{1}{3} > \frac{1}{4} > \cdots ,$$

that is, the sequence $s_i = \frac{1}{i}$ for $i \geq 0$. ∎

Example 4.5. Consider the theory $T_{\mathsf{cons}}^{\mathsf{PA}}$, which includes the axioms of T_{cons} and T_{PA} and the following axioms:

- $\forall\, \mathsf{atom}\ u, v.\ u \preceq_{\mathsf{c}} v \leftrightarrow u = v$ ($\preceq_{\mathsf{c}}$ (1))
- $\forall\, \mathsf{atom}\ u.\ \forall v.\ \neg\mathsf{atom}(v) \rightarrow \neg(v \preceq_{\mathsf{c}} u)$ ($\preceq_{\mathsf{c}}$ (2))
- $\forall\, \mathsf{atom}\ u.\ \forall v, w.\ u \preceq_{\mathsf{c}} \mathsf{cons}(v, w) \leftrightarrow u = v \lor u \preceq_{\mathsf{c}} w$ ($\preceq_{\mathsf{c}}$ (3))
- $\forall u_1, v_1, u_2, v_2.\ \mathsf{cons}(u_1, v_1) \preceq_{\mathsf{c}} \mathsf{cons}(u_2, v_2)$
  $\leftrightarrow (u_1 = u_2 \land v_1 \preceq_{\mathsf{c}} v_2) \lor \mathsf{cons}(u_1, v_1) \preceq_{\mathsf{c}} v_2$ ($\preceq_{\mathsf{c}}$ (4))
- $\forall x, y.\ x \prec_{\mathsf{c}} y \leftrightarrow x \preceq_{\mathsf{c}} y \land x \neq y$ ($\prec_{\mathsf{c}}$)
- $\forall\, \mathsf{atom}\ u.\ |u| = 1$ (length atom)
- $\forall u, v.\ |\mathsf{cons}(u, v)| = 1 + |v|$ (length list)

The first four axioms define the sublist relation $\preceq_{\mathsf{c}}$. $x \preceq_{\mathsf{c}} y$ holds iff x is a (not necessarily strict) sublist of y. The next axiom defines the strict sublist relation: $x \prec_{\mathsf{c}} y$ iff x is a strict sublist of y. The final two axioms define the length function, which returns the number of elements in a list.

    The strict sublist relation $\prec_{\mathsf{c}}$ is well-founded on the set of all lists. One can prove that the number of sublists of a list is finite; and that its set of strict sublists is a superset of the set of strict sublists of any of its sublists. Hence, there cannot be an infinite sequence of lists descending according to $\prec_{\mathsf{c}}$. ∎

    Well-founded induction generalizes complete induction to arbitrary theory T by allowing the use of any binary predicate $\prec$ that is well-founded in the domain of every T-interpretation. It is defined in the theory T with well-founded relation $\prec$ by the following schema

$$(\forall n. \ (\forall n'. \ n' \prec n \rightarrow F[n']) \rightarrow F[n]) \ \rightarrow \ \forall x. \ F[x]$$

for Σ-formulae $F[x]$ with only one free variable x. In other words, to prove the T-validity of $\forall x. \ F[x]$, it is sufficient to follow the **well-founded induction principle**:

- Assume as the **inductive hypothesis** that for arbitrary element n and for every element n' such that $n' \prec n$, $F[n']$ is T-valid. Then prove that $F[n]$ is T-valid.

Complete induction in T_{PA} of Section 4.2 is a specific instance of well-founded induction that uses the well-founded relation $<$.

A theory of lists augmented with the first five axioms of Example 4.5 has well-founded induction in which the well-founded relation is $\prec_c$.

Example 4.6. Consider proving the trivial property

$$\forall x. \ |x| \geq 1 \tag{4.16}$$

in $T_{\mathsf{cons}}^{\mathsf{PA}}$, which was defined in Example 4.5. We apply well-founded induction on x using the well-founded relation $\prec_c$ to prove

$$F[x] : \ |x| \geq 1 \ . \tag{4.17}$$

For the inductive hypothesis, assume that

$$\forall x'. \ x' \prec_c x \ \rightarrow \ \underbrace{|x'| \geq 1}_{F[x']} \ . \tag{4.18}$$

Consider two cases: either $\mathsf{atom}(x)$ or $\neg\mathsf{atom}(x)$.

In the first case $|x| = 1 \geq 1$ by (length atom).

In the second case x is not an atom, so $x = \mathsf{cons}(u, v)$ for some u, v by the (construction) axiom. Then

$$
\begin{aligned}
|x| &= |\mathsf{cons}(u, v)| \\
&= 1 + |v| &&\text{(length list)} \\
&\geq 1 + 1 &&\text{IH (4.18), } x' \mapsto v, \text{ since } v \prec_c \mathsf{cons}(u, v) \\
&\geq 1
\end{aligned}
$$

as desired. Exercise 4.2 asks the reader to prove formally that $\forall u, v. \ v \prec_c \mathsf{cons}(u, v)$.

This property is also easily proved using stepwise induction. ∎

In applying well-founded induction, we need not restrict ourselves to the intended domain D of a theory T. A useful class of well-founded relations are **lexicographic relations**. From a finite set of pairs of sets and well-founded relations $(S_1, \prec_1), \ldots, (S_m, \prec_m)$, construct the set

$$S = S_1 \times \cdots \times S_m \,,$$

and define the relation $\prec$:

$$(s_1, \ldots, s_m) \prec (t_1, \ldots, t_m) \Leftrightarrow \bigvee_{i=1}^{m} \left(s_i \prec_i t_i \land \bigwedge_{j=1}^{i-1} s_j = t_j \right)$$

for $s_i, t_i \in S_i$. That is, for elements $s : (s_1, \ldots, s_m)$, $t : (t_1, \ldots, t_m)$ of S, $s \prec t$ iff at some position i, $s_i \prec_i t_i$, and for all preceding positions j, $s_j = t_j$. For convenience, we abbreviate $(s_1, \ldots, s_m)$ by $\bar{s}$ and thus write, for example, $\bar{s} \prec \bar{t}$.

Lexicographic well-founded induction has the form

$$(\forall \bar{n}.\ (\forall \bar{n}'.\ \bar{n}' \prec \bar{n} \rightarrow F[\bar{n}']) \rightarrow F[\bar{n}]) \quad \rightarrow \quad \forall \bar{x}.\ F[\bar{x}]$$

for Σ-formula $F[\bar{x}]$ with only free variables $\bar{x} = \{x_1, \ldots, x_m\}$. Notice that the form of this induction principle is the same as well-founded induction. The only difference is that we are considering tuples $\bar{n} = (n_1, \ldots, n_m)$ rather than single elements n.

Example 4.7. Consider the following puzzle. You have a bag of red, yellow, and blue chips. If only one chip remains in the bag, you take it out. Otherwise, you remove two chips at random:

1. If one of the two removed chips is red, you do not put any chips in the bag.
2. If both of the removed chips are yellow, you put one yellow chip and five blue chips in the bag.
3. If one of the chips is blue and the other is not red, you put ten red chips in the bag.

These cases cover all possibilities for the two chips. Does this process always halt?

We prove the following property: *for all bags of chips, you can execute the choose-and-replace process only a finite number of times before the bag is empty.* Let the triple

$$(\#\text{yellow},\ \#\text{blue},\ \#\text{red})$$

represent the current state of the bag. Such a tuple is in the set of triples of natural numbers $S : \mathbb{N}^3$. Let $<_3$ be the natural lexicographic extension of $<$ to such triples. For example,

$$(11, 13, 3) \not<_3 (11, 9, 104) \quad \text{but} \quad (11, 9, 104) <_3 (11, 13, 3) \,.$$

We prove that for arbitrary bag state (y, b, r) represented by the triple of natural numbers y, b, and r, only a finite number of steps remain.

For the base cases, consider when the bag has no chips (state $(0,0,0)$) or only one chip (one of states $(1,0,0)$, $(0,1,0)$, or $(0,0,1)$). In the first case, you are done; in the second set of cases, only one step remains.

Assume for the inductive hypothesis that for any bag state (y',b',r') such that

$$(y',b',r') <_3 (y,b,r) ,$$

only a finite number of steps remain. Now remove two chips from the current bag, represented by state (y,b,r). Consider the three possible cases:

1. *If one of the two removed chips is red, you do not put any chips in the bag.* Then the new bag state is $(y-1,b,r-1)$, $(y,b-1,r-1)$, or $(y,b,r-2)$. Each is less than (y,b,r) by $<_3$.
2. *If both of the removed chips are yellow, you put one yellow chip and five blue chips in the bag.* Then the new bag state is $(y-1,b+5,r)$, which is less than (y,b,r) by $<_3$.
3. *If one of the chips is blue and the other is not red, you put ten red chips in the bag.* Then the new bag state is $(y-1,b-1,r+10)$ or $(y,b-2,r+10)$. Each is less than (y,b,r) by $<_3$.

In all cases, we can apply the inductive hypothesis to deduce that only a finite number of steps remain from the next state. Since only one step of the process is required to get to the next state, there are only a finite number of steps remaining from the current state (y,b,r). Hence, the process always halts. ∎

Example 4.8. Consider proving the property

$$\forall x,y.\ x \preceq_c y \ \rightarrow\ |x| \le |y| \tag{4.19}$$

in $T_{\text{cons}}^{\text{PA}}$. Let $\prec_c^2$ be the natural lexicographic extension of $\prec_c$ to pairs of lists. That is, $(x_1,y_1) \prec_c^2 (x_2,y_2)$ iff $x_1 \prec_c x_2 \lor (x_1 = x_2 \land y_1 \prec_c y_2)$.

We apply lexicographic well-founded induction to pairs (x,y) to prove

$$F[x,y]:\ x \preceq_c y \ \rightarrow\ |x| \le |y| . \tag{4.20}$$

For the inductive hypothesis, assume that

$$\forall x',y'.\ (x',y') \prec_c^2 (x,y) \ \rightarrow\ \underbrace{x' \preceq_c y' \ \rightarrow\ |x'| \le |y'|}_{F[x',y']} . \tag{4.21}$$

Now consider arbitrary lists x and y. Consider two cases: either $\text{atom}(x)$ or $\neg\text{atom}(x)$.

If $\text{atom}(x)$, then

$$|x| = 1 \qquad\qquad \text{(length atom)}$$
$$\le |y| \qquad\qquad \text{Example 4.6}$$

Hence, regardless of whether $x \preceq_c y$, we have that $|x| \leq |y|$ so that (4.20) holds.

If $\neg\mathsf{atom}(x)$, then consider two cases: either $\mathsf{atom}(y)$ or $\neg\mathsf{atom}(y)$. If $\mathsf{atom}(y)$, then

$$x \preceq_c y \Leftrightarrow \bot$$

by ($\preceq_c$ (2)); therefore, (4.20) holds trivially.

For the final case, we have that $\neg\mathsf{atom}(x)$ and $\neg\mathsf{atom}(y)$. Then $x = \mathsf{cons}(u_1, v_1)$ and $y = \mathsf{cons}(u_2, v_2)$ for some lists u_1, v_1, u_2, v_2. We have

$$
\begin{aligned}
x \preceq_c y &\Leftrightarrow \mathsf{cons}(u_1, v_1) \preceq_c \mathsf{cons}(u_2, v_2) && \text{assumption} \\
&\Leftrightarrow (u_1 = u_2 \ \wedge \ v_1 \preceq_c v_2) \ \vee \ \mathsf{cons}(u_1, v_1) \preceq_c v_2 && (\preceq_c (4))
\end{aligned}
$$

The disjunction suggests two possibilities. Consider the first disjunct. Because $v_1 \prec_c \mathsf{cons}(u_1, v_1) = x$, we have that

$$(v_1, v_2) \prec_c^2 (x, y) \ ,$$

allowing us to appeal to the inductive hypothesis (4.21): from $v_1 \preceq_c v_2$, deduce that $|v_1| \leq |v_2|$. Then with two applications of (length list), we have

$$|x| \leq |y| \ \Leftrightarrow \ 1 + |v_1| \leq 1 + |v_2| \ \Leftrightarrow \ |v_1| \leq |v_2| \ .$$

Therefore, $|x| \leq |y|$ and (4.20) holds for this case.

Suppose the second disjunct ($\mathsf{cons}(u_1, v_1) \preceq_c v_2$) holds. We again look to the inductive hypothesis (4.21). We have

$$(\mathsf{cons}(u_1, v_1), v_2) \prec_c^2 (x, y)$$

because $\mathsf{cons}(u_1, v_1) = x$ and $v_2 \prec_c \mathsf{cons}(u_2, v_2) = y$. Therefore, the inductive hypothesis tells us that $|x| \leq |v_2|$, while (length list) implies that $|v_2| < |y|$. In short,

$$|x| \leq |v_2| < |y| \ ,$$

which implies $|x| \leq |y|$ as desired, completing the proof.   ∎

Example 4.9. Augment the theory of Presburger arithmetic $T_\mathbb{N}$ (see Chapters 3 and 7) with the following axioms to define the Ackermann function:

- $\forall y. \ ack(0, y) = y + 1$ (ack left zero)
- $\forall x. \ ack(x + 1, 0) = ack(x, 1)$ (ack right zero)
- $\forall x, y. \ ack(x + 1, y + 1) = ack(x, ack(x + 1, y))$ (ack successor)

The Ackermann function grows quickly for increasing arguments:

- $ack(0, 0) = 1$
- $ack(1, 1) = 3$

- $ack(2,2) = 7$
- $ack(3,3) = 61$
- $ack(4,4) = 2^{2^{2^{2^{16}}}} - 3$

One might expect that proving properties about the Ackermann function would be difficult.

However, lexicographic well-founded induction allows us to reason about certain properties of the function. Define $<_2$ as the natural lexicographic extension of $<$ to pairs of natural numbers. Now consider input arguments to ack and the resulting arguments in recursive calls:

- (ack left zero) does not involve a recursive call.
- In (ack right zero), $(x+1, 0) >_2 (x, 1)$.
- In (ack successor),
    - $(x+1, y+1) >_2 (x+1, y)$, and
    - $(x+1, y+1) >_2 (x, ack(x+1, y))$.

As the arguments decrease according to $<_2$ with each level of recursion, we conclude that the computation of $ack(x, y)$ halts for every x and y. In Chapter 5, we show that finding well-founded relations is a general technique for showing that functions always halt.

Additionally, we can induct over the execution of ack to prove properties of the ack function itself. Let us prove that

$$\forall x, y.\ ack(x, y) > y \tag{4.22}$$

is $T_{\mathbb{N}}^{ack}$-valid. We apply lexicographic well-founded induction to the arguments of ack to prove

$$F[x, y] :\ ack(x, y) > y \tag{4.23}$$

for arbitrary natural numbers x and y. For the inductive hypothesis, assume that

$$\forall x', y'.\ (x', y') <_2 (x, y) \ \rightarrow\ \underbrace{ack(x', y') > y'}_{F[x', y']} . \tag{4.24}$$

Consider three cases: $x = 0$, $x > 0\ \land\ y = 0$, and $x > 0\ \land\ y > 0$.

If $x = 0$, then $ack(0, y) = y + 1 > y$ by (ack left zero), as desired.

If $x > 0\ \land\ y = 0$, then

$$ack(x, 0) = ack(x - 1, 1)$$

by (ack right zero). Since

$$(x' : x - 1,\ y' : 1) <_2 (x, y) ,$$

the inductive hypothesis (4.24) tells us that

$$ack(x-1,1) > 1 \ .$$

Therefore, we have

$$ack(x,0) = ack(x-1,1) > 1 \ ,$$

so $ack(x,0) > 0$ as desired.

For the final case, $x > 0 \ \wedge \ y > 0$, we have

$$ack(x,y) = ack(x-1, ack(x,y-1))$$

by (ack successor). Since

$$(x' : x-1, \ y' : ack(x,y-1)) <_2 (x,y) \ ,$$

the inductive hypothesis (4.24) implies that

$$ack(x-1, ack(x,y-1)) > ack(x,y-1) \ .$$

Furthermore, since

$$(x' : x, \ y' : y-1) <_2 (x,y) \ ,$$

the inductive hypothesis (4.24) implies that

$$ack(x,y-1) > y-1 \ .$$

All together, then, we have

$$ack(x,y) = ack(x-1, ack(x,y-1)) > ack(x,y-1) > y-1 \ ;$$

hence, $ack(x,y) > (y-1)+1 = y$, completing the proof. ∎

4.4 Structural Induction

Induction has many other applications outside of reasoning about the validity of first-order formulae. In this section, we introduce the proof technique of **structural induction** for proving properties about formulae themselves. Structural induction is applied in Section 2.7, in analyzing the quantifier elimination procedures of Chapter 7, and in other applications throughout the book.

Define the **strict subformula relation** over FOL formulae as follows: two formulae F_1 and F_2 are related by the strict subformula relation iff F_1 is a strict subformula of F_2. The strict subformula relation is well founded over the set of FOL formulae since every formula, having only a finite number of symbols, has only a finite number of strict subformulae; and each of its strict subformulae has fewer strict subformulae that it does. To prove a desired property of FOL formulae, instantiate the well-founded induction principle with the strict subformula relation:

- Assume as the **inductive hypothesis** that for arbitrary FOL formula F and for every strict subformula G of F, G has the desired property. Then prove that F has the property.

Since atoms do not have strict subformulae, they are treated as base cases. This induction principle is the **structural induction principle**.

Example 4.10. Exercise 1.3 asks the reader to prove that certain logical connectives are redundant in the presence of others. Formally, the exercise is asking the reader to prove the following claim: Every propositional formula F is equivalent to a propositional formula F' constructed with only the logical connectives $\top$, $\wedge$, and $\neg$.

There are three base cases to consider:

- The formula $\top$ can be represented directly as $\top$.
- The formula $\bot$ is equivalent to $\neg\top$.
- Any propositional variable P can be represented directly as P.

For the inductive step, consider formulae G, G_1, and G_2, and assume as the inductive hypothesis that each is equivalent to formulae G', G'_1, and G'_2, respectively, which are constructed only from the connectives $\top$, $\vee$, and $\neg$ (and propositional variables, of course). We show that each possible formulae that can be constructed from G, G_1, and G_2 with only one logical connective is equivalent to another constructed with only $\top$, $\vee$, and $\neg$:

- $\neg G$ is equivalent to $\neg G'$ from the inductive hypothesis.
- By considering the truth table in which the four possible valuations of G_1 and G_2 are considered, one can establish that $G_1 \vee G_2$ is equivalent to $\neg(\neg G'_1 \wedge \neg G'_2)$. By the inductive hypothesis, the latter formula is constructed only from propositional variables, $\top$, $\wedge$, and $\neg$.
- By similar reasoning, $G_1 \to G_2$ is equivalent to $\neg(G'_1 \wedge \neg G'_2)$, which satisfies the claim.
- Similar reasoning handles $G_1 \leftrightarrow G_2$ as well.

Hence, the claim is proved.

Note that the main argument is essentially similar to the answer that the reader might have provided in answering Exercise 1.3. Structural induction merely provides the basis for lifting the truth-table argument to a general statement about propositional formulae. ∎

Structural induction is also useful for reasoning about interpretations of formulae, as the following example shows.

Example 4.11. This example relies on several basic concepts of set theory; however, even the reader unfamiliar with set theory can understand the application of structural induction without understanding the actual claim.

Consider $\Sigma_{\mathbb{Q}}$-formulae $F[x_1, \ldots, x_n]$ in which the only predicate is $\leq$, the only logical connectives are $\vee$ and $\wedge$, and the only quantifier is $\forall$. We prove that the set of satisfying $T_{\mathbb{Q}}$-interpretations of F (intuitively, those $T_{\mathbb{Q}}$-interpretations that assign to $x_1, \ldots, x_n$ values from $\mathbb{Q}^n$ that satisfy F) describes a closed subset of $\mathbb{Q}^n$.

For the base case, consider any inequality $\alpha \leq \beta$ with free variables $x_1, \ldots, x_n$. From basic set theory, the set of satisfying points is closed.

For the inductive step, consider formulae G, G_1, and G_2 constructed as specified. Assume as the inductive hypothesis that the satisfying $T_{\mathbb{Q}}$-interpretations for each comprise closed sets. Consider applying the allowed logical connectives and quantifier:

- $G_1 \wedge G_2$: The set described by this formula is the set-theoretic intersection of the sets described by G_1 and G_2, and is thus closed by the inductive hypothesis and set theory.
- $G_1 \vee G_2$: Similarly, the set described by this formula is the set-theoretic union of the sets described by G_1 and G_2, and is thus closed by the inductive hypothesis and set theory.
- $\forall x.\ G$: Consider subformula G with free variable x (if x is not free in G, then the formula is equivalent to just G, which describes a closed set by the inductive hypothesis). For each value $\frac{a}{b} \in \mathbb{Q}$, consider the formula

$$G_{\frac{a}{b}} : G \wedge bx \leq a \wedge a \leq bx \ .$$

The set described by each $G_{\frac{a}{b}}$ is closed according to the inductive hypothesis and reasoning similar to the previous cases. From set theory, the conjunction of all such sets is still closed, so the set of satisfying $T_{\mathbb{Q}}$-interpretations of $\forall x.\ G$ describes a closed set.

The induction is complete, so the claim is proved.

Results from Chapter 7 prove that $\exists$ also preserves closed sets in $T_{\mathbb{Q}}$. ∎

Remark 4.12. Example 4.11 considers a subset of FOL formulae. However, this subset is by definition closed under conjunction, disjunction, and universal quantification: if F, F_1, and F_2 are in the subset, then so are $F_1 \wedge F_2$, $F_1 \vee F_2$, and $\forall x.\ F$; and conversely. In other words, all strict subformulae of a formula in the subset are also in the subset, so that structural induction is applicable.

The proof of Lemma 2.31 provides another example of the application of structural induction.

4.5 Summary

This chapter covers several induction principles in several first-order theories:

- *Stepwise induction* is presented in the context of integer arithmetic and lists. The induction principle requires defining a step such as adding one or constructing a list with one more element.

- *Complete induction* is presented in the context of integer arithmetic. The induction principle relies on the well-foundedness of the $<$ predicate. Rather than assuming that the desired property holds for one element n and proving the property for the case $n+1$ as in stepwise reduction, one assumes that the property holds for all elements $n' < n$ and proves that it holds for n. This stronger assumption sometime yields easier or more concise proofs.

- *Well-founded induction* generalizes complete induction to other theories; it is presented in the context of lists and lexicographic tuples. The induction principle requires a well-founded relation over the domain.

- *Structural induction* is an instance of well-founded induction in which the domain is formulae and the well-founded relation is the strict subformula relation.

Besides being an important tool for proving first-order validities, induction is the basis for both verification methodologies studied in Chapter 5. Structural induction also serves as the basis for the quantifier elimination procedures studied in Chapter 7.

Bibliographic Remarks

The induction proofs in Examples 4.1, 4.3, and 4.9 are taken from the text of Manna and Waldinger [55].

Blaise Pascal (1623–1662) and Jacob Bernoulli (1654–1705) are recognized as having formalized stepwise and complete induction, respectively. Less formal versions of induction appear in texts by Francesco Maurolico (1494–1575); Rabbi Levi Ben Gershon (1288–1344), who recognized induction as a distinct form of mathematical proof; Abu Bekr ibn Muhammad ibn al-Husayn Al-Karaji (953–1029); and Abu Kamil Shuja Ibn Aslam Ibn Mohammad Ibn Shaji (850–930) [97]. Some historians claim that Euclid may have applied induction informally.

Exercises

4.1 (T_{cons}^+). Prove the following in T_{cons}^+:

(a) $\forall u, v.\ \textit{flat}(u) \land \textit{flat}(v) \rightarrow \textit{flat}(concat(u, v))$
(b) $\forall u.\ \textit{flat}(u) \rightarrow \textit{flat}(rvs(u))$

4.2 ($T_{\text{cons}}^{\text{PA}}$). Prove or disprove the following in $T_{\text{cons}}^{\text{PA}}$:

(a) $\forall u.\ u \preceq_c u$
(b) $\forall u, v, w.\ \textsf{cons}(u, v) \preceq_c w \rightarrow v \preceq_c w$
(c) $\forall u, v.\ v \prec_c \textsf{cons}(u, v)$

4.3 $(T^+_{\text{cons}} \cup T^{\text{PA}}_{\text{cons}})$. Prove the following in $T^+_{\text{cons}} \cup T^{\text{PA}}_{\text{cons}}$:

(a) $\forall u, v.\ |concat(u, v)| = |u| + |v|$
(b) $\forall u.\ \mathit{flat}(u)\ \rightarrow\ |rvs(u)| = |u|$

4.4 (Chips). Does the process of Example 4.7 still halt if

(a) in Step 1, you return one red chip to the bag?
(b) in Step 1, you add one blue chip?
(c) in Step 1, you add one blue chip; and in Step 3, you return the blue chip to the bag but do not add any other chips?

4.5 (Strict sublist). Modify Example 4.8 to prove

$$\forall x, y.\ x \prec_c y\ \rightarrow\ |x| < |y|\ .$$

4.6 (Structural induction). Prove that every first-order formula F is equivalent to a first-order formula F' constructed with only the logical connectives $\top$, $\wedge$, and $\neg$ and the quantifier $\forall$.

4.7 (Finite number of sublists). Prove that the number of sublists of a list (defined in $T^{\text{PA}}_{\text{cons}}$) is finite.

4.8 (★ $\prec_c$ is well-founded). Prove that $\prec_c$, defined in $T^{\text{PA}}_{\text{cons}}$, is well-founded over lists. To avoid circularity, do not apply well-founded induction in this proof. *Hint*: Prove that $\prec_c$ is transitive and **irreflexive** $(\forall u.\ \neg(u \prec_c u))$; then apply Exercise 4.7.

Program Correctness: Mechanics

When examining the detail of the algorithm, it seems probable that the proof will be helpful in explaining not only what *is happening but* why.
— Tony Hoare
An Axiomatic Basis for Computer Programming, 1969

We are finally ready to apply FOL and induction to a real problem: specifying and proving properties of programs. In this chapter, we develop the three foundational methods that underly all verification and program analysis techniques. In the next chapter, we discuss strategies for applying them.

First, **specification** is the precise statement of properties that a program should exhibit. The language of FOL offers precision. The remaining task is to develop a scheme for embedding FOL statements into program text as **program annotations**. We focus on two forms of properties. **Partial correctness** properties, or **safety** properties, assert that certain states — typically, error states — cannot ever occur during the execution of a program. An important subset of this form of property is the partial correctness of programs: *if* a program halts, then its output satisfies some relation with its input. **Total correctness** properties, or **progress** properties, assert that certain states are eventually reached during program execution. Section 5.1 presents specification in the context of a simple programming language, pi.

The next foundational method is the **inductive assertion method** for proving partial correctness properties. The inductive assertion method is based on the mathematical induction of Chapter 4. To prove that every state during the execution of a program satisfies FOL formula F, prove as the base case that F holds at the beginning of execution; assume as the inductive hypothesis that F currently holds (at some point during the execution); and prove as the inductive step that F holds after one more step of the program. Section 5.2 discusses the mechanics for reducing a program with a partial correctness specification to this inductive argument. The challenge in applying this method is to discover additional annotations to make the induction go through. Chapter 6 discusses strategies for finding the extra information.

The third foundational method is the **ranking function method** for proving total correctness properties. Proving total correctness breaks down into two arguments. First, one proves that some partial correctness property holds using the inductive assertion method; second, one argues that some set of loops and recursive functions always halt. The ranking function method applies to the latter argument: one associates with each loop and recursive function a **ranking function** that maps the program variables to a well-founded domain (see Chapter 4); then one proves that whenever program control moves from one ranking function to the next, the value decreases according to the well-founded relation. Since the relation is well-founded, the looping and recursion must eventually halt. A typical total correctness property asserts that the program halts *and* its output satisfies some relation with its input. The ranking function method applies to the first conjunct (the program halts); the inductive assertion method applies to the second (its output satisfies some relation with its input). Section 5.3 presents the ranking function method.

We explain all concepts in this and the next chapter with a set of example programs that manipulate arrays. We chose these programs for several reasons. First, they should be familiar to most readers; the reader can thus focus on the verification methodology rather than on understanding new complex programs. Second, our correctness proofs rely heavily on the decision procedures that are discussed in Part II of this book. Finally, they are small but dense, allowing us to exhibit common techniques for proving interesting facts about programs. The reader should keep in mind, however, that the methods of this chapter underlie software and hardware analyses that are applied in practice.

The reader may find the contents of this chapter to be rather technical. Indeed, the transformation of an annotated program into a set of verification conditions is a purely mechanical task. Fortunately, a **verifying compiler** does this work in practice: it parses an annotated program, checking the syntax and semantics as usual, and generates a set of verification conditions. But just as learning how compilers work is important for understanding programming languages, learning how verifying compilers work is important for understanding verification and programming languages with annotations. Moreover, applying the steps of generating verification conditions provides practice in manipulating and understanding FOL formulae, a useful skill. Chapter 6 discusses strategies for writing annotations, a task that cannot be fully automated.

5.1 pi: A Simple Imperative Language

This section introduces the programming language pi, an imperative language with facilities for annotations. To allow us to focus on the fundamentals of program verification, pi lacks complicating features of typical imperative lan-

```
@pre ⊤
@post ⊤
bool LinearSearch(int[] a, int ℓ, int u, int e) {
    for @ ⊤
      (int i := ℓ; i ≤ u; i := i + 1) {
      if (a[i] = e) return true;
    }
    return false;
}
```

Fig. 5.1. LinearSearch

guages: its data types do not include pointer or reference types; and it does not allow global variables, although it does have global constants (see Exercise 6.5). After reading this chapter and Chapter 12, the interested reader should consult the wide literature on program analysis to learn how the techniques of these chapters extend to reasoning about standard programming languages.

5.1.1 The Language

Because pi is superficially a C-like language with restrictions, we present the essential features of pi through examples.

Example 5.1. Figure 5.1 lists the function LinearSearch, which searches the range $[\ell, u]$ of an array a of integers for a value e. It returns **true** iff the given array contains the value between the lower bound ℓ and upper bound u. It behaves correctly only if $0 \leq \ell$ and $u < |a|$; otherwise, the array a is accessed outside of its domain $[0, |a| - 1]$. $|a|$ denotes the length of array a.

Observe that most of the syntax is similar to C. For example, the **for** loop sets i to be ℓ initially and then executes the body of the loop and increments i by 1 as long as $i \leq u$. Also, an integer array has type **int**[], which is constructed from base type **int**. One syntactic difference occurs in assignment, which is written := to distinguish it from the equality predicate =. We use = as the equality predicate, rather than ==, to correspond to the standard equality predicate of FOL. Finally, unlike C, pi has type **bool** and constants **true** and **false**.

Notice the lines beginning with @. They are program annotations, which we discuss in detail in the next section.

In LinearSearch, a, ℓ, u, and e are the **formal parameters** (also, **parameters**) of the function. If LinearSearch is called as LinearSearch($b, 0, |b| - 1, v$), then b, 0, $|b| - 1$, and v are the **arguments**. ∎

Example 5.2. Figure 5.2 lists the recursive function BinarySearch, which searches a range $[\ell, u]$ of a sorted (weakly increasing: $a[i] \leq a[j]$ if $i \leq j$) array a of integers for a value e. Like LinearSearch, it returns **true** iff the

```
@pre ⊤
@post ⊤
bool BinarySearch(int[] a, int ℓ, int u, int e) {
    if (ℓ > u) return false;
    else {
        int m := (ℓ + u) div 2;
        if (a[m] = e) return true;
        else if (a[m] < e) return BinarySearch(a, m + 1, u, e);
        else return BinarySearch(a, ℓ, m − 1, e);
    }
}
```

Fig. 5.2. BinarySearch

given array contains the value in the range $[\ell, u]$. It behaves correctly only if $0 \leq \ell$ and $u < |a|$.

One level of recursion operates as follows. If the lower bound ℓ of the range is greater than the upper bound u, then the (empty) subarray cannot contain e, so it returns **false**. Otherwise, it examines the middle element $a[m]$ of the subarray: if it is e, then the subarray clearly contains e; otherwise, it recurses on the left half if $a[m] < e$ and on the right half if $a[m] > e$.

pi syntactically distinguishes between integer division and real division: for **int** variables a and b, write a **div** b instead of a/b. Integer division is defined as follows:

$$a \text{ div } b \stackrel{\text{def}}{=} \left\lfloor \frac{a}{b} \right\rfloor \,.$$

That is, a **div** b is equal to the greatest integer less than or equal to $\frac{a}{b}$ (the *floor* of $\frac{a}{b}$). ∎

Example 5.3. Figure 5.3 lists the function BubbleSort, which sorts an integer array. It works by "bubbling" the largest element of the left unsorted region of the array toward the sorted region on the right; this element then becomes the left element of the sorted region, enlarging the region by one cell. In Figure 5.4, for example, the first line shows an array in which the rightmost boxed cells comprise the sorted region and the other cells comprise the unsorted region. In the final line, the sorted region has been expanded by one cell.

Figure 5.4 lists a portion of a sample execution trace. The right two cells (5, 6) of the array have already been sorted. In the trace, the inner loop moves the largest element 4 of the unsorted region to the right to join the sorted region, which is indicated by the dotted rectangle. In the first two steps, $a[j] \leq a[j + 1]$ ($2 \leq 3$ and $3 \leq 4$), so the values of cell j and $j + 1$ are not swapped in either case. In the subsequent two steps, $a[j] > a[j + 1]$ ($4 > 1$ and $4 > 2$), causing a swap at each step. In the fifth step, the inner loop's guard $i < j$ no longer holds, so the inner loop exits and the outer

```
@pre ⊤
@post ⊤
int[] BubbleSort(int[] a₀) {
   int[] a := a₀;
   for @ ⊤
      (int i := |a| − 1; i > 0; i := i − 1) {
      for @ ⊤
         (int j := 0; j < i; j := j + 1) {
         if (a[j] > a[j + 1]) {
            int t := a[j];
            a[j] := a[j + 1];
            a[j + 1] := t;
         }
      }
   }
   return a;
}
```

Fig. 5.3. BubbleSort

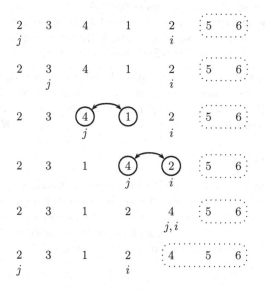

Fig. 5.4. Sample execution of BubbleSort

loop decrements i by 1. The sorted region has been expanded by one cell, as indicated by the final dotted rectangle. The last step shows the beginning of the next round of the inner loop.

Because pi does not have pointer or reference types, all data are passed by value, including arrays and structures. If BubbleSort were missing the **return**

```
typedef struct qs {
  int pivot;
  int[] array;
} qs;
```

Fig. 5.5. Structure qs

statement, then calling it would not have any discernible effect on the calling context. Additionally, pi does not allow updates to parameters, so BubbleSort assigns a_0 to a fresh variable a in the first line. This artificial requirement makes reasoning about functions easier: in annotations (see Section 5.1.2) throughout the function, one can always reference the input.   ■

In this book, our example programs manipulate arrays rather than recursive data structures. The reason is that we can express more interesting properties about arrays in the fragment of the theory of arrays studied in Chapter 11 than we can about lists in the fragment of the theory of recursive data structures studied in Chapter 9. This bias is a reflection of the structure and content of this book, not of what is theoretically possible.

However, we sometimes use records, a basic recursive data type, to allow a function to return multiple values. The following example illustrates such a record type, which is used in the program QuickSort (see Section 6.2).

Example 5.4. The structure qs of Figure 5.5 is a record with two fields: the *pivot* field of type int and the *array* field of type array. If x is a variable of type qs, then $x.pivot$ returns the value in its *pivot* field; also, $x.array[i] := v$ assigns v to position i of x's *array* field.   ■

5.1.2 Program Annotations

The most important feature of pi is the capacity for complex function annotations. An **annotation** is a FOL formula F whose free variables include only the program variables of the function in which the annotation occurs. An annotation F at location L asserts that F is true whenever program control reaches L. We discuss several forms of annotations in this section.

Function Specifications

The **function specification** of a function is a pair of annotations. The **function precondition** is a formula F whose free variables include only the formal parameters. It specifies what should be true upon entering the function — or, in other words, under what inputs the function is expected to work. The **function postcondition** is a formula G whose free variables include only the formal parameters and the special variable rv representing the return value of the function. The postcondition relates the function's output (the return value rv) to its input (the parameters).

```
@pre 0 ≤ ℓ  ∧  u < |a|
@post rv  ↔  ∃i. ℓ ≤ i ≤ u  ∧  a[i] = e
bool LinearSearch(int[] a, int ℓ, int u, int e) {
    for @ ⊤
        (int i := ℓ; i ≤ u; i := i + 1) {
        if (a[i] = e) return true;
    }
    return false;
}
```

Fig. 5.6. LinearSearch with function specification

```
@pre ⊤
@post rv  ↔  ∃i. 0 ≤ ℓ ≤ i ≤ u < |a|  ∧  a[i] = e
bool LinearSearch(int[] a, int ℓ, int u, int e) {
    if (ℓ < 0  ∨  u ≥ |a|) return false;
    for @ ⊤
        (int i := ℓ; i ≤ u; i := i + 1) {
        if (a[i] = e) return true;
    }
    return false;
}
```

Fig. 5.7. Robust LinearSearch with function specification

Example 5.5. In Example 5.1, we informally specified the behavior of Lin-earSearch as follows: LinearSearch returns true iff the array a contains the value e in the range $[\ell, u]$. It behaves correctly only when $\ell \geq 0$ and $u < |a|$.

Function specifications formalize such statements. Figure 5.6 presents Lin-earSearch with its specification. The precondition asserts that the lower bound ℓ should be at least 0 and that the upper bound u should be less than the length $|a|$ of the array a. The postcondition asserts that the return value rv is true iff $a[i] = e$ for some index $i \in [\ell, u]$ of a.   ∎

Example 5.6. A nontrivial precondition (a formula other than ⊤) is not al-ways acceptable, especially if a function is public to a module. Figure 5.7 lists a more robust version of linear search. The formula

$$0 \leq \ell \leq i \leq u < |a|$$

abbreviates

$$0 \leq \ell \wedge \ell \leq i \wedge i \leq u \wedge u < |a| \ .$$

A nontrivial precondition is sometimes acceptable for a function that is private to a module. The verification method of this chapter checks that every instance of a call to such a function obeys the precondition.   ∎

```
@pre 0 ≤ ℓ ∧ u < |a| ∧ sorted(a, ℓ, u)
@post rv ↔ ∃i. ℓ ≤ i ≤ u ∧ a[i] = e
bool BinarySearch(int[] a, int ℓ, int u, int e) {
  if (ℓ > u) return false;
  else {
    int m := (ℓ + u) div 2;
    if (a[m] = e) return true;
    else if (a[m] < e) return BinarySearch(a, m + 1, u, e);
    else return BinarySearch(a, ℓ, m − 1, e);
  }
}
```

Fig. 5.8. BinarySearch with function specification

```
@pre ⊤
@post sorted(rv, 0, |rv| − 1)
int[] BubbleSort(int[] a₀) {
  int[] a := a₀;
  for @ ⊤
    (int i := |a| − 1; i > 0; i := i − 1) {
    for @ ⊤
      (int j := 0; j < i; j := j + 1) {
      if (a[j] > a[j + 1]) {
        int t := a[j];
        a[j] := a[j + 1];
        a[j + 1] := t;
      }
    }
  }
  return a;
}
```

Fig. 5.9. BubbleSort with function specification

Example 5.7. Figure 5.8 lists BinarySearch with its specification. As expected, its postcondition is identical to the postcondition of LinearSearch. However, its precondition also states that the array a is sorted.

The **sorted** predicate is defined in the combined theory of integers and arrays, $T_{\mathbb{Z}} \cup T_A$:

$$\mathsf{sorted}(a, \ell, u) \Leftrightarrow \forall i, j. \, \ell \leq i \leq j \leq u \rightarrow a[i] \leq a[j] \,.$$

∎

Example 5.8. Figure 5.9 lists BubbleSort with its specification. Given any array, the returned array is sorted. Of course, other properties are desirable and could be specified as well. For example, the returned array rv should be a permutation of the original array a_0 (see Exercise 6.5). ∎

Section 5.2 presents a method for proving that a function satisfies its partial correctness specification: if the function precondition is satisfied and the function halts, then the function postcondition holds upon return. Section 5.3 discusses a method for proving that, additionally, the function always halts.

Loop Invariants

Each `for` loop and `while` loop has an attendant annotation called the **loop invariant**. A `while` loop

```
while
  @ F
  (⟨condition⟩) {
    ⟨body⟩
}
```

says to apply the ⟨body⟩ as long as ⟨condition⟩ holds. The assertion F must hold at the beginning of every iteration. It is evaluated before the ⟨condition⟩ is evaluated, so it must hold even on the final iteration when ⟨condition⟩ is `false`. Therefore, on entering the ⟨body⟩ of the loop,

$$F \ \wedge \ \langle condition \rangle$$

must hold, and on exiting the loop,

$$F \ \wedge \ \neg \langle condition \rangle$$

must hold.

To consider a `for` loop, translate the loop

```
for
  @ F
  (⟨initialize⟩; ⟨condition⟩; ⟨increment⟩) {
    ⟨body⟩
}
```

into the equivalent loop

```
⟨initialize⟩;
while
  @ F
  (⟨condition⟩) {
    ⟨body⟩
    ⟨increment⟩
}
```

F must hold after the ⟨initialize⟩ statement has been evaluated and, on each iteration, before the ⟨condition⟩ is evaluated.

```
@pre 0 ≤ ℓ ∧ u < |a|
@post rv ↔ ∃i. ℓ ≤ i ≤ u ∧ a[i] = e
bool LinearSearch(int[] a, int ℓ, int u, int e) {
  for
    @L :  ℓ ≤ i ∧ (∀j. ℓ ≤ j < i  →  a[j] ≠ e)
    (int i := ℓ; i ≤ u; i := i + 1) {
    if (a[i] = e) return true;
  }
  return false;
}
```

Fig. 5.10. LinearSearch with loop invariant

Example 5.9. Figure 5.10 lists LinearSearch with a nontrivial loop invariant at L. It asserts that whenever control reaches L, the loop index is at least ℓ and that $a[j] \neq e$ for previously examined indices j. ∎

Section 5.2 shows that loop invariants are crucial for constructing an inductive argument that a function obeys its specification.

Assertions

In pi, one can add an annotation anywhere. When an annotation is not a function precondition, function postcondition, or loop invariant, we call it an **assertion**. Assertions allow programmers to provide a formal comment. For example, if at the statement

$$i := i + k;$$

the programmer thinks that k is positive, then the programmer can add an assertion stating that supposition:

$$@ \ k > 0;$$
$$i := i + k;$$

Later, the programmer's hyothesis about k is verified with formal verification at compile time or with dynamic assertion tests at runtime.

Runtime assertions are a special class of assertions. In most programming languages, **runtime errors** include division by 0, modulo by 0, and dereference of null. In particular, division by 0 and modulo by 0 cause hardware exceptions, while only some languages, such as Java, catch a dereference of null. In pi, runtime errors include division by 0, modulo by 0, and accessing an array out of bounds. The pi compiler generates runtime assertions to catch runtime errors.

Example 5.10. Figure 5.11 lists LinearSearch with runtime assertions. The array read $a[i]$ is protected by the assertion that i is a legal index of a. ∎

```
@pre ⊤
@post ⊤
bool LinearSearch(int[] a, int ℓ, int u, int e) {
    for @ ⊤
        (int i := ℓ; i ≤ u; i := i + 1) {
        @ 0 ≤ i < |a|;
        if (a[i] = e) return true;
    }
    return false;
}
```

Fig. 5.11. LinearSearch with runtime assertions

```
@pre ⊤
@post ⊤
bool BinarySearch(int[] a, int ℓ, int u, int e) {
    if (ℓ > u) return false;
    else {
        @ 2 ≠ 0;
        int m := (ℓ + u) div 2;
        @ 0 ≤ m < |a|;
        if (a[m] = e) return true;
        else {
            @ 0 ≤ m < |a|;
            if (a[m] < e) return BinarySearch(a, m + 1, u, e);
            else return BinarySearch(a, ℓ, m − 1, e);
        }
    }
}
```

Fig. 5.12. BinarySearch with runtime assertions

Example 5.11. Figure 5.12 lists BinarySearch with runtime assertions. The first assertion protects the division: it asserts that $2 \neq 0$, which clearly holds. The next two assertions protect the array reads.   ■

Example 5.12. Figure 5.13 lists BubbleSort with compiler-generated runtime assertions. All assertions protect array accesses. The first two runtime assertions are sufficient to protect all array accesses. Figure 5.14 lists a concise version.   ■

5.2 Partial Correctness

Having specified and implemented each function of a program, we would like to prove that the functions obey their specifications (from another perspective,

```
@pre ⊤
@post ⊤
int[] BubbleSort(int[] a₀) {
    int[] a := a₀;
    for @ ⊤
        (int i := |a| − 1; i > 0; i := i − 1) {
        for @ ⊤
            (int j := 0; j < i; j := j + 1) {
            @ 0 ≤ j < |a|;
            @ 0 ≤ j + 1 < |a|;
            if (a[j] > a[j + 1])  {
                @ 0 ≤ j < |a|;
                int t := a[j];
                @ 0 ≤ j < |a|;
                @ 0 ≤ j + 1 < |a|;
                a[j] := a[j + 1];
                @ 0 ≤ j + 1 < |a|;
                a[j + 1] := t;
            }
        }
    }
    return a;
}
```

Fig. 5.13. BubbleSort with runtime assertions

that their specifications reflect their actual behavior). A function is **partially correct** if when the function's precondition is satisfied on entry, its postcondition is satisfied when the function returns (if it ever does). In general, functions may not halt: a loop's guard could be incorrect, or a recursive function could fail to handle a particular base case. Section 5.3 discusses how to prove that a function always halts.

We present the **inductive assertion method** for proving that a program is partially correct. The method reduces each function and its annotations to a finite set of **verification conditions** (**VC**s), which are FOL formulae. If all of a function's VCs are valid, then the function obeys its specification. The reduction occurs in two stages: first, each function of the annotated program is broken down into a finite set of **basic paths** (Sections 5.2.1 and 5.2.2); second, each basic path generates a verification condition (Section 5.2.4). Sections 5.2.3 and 5.2.5 provide a more abstract view of the inductive assertion method.

Loops complicate proofs of partial correctness because they create an unbounded number of paths from function entry to exit. Recursive functions similarly complicate proofs. A **path** is a sequence of program statements. For loops, loop invariants cut the paths into a finite set of basic paths, while for recursive functions, the function specification of the recursive function cuts the paths. In this section, we assume that we are given function specifications

```
@pre ⊤
@post ⊤
int[] BubbleSort(int[] a₀) {
    int[] a := a₀;
    for @ ⊤
        (int i := |a| − 1; i > 0; i := i − 1) {
        for @ ⊤
            (int j := 0; j < i; j := j + 1) {
            @ 0 ≤ j < |a| ∧ 0 ≤ j + 1 < |a|;
            if (a[j] > a[j + 1]) {
                int t := a[j];
                a[j] := a[j + 1];
                a[j + 1] := t;
            }
        }
    }
    return a;
}
```

Fig. 5.14. BubbleSort with compressed runtime assertions

```
@pre 0 ≤ ℓ ∧ u < |a|
@post rv ↔ ∃i. ℓ ≤ i ≤ u ∧ a[i] = e
bool LinearSearch(int[] a, int ℓ, int u, int e) {
    for
        @L : ℓ ≤ i ∧ (∀j. ℓ ≤ j < i → a[j] ≠ e)
        (int i := ℓ; i ≤ u; i := i + 1) {
        if (a[i] = e) return true;
    }
    return false;
}
```

Fig. 5.15. LinearSearch with loop invariants

and loop invariants and concentrate on the task of generating the corresponding verification conditions. In practice, this task is performed by a verifying compiler. Chapter 6 discusses strategies for constructing specifications and loop invariants.

5.2.1 Basic Paths: Loops

A **basic path** is a sequence of instructions that begins at the function precondition or a loop invariant and ends at a loop invariant, an assertion, or the function postcondition. Moreover, a loop invariant can only occur at the beginning or the ending of a basic path. Thus, basic paths do not cross loops. The following examples illustrate the characteristics of basic paths.

Example 5.13. Figure 5.15 lists an annotated version of LinearSearch. Its basic paths are the following. The first basic path starts at the function precondition, enters the **for** loop via the initialization statement, and ends at the loop invariant L:

$$\text{(1)}$$

@pre $0 \leq \ell \ \land \ u < |a|$
$i := \ell$;
@L : $\ell \leq i \ \land \ (\forall j. \ \ell \leq j < i \ \rightarrow \ a[j] \neq e)$

The second basic path begins at the loop invariant at L, passes the loop guard $i \leq u$, passes the guard $a[i] = e$ of the **if** statement, executes the **return** (of **true**), and ends at the postcondition:

$$\text{(2)}$$

@L : $\ell \leq i \ \land \ (\forall j. \ \ell \leq j < i \ \rightarrow \ a[j] \neq e)$
assume $i \leq u$;
assume $a[i] = e$;
$rv := \textbf{true}$;
@post $rv \ \leftrightarrow \ \exists j. \ \ell \leq j \leq u \ \land \ a[j] = e$

This path exhibits two new aspects of basic paths. First, **return** statements become assignments to the special variable rv representing the return value.

Second, guards arising in program statements (in **for** loop guards, **while** loop guards, or **if** statements) become **assume statements** in basic paths. An assume statement **assume** c in a basic path means that the remainder of the basic path is executed only if the condition c holds at **assume** c. Each guard with condition c results in two assumptions: the guard holds (c) or it does not hold ($\neg c$). Therefore, each guard produces two paths with the same prefix up to the guard. They diverge on the assumption: one basic path has the statement **assume** c, and the other has the statement **assume** $\neg c$. These assumptions and the control structure of the program determine the construction of the remainder of the basic paths.

For example, the third path has the same prefix as **(2)** but makes the opposite assumption at the **if** statement guard: it assumes $a[i] \neq e$ rather than $a[i] = e$. Therefore, this path loops back around to the loop invariant:

$$\text{(3)}$$

@L : $\ell \leq i \ \land \ (\forall j. \ \ell \leq j < i \ \rightarrow \ a[j] \neq e)$
assume $i \leq u$;
assume $a[i] \neq e$;
$i := i + 1$;
@L : $\ell \leq i \ \land \ (\forall j. \ \ell \leq j < i \ \rightarrow \ a[j] \neq e)$

The final basic path has the same prefix as **(2)** and **(3)** but makes the opposite assumption at the **for** loop guard: it assumes $i > u$ rather than $i \leq u$. Therefore, this path exits the loop and returns **false**:

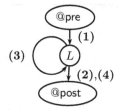

Fig. 5.16. Visualization of basic paths of LinearSearch

$$(4)$$

$@L: \ell \leq i \,\wedge\, (\forall j.\ \ell \leq j < i \;\rightarrow\; a[j] \neq e)$
assume $i > u$;
$rv := $ **false**;
$@post\ rv \,\leftrightarrow\, \exists j.\ \ell \leq j \leq u \,\wedge\, a[j] = e$

To avoid forgetting a basic path, we list paths in a depth-first order. When a guard is encountered, assume that it holds and generate the resulting paths; then assume that it does not hold and generate the resulting paths. In this example, the loop guard $i \leq u$ in **(2)** is first encountered; **(2)** and **(3)** follow from the assumption that the loop guard holds, while **(4)** follows from the assumption that it does not hold. The **if** statement guard $a[i] = e$ is next encountered in **(2)**; **(2)** follows from the assumption that it holds, while **(3)** follows from the assumption that it does not hold. Figure 5.16 visualizes these basic paths. ∎

Example 5.14. Figure 5.17 lists BubbleSort with loop invariants. The outer loop invariant at L_1 asserts that

- i is in the range $[-1, |a| - 1]$ (if $|a| = 0$, then i is initially -1);
- a is sorted in the range $[i, |a| - 1]$;
- and a is **partitioned** such that each element in the range $[0, i]$ is at most (less than or equal to) each element in the range $[i + 1, |a| - 1]$.

Its inner loop invariant at L_2 asserts that

- i is in the range $[1, |a| - 1]$, and j is in the range $[0, i]$;
- a is sorted in the range $[i, |a| - 1]$ as in the outer loop;
- a is partitioned as in the outer loop;
- and a is also partitioned such that each element in the range $[0, j - 1]$ is at most $a[j]$.

The **partitioned** predicate is defined in the theory $T_{\mathbb{Z}} \cup T_A$:

$\text{partitioned}(a, \ell_1, u_1, \ell_2, u_2)$
$\quad \leftrightarrow \forall i, j.\ \ell_1 \leq i \leq u_1 < \ell_2 \leq j \leq u_2 \;\rightarrow\; a[i] \leq a[j]\ .$

```
@pre ⊤
@post sorted(rv, 0, |rv| − 1)
int[] BubbleSort(int[] a₀) {
    int[] a := a₀;
    for
            ⎡ −1 ≤ i < |a|                            ⎤
    @L₁ :  ⎢ ∧ partitioned(a, 0, i, i + 1, |a| − 1)  ⎥
            ⎣ ∧ sorted(a, i, |a| − 1)                 ⎦
    (int i := |a| − 1; i > 0; i := i − 1) {
        for
                ⎡ 1 ≤ i < |a| ∧ 0 ≤ j ≤ i                ⎤
        @L₂ :  ⎢ ∧ partitioned(a, 0, i, i + 1, |a| − 1)  ⎥
                ⎢ ∧ partitioned(a, 0, j − 1, j, j)        ⎥
                ⎣ ∧ sorted(a, i, |a| − 1)                 ⎦
        (int j := 0; j < i; j := j + 1) {
        if (a[j] > a[j + 1]) {
            int t := a[j];
            a[j] := a[j + 1];
            a[j + 1] := t;
        }
        }
    }
    return a;
}
```

Fig. 5.17. BubbleSort with loop invariants

Performing a depth-first exploration, the first basic path starts at the precondition and ends at the outer loop invariant at L_1:

$$\text{(1)}$$

```
@pre ⊤;
a := a₀;
i := |a| − 1;
@L₁ : −1 ≤ i < |a| ∧ partitioned(a, 0, i, i + 1, |a| − 1) ∧ sorted(a, i, |a| − 1)
```

The second basic path starts at L_1 and ends at the inner loop invariant at L_2 (recall that the annotation is checked after the loop initialization $j := 0$):

$$\text{(2)}$$

```
@L₁ : −1 ≤ i < |a| ∧ partitioned(a, 0, i, i + 1, |a| − 1) ∧ sorted(a, i, |a| − 1)
assume i > 0;
j := 0;
        ⎡ 1 ≤ i < |a| ∧ 0 ≤ j ≤ i ∧ partitioned(a, 0, i, i + 1, |a| − 1) ⎤
@L₂ :  ⎣ ∧ partitioned(a, 0, j − 1, j, j) ∧ sorted(a, i, |a| − 1)        ⎦
```

The third and fourth basic paths follow the inner loop, each handling one assumption on the guard $a[j] > a[j + 1]$ of the if statement:

---
(3)

$@L_2 : \begin{bmatrix} 1 \leq i < |a| \ \wedge \ 0 \leq j \leq i \ \wedge \ \text{partitioned}(a, 0, i, i+1, |a|-1) \\ \wedge \ \text{partitioned}(a, 0, j-1, j, j) \ \wedge \ \text{sorted}(a, i, |a|-1) \end{bmatrix}$

assume $j < i$;
assume $a[j] > a[j+1]$;
$t := a[j]$;
$a[j] := a[j+1]$;
$a[j+1] := t$;
$j := j+1$;
$@L_2 : \begin{bmatrix} 1 \leq i < |a| \ \wedge \ 0 \leq j \leq i \ \wedge \ \text{partitioned}(a, 0, i, i+1, |a|-1) \\ \wedge \ \text{partitioned}(a, 0, j-1, j, j) \ \wedge \ \text{sorted}(a, i, |a|-1) \end{bmatrix}$

---
(4)

$@L_2 : \begin{bmatrix} 1 \leq i < |a| \ \wedge \ 0 \leq j \leq i \ \wedge \ \text{partitioned}(a, 0, i, i+1, |a|-1) \\ \wedge \ \text{partitioned}(a, 0, j-1, j, j) \ \wedge \ \text{sorted}(a, i, |a|-1) \end{bmatrix}$

assume $j < i$;
assume $a[j] \leq a[j+1]$;
$j := j+1$;
$@L_2 : \begin{bmatrix} 1 \leq i < |a| \ \wedge \ 0 \leq j \leq i \ \wedge \ \text{partitioned}(a, 0, i, i+1, |a|-1) \\ \wedge \ \text{partitioned}(a, 0, j-1, j, j) \ \wedge \ \text{sorted}(a, i, |a|-1) \end{bmatrix}$

The fifth basic path starts at L_2, exits the inner loop, and decrements i on its way to L_1:

---
(5)

$@L_2 : \begin{bmatrix} 1 \leq i < |a| \ \wedge \ 0 \leq j \leq i \ \wedge \ \text{partitioned}(a, 0, i, i+1, |a|-1) \\ \wedge \ \text{partitioned}(a, 0, j-1, j, j) \ \wedge \ \text{sorted}(a, i, |a|-1) \end{bmatrix}$

assume $j \geq i$;
$i := i-1$;
$@L_1 : \ -1 \leq i < |a| \ \wedge \ \text{partitioned}(a, 0, i, i+1, |a|-1) \ \wedge \ \text{sorted}(a, i, |a|-1)$

The final basic path starts at L_1, exits the outer loop, and then exits the function, returning the (presumably sorted) array a:

---
(6)

$@L_1 : \ -1 \leq i < |a| \ \wedge \ \text{partitioned}(a, 0, i, i+1, |a|-1) \ \wedge \ \text{sorted}(a, i, |a|-1)$

assume $i \leq 0$;
$rv := a$;
@post $\text{sorted}(rv, 0, |rv|-1)$

Figure 5.18 visualizes these basic paths. ∎

Example 5.15. Figure 5.19 lists BubbleSort with runtime assertions at L_3 and a different set of loop invariants at L_1 and L_2 relevant for proving the runtime assertions. Six basic paths correspond in structure to those of Figure 5.18, although their content varies based on the new precondition, postcondi-

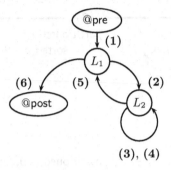

Fig. 5.18. Visualization of basic paths of BubbleSort

```
@pre ⊤
@post ⊤
int[] BubbleSort(int[] a₀) {
    int[] a := a₀;
    for
        @L₁ : −1 ≤ i < |a|
        (int i := |a| − 1; i > 0; i := i − 1) {
        for
            @L₂ : 0 < i < |a| ∧ 0 ≤ j ≤ i
            (int j := 0; j < i; j := j + 1) {
            @L₃ : 0 ≤ j < |a| ∧ 0 ≤ j + 1 < |a|;
            if (a[j] > a[j + 1])  {
                int t := a[j];
                a[j] := a[j + 1];
                a[j + 1] := t;
            }
        }
    }
    return a;
}
```

Fig. 5.19. BubbleSort with runtime assertions

---

tion, and loop invariants. These basic paths ignore the runtime assertion at L_3. Then one additional basic path ends at the runtime assertion:

$$\text{(7)}$$

$@L_2 :\ 0 < i < |a| \ \wedge \ 0 \le j \le i$
assume $j < i$;
$@L_3 :\ 0 \le j < |a| \ \wedge \ 0 \le j + 1 < |a|$

∎

```
@pre 0 ≤ ℓ ∧ u < |a| ∧ sorted(a, ℓ, u)
@post rv ↔ ∃i. ℓ ≤ i ≤ u ∧ a[i] = e
bool BinarySearch(int[] a, int ℓ, int u, int e) {
    if (ℓ > u) return false;
    else {
        int m := (ℓ + u) div 2;
        if (a[m] = e) return true;
        else if (a[m] < e) {
            @R₁ : 0 ≤ m + 1 ∧ u < |a| ∧ sorted(a, m + 1, u);
            return BinarySearch(a, m + 1, u, e);
        } else {
            @R₂ : 0 ≤ ℓ ∧ m − 1 < |a| ∧ sorted(a, ℓ, m − 1);
            return BinarySearch(a, ℓ, m − 1, e);
        }
    }
}
```

Fig. 5.20. BinarySearch with function call assertions

5.2.2 Basic Paths: Function Calls

Like loops, recursive functions create an unbounded number of paths within
programs. But just as loop invariants cut loops to produce a finite number of
basic paths, function specifications cut function calls.

Recall that the function postcondition is a relation between the return
value rv and the formal parameters. A function's postcondition summarizes
the effects of calling it. We use these summaries to replace function calls in
basic paths.

Remark 5.16. The postconditions of the functions of a program need only
include information that is relevant for proving the given specification, so the
summaries may be incomplete. Ignoring irrelevant aspects of functions reduces
the size of annotations. Chapter 6 discusses techniques for developing function
specifications.

The replacement of function calls by function summaries makes the listing
of basic paths (and the resulting analysis described in Section 5.2.4) local to
functions. Basic paths do not span multiple functions. However, recall that the
function postcondition is guaranteed to hold on return only when the function
precondition is satisfied on entry. To ensure that the precondition is satisfied,
each instance of a function call generates an extra basic path in which the
called function's precondition is asserted. An example clarifies this discussion.

Example 5.17. Figure 5.8 lists BinarySearch with its function specification.
BinarySearch contains two (recursive) function calls. In Figure 5.20, each function call is protected by a **function call assertion** at R_1 and R_2. Each assertion is constructed by applying a substitution to BinarySearch's precondition

$$F[a, \ell, u, e] : \ 0 \le \ell \ \wedge \ u < |a| \ \wedge \ \mathsf{sorted}(a, \ell, u) \ .$$

The first function call is $\mathsf{BinarySearch}(a, m+1, u, e)$, so the function call assertion at R_1 is $F\sigma_1$, where

$$\sigma_1 : \ \{a \mapsto a, \ \ell \mapsto m+1, \ u \mapsto u, \ e \mapsto e\} \ .$$

The notation of Section 1.5 allows us to write $F[a, m+1, u, e]$.

The second function call is $\mathsf{BinarySearch}(a, \ell, m-1, e)$, so the function call assertion at R_2 is $F[a, \ell, m-1, e]$. These assertions are treated in the same way as other assertions, such as runtime assertions. So far, we have the following basic paths:

---------------------------------- **(1)** ----------------------------------

@pre $0 \le \ell \ \wedge \ u < |a| \ \wedge \ \mathsf{sorted}(a, \ell, u)$
assume $\ell > u$;
$rv := \mathsf{false}$;
@post $rv \ \leftrightarrow \ \exists i. \ \ell \le i \le u \ \wedge \ a[i] = e$

---------------------------------- **(2)** ----------------------------------

@pre $0 \le \ell \ \wedge \ u < |a| \ \wedge \ \mathsf{sorted}(a, \ell, u)$
assume $\ell \le u$;
$m := (\ell + u) \ \mathsf{div} \ 2$;
assume $a[m] = e$;
$rv := \mathsf{true}$;
@post $rv \ \leftrightarrow \ \exists i. \ \ell \le i \le u \ \wedge \ a[i] = e$

---------------------------------- **(3)** ----------------------------------

@pre $0 \le \ell \ \wedge \ u < |a| \ \wedge \ \mathsf{sorted}(a, \ell, u)$
assume $\ell \le u$;
$m := (\ell + u) \ \mathsf{div} \ 2$;
assume $a[m] \ne e$;
assume $a[m] < e$;
@R_1 : $0 \le m+1 \ \wedge \ u < |a| \ \wedge \ \mathsf{sorted}(a, m+1, u)$

---------------------------------- **(5)** ----------------------------------

@pre $0 \le \ell \ \wedge \ u < |a| \ \wedge \ \mathsf{sorted}(a, \ell, u)$
assume $\ell \le u$;
$m := (\ell + u) \ \mathsf{div} \ 2$;
assume $a[m] \ne e$;
assume $a[m] \ge e$;
@R_2 : $0 \le \ell \ \wedge \ m-1 < |a| \ \wedge \ \mathsf{sorted}(a, \ell, m-1)$

Because BinarySearch lacks loops, each basic path starts at the function precondition.

It remains to consider paths (4) and (6), which pass through the recursive function calls and end at the postcondition. Paths (3) and (5) end in the function call assertions at R_1 and R_2 protecting these function calls. Since they assert that the called BinarySearch's precondition holds, we can assume that the returned values obey the postcondition of BinarySearch in each of the calling contexts. Therefore, we can use the function postcondition as a summary of the function call:

$$\text{(4)}$$

@pre $0 \leq \ell \ \wedge \ u < |a| \ \wedge \ \mathsf{sorted}(a, \ell, u)$
assume $\ell \leq u$;
$m := (\ell + u) \ \mathbf{div} \ 2$;
assume $a[m] \neq e$;
assume $a[m] < e$;
assume $v_1 \leftrightarrow \exists i. \ m + 1 \leq i \leq u \ \wedge \ a[i] = e$;
$rv := v_1$;
@post $rv \leftrightarrow \exists i. \ \ell \leq i \leq u \ \wedge \ a[i] = e$

The lines

assume $v_1 \leftrightarrow \exists i. \ m + 1 \leq i \leq u \ \wedge \ a[i] = e$;
$rv := v_1$;

arise as follows. First, translate the **return** statement

return $\mathsf{BinarySearch}(a, m + 1, u, e)$;

into an assignment to rv, as usual:

$rv := \mathsf{BinarySearch}(a, m + 1, u, e)$;

Next, given that the precondition holds (from path (3)), assume that the postcondition holds. Therefore, summarize the function call with a relation based on BinarySearch's postcondition,

$$G[a, \ell, u, e, rv] : \ rv \leftrightarrow \exists i. \ \ell \leq i \leq u \ \wedge \ a[i] = e \ .$$

Specifically, the relation is $G[a, m + 1, u, e, v_1]$, where v_1 is a fresh variable that captures the return value. In the basic path, assume this relation; then use the return value v_1 in the assignment:

assume $G[a, m + 1, u, e, v_1]$;
$rv := v_1$;

These are the penultimate lines of (4). Hence, (4) replaces the function call $\mathsf{BinarySearch}(a, m + 1, u, e)$ with a summary based on the function postcondition. Now reasoning about the basic path does not require reasoning about all of BinarySearch at once.

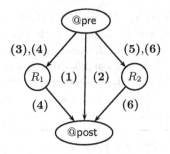

Fig. 5.21. Visualization of basic paths of BinarySearch

Construct the final basic path for the function call BinarySearch$(a, \ell, m - 1, e)$ similarly:

---

(6)

@pre $0 \leq \ell \wedge u < |a| \wedge$ sorted(a, ℓ, u)
assume $\ell \leq u$;
$m := (\ell + u)$ div 2;
assume $a[m] \neq e$;
assume $a[m] \geq e$;
assume $v_2 \leftrightarrow \exists i.\ \ell \leq i \leq m - 1 \wedge a[i] = e$;
$rv := v_2$;
@post $rv \leftrightarrow \exists i.\ \ell \leq i \leq u \wedge a[i] = e$

Again, v_2 is a fresh variable.

Figure 5.21 visualizes these basic paths. Paths **(4)** and **(6)** are shown to pass through locations R_1 and R_2, respectively.   ∎

For the general case, consider function f with prototype

@pre $F[p_1, \ldots, p_n]$
@post $G[p_1, \ldots, p_n, rv]$
type$_0$ f(type$_1$ p_1, ..., type$_n$ p_n)

Suppose that f is called in context

$w := f(e_1, \ldots, e_n)$;

where $e_1, \ldots, e_n$ are expressions. Then augment the calling context with the function call assertion:

@ $F[e_1, \ldots, e_n]$;
$w := f(e_1, \ldots, e_n)$;

Treat this new assertion the same as any assertion: it results in at least one basic path ending in

...
@ $F[e_1, \ldots, e_n]$

Finally, in basic paths that pass through the function call, replace the function call by an assumption and assignment constructed from the postcondition, where v is a fresh variable:

```
...
assume G[e₁,...,eₙ,v];
w := v;
...
```

Note that rv need not have type bool as in BinarySearch. For example, for a function with prototype

```
@pre ⊤
@post rv ≥ x
int g(int x)
```

the statement

```
w := g(n + 1);
```

is summarized in basic paths as follows:

```
assume v ≥ n + 1;
w := v;
```

5.2.3 Program States

Before presenting the final step in proving partial correctness, we formalize program state. A program **state** s is an assignment of values of the proper type to all variables. The program variables include a distinguished variable pc, the **program counter**. It holds the current location of control.

Example 5.18. The state

$$s : \{pc \mapsto L_1, \ a \mapsto [2; 0; 1], \ i \mapsto 2, \ j \mapsto 0, \ t \mapsto 2, \ rv \mapsto []\}$$

is a state of BubbleSort in which control resides at L_1. ∎

A state can be extended to a logical interpretation. Suppose that T is the theory that captures the functions ($+$, $-$, etc.) and predicates ($=$, $<$, etc.) of the program. Extend a state s to a logical T-interpretation $I : (D_I, \alpha_I)$: let D_I be all values of the program types; and construct α_I by using the assignments of s and adding assignments for all logical functions and predicates so that I is a T-interpretation. Subsequently, when we say a state, we mean either the assignment of program variables to values or the extension to a T-interpretation for the appropriate theory T, depending on the context. When we write $s \models F$, we mean that $I \models F$ for a T-interpretation I extending s.

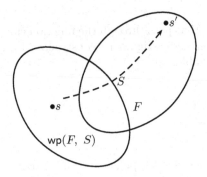

Fig. 5.22. Weakest precondition

Example 5.19. To extend

$$s: \{pc \mapsto L_1,\ a \mapsto [2;0;1],\ i \mapsto 2,\ j \mapsto 0,\ t \mapsto 2,\ rv \mapsto []\}$$

to a $(T_{\mathbb{Z}} \cup T_A)$-interpretation $I : (D_I, \alpha_I)$, let D_I be the set of all integers and arrays of integers; and for α_I, assign the standard functions to $\cdot[\cdot]$, $\cdot\langle\cdot \triangleleft \cdot\rangle$, $+$, $-$, *etc.*   ∎

5.2.4 Verification Conditions

Our goal is to reduce an annotated function to a finite set of FOL formulae, called **verification conditions**, such that their validity implies that the function's behavior agrees with its annotations. The reduction to basic paths reduces reasoning about the function to reasoning about a finite set of basic paths. The final reduction from basic paths to VCs requires a mechanism for incorporating the effects of program statements into FOL formulae. The **weakest precondition** predicate transformer is the mechanism. A **predicate transformer** p is a function

$$p : \text{FOL} \times \text{stmts} \to \text{FOL}$$

that maps a FOL formula $F \in \text{FOL}$ and program statement $S \in \text{stmts}$ to a FOL formula.

The weakest precondition $\text{wp}(F, S)$ has the defining characteristic that if state s is such that

$$s \models \text{wp}(F, S)$$

and if statement S is executed on state s to produce state s', then

$$s' \models F\ .$$

This situation is visualized in Figure 12.1(a). The region labeled F is the set of states that satisfy F; similarly, the region labeled $\text{wp}(F, S)$ is the set of states that satisfy $wp(F, S)$. Every state s on which executing statement S leads to a state s' in the F region must be in the $wp(F, S)$ region.

Define the weakest precondition for the two statement types of basic paths introduced in Section 5.2.1:

- *Assumption*: What must hold before statement `assume` c is executed to ensure that F holds afterward? If $c \to F$ holds before, then satisfying c in `assume` c guarantees that F holds afterward:

  $$wp(F, \text{assume } c) \; \Leftrightarrow \; c \to F$$

- *Assignment*: What must hold before statement $v := e$ is executed to ensure that $F[v]$ holds afterward? If $F[e]$ holds before, then assigning e to v with $v := e$ makes $F[v]$ hold afterward:

  $$wp(F[v], \; v := e) \; \Leftrightarrow \; F[e]$$

For a sequence of statements $S_1; \ldots; S_n$, define

$$wp(F, \; S_1; \ldots; S_n) \; \Leftrightarrow \; wp(wp(F, \; S_n), \; S_1; \ldots; S_{n-1}) \,.$$

The weakest precondition moves a formula backward over a sequence of statements: for F to hold after executing $S_1; \ldots; S_n$, $wp(F, \; S_1; \ldots; S_n)$ must hold before executing the statements. Because basic paths have only assumption and assignment statements, the definition of wp is complete.

Then the **verification condition** of basic path

@ F
$S_1;$

$\vdots$

$S_n;$
@ G

---

is

$$F \; \to \; wp(G, \; S_1; \ldots; S_n) \,.$$

Its validity implies that when F holds before the statements of the path are executed, then G holds afterward. Traditionally, this verification condition is denoted by the **Hoare triple**

$$\{F\}S_1; \ldots; S_n\{G\} \,.$$

Example 5.20. Consider the basic path

---
(1)

@ $x \geq 0$
$x := x + 1;$
@ $x \geq 1$

The VC is

$$\{x \geq 0\}x := x + 1\{x \geq 1\} : \ x \geq 0 \ \rightarrow \ \mathsf{wp}(x \geq 1, \ x := x + 1)$$

so compute

$$\begin{aligned}
&\mathsf{wp}(x \geq 1, \ x := x + 1) \\
&\Leftrightarrow \ (x \geq 1)\{x \mapsto x + 1\} \\
&\Leftrightarrow \ x + 1 \geq 1 \\
&\Leftrightarrow \ x \geq 0
\end{aligned}$$

Simplifying the VC based on this computation produces

$$x \geq 0 \ \rightarrow \ x \geq 0 \ ,$$

which is clearly $T_{\mathbb{Z}}$-valid. ∎

Example 5.21. We generate the VC corresponding to basic path **(2)** in Example 5.13 (LinearSearch):

───────────────────────── **(2)** ─────────────────────────

$@L: \ F: \ \ell \leq i \ \wedge \ (\forall j. \ \ell \leq j < i \ \rightarrow \ a[j] \neq e)$
$S_1: \ \textbf{assume } i \leq u;$
$S_2: \ \textbf{assume } a[i] = e;$
$S_3: \ rv := \textbf{true};$
$@\text{post } G: \ rv \ \leftrightarrow \ \exists j. \ \ell \leq j \leq u \ \wedge \ a[j] = e$

───

The VC is

$$F \ \rightarrow \ \mathsf{wp}(G, \ S_1; S_2; S_3) \ ,$$

so compute

$$\begin{aligned}
&\mathsf{wp}(G, \ S_1; S_2; S_3) \\
&\Leftrightarrow \ \mathsf{wp}(\mathsf{wp}(rv \ \leftrightarrow \ \exists j. \ \ell \leq j \leq u \ \wedge \ a[j] = e, \ rv := \textbf{true}), \ S_1; S_2) \\
&\Leftrightarrow \ \mathsf{wp}(\textbf{true} \ \leftrightarrow \ \exists j. \ \ell \leq j \leq u \ \wedge \ a[j] = e, \ S_1; S_2) \\
&\Leftrightarrow \ \mathsf{wp}(\exists j. \ \ell \leq j \leq u \ \wedge \ a[j] = e, \ S_1; S_2) \\
&\Leftrightarrow \ \mathsf{wp}(\mathsf{wp}(\exists j. \ \ell \leq j \leq u \ \wedge \ a[j] = e, \ \textbf{assume } a[i] = e), \ S_1) \\
&\Leftrightarrow \ \mathsf{wp}(a[i] = e \ \rightarrow \ \exists j. \ \ell \leq j \leq u \ \wedge \ a[j] = e, \ S_1) \\
&\Leftrightarrow \ \mathsf{wp}(a[i] = e \ \rightarrow \ \exists j. \ \ell \leq j \leq u \ \wedge \ a[j] = e, \ \textbf{assume } i \leq u) \\
&\Leftrightarrow \ i \leq u \ \rightarrow \ (a[i] = e \ \rightarrow \ \exists j. \ \ell \leq j \leq u \ \wedge \ a[j] = e)
\end{aligned}$$

Replacing F and $\mathsf{wp}(G, \ S_1; S_2; S_3)$ according to the computed formula results in the VC

$$\begin{aligned}
&\ell \leq i \ \wedge \ (\forall j. \ \ell \leq j < i \ \rightarrow \ a[j] \neq e) \\
&\quad \rightarrow \ (i \leq u \ \rightarrow \ (a[i] = e \ \rightarrow \ \exists j. \ \ell \leq j \leq u \ \wedge \ a[j] = e))
\end{aligned}$$

or, equivalently,

$$\begin{aligned}
&\ell \leq i \ \wedge \ (\forall j. \ \ell \leq j < i \ \rightarrow \ a[j] \neq e) \ \wedge \ i \leq u \ \wedge \ a[i] = e \\
&\quad \rightarrow \ \exists j. \ \ell \leq j \leq u \ \wedge \ a[j] = e
\end{aligned}$$

according to the equivalence

$$F_1 \wedge F_2 \;\rightarrow\; (F_3 \rightarrow (F_4 \rightarrow F_5)) \;\Leftrightarrow\; (F_1 \wedge F_2 \wedge F_3 \wedge F_4) \;\rightarrow\; F_5 \ .$$

This formula is $(T_{\mathbb{Z}} \cup T_A)$-valid. ∎

Example 5.22. For basic path **(3)** of Example 5.13 (LinearSearch),

─────────────────────── **(3)** ───────────────────────

@L : F : $\ell \le i \ \wedge \ (\forall j. \ \ell \le j < i \ \rightarrow \ a[j] \ne e)$
S_1 : assume $i \le u$;
S_2 : assume $a[i] \ne e$;
S_3 : $i := i + 1$;
@L : G : $\ell \le i \ \wedge \ (\forall j. \ \ell \le j < i \ \rightarrow \ a[j] \ne e)$

───

we use a different strategy to compute the corresponding VC

$$F \;\rightarrow\; \mathsf{wp}(G, \ S_1; S_2; S_3) \ .$$

We collect all modifications to G during applications of wp and then apply them all at once. Compute

$\mathsf{wp}(G, \ S_1; S_2; S_3)$
$\Leftrightarrow \ \mathsf{wp}(\mathsf{wp}(G, \ i := i + 1), \ S_1; S_2)$
$\Leftrightarrow \ \mathsf{wp}(G\{i \mapsto i+1\}, \ S_1; S_2)$
$\Leftrightarrow \ \mathsf{wp}(\mathsf{wp}(G\{i \mapsto i+1\}, \ \text{assume } a[i] \ne e), \ S_1)$
$\Leftrightarrow \ \mathsf{wp}(a[i] \ne e \ \rightarrow \ G\{i \mapsto i+1\}, \ S_1)$
$\Leftrightarrow \ \mathsf{wp}(a[i] \ne e \ \rightarrow \ G\{i \mapsto i+1\}, \ \text{assume } i \le u)$
$\Leftrightarrow \ i \le u \ \rightarrow \ a[i] \ne e \ \rightarrow \ G\{i \mapsto i+1\}$

Then the VC is

$$F \;\rightarrow\; i \le u \;\rightarrow\; a[i] \ne e \;\rightarrow\; G\{i \mapsto i+1\} \ ,$$

or

$$\ell \le i \ \wedge \ (\forall j. \ \ell \le j < i \ \rightarrow \ a[j] \ne e) \ \wedge \ i \le u \ \wedge \ a[i] \ne e$$
$$\rightarrow \ \ell \le i+1 \ \wedge \ \forall j. \ \ell \le j < i+1 \ \rightarrow \ a[j] \ne e \ ,$$

which is $(T_{\mathbb{Z}} \cup T_A)$-valid. ∎

Example 5.23. Consider basic path **(2)** of Example 5.17 (BinarySearch):

─────────────────────── **(2)** ───────────────────────

@pre F : $0 \le \ell \ \wedge \ u < |a| \ \wedge \ \mathsf{sorted}(a, \ell, u)$
S_1 : assume $\ell \le u$;
S_2 : $m := (\ell + u)$ div 2;
S_3 : assume $a[m] = e$;
S_4 : $rv := \text{true}$;
@post G : $rv \ \leftrightarrow \ \exists i. \ \ell \le i \le u \ \wedge \ a[i] = e$

───

The VC is

$$F \;\rightarrow\; \mathsf{wp}(G,\; S_1; S_2; S_3; S_4)\;,$$

so compute

$$
\begin{aligned}
&\mathsf{wp}(G,\; S_1; S_2; S_3; S_4)\\
&\Leftrightarrow \mathsf{wp}(\mathsf{wp}(G,\; rv := \mathbf{true}),\; S_1; S_2; S_3)\\
&\Leftrightarrow \mathsf{wp}(G\{rv \mapsto \mathbf{true}\},\; S_1; S_2; S_3)\\
&\Leftrightarrow \mathsf{wp}(\mathsf{wp}(G\{rv \mapsto \mathbf{true}\},\; \mathbf{assume}\ a[m] = e),\; S_1; S_2)\\
&\Leftrightarrow \mathsf{wp}(a[m] = e\ \rightarrow\ G\{rv \mapsto \mathbf{true}\},\; S_1; S_2)\\
&\Leftrightarrow \mathsf{wp}(\mathsf{wp}(a[m] = e\ \rightarrow\ G\{rv \mapsto \mathbf{true}\},\; m := (\ell + u)\ \mathbf{div}\ 2),\; S_1)\\
&\Leftrightarrow \mathsf{wp}((a[m] = e\ \rightarrow\ G\{rv \mapsto \mathbf{true}\})\{m \mapsto (\ell + u)\ \mathbf{div}\ 2\},\; S_1)\\
&\Leftrightarrow \mathsf{wp}((a[m] = e\ \rightarrow\ G\{rv \mapsto \mathbf{true}\})\{m \mapsto (\ell + u)\ \mathbf{div}\ 2\}\\
&\quad\ , \; \mathbf{assume}\ \ell \le u)\\
&\Leftrightarrow \ell \le u\ \rightarrow\ (a[m] = e\ \rightarrow\ G\{rv \mapsto \mathbf{true}\})\{m \mapsto (\ell + u)\ \mathbf{div}\ 2\}
\end{aligned}
$$

Applying the substitutions produces

$$\ell \le u\ \rightarrow\ a[(\ell + u)\ \mathbf{div}\ 2] = e\ \rightarrow\ G\{rv \mapsto \mathbf{true},\ m \mapsto (\ell + u)\ \mathbf{div}\ 2\}\;.$$

Simplifying the VC accordingly

$$
\begin{aligned}
&0 \le \ell \wedge u < |a| \wedge \mathsf{sorted}(a, \ell, u) \wedge \ell \le u \wedge a[(\ell + u)\ \mathbf{div}\ 2] = e\\
&\rightarrow\ \exists i.\ \ell \le i \le u \wedge a[i] = e
\end{aligned}
$$

reveals that it is $(T_{\mathbb{Z}} \cup T_A)$-valid: $\ell \le u$ from the antecedent implies that $\ell \le (\ell + u)\ \mathbf{div}\ 2 \le u$, so that $a[(\ell + u)\ \mathbf{div}\ 2] = e$ implies that $\exists i.\ \ell \le i \le u \wedge a[i] = e$. ∎

Example 5.24. Consider basic path **(3)** of Example 5.14 (BubbleSort):

-------------------------------- **(3)** --------------------------------

$$@L_2:\ F:\ \begin{bmatrix} 1 \le i < |a| \wedge 0 \le j \le i\\ \wedge\ \mathsf{partitioned}(a, 0, i, i+1, |a|-1)\\ \wedge\ \mathsf{partitioned}(a, 0, j-1, j, j) \wedge \mathsf{sorted}(a, i, |a|-1) \end{bmatrix}$$

$S_1:$ **assume** $j < i$;
$S_2:$ **assume** $a[j] > a[j+1]$;
$S_3:$ $t := a[j]$;
$S_4:$ $a[j] := a[j+1]$;
$S_5:$ $a[j+1] := t$;
$S_6:$ $j := j + 1$;

$$@L_2:\ G:\ \begin{bmatrix} 1 \le i < |a| \wedge 0 \le j \le i\\ \wedge\ \mathsf{partitioned}(a, 0, i, i+1, |a|-1)\\ \wedge\ \mathsf{partitioned}(a, 0, j-1, j, j) \wedge \mathsf{sorted}(a, i, |a|-1) \end{bmatrix}$$

The VC is

$$F\ \rightarrow\ \mathsf{wp}(G,\; S_1; S_2; S_3; S_4; S_5; S_6)$$

so compute

$\mathsf{wp}(G,\ S_1; S_2; S_3; S_4; S_5; S_6)$
$\Leftrightarrow\ \mathsf{wp}(\mathsf{wp}(G,\ j := j+1),\ S_1; S_2; S_3; S_4; S_5)$
$\Leftrightarrow\ \mathsf{wp}(G\{j \mapsto j+1\},\ S_1; S_2; S_3; S_4; S_5)$
$\Leftrightarrow\ \mathsf{wp}(\mathsf{wp}(G\{j \mapsto j+1\},\ a[j+1] := t),\ S_1; S_2; S_3; S_4)$
$\Leftrightarrow\ \mathsf{wp}(G\{j \mapsto j+1\}\{a \mapsto a\langle j+1 \lhd t\rangle\},\ S_1; S_2; S_3; S_4)$

Array assignment $a[j+1] := t$ translates to the functional substitution $\{a \mapsto a\langle j+1 \lhd t\rangle\}$ according to the theory of arrays, T_A. That is, the assignment is modeled by substituting $a\langle j+1 \lhd t\rangle$ for every instance a affected by the assignment. Continuing,

$\Leftrightarrow\ \mathsf{wp}(G\{j \mapsto j+1,\ a \mapsto a\langle j+1 \lhd t\rangle\},\ S_1; S_2; S_3; S_4)$
$\Leftrightarrow\ \mathsf{wp}(\mathsf{wp}(G\{j \mapsto j+1,\ a \mapsto a\langle j+1 \lhd t\rangle\},\ a[j] := a[j+1])$
$\qquad,\ S_1; S_2; S_3)$
$\Leftrightarrow\ \mathsf{wp}(G\{j \mapsto j+1,\ a \mapsto a\langle j+1 \lhd t\rangle\}\{a \mapsto a\langle j \lhd a[j+1]\rangle\}$
$\qquad,\ S_1; S_2; S_3)$
$\Leftrightarrow\ \mathsf{wp}(G\{j \mapsto j+1,\ a \mapsto a\langle j \lhd a[j+1]\rangle\langle j+1 \lhd t\rangle\},\ S_1; S_2; S_3)$

The array assignment S_4 similarly translates to a substitution. Composing the two substitutions produces the substitution in which the doubly-modified array $a\langle j \lhd a[j+1]\rangle\langle j+1 \lhd t\rangle$ replaces a. Then

$\Leftrightarrow\ \mathsf{wp}(\mathsf{wp}(G\{j \mapsto j+1,\ a \mapsto a\langle j \lhd a[j+1]\rangle\langle j+1 \lhd t\rangle\},\ t := a[j])$
$\qquad,\ S_1; S_2)$
$\Leftrightarrow\ \mathsf{wp}(G\{j \mapsto j+1,\ a \mapsto a\langle j \lhd a[j+1]\rangle\langle j+1 \lhd t\rangle\}\{t \mapsto a[j]\}$
$\qquad,\ S_1; S_2)$
$\Leftrightarrow\ \mathsf{wp}(G\{j \mapsto j+1,\ a \mapsto a\langle j \lhd a[j+1]\rangle\langle j+1 \lhd a[j]\rangle,\ t \mapsto a[j]\}$
$\qquad,\ S_1; S_2)$

Here, the composition of substitutions results in applying $\{t \mapsto a[j]\}$ to the term $a\langle j \lhd a[j+1]\rangle\langle j+1 \lhd t\rangle$, which contains t. To finish,

$\Leftrightarrow\ \mathsf{wp}(\mathsf{wp}(G\{j \mapsto j+1,\ a \mapsto a\langle j \lhd a[j+1]\rangle\langle j+1 \lhd a[j]\rangle,\ t \mapsto a[j]\}$
$\qquad,\ \texttt{assume}\ a[j] > a[j+1])$
$\qquad,\ S_1)$
$\Leftrightarrow\ \mathsf{wp}(a[j] > a[j+1]$
$\qquad \to\ G\{j \mapsto j+1,\ a \mapsto a\langle j \lhd a[j+1]\rangle\langle j+1 \lhd a[j]\rangle,\ t \mapsto a[j]\}$
$\qquad,\ S_1)$
$\Leftrightarrow\ \mathsf{wp}(a[j] > a[j+1]$
$\qquad \to\ G\{j \mapsto j+1,\ a \mapsto a\langle j \lhd a[j+1]\rangle\langle j+1 \lhd a[j]\rangle,\ t \mapsto a[j]\}$
$\qquad,\ \texttt{assume}\ j < i)$
$\Leftrightarrow\ j < i\ \to\ a[j] > a[j+1]$
$\qquad \to\ G\{j \mapsto j+1,\ a \mapsto a\langle j \lhd a[j+1]\rangle\langle j+1 \lhd a[j]\rangle,\ t \mapsto a[j]\}$
$\Leftrightarrow\ j < i\ \land\ a[j] > a[j+1]$
$\qquad \to\ G\{j \mapsto j+1,\ a \mapsto a\langle j \lhd a[j+1]\rangle\langle j+1 \lhd a[j]\rangle,\ t \mapsto a[j]\}$

Finally, applying the substitution

$$\sigma: \{j \mapsto j + 1, \ a \mapsto a\langle j \lhd a[j+1]\rangle\langle j+1 \lhd a[j]\rangle, \ t \mapsto a[j]\}$$

to G produces $G\sigma$:

$$1 \le i < |a\langle j \lhd a[j+1]\rangle\langle j+1 \lhd a[j]\rangle| \ \land \ 0 \le j+1 \le i$$
$$\land \ \text{partitioned}(a\langle j \lhd a[j+1]\rangle\langle j+1 \lhd a[j]\rangle, 0, i, i+1,$$
$$|a\langle j \lhd a[j+1]\rangle\langle j+1 \lhd a[j]\rangle| - 1)$$
$$\land \ \text{partitioned}(a\langle j \lhd a[j+1]\rangle\langle j+1 \lhd a[j]\rangle, 0, j, j+1, j+1)$$
$$\land \ \text{sorted}(a\langle j \lhd a[j+1]\rangle\langle j+1 \lhd a[j]\rangle, i, |a\langle j \lhd a[j+1]\rangle\langle j+1 \lhd a[j]\rangle| - 1)$$

The **length function** $| \cdot |$ obeys the following axiom:

$$\forall a, i, e. \ |a\langle i \lhd e\rangle| = |a| \qquad\qquad \text{(array length)}$$

In other words, modifying an array's elements does not change its size. Under this axiom, $G\sigma$ is equivalent to

$$1 \le i < |a| \ \land \ 0 \le j+1 \le i$$
$$\land \ \text{partitioned}(a\langle j \lhd a[j+1]\rangle\langle j+1 \lhd a[j]\rangle, 0, i, i+1, |a| - 1)$$
$$\land \ \text{partitioned}(a\langle j \lhd a[j+1]\rangle\langle j+1 \lhd a[j]\rangle, 0, j, j+1, j+1)$$
$$\land \ \text{sorted}(a\langle j \lhd a[j+1]\rangle\langle j+1 \lhd a[j]\rangle, i, |a| - 1)$$

Thus, the VC is

$$
\begin{bmatrix}
1 \le i < |a| \ \land \ 0 \le j \le i \\
\land \ \text{partitioned}(a, 0, i, i+1, |a| - 1) \\
\land \ \text{partitioned}(a, 0, j-1, j, j) \\
\land \ \text{sorted}(a, i, |a| - 1) \\
\land \ j < i \ \land \ a[j] > a[j+1]
\end{bmatrix}
$$
$$
\rightarrow
\begin{bmatrix}
1 \le i < |a| \ \land \ 0 \le j+1 \le i \\
\land \ \text{partitioned}(a\langle j \lhd a[j+1]\rangle\langle j+1 \lhd a[j]\rangle, 0, i, i+1, |a| - 1) \\
\land \ \text{partitioned}(a\langle j \lhd a[j+1]\rangle\langle j+1 \lhd a[j]\rangle, 0, j, j+1, j+1) \\
\land \ \text{sorted}(a\langle j \lhd a[j+1]\rangle\langle j+1 \lhd a[j]\rangle, i, |a| - 1)
\end{bmatrix}
$$

which is $(T_{\mathbb{Z}} \cup T_A)$-valid.   ∎

5.2.5 *P*-Invariant and *P*-Inductive

Let us consider the inductive assertion method abstractly.

A **program** is a set of functions with some distinguished **entry function**. Let P be a program with distinguished entry function f such that f has function precondition F_{pre} and initial location L_0. A **computation** of program P, or a P-computation, is a sequence of states

$$s_0, s_1, s_2, \ldots$$

such that

1. $s_0[pc] = L_0$ and $s_0 \models F_{\text{pre}}$;
2. and for each index i, s_{i+1} is a result of executing the instruction at $s_i[pc]$ on state s_i.

The notation $s_i[pc]$ indicates the value of pc given by state s_i. A computation may be finite or infinite. Infinite computations arise when a program contains a function that does not always halt (either through recursion or looping).

A formula F annotating location L of program P is P-**invariant** (also, is an invariant of P, or is a P-invariant) iff for all P-computations $s_0, s_1, s_2, \ldots$ and for each index i, if $s_i[pc] = L$ then $s_i \models F$. The annotations of P are P-invariant iff each annotation is P-invariant. This definition is not implementable: checking if F is P-invariant requires checking an infinite number of P-computations in general, even if all computations are finite.

Instead, we use the inductive assertion method introduced in this chapter. If all verification conditions generated from program P are T-valid (in the proper theory T), then the annotations are P-**inductive** (also, are inductive P-invariants) and therefore P-invariant. In summary, we have the following theorem.

Theorem 5.25 (Verification Conditions). *If for every basic path*

$@L_i : \ F$
$S_1;$
$\vdots$
$S_n;$
$@L_j : \ G$

---

of program P, the verification condition

$$\{F\}S_1; \ldots; S_n\{G\}$$

is valid (in the appropriate theory), then the annotations are P-invariant. In particular, the annotations are P-inductive.

In other words, when P's annotations are P-inductive, each function of P obeys its specification.

Henceforth, when P is obvious from the context, we say invariant instead of P-invariant and inductive instead of P-inductive.

5.3 Total Correctness

Partial correctness is just one step in proving the **total correctness** of a function or program. Total correctness of a function asserts that if the input satisfies the function precondition, then the function *eventually halts* and produces output that satisfies its function postcondition. In other words, total correctness requires proving partial correctness and that the function always halts on input satisfying its precondition. We focus now on the latter task.

Proving function termination is based on well-founded relations (see Chapter 4). Define a set S with a well-founded relation $\prec$. Then find a function δ mapping program states to S such that δ decreases according to $\prec$ along every basic path. Since $\prec$ is well-founded, there cannot exist an infinite sequence of program states; otherwise, they would map to an infinite decreasing sequence in S. The function δ is called a **ranking function**.

Choosing Well-Founded Relations and Ranking Functions

The concept of well-founded relations is the fundamental principle of this method. The ranking function itself is really just a convenience. One could directly construct a well-founded relation over the program states and show that the output state of each basic path is less than the input state according to this relation. However, it is often conceptually easier to find a function that maps states to a known set S with a known well-founded relation $\prec$. For example, we usually choose as S the set of n-tuples of natural numbers and as $\prec$ the lexicographic extension $<_n$ of $<$ to n-tuples of natural numbers, where n varies according to the application.

As with partial correctness, we consider total correctness in the context of loops first and then in the context of recursion. Section 6.2 examines a program with both loops and recursion.

Example 5.26. Figure 5.23 lists BubbleSort with ranking annotations. It contains one new type of annotation: $\downarrow (i+1, i+1)$ and $\downarrow (i+1, i-j)$ assert that the functions $(i+1, i+1)$ and $(i+1, i-j)$, respectively, are ranking functions. These functions map states of BubbleSort onto pairs of natural numbers $S : \mathbb{N}^2$ with well-founded relation $<_2$. Intuitively, we have captured two separate arguments. The outer loop eventually finishes because i decreases to 0; hence $i+1$ decreases as well. Why do we use $i+1$ rather than i? When $|a| = 0$, the initial assignment to i is -1. While $i+1$ is always nonnegative, i is not; and recall that we want to map into the natural numbers. The inner loop halts because j increases to i; hence $i - j$ decreases to 0. Therefore, our intuition tells us that $i+1$ is important for the outer loop, and $i-j$ is important for the inner loop.

Placing these two functions $i+1$ and $i-j$ together as a pair $(i+1, i-j)$ provides the annotation for the inner loop. We expect $i+1$ to remain constant while the inner loop is executing and decreasing $i-j$. For the annotation of the outer loop, we note that $i+1 > i-j = i-0 = i$ on entry to the inner loop, so that $(i+1, i+1) >_2 (i+1, i-j)$.

The loop annotations assert that the ranking functions $(i+1, i+1)$ and $(i+1, i-j)$ map program states to pairs of natural numbers. Hence, we need to prove that the loop annotations are inductive using the inductive assertion

```
@pre ⊤
@post ⊤
int[] BubbleSort(int[] a₀) {
    int[] a := a₀;
    for
        @L₁ : i + 1 ≥ 0
        ↓ (i + 1, i + 1)
        (int i := |a| − 1; i > 0; i := i − 1) {
        for
            @L₂ : i + 1 ≥ 0 ∧ i − j ≥ 0
            ↓ (i + 1, i − j)
            (int j := 0; j < i; j := j + 1) {
            if (a[j] > a[j + 1]) {
                int t := a[j];
                a[j] := a[j + 1];
                a[j + 1] := t;
            }
        }
    }
    return a;
}
```

Fig. 5.23. BubbleSort with annotations to prove termination

method. We leave this step to the reader. It only remains to prove that the functions decrease along each basic path.

The relevant basic paths are the following:

─────────────────────── **(1)** ───────────────────────

$@L_1 : i + 1 ≥ 0$
$↓ L_1 : (i + 1, i + 1)$
assume $i > 0$;
$j := 0$;
$↓ L_2 : (i + 1, i − j)$

─────────────────────── **(2)** ───────────────────────

$@L_2 : i + 1 ≥ 0 ∧ i − j ≥ 0$
$↓ L_2 : (i + 1, i − j)$
assume $j < i$;
assume $a[j] > a[j + 1]$;
$t := a[j]$;
$a[j] := a[j + 1]$;
$a[j + 1] := t$;
$j := j + 1$;
$↓ L_2 : (i + 1, i − j)$

---
(3) ---

@L_2 : $i+1 \geq 0 \ \wedge \ i-j \geq 0$
↓L_2 : $(i+1, i-j)$
assume $j < i$;
assume $a[j] \leq a[j+1]$;
$j := j+1$;
↓L_2 : $(i+1, i-j)$

---
(4) ---

@L_2 : $i+1 \geq 0 \ \wedge \ i-j \geq 0$
↓L_2 : $(i+1, i-j)$
assume $j \geq i$;
$i := i-1$;
↓L_1 : $(i+1, i+1)$

The paths entering and exiting the outer loop at L_1 are not relevant for the termination argument. The entering path does not begin with a ranking function annotation, so there is nothing to prove. The exiting path leads to the **return** statement.

For termination purposes, paths **(2)** and **(3)** can be treated the same:

@L_2 : $i+1 \geq 0 \ \wedge \ i-j \geq 0$
↓L_2 : $(i+1, i-j)$
assume $j < i$;
. . .
$j := j+1$;
↓L_2 : $(i+1, i-j)$

The excluded statements do not impact the value of the ranking functions. ∎

Verification Conditions

A basic path beginning and ending with a ranking function

@ F
↓ $\delta[\bar{x}]$
S_1;
⋮
S_k;
↓ $\kappa[\bar{x}]$

---

induces a verification condition

$$F \;\rightarrow\; \mathsf{wp}(\kappa \prec \delta[\overline{x}_0], \; S_1; \cdots ; S_k)\{\overline{x}_0 \mapsto \overline{x}\} \;.$$

In words, we must prove that the value of κ after executing statements $S_1; \cdots ; S_k$ is less than the value of δ before executing the statements. Therefore, we rename the variables of δ to something new ($\overline{x}_0$ in this case), compute the weakest precondition of $\kappa \prec \delta[\overline{x}_0]$ across the statements $S_1; \cdots ; S_k$, and then rename the new variables back to their original names ($\overline{x}$ in this case). This renaming process preserves the value of $\delta[\overline{x}]$ in its context. The annotation F can provide extra invariant information with which to prove this relation.

Example 5.27. Let us return to the proof of Example 5.26 that BubbleSort halts. Path **(1)** induces the following verification condition:

$$i + 1 \geq 0 \;\wedge\; i > 0 \;\rightarrow\; (i + 1, i - 0) <_2 (i + 1, i + 1) \,,$$

which is valid. Paths **(2)** and **(3)** induce the verification condition:

$$i + 1 \geq 0 \;\wedge\; i - j \geq 0 \;\wedge\; j < i \;\rightarrow\; (i + 1, i - (j + 1)) <_2 (i + 1, i - j) \,,$$

which is valid. Finally, **(4)** induces the verification condition

$$i + 1 \geq 0 \;\wedge\; i - j \geq 0 \;\wedge\; j \geq i \;\rightarrow\; ((i - 1) + 1, (i - 1) + 1) <_2 (i + 1, i - j) \,,$$

which is also valid. Hence, BubbleSort always halts. Combined with the proof of the sortedness property, we can now say that BubbleSort is totally correct with respect to its specification: it always halts and returns a sorted array.

Let us work through the construction of the final verification condition for basic path **(4)**. First, replace i and j with i_0 and j_0, respectively, in the function annotating L_2: $(i_0 + 1, i_0 - j_0)$. Then compute

$$
\begin{aligned}
&\mathsf{wp}((i + 1, i + 1) <_2 (i_0 + 1, i_0 - j_0), \; \mathsf{assume}\ j \geq i; \; i := i - 1) \\
\Leftrightarrow\; &\mathsf{wp}(((i - 1) + 1, (i - 1) + 1) <_2 (i_0 + 1, i_0 - j_0), \; \mathsf{assume}\ j \geq i) \\
\Leftrightarrow\; &j \geq i \;\rightarrow\; (i, i) <_2 (i_0 + 1, i_0 - j_0)
\end{aligned}
$$

Now, having preserved the original value of $(i + 1, i - j)$ at L_2, replace i_0 and j_0 with i and j, respectively:

$$j \geq i \;\rightarrow\; (i, i) <_2 (i + 1, i - j) \,.$$

Noting that **(4)** begins by asserting $i + 1 \geq 0 \;\wedge\; i - j \geq 0$, we have our verification condition:

$$i + 1 \geq 0 \;\wedge\; i - j \geq 0 \;\wedge\; j \geq i \;\rightarrow\; (i, i) <_2 (i + 1, i - j) \,.$$

In this proof, the loop annotations (other than the ranking functions) do not have any bearing on the termination argument. Their purpose is only to prove that the given functions map to the natural numbers. ∎

```
@pre u − ℓ + 1 ≥ 0
@post ⊤
↓ u − ℓ + 1
bool BinarySearch(int[] a, int ℓ, int u, int e) {
    if (ℓ > u) return false;
    else {
        int m := (ℓ + u) div 2;
        if (a[m] = e) return true;
        else if (a[m] < e) return BinarySearch(a, m + 1, u, e);
        else return BinarySearch(a, ℓ, m − 1, e);
    }
}
```

Fig. 5.24. BinarySearch always halts

Besides loops, recursion is another source of nontermination and hence requires ranking annotations as well. Again, we break the termination argument down to the level of basic paths.

Example 5.28. Figure 5.24 lists the BinarySearch function. $u - \ell + 1$ maps the formal parameters of BinarySearch to $S : \mathbb{N}$ with well-founded relation $<$. Why do we use $u - \ell + 1$ as the ranking function? Intuitively, the interval $[\ell, u]$ shortens at each level of recursion, so $u - \ell$ is a good guess at a ranking function. However, it may be that $\ell > u$ so that $u - \ell$ does not map into $\mathbb{N}$; but in this case $\ell = u + 1$, so $u - \ell + 1$ does map into $\mathbb{N}$.

We now need to prove two properties of $u - \ell + 1$:

1. Because $u - \ell + 1$ has type int, we must prove that $u - \ell + 1$ in fact maps to $\mathbb{N}$: whenever $u - \ell + 1$ is evaluated at function entry, it must be the case that $u - \ell + 1 \geq 0$.
2. We must prove that $u - \ell + 1$ decreases from function entry to each recursive call.

The function precondition asserts the first property, so we need only prove that the function specification is inductive as usual. To prove the second property, we reduce the argument to basic paths: $u - \ell + 1$ should decrease across each basic path.

Convince yourself that the annotations other than the ranking argument are inductive.

We now consider the ranking argument. The relevant basic paths of the function are the following:

$$\text{───────────────── (1) ─────────────────}$$

@pre $u - \ell + 1 \geq 0$
↓ $u - \ell + 1$
assume $\ell \leq u$;
$m := (\ell + u)$ **div** 2;
assume $a[m] \neq e$;
assume $a[m] < e$;
↓ $u - (m + 1) + 1$

$$\text{───────────────── (2) ─────────────────}$$

@pre $u - \ell + 1 \geq 0$
↓ $u - \ell + 1$
assume $\ell \leq u$;
$m := (\ell + u)$ **div** 2;
assume $a[m] \neq e$;
assume $a[m] \geq e$;
↓ $(m - 1) - \ell + 1$

Two other basic paths exist from function entry to the first two **return** statements; however, as the recursion ends at each, they are irrelevant to the termination argument.

The basic paths induce two verification conditions. Before examining them, notice that the **assume** statements about $a[m]$ are irrelevant to the termination argument. Now, the first VC is

$$u - \ell + 1 \geq 0 \;\wedge\; \ell \leq u \;\wedge\; \cdots$$
$$\rightarrow \; u - (((\ell + u) \text{ div } 2) + 1) + 1 < u - \ell + 1 \,,$$

where $\cdots$ elides the literals involving $a[m]$. It is $T_{\mathbb{Z}}$-valid. The VC

$$u - \ell + 1 \geq 0 \;\wedge\; \ell \leq u \;\wedge\; \cdots$$
$$\rightarrow \; (((\ell + u) \text{ div } 2) - 1) - \ell + 1 < u - \ell + 1$$

for the second basic path is also $T_{\mathbb{Z}}$-valid, so BinarySearch halts on all input in which ℓ is initially at most $u + 1$.

Section 6.2 provides an alternative to using the awkward ranking function $u - \ell + 1$. Additionally, the argument proves termination on all input. ∎

5.4 Summary

This chapter introduces the specification and verification of sequential programs. It covers:

- The programming language pi.

- *Program specification.* Specifying a program involves writing *function pre-conditions* and *function postconditions* as first-order assertions. A function precondition asserts on which inputs the function is defined, while a function postcondition asserts the form of the returned data. Other annotations: loop invariants, assertions, runtime assertions.
- *Partial correctness*, which guarantees that if a function halts and the input satisfied the function precondition, then its returned value satisfies the function postcondition. Partial correctness is proved via an inductive argument. Additional annotations strengthen the inductive hypothesis. Basic paths, program state, verification conditions, inductive invariants.
- *Total correctness*, which guarantees additionally that the program or function always halts. Total correctness requires mapping, via a ranking function, program states to a domain with a well-founded relation and proving that the mapped values in the domain decrease as computation progresses. Typically, proving termination requires additional partial correctness annotations.

Chapter 6 discusses strategies for applying the techniques of this chapter.

The methods introduced in this chapter are fundamental to verification of software and hardware. However, we present them in a simple context. Decades of research have made much more possible.

The validity of verification conditions listed in examples or produced by programs in the chapter are all decided using the decision procedures discussed in Part II. We have focused on specifications that can be expressed in the fragments of theories introduced in Chapter 3. More complex specifications may require general mechanical theorem proving. However, mechanical theorem provers often rely on the decision procedures of Part II when possible for speed and to minimize human interaction.

Chapter 12 introduces algorithms for deducing annotations.

Bibliographic Remarks

Formally proving program correctness has been a subject of active research for five decades. McCarthy argues in [59, 58] for a "mathematical science of computation". Floyd [34] and Hoare [39] introduce the main concepts for proving property invariance and termination. In particular, they develop *Floyd-Hoare logic*. Manna describes a verification style similar to ours [52]. The *weakest precondition* predicate transformer was first formalized by Dijkstra [28].

King describes in his thesis [50] the idea of a *verifying compiler*, which generates and proves during compilation the verification conditions that arise from program annotations. See [27] for a discussion of the *Extended Static Checker*, a verifying compiler for Java.

```
@pre p(a₀)
@post sorted(rv, 0, |rv| − 1)
int[] InsertionSort(int[] a₀) {
    int[] a := a₀;
    for
        @ r₁(a, a₀, i, j)
        (int i := 1; i < |a|; i := i + 1) {
        int t := a[i];
        for
            @ r₂(a, a₀, i, j)
            (int j := i − 1; j ≥ 0; j := j − 1) {
            if (a[j] ≤ t) break;
            a[j + 1] := a[j];
        }
        a[j + 1] := t;
    }
    return a;
}
```

Fig. 5.25. InsertionSort for Exercise 5.1(a)

Exercises

5.1 (Basic paths). For each of the following functions, replace each @pre $\top$ with a fresh predicate p over the function parameters, each @post $\top$ with a fresh predicate q over rv and the function parameters, and each @ $\top$ with a fresh predicate r over the function variables. As an example, see Figure 5.25 for the replacements for part (a). Then list the basic paths.

(a) InsertionSort of Figure 6.8.
(b) merge of Figure 6.9.
(c) ms of Figure 6.9.

5.2 (Weakest precondition). Compute the following formulae:

(a) $\mathrm{wp}(x \geq 0, \ x := x − k; \ \mathbf{assume} \ k \leq 1)$
(b) $\mathrm{wp}(x \geq 0, \ \mathbf{assume} \ k \leq x; \ x := x − k)$
(c) $\mathrm{wp}(x \geq 0, \ x := x − k; \ \mathbf{assume} \ k \leq x)$
(d) $\mathrm{wp}(x + 2y \geq 3, \ x := x + 1; \ \mathbf{assume} \ x > 0; \ y := y + x)$

5.3 (Verification condition generation). Generate the VCs for the following basic paths:

$$(1)$$

```
@ x > 0;
x := x − k;
assume k ≤ 1;
@ x ≥ 0;
```

———————————————————— (2) ————————————————————

@ ⊤;
assume $k \leq x$;
$x := x - k$;
@ $x \geq 0$;

———————————————————— (3) ————————————————————

@ ⊤;
$x := x - k$;
assume $k \leq x$;
@ $x \geq 0$;

———————————————————— (4) ————————————————————

@ $k \geq 0$;
$x := x - k$;
assume $k \leq x$;
@ $x \geq 0$;

———————————————————— (5) ————————————————————

@ $y \geq 0$;
$x := x + 1$;
assume $x > 0$;
$y := y + x$;
@ $x + 2y \geq 3$;

Which are $T_{\mathbb{Z}}$-valid? Which are $T_{\mathbb{Q}}$-valid?

5.4 (Verification conditions). For each basic path generated in Exercise 5.1, list the corresponding VCs.

5.5 (Public functions). Example 5.6 asserts that a function that is accessible outside a module should have a reasonable function precondition, such as ⊤. Implement verified public wrapper functions to LinearSearch and BinarySearch for searching an entire array. The function preconditions should be reasonable.

5.6 (The div function). Integer division, even by a constant, is not a function of $T_{\mathbb{Z}}$; however, it is useful for reasoning about programs like BinarySearch. Show how basic paths that include the div function can be altered to use only standard linear arithmetic. *Hint*: Use an additional assume statement. How does this change affect the resulting VCs?

5.7 (Ackermann function). Implement the *ack* function of Example 4.9 as a pi program and prove that it always halts.

6

Program Correctness: Strategies

The basis of our approach is the notion of an interpretation of a program: that is, an association of a proposition with each connection in the flow of control through a program.

— Robert W. Floyd
Assigning Meanings to Programs, 1967

As in other applications of mathematical induction (see Example 4.1), the main challenge in applying the inductive assertion method is discovering extra information to make the inductive argument succeed. Consider a typical partial correctness property that asserts that a function's output satisfies some relation with its input. Assuming this property as the inductive hypothesis does not provide any information about how the function behaves between entry and exit. It is a weak hypothesis. Therefore, one must provide more information about the function in the form of additional program annotations. Section 6.1 discusses strategies for discovering this additional information. Section 6.2 applies the strategies to prove that QuickSort always returns a sorted array.

6.1 Developing Inductive Annotations

The machinery presented in Section 5.2 automatically reduces an annotated function to a finite set of verification conditions. Furthermore, the decision procedures discussed in Part II of this text make deciding the validity of many verification conditions an automatable task. For example, all verification conditions in this text fall within decidable fragments of FOL, unless otherwise noted. Thus, determining if a program's annotations are inductive can be automated in many cases. Ongoing research in decision procedures continually expands the set of annotations that produce decidable verification conditions.

Developing annotations is a different matter. As expected, writing a function specification requires human ingenuity, just as implementing the function requires it. Of course, simple assertions, such as that a program is free of run-time errors, can be generated automatically.

Writing the loop invariants also requires human ingenuity. A certain level of human intervention is acceptable: the programmer ought to know certain facts about her/his code. Loop invariants often capture insights into how the code works and what it accomplishes. Developing the implementation and annotations simultaneously results in more robust systems. Finally, annotations formally document code, facilitating better development in team projects.

However, Section 5.2.5 points out a fundamental limitation of the inductive assertion method of program verification: loop invariants must be inductive for the corresponding verification conditions to be valid, not just invariant. Consequently, the programmer can assert many facts that are indeed invariant; yet if the annotations are not inductive, the facts cannot be proved.

Much research addresses automatic (inductive) invariant discovery. For example, algorithms exist for discovering linear and polynomial relations among integer and real variables. Such invariants can, for example, provide loop index bounds, prove the lack of division by 0, or prove that an index into an array is within bounds. Other methods exist for discovering the "shape" of memory in programming languages with pointers, allowing, for example, the partially automated analysis of linked lists. One of the most important roles of automatic invariant discovery is strengthening the programmer's annotations into inductive annotations. Chapter 12 introduces invariant generation procedures. However, no set of algorithms will ever fully replace humans in writing verified software.

In this section, we suggest structured techniques for developing inductive annotations to prove partial correctness. We emphasize that the methods are just heuristics: human ingenuity is still the most important ingredient in forming proofs.

6.1.1 Basic Facts

To begin a proof, include basic facts in loop invariants. Basic facts include loop index ranges and other "obvious" facts. To be inductive, complex assertions usually require these basic facts. We illustrate the development of basic facts through several examples.

Example 6.1. Consider the loop of LinearSearch(see also Figure 5.1):

```
for
  @L : ⊤
  (int i := ℓ; i ≤ u; i := i + 1) {
  if (a[i] = e) return true;
}
```

Based on the initialization of i, the loop guard, and that i is only modified by being incremented in the loop update, we know that at L,

$\ell \leq i \leq u + 1$.

Notice the upper bound. It is a common mistake to forget that on the final iteration, the loop guard is not true. Our basic annotation of the loop is the following:

```
for
    @L :  ℓ ≤ i ≤ u + 1
    (int i := ℓ; i ≤ u; i := i + 1) {
    if (a[i] = e) return true;
}
```

■

Example 6.2. Consider the loops of BubbleSort (see also Figure 5.3):

```
for
    @L₁ :  ⊤
    (int i := |a| − 1; i > 0; i := i − 1) {
    for
        @L₂ :  ⊤
        (int j := 0; j < i; j := j + 1) {
        if (a[j] > a[j + 1])  {
            int t := a[j];
            a[j] := a[j + 1];
            a[j + 1] := t;
        }
    }
}
```

The outer loop index i ranges according to

$$-1 \leq i < |a|$$

Why -1? If $|a| = 0$, then $|a| - 1 = -1$ so that i is initially -1. Keep in mind that "corner cases" like this one are just as important as normal cases (and perhaps even more important when considering correctness: corner cases are often the source of bugs). In the inner loop, the range of i is more restricted:

$$0 < i < |a|$$

because of the outer loop guard.

In the inner loop, j ranges according to

$$0 \leq j \leq i .$$

Therefore, our basic annotation of the two loops is the following:

```
for
  @L₁ : -1 ≤ i < |a|
  (int i := |a| − 1; i > 0; i := i − 1) {
  for
    @L₂ : 0 < i < |a| ∧ 0 ≤ j ≤ i
    (int j := 0; j < i; j := j + 1) {
    if (a[j] > a[j + 1])  {
       int t := a[j];
       a[j] := a[j + 1];
       a[j + 1] := t;
    }
  }
}
```

Note that the loops modify just the elements of a, not a itself. Therefore, we could add the annotation

$$|a| = |a_0|$$

to both loops. Such an annotation would be useful if the postcondition asserted, for example, that

$$|rv| = |a_0| \ .$$

For the property that we address ($\mathsf{sorted}(rv, 0, |rv| - 1)$), this annotation is not useful.   ∎

6.1.2 The Precondition Method

Basic facts provide a foundation for more interesting information. The **precondition method** (also called the "backward substitution" or "backward propagation" method) is a strategy for developing more interesting information in a structured way. Again, we emphasize that the method is a heuristic, not an algorithm: it provides some guidance for the human rather than replacing the human's intuition and ingenuity.

The precondition method consists of the following steps:

1. Identify a fact F that is known at one location L in the function (@L : F) but that is not supported by annotations earlier in the function.
2. Repeat:
   a) Compute the weakest preconditions of F backward through the function, ending at loop invariants or at the beginning of the function.
   b) At each new annotation location L', generalize the new facts to new formula F' (@L' : F').

We illustrate the technique through examples.

Example 6.3. Consider the loop of LinearSearch (see also Figure 5.1), annotated with basic facts:

```
for
    @L : ℓ ≤ i ≤ u + 1
    (int i := ℓ; i ≤ u; i := i + 1) {
        if (a[i] = e) return true;
    }
    return false;
```

The postcondition of LinearSearch is

$$rv \leftrightarrow \exists i. \ \ell \leq i \leq u \land a[i] = e \ .$$

Consider basic path **(4)** of Example 5.13 but with the current loop invariant substituted for the first assertion:

$$\text{———————— (4) ————————}$$

$$@L : F_1 : \ell \leq i \leq u + 1$$
$$S_1 : \text{assume } i > u;$$
$$S_2 : rv := \text{false};$$
$$@\text{post } F_2 : rv \leftrightarrow \exists j. \ \ell \leq j \leq u \land a[j] = e$$

Note that we continue to number basic paths as they were numbered in Example 5.13. The VC

$$\{F_1\}S_1; S_2\{F_2\} : \ell \leq i \leq u + 1 \land i > u \ \rightarrow \ \neg(\exists j. \ \ell \leq j \leq u \land a[j] = e)$$

is not $(T_\mathbb{Z} \cup T_A)$-valid. Essentially, the antecedent does not assert anything useful about the content of a. Write the consequent as

$$F : \forall j. \ \ell \leq j \leq u \ \rightarrow \ a[j] \neq e$$

by pushing in the negation. F says that if LinearSearch exits via S_2, then no element of a in the range $[\ell, u]$ is e. But F is not supported by the current loop invariant at L. In short, F_2 is a fact that is not supported by earlier annotations.

Having identified an unsupported fact, we compute preconditions. To propagate F_2 back to the loop invariant, compute

$$\text{wp}(F_2, \ S_1; S_2)$$
$$\Leftrightarrow \text{wp}(\text{wp}(F_2, \ rv := \text{false}), \ S_1)$$
$$\Leftrightarrow \text{wp}(F_2\{rv \mapsto \text{false}\}, \ S_1)$$
$$\Leftrightarrow \text{wp}(F_2\{rv \mapsto \text{false}\}, \ \text{assume } i > u)$$
$$\Leftrightarrow i > u \ \rightarrow \ F_2\{rv \mapsto \text{false}\}$$
$$\Leftrightarrow i > u \ \rightarrow \ \forall j. \ \ell \leq j \leq u \ \rightarrow \ a[j] \neq e$$

The final formula

$$G : i > u \;\rightarrow\; \forall j.\; \ell \le j \le u \;\rightarrow\; a[j] \ne e \;,$$

in particular the antecedent $i > u$, and some intuition suggests the generalization

$$G' : \forall j.\; \ell \le j < i \;\rightarrow\; a[j] \ne e \;.$$

We compute one backward iteration through the loop to increase our confidence:

$$\text{────────────── (3) ──────────────}$$

```
@L :  H : ?
S₁ :  assume i ≤ u;
S₂ :  assume a[i] ≠ e;
S₃ :  i := i + 1;
@L :  G :  i > u  →  ∀j. ℓ ≤ j ≤ u  →  a[j] ≠ e
```

Then

$$
\begin{aligned}
&\mathsf{wp}(G,\; S_1; S_2; S_3)\\
\Leftrightarrow\;& \mathsf{wp}(\mathsf{wp}(G,\; i := i+1),\; S_1; S_2)\\
\Leftrightarrow\;& \mathsf{wp}(G\{i := i+1\},\; S_1; S_2)\\
\Leftrightarrow\;& \mathsf{wp}(\mathsf{wp}(G\{i := i+1\},\; \mathtt{assume}\; a[i] \ne e),\; S_1)\\
\Leftrightarrow\;& \mathsf{wp}(a[i] \ne e \;\rightarrow\; G\{i := i+1\},\; S_1)\\
\Leftrightarrow\;& \mathsf{wp}(a[i] \ne e \;\rightarrow\; G\{i := i+1\},\; \mathtt{assume}\; i \le u)\\
\Leftrightarrow\;& i \le u \;\rightarrow\; a[i] \ne e \;\rightarrow\; G\{i := i+1\}\\
\Leftrightarrow\;& i \le u \;\wedge\; a[i] \ne e \;\wedge\; i+1 > u \;\rightarrow\; \forall j.\; \ell \le j \le u \;\rightarrow\; a[j] \ne e\\
\Leftrightarrow\;& i = u \;\wedge\; a[u] \ne e \;\rightarrow\; \forall j.\; \ell \le j \le u \;\rightarrow\; a[j] \ne e\\
\Leftrightarrow\;& i = u \;\wedge\; a[u] \ne e \;\rightarrow\; \forall j.\; \ell \le j \le u - 1 \;\rightarrow\; a[j] \ne e\\
\Leftrightarrow\;& i = u \;\wedge\; a[u] \ne e \;\rightarrow\; \forall j.\; \ell \le j \le i - 1 \;\rightarrow\; a[j] \ne e
\end{aligned}
$$

To obtain the second-to-last line from the third-to-last, note that the antecedent already asserts that $a[u] \ne e$; hence, its occurrence as the case $j = u$ of $\forall j.\; \ell \le j \le u \cdots$ is redundant. The final line is realized by applying the equality $i = u$ to the upper bound on j. As we suspected, it seems that the right bound on j should be related to the progress of i, rather than being fixed to u. This observation from computing the weakest precondition matches our intuition. One trick to generalize assertions is to *replace fixed terms (bounds, indices, etc.) with terms that evolve according to the loop counter.*

Thus, we settle on the formula

$$G' : \forall j.\; \ell \le j < i \;\rightarrow\; a[j] \ne e \;.$$

That is, all previously checked entries of a do not equal e. We add this assertion to the loop invariant:

```
for
    @L :  ℓ ≤ i ≤ u + 1  ∧  (∀j. ℓ ≤ j < i  →  a[j] ≠ e)
    (int i := ℓ; i ≤ u; i := i + 1) {
    if (a[i] = e) return true;
}
```

The result is similar to the annotation in Figure 5.15. Generating and checking the corresponding VCs reveals that the annotations are inductive. ∎

Example 6.4. Consider the version of BinarySearch of Figure 5.12 that contains runtime assertions but has only a trivial function specification $\top$. Using the precondition method, we infer a function precondition that makes the annotations inductive. Contexts that call BinarySearch are then forced to obey this function precondition, guaranteeing a lack of runtime errors.

Consider the path from function entry to the assertion protecting the array access:

$$(\cdot)$$

@pre $H : ?$
$S_1 :$ assume $\ell \leq u$;
$S_2 : m := (\ell + u)$ div 2;
@ $F : 0 \leq m < |a|$

Compute

$$\begin{aligned}
&\text{wp}(F, \ S_1; S_2) \\
&\Leftrightarrow \ \text{wp}(\text{wp}(F, \ m := (\ell + u) \text{ div } 2), \ S_1) \\
&\Leftrightarrow \ \text{wp}(F\{m \mapsto (\ell + u) \text{ div } 2\}, \ S_1) \\
&\Leftrightarrow \ \text{wp}(F\{m \mapsto (\ell + u) \text{ div } 2\}, \ \text{assume } \ell \leq u) \\
&\Leftrightarrow \ \ell \leq u \ \rightarrow \ F\{m \mapsto (\ell + u) \text{ div } 2\} \\
&\Leftrightarrow \ \ell \leq u \ \rightarrow \ 0 \leq (\ell + u) \text{ div } 2 < |a| \\
&\Leftarrow \ 0 \leq \ell \wedge u < |a|
\end{aligned}$$

The final line implies the penultimate line, for if $0 \leq \ell \wedge u < |a|$ and $\ell \leq u$, then both $0 \leq \ell < |a|$ and $0 \leq u < |a|$; hence, their mean is also in the range $[0, |a| - 1]$. Therefore, it is guaranteed that

$$0 \leq \ell \wedge u < |a| \ \rightarrow \ \text{wp}(F, \ S_1; S_2)$$

is $T_{\mathbb{Z}}$-valid.

The formula $0 \leq \ell \wedge u < |a|$ appears as the function precondition in Figure 6.1. The annotations are inductive, proving that the runtime assertion $0 \leq m < |a|$ holds in every execution of BinarySearch in which the precondition $0 \leq \ell \wedge u < |a|$ is satisfied. ∎

Example 6.5. Consider the following code fragment of BubbleSort (see also Figure 5.3)

```
@pre 0 ≤ ℓ ∧ u < |a|
@post ⊤
bool BinarySearch(int[] a, int ℓ, int u, int e) {
    if (ℓ > u) return false;
    else {
        @ 2 ≠ 0;
        int m := (ℓ + u) div 2;
        @ 0 ≤ m < |a|;
        if (a[m] = e) return true;
        else if (a[m] < e) return BinarySearch(a, m + 1, u, e);
        else return BinarySearch(a, ℓ, m − 1, e);
    }
}
```

Fig. 6.1. BinarySearch with runtime assertions

```
    for
        @L₁ :  −1 ≤ i < |a|
        (int i := |a| − 1; i > 0; i := i − 1) {
        for
            @L₂ :  0 < i < |a| ∧ 0 ≤ j ≤ i
            (int j := 0; j < i; j := j + 1) {
            if (a[j] > a[j + 1]) {
                int t := a[j];
                a[j] := a[j + 1];
                a[j + 1] := t;
            }
        }
    }
    return a;
```

and its postcondition

$$F : \mathsf{sorted}(rv, 0, |rv| - 1) .$$

Consider the path

────────────────────────────── (6) ──────────────────────────────

```
@L₁ :  G : ?
S₁ :  assume i ≤ 0;
S₂ :  rv := a;
@post F :  sorted(rv, 0, |rv| − 1)
```

Computing $\mathsf{wp}(F, S_1; S_2)$ produces the formula

$$F' : i \leq 0 \;\rightarrow\; \mathsf{sorted}(a, 0, |a| - 1) ,$$

which tells us (not surprisingly) that a should be sorted upon exiting the outer loop. Observe the index variable of the outer loop: it starts at $|a| - 1$

and decrements down to 0. Therefore, recalling the trick to *replace fixed terms (bounds, indices, etc.) with terms that evolve according to the loop counter* suggests the following generalization of F':

$G :$ $\mathsf{sorted}(a, i, |a| - 1)$.

G trivially holds upon entering the outer loop; moreover, it follows from the behavior of i that progress is made by working down the array. The outer loop invariant L_1 should include G. Thus, we have

$@L_1 :$ $-1 \leq i < |a| \;\wedge\; \mathsf{sorted}(a, i, |a| - 1)$

so far.

Propagate G via wp to the inner loop along the path from the exit of the inner loop L_2 to the top of the outer loop L_1:

-- **(5)** --

$@L_2 :$ $H : ?$
$S_1 :$ **assume** $j \geq i$;
$S_2 :$ $i := i - 1$;
$@L_1 :$ $G :$ $\mathsf{sorted}(a, i, |a| - 1)$

The result at L_2 is the formula

$H' :$ $j \geq i \;\rightarrow\; \mathsf{sorted}(a, i - 1, |a| - 1)$,

which states that when the inner loop has *finished*, the range $[i - 1, |a| - 1]$ is sorted. Immediately generalizing H' to

$H'' :$ $\mathsf{sorted}(a, i - 1, |a| - 1)$

is too strong. For suppose H'' were to annotate the inner loop at L_2, and consider the path

-- **(2)** --

$@L_1 :$ $G :$ $\mathsf{sorted}(a, i, |a| - 1)$
$S_1 :$ **assume** $i > 0$;
$S_2 :$ $j := 0$;
$@L_2 :$ $H'' :$ $\mathsf{sorted}(a, i - 1, |a| - 1)$

Computing

$G \;\rightarrow\; \mathsf{wp}(H'', \mathbf{assume}\ i > 0;\ j := 0)$

produces

$\mathsf{sorted}(a, i, |a| - 1) \;\wedge\; i > 0 \;\rightarrow\; \mathsf{sorted}(a, i - 1, |a| - 1)$,

which is not $(T_{\mathbb{Z}} \cup T_{\mathsf{A}})$-valid. All we know at L_1 (with respect to sortedness of a) is $G :$ $\mathsf{sorted}(a, i, |a| - 1)$. Essentially, $\mathsf{sorted}(a, i - 1, |a| - 1)$ at L_2 is a special case that definitely holds only when the inner loop has finished. Therefore, we generalize H' to the weaker assertion H : $\mathsf{sorted}(a, i, |a| - 1)$, which claims that a smaller subrange of a is sorted.

At this point, we have annotated the loops of BubbleSort as follows:

```
for
    @L₁ : −1 ≤ i < |a| ∧ sorted(a, i, |a| − 1)
    (int i := |a| − 1;  i > 0;  i := i − 1) {
    for
        @L₂ : 0 < i < |a| ∧ 0 ≤ j ≤ i ∧ sorted(a, i, |a| − 1)
        (int j := 0;  j < i;  j := j + 1) {
        if (a[j] > a[j + 1])  {
            int t := a[j];
            a[j] := a[j + 1];
            a[j + 1] := t;
        }
    }
}
```

The resulting VCs are not valid. Further annotations require some insight on our part, which leads us to the next section.   ∎

6.1.3 A Strategy

In general, proofs require insights beyond generalizing formulae obtained through the precondition method. We adopt the following strategy when proving partial correctness.

First, decompose the function specification into atomic properties. Then analyze each atomic property. For example, to prove that BubbleSort returns a sorted array that is a permutation of the input, study the sortedness property and permutation property separately. In some cases, several atomic properties may have to be examined together to complete the proof. For each basic property, apply the following steps:

1. Assert basic facts (Section 6.1.1).
2. Repeat:
    a) Use the precondition method to propagate annotations (Section 6.1.2).
    b) Formalize an insight.

The second step suggests applying the precondition method until nothing more can be learned. Then pause, understand another essential fact about the program, and resume applying the precondition method.

While Chapter 12 discusses the foundations of algorithms for automatically generating inductive annotations, the reader should be aware that even the best of these algorithms cannot approach the abilities of a human. Take heart! Experience has shown that students quickly become adept at annotating programs.

Example 6.6. We resume our analysis of BubbleSort from Example 6.5. Some cogitation (and observation of sample traces; see Figure 5.4) suggests that BubbleSort exhibits the following behavior: the inner loop propagates the largest value of the unsorted region to the right side of the unsorted region, thus expanding the sorted region. At every iteration, j is the index of the largest value found so far. In other words, all values in the range $[0, j-1]$ are at most $a[j]$:

$$F : \; \mathsf{partitioned}(a, 0, j-1, j, j) \; .$$

This observations should be added as an annotation at L_2. Having gained new insight into BubbleSort, we return to the precondition method and propagate F back to the outer loop at L_1 along the path

$$\text{——————(2)——————}$$

$@L_1 : \; H : ?$
$S_1 : \; \mathsf{assume} \; i > 0;$
$S_2 : \; j := 0;$
$@L_2 : \; F : \; \mathsf{partitioned}(a, 0, j-1, j, j)$

resulting in the new annotation

$$\mathsf{wp}(F, \; S_1; S_2) : \; i > 0 \; \rightarrow \; \mathsf{partitioned}(a, 0, -1, 0, 0)$$

at L_1. The result is trivially valid according to the definition of partitioned, so it does not contribute any new information. Thus, we finish this round of Step 2 with the annotations

```
for
    @L₁ :  −1 ≤ i < |a| ∧ sorted(a, i, |a| − 1)
    (int i := |a| − 1;  i > 0;  i := i − 1) {
    for
             ⎡ 0 < i < |a| ∧ 0 ≤ j ≤ i                              ⎤
    @L₂ :  ⎢ ∧ partitioned(a, 0, j − 1, j, j) ∧ sorted(a, i, |a| − 1) ⎥
             ⎣                                                       ⎦
        (int j := 0;  j < i;  j := j + 1) {
        if (a[j] > a[j + 1]) {
            int t := a[j];
            a[j] := a[j + 1];
            a[j + 1] := t;
        }
    }
}
```

The annotations are not yet inductive.

Some further meditation enlightens us with the following: the sorted region must contain the largest elements of a, for the inner loop has assiduously moved the largest element of the unsorted region to the sorted region. In other words, the sorted range $[i+1, |a|-1]$ contains the largest elements of a:

$$G: \text{ partitioned}(a, 0, i, i+1, |a|-1) \ .$$

This observation should be added as an annotation at L_1. Now we propagate G from L_1 to L_2. Recall from Example 6.5 that our propagation of $\text{sorted}(a, i, |a|-1)$ to the inner loop was unsuccessful. Similarly,

$$\text{wp}(G, \text{ assume } j \geq i; \ i := i-1)$$
$$\Leftrightarrow \ j \geq i \ \to \ \text{partitioned}(a, 0, i-1, i, |a|-1)$$

for the path

$$(5)$$

```
@L₂ :  H : ?
assume j ≥ i;
i := i − 1;
@L₁ :  G :  partitioned(a, 0, i, i + 1, |a| − 1)
```

cannot be generalized to

$$\text{partitioned}(a, 0, i-1, i, |a|-1) \ .$$

Instead, consider the path from L_1 to L_2:

$$(2)$$

```
@L₁ :  G :  partitioned(a, 0, i, i + 1, |a| − 1)
S₁ :  assume i > 0;
S₂ :  j := 0;
@L₂ :  H : ?
```

Find the strongest formula H that can annotate the inner loop such that the VC

$$\text{partitioned}(a, 0, i, i+1, |a|-1) \ \to \ \text{wp}(H, \ S_1; S_2)$$

for the path is valid. In other words, seek a formula H annotating the inner loop that is supported by the annotation G of the outer loop. The strongest such formula is G itself.

These new annotations result in Figure 5.17.   ■

6.2 Extended Example: QuickSort

In this section, we bring together the concepts studied in this and the last chapters through a single example. We prove that QuickSort always halts and returns a sorted array. We argue at the level of annotations, leaving a computer or the reader to check the VCs.

Figure 6.2 lists the high-level functions of QuickSort. QuickSort is a wrapper function (or public interface) for the recursive function qsort, which sorts array a_0 in the range $[\ell, u]$. As in BubbleSort, the first line of qsort assigns a_0 to an

```
typedef struct qs {
    int pivot;
    int[] array;
} qs;
```

@pre ⊤
@post sorted$(rv, 0, |rv| - 1)$
```
int[] QuickSort(int[] a) {
    return qsort(a, 0, |a| - 1);
}
```

@pre ⊤
@post ⊤
```
int[] qsort(int[] a₀, int ℓ, int u) {
    int[] a := a₀;
    if (ℓ ≥ u) return a;
    else {
        qs p := partition(a, ℓ, u);
        a := p.array;
        a := qsort(a, ℓ, p.pivot - 1);
        a := qsort(a, p.pivot + 1, u);
        return a;
    }
}
```

Fig. 6.2. Main functions of QuickSort

array a because qsort modifies a (recall that pi does not allow parameters to be modified). The qs data structure holds the two data that the partition function, listed in Figure 6.3, returns: the pivot index $pivot$ and the partitioned array $array$.

One level of recursion of qsort works as follows. If $\ell \geq u$, then the trivial range $[\ell, u]$ of a_0 is already sorted. Otherwise, partition chooses a *pivot index* $pi \in [\ell, u]$, remembering the *pivot value* $a[pi]$ as pv. It then swaps cells pi and u of a so that the randomly chosen pivot now appears on the right side of the $[\ell, u]$ subarray. random has the following prototype:

@pre $\ell \leq u$
@post $\ell \leq rv \leq u$
int random(int ℓ, int u);

The for loop of partition partitions a such that all elements at most pv are on the left and all elements greater than pv are on the right. Within the loop, $j < u$, so that the pivot value pv, stored in $a[u]$, remains untouched. When the loop finishes, if $i < u - 1$, then the value $a[i + 1]$ is the first value greater than pv; otherwise, all elements of a are at most pv. Finally, partition

```
@pre ⊤
@post ⊤
qs partition(int[] a₀, int ℓ, int u) {
    int[] a := a₀;
    int pi := random(ℓ, u);
    int pv := a[pi];
    a[pi] := a[u];
    a[u] := pv;

    int i := ℓ - 1;
    for @ ⊤
        (int j := ℓ; j < u; j := j + 1) {
        if (a[j] ≤ pv) {
            i := i + 1;
            t := a[i];
            a[i] := a[j];
            a[j] := t;
        }
    }

    t := a[i + 1];
    a[i + 1] := a[u];
    a[u] := t;
    return
        { pivot = i + 1;
          a = a;
        };
}
```

Fig. 6.3. QuickSort's partition function

swaps the pivot value $a[u]$ with $a[i + 1]$ so that a is partitioned as follows in the range $[ℓ, u]$: cells to the left of $i + 1$ have value at most pv; $a[i + 1] = pv$; and cells to the right of $i + 1$ have value greater than pv. It returns the pivot index $i + 1$ and the partitioned array a via an instance of the qs data type.

Finally, qsort recursively sorts the subarrays to the left and to the right of the pivot index.

Figure 6.4 presents a sample trace. In the first line, partition chooses the second cell as the pivot and swaps it with cell u. The subsequent six lines follow the partition's loop as it partitions elements according to pv. The penultimate line shows the swap that brings the pivot element into the pivot position. The final line shows the state of the array when it is returned to qsort. qsort calls itself recursively on the two indicated subarrays. We encourage the reader to understand QuickSort and the sample trace before reading further.

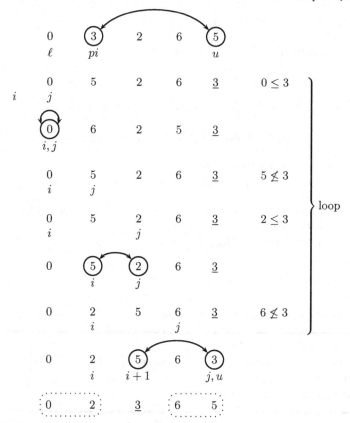

Fig. 6.4. Sample execution of QuickSort

6.2.1 Partial Correctness

We prove that if QuickSort halts, then it returns a sorted array. First, we develop the function specifications for qsort and partition so that QuickSort and qsort have inductive annotations. We then leave the annotation of the loop of partition as Exercise 6.3.

First, annotate qsort and partition with their function specifications. To avoid runtime errors, the function preconditions should include

$$0 \le \ell \ \wedge \ u < |a_0| \ .$$

Next, while the returned array is not the same as the input array a_0 in either function, we know that their lengths are the same:

$$|rv| = |a_0| \ .$$

We also observe that neither qsort nor partition modify the array outside of the range $[\ell, u]$. Thus, we note in the function postcondition that

$$\text{beq}(rv, a_0, 0, \ell - 1) \ \wedge \ \text{beq}(rv, a_0, u + 1, |a_0| - 1) \ .$$

The **bounded equality** predicate beq is defined

$$\text{beq}(a, b, k_1, k_2) \ \Leftrightarrow \ \forall i. \ k_1 \leq i \leq k_2 \ \rightarrow \ a[i] = b[i]$$

in the theory $T_{\mathbb{Z}} \cup T_A$. It asserts that two arrays are equal in the index range $[k_1, k_2]$.

The annotations for partition vary slightly because of its return type:

$$|rv.array| = |a_0| \ \wedge \ \text{beq}(rv.array, a_0, 0, \ell - 1)$$
$$\wedge \ \text{beq}(rv.array, a_0, u + 1, |a_0| - 1)$$

Since partition returns an integer (*pivot*) and an array (*array*) in a **qs** structure, the postcondition asserts facts about *rv.array*.

To finish with qsort, formalize that qsort sorts the range $[\ell, u]$ of the given array:

$$\text{sorted}(rv, \ell, u) \ .$$

So far, then, we have specified qsort as follows:

@pre $0 \leq \ell \ \wedge \ u < |a_0|$

@post $\left[\begin{array}{l} |rv| = |a_0| \ \wedge \ \text{beq}(rv, a_0, 0, \ell - 1) \ \wedge \ \text{beq}(rv, a_0, u + 1, |a_0| - 1) \\ \wedge \ \text{sorted}(rv, \ell, u) \end{array} \right]$

int[] qsort(int[] a_0, int ℓ, int u)

To finish the specification of partition, recall that partition is intended to return an array that is partitioned around the pivot element. Therefore, let us formalize the description that we gave above. Observe that the specification of random guarantees that

$$\ell \leq rv.pivot \leq u \ ,$$

as desired. Now, for the left subarray,

$$\forall i. \ \ell \leq i < rv.pivot \ \rightarrow \ rv.array[i] \leq rv.array[rv.pivot] \ ,$$

or, as a partition,

$$\text{partitioned}(rv.array, \ell, rv.pivot - 1, rv.pivot, rv.pivot) \ ,$$

while for the right subarray,

$$\forall i. \ rv.pivot < i \leq u \ \rightarrow \ rv.array[rv.pivot] < rv.array[i] \ .$$

We weaken this assertion slightly to

$$\text{partitioned}(rv.array, rv.pivot, rv.pivot, rv.pivot + 1, u) \ ,$$

which does not capture the strict inequality but is more convenient for reasoning. For partition, we have thus specified the following:

@pre $0 \leq \ell \wedge u < |a_0|$

@post $\begin{bmatrix} |rv.array| = |a_0| \wedge \text{beq}(rv.array, a_0, 0, \ell - 1) \\ \wedge \text{beq}(rv.array, a_0, u + 1, |a_0| - 1) \\ \wedge \ell \leq rv.pivot \leq u \\ \wedge \text{partitioned}(rv.array, \ell, rv.pivot - 1, rv.pivot, rv.pivot) \\ \wedge \text{partitioned}(rv.array, rv.pivot, rv.pivot, rv.pivot + 1, u) \end{bmatrix}$

qs partition(int$[]$ a_0, int ℓ, int u)

Let us step back a moment. Essentially, we have specified that qsort does not modify the array outside of the range $[\ell, u]$. Regarding the subarray given by $[\ell, u]$, all we have asserted is that it is sorted in the returned array. Focus on the recursive calls to qsort: is knowing that the ranges $[\ell, p.pivot - 1]$ and $[p.pivot + 1, u]$ of a are sorted enough to conclude that the range $[\ell, u]$ is sorted when a is returned? In other words, is the VC corresponding to the following basic path valid? The basic path follows the path from the precondition to the second **return** statement, using the function call abstraction introduced in Section 5.2.1 to abstract away functions calls:

$$(\cdot)$$

@pre $0 \leq \ell \wedge u < |a_0|$

$a := a_0;$

assume $\ell < u;$

assume $\begin{bmatrix} |v_1.array| = |a| \wedge \text{beq}(v_1.array, a, 0, \ell - 1) \\ \wedge \text{beq}(v_1.array, a, u + 1, |a| - 1) \\ \wedge \ell \leq v_1.pivot \leq u \\ \wedge \text{partitioned}(v_1.array, \ell, v_1.pivot - 1, v_1.pivot, v_1.pivot) \\ \wedge \text{partitioned}(v_1.array, v_1.pivot, v_1.pivot, v_1.pivot + 1, u) \end{bmatrix};$

$p := v_1;$

$a := p.array;$

assume $\begin{bmatrix} |v_2| = |a| \wedge \text{beq}(v_2, a, 0, \ell - 1) \wedge \text{beq}(v_2, a, p.pivot, |a| - 1) \\ \wedge \text{sorted}(v_2, \ell, p.pivot - 1) \end{bmatrix};$

$a := v_2;$

assume $\begin{bmatrix} |v_3| = |a| \wedge \text{beq}(v_3, a, 0, p.pivot) \wedge \text{beq}(v_3, a, u + 1, |a| - 1) \\ \wedge \text{sorted}(v_3, p.pivot + 1, u) \end{bmatrix};$

$a := v_3;$

$rv := a;$

@ $\begin{bmatrix} |rv| = |a_0| \wedge \text{beq}(rv, a_0, 0, \ell - 1) \wedge \text{beq}(rv, a_0, u + 1, |a_0| - 1) \\ \wedge \text{sorted}(rv, \ell, u) \end{bmatrix}$

The corresponding VC is not valid. The assumptions about v_1, v_2, and v_3 are not strong enough to imply that the range $[\ell, u]$ of rv is sorted.

The standard approach to addressing this problem is to reason simultaneously that qsort returns an array that is a permutation of its input array (a permuted array contains the same elements as the original array but possibly in a different order). However, reasoning about permutations presents a problem. A straightforward formalization of permutation is not possible in FOL, instead requiring second-order logic. We could assert that the output is a **weak permutation** of the input: all values occurring in the input array occur in the output array but possibly with a varying number of occurrences. Formally,

$$\forall e. \ (\exists i. \ a_0[i] = e) \ \leftrightarrow \ (\exists j. \ rv[j] = e) \ .$$

In Exercise 6.5, we ask the reader to explore an approximation to weak permutation.

However, that the elements are permuted is a stronger statement than necessary to prove sortedness. Instead, notice that QuickSort imposes a larger partitioning of the intermediate arrays than we have previously observed in our analysis. At every level of recursion of qsort, the elements of a_0 in the range $[\ell, u]$ are at least the elements to their left and at most the elements to their right. Formally, we strengthen the specification of qsort as follows:

$$@\text{pre} \begin{bmatrix} 0 \leq \ell \ \wedge \ u < |a_0| \\ \wedge \ \text{partitioned}(a_0, 0, \ell - 1, \ell, u) \\ \wedge \ \text{partitioned}(a_0, \ell, u, u + 1, |a_0| - 1) \end{bmatrix}$$

$$@\text{post} \begin{bmatrix} |rv| = |a_0| \ \wedge \ \text{beq}(rv, a_0, 0, \ell - 1) \ \wedge \ \text{beq}(rv, a_0, u + 1, |a_0| - 1) \\ \wedge \ \text{partitioned}(rv, 0, \ell - 1, \ell, u) \\ \wedge \ \text{partitioned}(rv, \ell, u, u + 1, |rv| - 1) \\ \wedge \ \text{sorted}(rv, \ell, u) \end{bmatrix}$$

int[] qsort(int[] a_0, int ℓ, int u)

Of course, now the specification of partition must be strengthened to carry this reasoning through the main basic path of qsort:

$$@\text{pre} \begin{bmatrix} 0 \leq \ell \ \wedge \ u < |a_0| \\ \wedge \ \text{partitioned}(a_0, 0, \ell - 1, \ell, u) \\ \wedge \ \text{partitioned}(a_0, \ell, u, u + 1, |a_0| - 1) \end{bmatrix}$$

$$@\text{post} \begin{bmatrix} |rv.array| = |a_0| \ \wedge \ \text{beq}(rv.array, a_0, 0, \ell - 1) \\ \wedge \ \text{beq}(rv.array, a_0, u + 1, |a_0| - 1) \\ \wedge \ \text{partitioned}(rv.array, 0, \ell - 1, \ell, u) \\ \wedge \ \text{partitioned}(rv.array, \ell, u, u + 1, |rv.array| - 1) \\ \wedge \ \ell \leq rv.pivot \leq u \\ \wedge \ \text{partitioned}(rv.array, \ell, rv.pivot - 1, rv.pivot, rv.pivot) \\ \wedge \ \text{partitioned}(rv.array, rv.pivot, rv.pivot, rv.pivot + 1, u) \end{bmatrix}$$

qs partition(int[] a_0, int ℓ, int u)

That is, partition preserves this partitioning even as it manipulates the elements in the range $[\ell, u]$. Indeed, partition itself imposes the necessary partitioning for the next level of recursion, which we already observed earlier as the final partitioned assertions of the function postcondition.

The annotations of QuickSort and qsort are inductive. Exercise 6.3 asks the reader to finish the proof by annotating the for loop of partition so that the annotations of partition are also inductive.

6.2.2 Total Correctness

To prove total correctness — that QuickSort actually returns a sorted arrays — we need to prove that QuickSort always halts. Our implementation of QuickSort has both recursive behavior in function qsort and looping behavior in function partition. We must analyze both possible sources of nontermination.

To prove that the loop in partition always halts, let us use the obvious ranking function of $\delta_1 : u - j$ suggested by the structure of the loop. δ_1 clearly maps the program state to $\mathbb{Z}$, but we prove the stronger fact that δ_1 actually maps the program state to $\mathbb{N}$ with well-founded relation $<$. In particular, we prove that

- $u - j \geq 0$ is a loop invariant;
- and $u - j$ decreases on each iteration.

Annotating the loop with the bounds on j suggested by the loop structure proves that the loop always halts:

---

for
    $@L_1 : \ell \leq j \wedge j \leq u$
    $\downarrow \delta_1 : u - j$
    (int $j := \ell;\ j < u;\ j := j + 1$)

Proving that the recursion of qsort always halts is superficially more difficult. The argument that we would like to make is that $u - \ell$ decreases on each recursive call, which requires proving that the pivot value returned by partition lies within the range $[\ell, u]$.

Observe, however, that $u - \ell$ may be negative when qsort is called with $\ell > u$. But in this case, $\ell = u + 1$, for either $|a_0| = 0$, and qsort was called from QuickSort; or $p.pivot = \ell$ or $p.pivot = u$, and qsort was called recursively. More generally, we can establish that $u - \ell + 1 \geq 0$ is an invariant of qsort. Hence, $\delta_2 : u - \ell + 1$ is our proposed ranking function that maps the program states to $\mathbb{N}$ with well-founded relation $<$.

Figure 6.5 formalizes the arguments that δ_1 and δ_2 are ranking functions. Notice that bounds on i are proved as loop invariants at L_1. These bounds imply that $rv.pivot$ lies within the range $[\ell, u]$ as required.

One trick that would avoid reasoning about the case in which $\ell > u$ is to cut the recursion at a point within qsort rather than at function entry. Figure 6.6 provides an alternate argument in which the ranking function labels the

```
@pre u − ℓ + 1 ≥ 0
@post ⊤
↓ δ₂ :  u − ℓ + 1
int[] qsort(int[] a₀, int ℓ, int u) {
    int[] a := a₀;
    if (ℓ ≥ u) return a;
    else {
        qs p := partition(a, ℓ, u);
        a := p.array;
        a := qsort(a, ℓ, p.pivot − 1);
        a := qsort(a, p.pivot + 1, u);
        return a;
    }
}


@pre ℓ ≤ u
@post ℓ ≤ rv.pivot ∧ rv.pivot ≤ u
qs partition(int[] a₀, int ℓ, int u) {
    ⋮

    int i := ℓ − 1;
    for
        @L₁ : ℓ ≤ j ∧ j ≤ u ∧ ℓ − 1 ≤ i ∧ i < j
        ↓ δ₁ :  u − j
        (int j := ℓ; j < u; j := j + 1) {

        ⋮

    }

    ⋮

    return
        { pivot = i + 1;
          a = a;
        };
}
```

Fig. 6.5. QuickSort always halts

else branch in qsort. The first branch terminates the recursion. partition is annotated as in Figure 6.5.

6.3 Summary

This chapter presents strategies for specifying and proving the correctness of sequential programs. It covers:

- *Strategies* for proving partial correctness. The need for strengthening annotations. Basic facts; the precondition method.

```
@pre ⊤
@post ⊤
int[] qsort(int[] a₀, int ℓ, int u) {
    int[] a := a₀;
    if (ℓ ≥ u) return a;
    else {
        ↓ δ₃ :  u − ℓ
        qs p := partition(a, ℓ, u);
        a := p.array;
        a := qsort(a, ℓ, p.pivot − 1);
        a := qsort(a, p.pivot + 1, u);
        return a;
    }
}
```

Fig. 6.6. Alternate argument that QuickSort always halts

```
@pre ⊤
@post ∀i. 0 ≤ i < |rv|  →  rv[i] ≥ 0
int[] abs(int[] a₀) {
    int[] a := a₀;
    for @ ⊤
        (int i := 0; i < |a|; i := i + 1) {
        if (a[i] < 0) {
            a[i] := − a[i];
        }
    }
    return a;
}
```

Fig. 6.7. Computing the absolute value of elements of a_0

- A full proof that QuickSort returns a sorted array.

Bibliographic Remarks

QuickSort was discovered by Tony Hoare, who also proposed specifying and verifying programs using FOL [39].

Exercises

6.1 (Absolute value). Prove the partial correctness of abs in Figure 6.7. That is, annotate the function; list basic paths and verification conditions; and argue that the VCs are valid.

```
@pre ⊤
@post sorted(rv, 0, |rv| − 1)
int[] InsertionSort(int[] a₀) {
    int[] a := a₀;
    for @ ⊤
        (int i := 1; i < |a|; i := i + 1) {
        int t := a[i];
        for @ ⊤
            (int j := i − 1; j ≥ 0; j := j − 1) {
            if (a[j] ≤ t) break;
            a[j + 1] := a[j];
        }
        a[j + 1] := t;
    }
    return a;
}
```

Fig. 6.8. InsertionSort

6.2 (InsertionSort). Prove the partial correctness of InsertionSort. That is, annotate the function; list basic paths and verification conditions; and argue that the VCs are valid. See Figure 6.8.

As in other languages, the **break** statement moves control to the loop exit.

6.3 (QuickSort). Finish the proof of the sortedness property of QuickSort. That is, annotate partition of Figure 6.3 so that its precondition and postcondition annotations given at the end of Section 6.2 are inductive.

6.4 (MergeSort). Prove the partial correctness of MergeSort. See Figure 6.9. The function merge uses the pi keyword **new**, which allocates an array of the specified size. Therefore, it is known after the allocation to buf that $|buf| = u − \ell + 1$.

First, deduce the function specifications for ms and merge by focusing on MergeSort and ms. Prove MergeSort and ms correct with respect to these annotations. Then analyze merge.

Since MergeSort is fairly long, you need not list basic paths and VCs. Just present MergeSort with its inductive annotations.

6.5 (Weak permutation). Define **weak permutation** as follows:

$$\forall e. \ (\exists i. \ a[i] = e) \ \leftrightarrow \ (\exists j. \ b[j] = e) \ . \tag{6.1}$$

Unfortunately, the decision procedures for arrays discussed in Chapter 11 cannot decide the validity of VCs arising from wperm annotations, as such VCs fall outside of the studied fragments of T_A. Instead, we describe an approximation.

Consider annotating BubbleSort as in Figure 6.10. The `define` keyword defines a global constant. In this case, e is defined to have some nondeterministic value; that is, e stands for an arbitrary integer. The annotations then use this e in wperm literals, where wperm is defined as follows:

$$\mathsf{wperm}(a, a_0, e) \Leftrightarrow (\exists i.\ a[i] = e) \leftrightarrow (\exists j.\ a_0[j] = e) .$$

Compared to the full definition (6.1) of weak permutation, wperm does not have a universally quantified variable e; instead, it uses a given expression e, in this case the global constant e.

(a) Argue that the annotations of Figure 6.10 are inductive. That is, list the VCs and argue their validity.

(b) Argue that the annotations imply that BubbleSort actually satisfies the weakest permutation property. That is, prove that the validity of the VC

$$\mathsf{wperm}(a, a_0, e) \wedge a' = \ldots \rightarrow \mathsf{wperm}(a', a_0, e)$$

implies the validity of the VC

$$(\forall e.\ (\exists i.\ a[i] = e) \leftrightarrow (\exists j.\ a_0[j] = e)) \wedge a' = \ldots$$
$$\rightarrow (\forall e.\ (\exists i.\ a'[i] = e) \leftrightarrow (\exists j.\ a_0[j] = e)) .$$

(c) Can this approximation be used to prove the weakest permutation property of
    (i) InsertionSort (Figure 6.8)?
    (ii) MergeSort (Figure 6.9)?
    (iii) QuickSort (Section 6.2)?
    If so, prove it. If not, explain why not.

6.6 (Sets with arrays). Implement an API (**application programming interface**) for manipulating sets. The underlying data structure of the implementation is arrays.

(a) Prove the correctness of the union function of Figure 6.11 by adding inductive annotations.

(b) Implement and specify and prove the correctness of an intersection function, which takes two arrays a_0 and b_0 and returns the intersection of the sets they represent.

(c) Implement and specify and prove the correctness of a subset function, which takes two arrays a_0 and b_0 and returns **true** iff the first set, represented by a_0, is a subset of the second set, represented by b_0.

6.7 (Sets with sorted arrays). Implement an API for manipulating sets. The underlying data structure of the implementation is sorted arrays.

(a) Prove the correctness of the union function of Figure 6.12 by adding inductive annotations.

(b) Implement and specify and prove the correctness of an intersection function, which takes two sorted arrays a_0 and b_0 and returns the intersection of the sets they represent as a sorted set.

(c) Implement and specify and prove the correctness of a subset function, which takes two sorted arrays a_0 and b_0 and returns true iff the first set, represented by a_0, is a subset of the second set, represented by b_0.

6.8 (QuickSort halts). Provide the basic paths and verification conditions for the proof of Section 6.2.2 that QuickSort always halts.

6.9 (Intuitive ranking functions). Following the proof that the recursion of qsort halts, move the location of the ranking function annotations in the following functions to produce more intuitive arguments:

(a) BinarySearch, Figure 5.2
(b) BubbleSort, Figure 5.3
(c) InsertionSort, Figure 6.8

6.10 (Fewer annotations). Notice in the annotated BubbleSort of Figure 5.17 that there are only a finite number of basic paths from function entry to L_2, from L_2 to function exit, and from L_2 back to itself.

(a) List these basic paths.
(b) Annotate only the inner loop of BubbleSort so that the VCs corresponding to the basic paths of (a) are valid.
(c) Treat InsertionSort of Figure 5.25 similarly.
(d) Similarly, annotate only the inner loop of BubbleSort with a ranking annotation.
(e) Treat InsertionSort similarly.

```
@pre ⊤
@post sorted(rv, 0, |rv| − 1)
int[] MergeSort(int[] a) {
    return ms(a, 0, |a| − 1);
}

@pre ⊤
@post ⊤
int[] ms(int[] a₀, int ℓ, int u) {
    int[] a := a₀;
    if (ℓ ≥ u) return a;
    else {
        int m := (ℓ + u) div 2;
        a := ms(a, ℓ, m);
        a := ms(a, m + 1, u);
        a := merge(a, ℓ, m, u);
        return a;
    }
}

@pre ⊤
@post ⊤
int[] merge(int[] a₀, int ℓ, int m, int u) {
    int[] a := a₀, buf := new int[u − ℓ + 1];
    int i := ℓ, j := m + 1;
    for @ ⊤
        (int k := 0; k < |buf|; k := k + 1) {
        if (i > m) {
            buf[k] := a[j];
            j := j + 1;
        } else if (j > u) {
            buf[k] := a[i];
            i := i + 1;
        } else if (a[i] ≤ a[j]) {
            buf[k] := a[i];
            i := i + 1;
        } else {
            buf[k] := a[j];
            j := j + 1;
        }
    }
    for @ ⊤
        (k := 0; k < |buf|; k := k + 1) {
        a[ℓ + k] := buf[k];
    }
    return a;
}
```

Fig. 6.9. MergeSort

```
define int e = ?;

@pre ⊤
@post wperm(a, a₀, e)
int[] BubbleSort(int[] a₀) {
    int[] a := a₀;
    for
        @L₁ :  −1 ≤ i < |a|  ∧  wperm(a, a₀, e)
        (int i := |a| − 1;  i > 0;  i := i − 1) {
        for
            @L₂ :  0 ≤ j < i  ∧  i < |a|  ∧  wperm(a, a₀, e)
            (int j := 0;  j < i;  j := j + 1) {
            if (a[j] > a[j + 1])  {
                int t := a[j];
                a[j] := a[j + 1];
                a[j + 1] := t;
            }
        }
    }
    return a;
}
```

Fig. 6.10. BubbleSort with annotations for weak permutation

```
define int e = ?;

@pre ⊤
@post [ (∃i. 0 ≤ i < |rv|  ∧  rv[i] = e)
        ↔ (∃i. 0 ≤ i < |a₀|  ∧  a₀[i] = e)  ∨  (∃i. 0 ≤ i < |b₀|  ∧  b₀[i] = e) ]
int[] union(int[] a₀, int[] b₀) {
    int[] u := new int[|a₀| + |b₀|];
    int j := 0;
    for @ ⊤
        (int i = 0;  i < |a₀|;  i := i + 1) {
        u[j] := a₀[i];
        j := j + 1;
    }
    for @ ⊤
        (int i = 0;  i < |b₀|;  i := i + 1) {
        u[j] := b₀[i];
        j := j + 1;
    }
    return u;
}
```

Fig. 6.11. Function union of the linear set implementation

```
define int e = ?;
```

$$\text{@pre } \mathsf{sorted}(a_0, 0, |a_0| - 1) \ \wedge \ \mathsf{sorted}(b_0, 0, |b_0| - 1)$$

$$\text{@post } \left[\begin{array}{l} \mathsf{sorted}(rv, 0, |rv| - 1) \\ \wedge \ \left[\begin{array}{l} (\exists i. \ 0 \leq i < |a_0| \ \wedge \ a_0[i] = e) \ \vee \ (\exists i. \ 0 \leq i < |b_0| \ \wedge \ b_0[i] = e) \\ \leftrightarrow \ (\exists i. \ 0 \leq i < |rv| \ \wedge \ rv[i] = e) \end{array} \right] \end{array} \right]$$

```
int[] union(int[] a₀, int[] b₀) {
  int[] u := new int[|a₀| + |b₀|];
  int i := 0, j := 0;
  for @ ⊤
    (int k = 0; k < |u|; k := k + 1) {
    if (i ≥ |a₀|) {
      u[k] := b₀[j];
      j := j + 1;
    }
    else if (j ≥ |b₀|) {
      u[k] := a₀[i];
      i := i + 1;
    }
    else if (a₀[i] ≤ b₀[j]) {
      u[k] := a₀[i];
      i := i + 1;
    }
    else {
      u[k] := b₀[j];
      j := j + 1;
    }
  }
  return u;
}
```

Fig. 6.12. Function union of the sorted set implementation

Part II

Algorithmic Reasoning

It is reasonable to hope that the relationship between computation and mathematical logic will be as fruitful in the next century as that between analysis and physics in the last. The development of this relationship demands a concern for both applications and mathematical elegance.

— John McCarthy
A Basis for a Mathematical Theory of Computation, 1963

Having established in Part I the mathematical foundations for precision in designing and implementing software and hardware systems, we turn in Part II to the task of automating some of the required logical reasoning.

Chapters 7–10 discuss decision procedures for many of the theories and fragments of theories introduced in Chapter 3. These decision procedures automate the task of proving the verification conditions of Chapters 5 and 6. Chapter 7 applies the method of quantifier elimination to decide validity in $T_{\mathbb{Z}}$ and $T_{\mathbb{Q}}$. Chapters 8 and 9 focus on decision procedures for the quantifier-free fragments of the theories $T_{\mathbb{Q}}$, T_{E}, T_{cons}, and T_{A}. In Chapter 10, these procedures are combined in the Nelson-Oppen framework to address formulae with symbols of multiple signatures. The treatment of arrays in Chapter 11 looks beyond the quantifier-free fragment, but we show how the combination method of Chapter 10 still applies.

Chapter 12 turns to automating the inductive assertion method of Chapter 5. It presents a methodology for constructing algorithms that learn inductive facts about software. These algorithms reduce the burden on the engineer to provide annotations.

Quantified Linear Arithmetic

Whilst in [Presburger arithmetic] one can only state rather simple theorems, yet an efficient algorithm... is useful in that it can quickly dispose of a host of the simpler formulas..., leaving only the more complex to be dealt with by some more general theorem prover or by the human.

— David C. Cooper
Theorem Proving in Arithmetic Without Multiplication, 1972

Recall from Chapter 3 that satisfiability in the theories of linear integer arithmetic $T_{\mathbb{Z}}$ and linear rational (or real) arithmetic $T_{\mathbb{Q}}$ is decidable. This chapter explores a common method of deciding satisfiability of arbitrarily quantified formulae in decidable theories in the context of $T_{\mathbb{Z}}$ and $T_{\mathbb{Q}}$.

A **quantifier elimination procedure** is an algorithm that constructs from a given formula an equivalent quantifier-free formula. When the given formula does not have any free variables, the atoms of the resulting formula are applications of predicates to constant terms such as $3 < 5$. If the truth value of these constant terms is decidable, a quantifier elimination procedure provides a basis for a satisfiability decidable procedure. When the given formula contains free variables, the resulting quantifier-free formula contains a subset of these free variables.

Section 7.1 presents the method of quantifier elimination in an abstract context. Sections 7.2 and 7.3 then present quantifier elimination methods for the theory of integers $T_{\mathbb{Z}}$ and the theory of rationals $T_{\mathbb{Q}}$, respectively. The complexity results of Section 7.4 suggest that these algorithms are near-optimal in time complexity, although quantifier-elimination methods are, in general, computationally expensive.

Sections 7.2.4 and 7.2.5 discuss optimizations for the integer case that are particularly effective when the given formula has only existential quantifiers or only universal quantifiers. With these optimizations, the quantifier elimination method for $T_{\mathbb{Z}}$ is our main decision procedure for the quantifier-free fragment of $T_{\mathbb{Z}}$. However, the case for $T_{\mathbb{Q}}$ is different: Chapter 8 presents a special decision procedure for the quantifier-free fragment of $T_{\mathbb{Q}}$.

7.1 Quantifier Elimination

7.1.1 Quantifier Elimination

Quantifier elimination (QE) is the main technique that underlies the algorithms of this chapter. As the name suggests, the idea is to eliminate quantifiers of a formula F until only a quantifier-free formula G that is equivalent to F remains.

Formally, a theory T **admits quantifier elimination** if there is an algorithm that, given Σ-formula F, returns a quantifier-free Σ-formula G that is T-equivalent to F. Then T is decidable if satisfiability in the quantifier-free fragment of T is decidable.

Example 7.1. Consider the $\Sigma_{\mathbb{Q}}$-formula

$$F : \exists x.\ 2x = y\ ,$$

which expresses the set of rationals y that can be halved. Intuitively, all rationals can be halved, so a quantifier-free $T_{\mathbb{Q}}$-equivalent formula is

$$G : \top\ ,$$

which expresses the set of all rationals. Also, G states that F is valid. ∎

Example 7.2. Consider the $\Sigma_{\mathbb{Z}}$-formula

$$F : \exists x.\ 2x = y\ ,$$

which expresses the set of integers y that can be halved (to produce another integer). Intuitively, only even integers can be halved. Can you think of a quantifier-free $T_{\mathbb{Z}}$-equivalent formula to F? In fact, no such formula exists. Later, we introduce an augmented theory of integers that contains a countably infinite number of divisibility predicates. For example, in this extended theory, an equivalent formula to F is

$$G : 2 \mid y\ ,$$

which expresses the set of even integers: integers that are divisible by 2. ∎

7.1.2 A Simplification

In developing a QE algorithm for theory T, we need only consider formulae of the form $\exists x.\ F$ for quantifier-free formula F. For given arbitrary formula G, choose the innermost quantified formula $\exists x.\ H$ or $\forall x.\ H$. In the latter case, rewrite $\forall x.\ H$ as $\neg(\exists x.\ \neg H)$ and focus on the subformula $\exists x.\ \neg H$ inside the negation.

In both the existential and universal cases, we now have a formula of the form $\exists x.\ F$ to which we apply the QE algorithm to find T-equivalent and quantifier-free formula H'. In the existential case, replace $\exists x.\ H$ in G with H'. In the universal case, replace $\forall x.\ H$ in G with $\neg H'$.

Example 7.3. Consider the Σ-formula

$$G_1 :\ \exists x.\ \forall y.\ \exists z.\ F_1[x, y, z]\ ,$$

and assume that T admits quantifier elimination. The innermost quantified formula is $\exists z.\ F_1[x, y, z]$. Applying the QE algorithm for T to this subformula returns $F_2[x, y]$:

$$G_2 :\ \exists x.\ \forall y.\ F_2[x, y]\ .$$

The innermost quantified formula is now $\forall y.\ F_2[x, y]$; rewriting, we have

$$G_3 :\ \exists x.\ \neg(\exists y.\ \neg F_2[x, y])\ .$$

Applying the QE algorithm to the existential subformula $\exists y.\ \neg F_2[x, y]$ produces $F_3[x]$. We now have

$$G_4 :\ \exists x.\ \neg F_3[x]\ .$$

Finally, applying the QE algorithm one more time to G_4 produces a quantifier-free formula G_5. G_5 is T-equivalent to G_1. ∎

7.2 Quantifier Elimination over Integers

We now turn to the theory of integers $T_{\mathbb{Z}}$. Presburger showed this theory to be decidable in 1929. We discuss the QE procedure of Cooper, first described in 1971.

7.2.1 Augmented Theory of Integers

Recall that $T_{\mathbb{Z}}$ has the following signature:

$$\Sigma_{\mathbb{Z}} :\ \{\ldots, -2, -1, 0, 1, 2, \ldots, -3\cdot, -2\cdot, 2\cdot, 3\cdot, \ldots, +, -, =, <\}\ ,$$

where

- ..., -2, -1, 0, 1, 2, ... are constants, intended to be assigned the obvious corresponding values in the intended domain $\mathbb{Z}$;
- ..., $-3\cdot$, $-2\cdot$, $2\cdot$, $3\cdot$, ... are unary functions, intended to represent constant coefficients (*e.g.*, $2 \cdot x$, abbreviated $2x$);
- $+$ and $-$ are binary functions, intended to represent the obvious corresponding functions over $\mathbb{Z}$;
- $=$ and $>$ are binary predicates, intended to represent the obvious corresponding predicates over $\mathbb{Z}$.

Example 7.2 claims that the $\Sigma_{\mathbb{Z}}$-formula $\exists x. \; 2x = y$ does not have a $T_{\mathbb{Z}}$-equivalent quantifier-free formula. The following lemma proves a more general claim.

Lemma 7.4. *Consider quantifier-free $\Sigma_{\mathbb{Z}}$-formula F such that* $\mathsf{free}(F) = \{y\}$. *F represents the set of integers*

$$S: \{n \in \mathbb{Z} \; : \; F\{y \mapsto n\} \text{ is } T_{\mathbb{Z}}\text{-valid}\} \;.$$

Either $S \cap \mathbb{Z}^+$ or $\mathbb{Z}^+ \setminus S$ is finite.

$\mathbb{Z}^+$ is the set of positive integers; $\cap$ and $\setminus$ are set intersection and complement, respectively. The lemma says that every quantifier-free $\Sigma_{\mathbb{Z}}$-formula with only one free variable represents a set of integers S such that either the subset of positive integers in S has finite cardinality or the set of positive integers not in S has finite cardinality. Exercise 7.1 asks the reader to prove this lemma.

Consider again the case of $\exists x. \; 2x = y$, and let S be the set of integers satisfying the formula, namely the even integers. Since both the set of positive even integers $S \cap \mathbb{Z}^+$ and the set of positive odd integers $\mathbb{Z}^+ \setminus S$ are infinite, the set of even integers cannot be represented in $T_{\mathbb{Z}}$ by a quantifier-free formula according to the lemma. Therefore, there is no quantifier-free $\Sigma_{\mathbb{Z}}$-formula that is $T_{\mathbb{Z}}$-equivalent to $\exists x. \; 2x = y$, and thus $T_{\mathbb{Z}}$ does not admit QE.

To circumvent this problem, we augment the theory $T_{\mathbb{Z}}$ with an infinite but countable number of unary **divisibility predicates**

$$k \mid \cdot \quad \text{for } k \in \mathbb{Z}^+ \;;$$

that is, a predicate exists for each positive integer k. The intended interpretation of $k \mid x$ is that it holds iff k divides x without any remainder. For example,

$$x > 1 \; \wedge \; y > 1 \; \wedge \; 2 \mid x + y$$

is satisfiable (choose $x = 2$ and $y = 2$), but

$$\neg(2 \mid x) \; \wedge \; 4 \mid x$$

is not satisfiable.

The augmented theory $\widehat{T_{\mathbb{Z}}}$ extends the signature of $T_{\mathbb{Z}}$ with these divisibility predicates. Additionally, the predicates are defined by the countable set of axioms

$$\forall x.\ k \mid x\ \leftrightarrow\ \exists y.\ x = ky \qquad\qquad\text{(divides)}$$

for $k \in \mathbb{Z}^+$. The next section shows that $\widehat{T_{\mathbb{Z}}}$ admits QE.

7.2.2 Cooper's Method

In this section, we present the basic form of Cooper's quantifier elimination method. In the subsequent sections, we examine a set of optimizations.

The algorithm is given a $\widehat{\Sigma_{\mathbb{Z}}}$-formula $\exists x.\ F[x]$ as input, where F is quantifier-free but may contain free variables in addition to x. It then proceeds to construct a quantifier-free $\widehat{\Sigma_{\mathbb{Z}}}$-formula that is $\widehat{T_{\mathbb{Z}}}$-equivalent to $\exists x.\ F[x]$ according to the following steps.

Step 1

Put $F[x]$ in NNF. The output $\exists x.\ F_1[x]$ is $\widehat{T_{\mathbb{Z}}}$-equivalent to $\exists x.\ F[x]$ and is such that F_1 is a positive Boolean combination (only $\wedge$ and $\vee$) of literals.

Step 2

Replace literals according to the following $\widehat{T_{\mathbb{Z}}}$-equivalences, applied from left to right:

$$
\begin{aligned}
s = t &\Leftrightarrow s < t + 1 \wedge t < s + 1 \\
\neg(s = t) &\Leftrightarrow s < t \vee t < s \\
\neg(s < t) &\Leftrightarrow t < s + 1
\end{aligned}
$$

The output $\exists x.\ F_2[x]$ is $\widehat{T_{\mathbb{Z}}}$-equivalent to $\exists x.\ F[x]$ and contains only literals of the form

$$s < t, \quad k \mid t, \quad \text{or} \quad \neg(k \mid t),$$

where s, t are $\widehat{\Sigma_{\mathbb{Z}}}$-terms and $k \in \mathbb{Z}^+$.

Example 7.5. Applying the $\widehat{T_{\mathbb{Z}}}$-equivalences to

$$\neg(x < y)\ \wedge\ \neg(x = y + 3)$$

produces the $\widehat{T_{\mathbb{Z}}}$-equivalent formula

$$y < x + 1\ \wedge\ (x < y + 3\ \vee\ y + 3 < x).$$

■

Step 3

Collect terms containing x so that literals have the form

$$hx < t, \quad t < hx, \quad k \mid hx + t, \quad \text{or} \quad \neg(k \mid hx + t),$$

where t is a term that does not contain x and $h, k \in \mathbb{Z}^+$. The output is the formula $\exists x.\ F_3[x]$, which is $\widehat{T_{\mathbb{Z}}}$-equivalent to $\exists x.\ F[x]$.

Example 7.6. Collecting terms in

$$x + x + y < z + 3z + 2y - 4x$$

produces the $\widehat{T_{\mathbb{Z}}}$-equivalent formula

$$6x < 4z + y .$$

∎

Step 4

Let

$$\delta' = \text{lcm}\{h\ :\ h \text{ is a coefficient of } x \text{ in } F_3[x]\} ,$$

where lcm returns the least common multiple of the set. Multiply atoms in $F_3[x]$ by constants so that δ' is the coefficient of x everywhere:

$$
\begin{array}{llll}
hx < t & \Leftrightarrow & \delta'x < h't & \text{where} \quad h'h = \delta' \\
t < hx & \Leftrightarrow & h't < \delta'x & \text{where} \quad h'h = \delta' \\
k \mid hx + t & \Leftrightarrow & h'k \mid \delta'x + h't & \text{where} \quad h'h = \delta' \\
\neg(k \mid hx + t) & \Leftrightarrow & \neg(h'k \mid \delta'x + h't) & \text{where} \quad h'h = \delta'
\end{array}
$$

Notice the abuse of notation: $h'k \mid \cdot$ is a different (unary) predicate than $k \mid \cdot$. This rewriting results in formula F_3' in which all occurrences of x occur in terms $\delta'x$. Replace $\delta'x$ terms with a fresh variable x' to form F_3'':

$$F_3'' :\ F_3'\{\delta'x \mapsto x'\} .$$

Finally, construct

$$\exists x'.\ \underbrace{F_3''[x'] \wedge \delta' \mid x'}_{F_4[x']} .$$

The divisibility literal constrains the fresh variable x' to be divisible by δ', which exactly captures the values of $\delta'x$.

$\exists x'.\ F_4[x']$ is $\widehat{T_{\mathbb{Z}}}$-equivalent to $\exists x.\ F[x]$. Moreover, each literal of $F_4[x']$ that contains x' has one of the following forms:

(A) $x' < a$
(B) $b < x'$
(C) $h \mid x' + c$
(D) $\neg(k \mid x' + d)$

where a, b, c, d are terms that do not contain x, and $h, k \in \mathbb{Z}^+$.

Step 5

Construct the **left infinite projection** $F_{-\infty}[x']$ from $F_4[x']$ by replacing

(A) literals $x' < a$ by $\top$

and

(B) literals $b < x'$ by $\bot$.

The idea is that very small numbers (the left side of the "number line") satisfy (A) literals but not (B) literals.

Let

$$\delta = \text{lcm} \left\{ \begin{array}{l} h \text{ of (C) literals } h \mid x' + c \\ k \text{ of (D) literals } \neg(k \mid x' + d) \end{array} \right\}$$

and B be the set of b terms appearing in (B) literals. Construct

$$F_5 : \bigvee_{j=1}^{\delta} F_{-\infty}[j] \ \vee \ \bigvee_{j=1}^{\delta} \bigvee_{b \in B} F_4[b+j] \ .$$

F_5 is quantifier-free and $\widehat{T_{\mathbb{Z}}}$-equivalent to $\exists x. \ F[x]$.

Step 5 is the trickiest part of the procedure, so let us focus on this step. The first major disjunct of F_5 contains only divisibility literals. It asserts that an infinite number of small numbers n satisfy $F_4[n]$. For if there exists one number n that satisfies the Boolean combination of divisibility literals in $F_{-\infty}$, then every $n - \lambda\delta$, for $\lambda \in \mathbb{Z}^+$, also satisfies $F_{-\infty}$.

The second major disjunct asserts that there is a least $n \in \mathbb{Z}$ that satisfies $F_4[n]$. This least n is determined by the b terms of the (B) literals.

More formerly, consider the following **periodicity property** of the divisibility predicates:

If $m \mid \delta$, then $m \mid n$ iff $m \mid n + \lambda\delta$ for all $\lambda \in \mathbb{Z}$.

In other words, $m \mid \cdot$ cannot distinguish between the cases $m \mid n$ and $m \mid n + \lambda\delta$. Since δ is chosen in Step 5 to be the least common multiple of the integers h and k of the divides predicates, no divides literal in F_5 can distinguish between two integers n and $n + \lambda\delta$, for any $\lambda \in \mathbb{Z}$.

With this property in mind, consider the first major disjunct of F_5 again. If $n \in \mathbb{Z}$ satisfies $F[n]$, then so does $n - \lambda\delta$ for $\lambda \in \mathbb{Z}^+$. Then surely a small enough number exists that satisfies all (A) literals and falsifies all (B) literals of F_4, mirroring the construction of $F_{-\infty}$.

For the second major disjunct, suppose that some number n satisfies $F_4[n]$. Decreasing this number continues to satisfy the same (A) literals. It cannot decrease past some value b^* without changing the truth of some (B) literal.

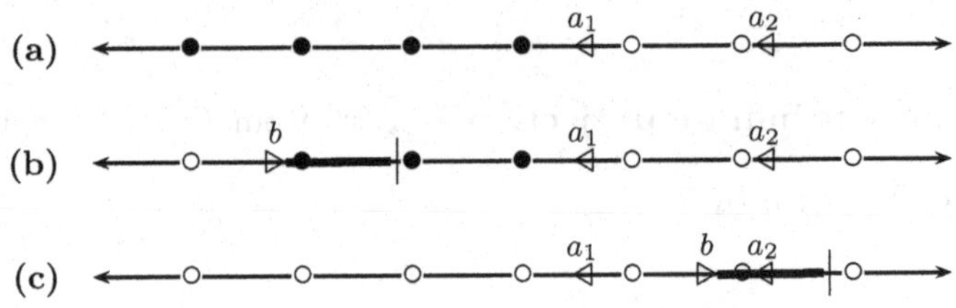

Fig. 7.1. (a) Left infinite projection **(b)** δ-interval **(c)** false

However, according to the periodicity rule, there exists a satisfying integer n' within the δ-interval to the right of b^*.

Figure 7.1 illustrates several situations when a, b, c, and d terms are constant. Circles represent points that satisfy the divides constraints; solid circles in particular represent satisfying points. Figure 7.1(a) illustrates a formula $x < a_1 \wedge x < a_2 \wedge \delta \mid x$: each left-pointing triangle represents a $x < a_i$ literal. The left infinite projection is satisfied. Figure 7.1(b) illustrates an additional $x > b$ literal; now, the δ-interval following the right-pointing triangle at b is searched. It contains a satisfying point. Finally, $b > a_1$ in Figure 7.1(c), so the δ-interval does not contain a satisfying point.

Example 7.7. Consider $\widehat{\Sigma_\mathbb{Z}}$-formula

$$\exists x. \; \underbrace{3x - 2y + 1 > -y \wedge 2x - 6 < z \wedge 4 \mid 5x + 1}_{F[x]} \;.$$

After Step 3, we have

$$\exists x. \; \underbrace{2x < z + 6 \wedge y - 1 < 3x \wedge 4 \mid 5x + 1}_{F_3[x]} \;.$$

Collecting coefficients of x in Step 4, we find

$$\delta' = \mathsf{lcm}\{2, 3, 5\} = 30 \;.$$

Multiplying when necessary, we rewrite the formula so that 30 is the coefficient of every occurrence of x:

$$\exists x. \; 30x < 15z + 90 \wedge 10y - 10 < 30x \wedge 24 \mid 30x + 6 \;.$$

Replacing $30x$ with fresh x' and conjoining a divides atom completes Step 4:

$$\exists x'. \; \underbrace{x' < 15z + 90 \wedge 10y - 10 < x' \wedge 24 \mid x' + 6 \wedge 30 \mid x'}_{F_4[x']} \;.$$

For Step 5, construct the left infinite projection

$$F_{-\infty}[x]: \; \top \wedge \bot \wedge 24 \mid x' + 6 \wedge 30 \mid x' \;,$$

which simplifies to $\bot$. Compute

$$\delta = \text{lcm}\{24, 30\} = 120$$

and

$$B = \{10y - 10\} \ .$$

Then replacing x' by $10y - 10 + j$ in $F_4[x']$ produces

$$F_5 : \bigvee_{j=1}^{120} \left[\begin{array}{l} 10y - 10 + j < 15z + 90 \ \wedge \ 10y - 10 < 10y - 10 + j \\ \wedge \ 24 \mid 10y - 10 + j + 6 \ \wedge \ 30 \mid 10y - 10 + j \end{array} \right]$$

which simplifies to

$$F_5 : \bigvee_{j=1}^{120} \left[\begin{array}{l} 10y + j < 15z + 100 \ \wedge \ 0 < j \\ \wedge \ 24 \mid 10y + j - 4 \ \wedge \ 30 \mid 10y + j - 10 \end{array} \right] \ .$$

F_5 is quantifier-free and $\widehat{T_\mathbb{Z}}$-equivalent to $\exists x. \ F[x]$. ∎

Example 7.8. Consider again the formula defining the set of even integers:

$$\exists x. \ \underbrace{2x = y}_{F[x]} \ .$$

Rewriting according to Steps 2 and 3 produces

$$\exists x. \ y - 1 < 2x \ \wedge \ 2x < y + 1 \ .$$

Then

$$\delta' = \text{lcm}\{2, 2\} = 2 \ ,$$

so Step 4 completes with

$$\exists x'. \ \underbrace{y - 1 < x' \ \wedge \ x' < y + 1 \ \wedge \ 2 \mid x'}_{F_4[x']} \ .$$

Computing the left infinite projection $F_{-\infty}$ produces $\bot$, as $F_4[x']$ contains a **(B)** literal as a conjunct. However,

$$\delta = \text{lcm}\{2\} = 2$$

and

$$B = \{y - 1\} \ ,$$

so

$$F_5 : \bigvee_{j=1}^{2} (y - 1 < y - 1 + j \ \wedge \ y - 1 + j < y + 1 \ \wedge \ 2 \mid y - 1 + j) \ .$$

Simplifying, we find

$$F_5 : \bigvee_{j=1}^{2} (0 < j \ \wedge \ j < 2 \ \wedge \ 2 \mid y + j - 1) \ ,$$

and then

$$F_5 : \ 2 \mid y \ ,$$

which is quantifier-free and $\widehat{T_\mathbb{Z}}$-equivalent to $\exists x. \ F[x]$.   ■

Example 7.9. Consider the formula

$$\exists x. \ \underbrace{(3x + 1 < 10 \ \vee \ 7x - 6 > 7) \ \wedge \ 2 \mid x}_{F[x]} \ .$$

Rewriting to isolate x terms produces

$$\exists x. \ (3x < 9 \ \vee \ 13 < 7x) \ \wedge \ 2 \mid x \ ,$$

so

$$\delta' = \mathsf{lcm}\{3, 7\} = 21 \ .$$

After multiplying coefficients by proper constants,

$$\exists x. \ (21x < 63 \ \vee \ 39 < 21x) \ \wedge \ 42 \mid 21x \ ,$$

we replace $21x$ by x':

$$\exists x'. \ \underbrace{(x' < 63 \ \vee \ 39 < x') \ \wedge \ 42 \mid x' \ \wedge \ 21 \mid x'}_{F_4[x']} \ .$$

Then

$$F_{-\infty}[x'] : \ (\top \ \vee \ \bot) \ \wedge \ 42 \mid x' \ \wedge \ 21 \mid x' \ ,$$

or, simplifying,

$$F_{-\infty}[x'] : \ 42 \mid x' \ \wedge \ 21 \mid x' \ .$$

Finally,

$$\delta = \mathsf{lcm}\{21, 42\} = 42$$

and

$$B = \{39\} \ ,$$

so

$$F_5 : \quad \begin{matrix} \overset{42}{\underset{j=1}{\bigvee}} (42 \mid j \ \wedge \ 21 \mid j) \ \vee \\ \overset{42}{\underset{j=1}{\bigvee}} ((39 + j < 63 \ \vee \ 39 < 39 + j) \ \wedge \ 42 \mid 39 + j \ \wedge \ 21 \mid 39 + j) \ . \end{matrix}$$

Since $42 \mid 42$ and $21 \mid 42$, the left main disjunct simplifies to $\top$, so that $\exists x. \ F[x]$ is $\widehat{T_{\mathbb{Z}}}$-equivalent to $\top$. Thus, F is $\widehat{T_{\mathbb{Z}}}$-valid. ■

Theorem 7.10 (Correct). *Given $\widehat{\Sigma_{\mathbb{Z}}}$-formula $\exists x. \ F[x]$ in which F is quantifier-free, Cooper's method returns a $\widehat{T_{\mathbb{Z}}}$-equivalent quantifier-free formula.*

Proof. The transformations of the first four steps produce formula F_4. By inspection, we assert that in $\widehat{T_{\mathbb{Z}}}$

$$\exists x. \ F[x] \ \Leftrightarrow \ \exists x. \ F_4[x] \ .$$

The focus of the proof is to prove that $\exists x. \ F_4[x] \ \Leftrightarrow \ F_5$ in $\widehat{T_{\mathbb{Z}}}$:

$$\exists x. \ F_4[x] \ \Leftrightarrow \ \overset{\delta}{\underset{j=1}{\bigvee}} F_{-\infty}[j] \ \vee \ \overset{\delta}{\underset{j=1}{\bigvee}} \underset{b \in B}{\bigvee} F_4[b + j] \ .$$

We accomplish the proof in two steps.

1. $F_5 \Rightarrow \exists x. \ F_4[x]$: We assume the existence of an interpretation I such that $I \models F_5$ and prove that $I \models \exists x. \ F_4[x]$.
2. $\exists x. \ F_4[x] \Rightarrow F_5$: We assume the existence of an interpretation I such that $I \models \exists x. \ F_4[x]$ and prove that $I \models F_5$.

Assume then that $I \models F_5$, so that one of the disjuncts of F_5 is true under I. If one of the second set of disjuncts is true, say $F_4[b^* + j^*]$, then

$$I \triangleleft \{x \mapsto b^* + j^*\} \ \models \ F_4[x]$$
$$I \ \models \ \exists x. \ F_4[x] \ .$$

Otherwise, one of the first set of disjuncts is true, so for some $j^* \in [1, \delta]$, $I \triangleleft \{x \mapsto j^*\} \models F_{-\infty}[x]$. By construction of $F_{-\infty}$, there is some $\lambda > 0$ such that $I \triangleleft \{x \mapsto j^* - \lambda\delta\} \models F_4[x]$. That is, there is some $j^* - \lambda\delta$ that is so small that the inequality literals of F_4 evaluate under $I \triangleleft \{x \mapsto j^* - \lambda\delta\}$ exactly as in the construction of $F_{-\infty}$. Thus, $I \models \exists x. \ F_4[x]$ in this case as well.

For the other direction, assume that $I \models \exists x. \ F_4[x]$. Thus, some $n \in \mathbb{Z}$ exists such that $I \triangleleft \{x \mapsto n\} \models F_4[x]$. If for some $b^* \in B$ and $j^* \in [1, \delta]$,

$I \models n = b^* + j^*$, then $I \models F_4[b^* + j^*]$. As $F_4[b^* + j^*]$ is a disjunct of F_5, $I \models F_5$.

Otherwise, consider whether $I \vartriangleleft \{x \mapsto n - \delta\} \models F_4[x]$. If not, then one of the **(B)** literals, say $b^* < x$ for some $b^* \in B$, of F_4 becomes false under I in the transition from n to $n - \delta$. But then $I \models n = b^* + j^*$ for some $j^* \in [1, \delta]$, contradicting our assumption that n is not equal to some $b^* + j^*$. Hence, it must be the case that $I \vartriangleleft \{x \mapsto n - \delta\} \models F_4[x]$.

By induction using this argument, we find that $I \vartriangleleft \{x \mapsto n - \lambda\delta\} \models F_4[x]$ for all $\lambda > 0$. For some λ, $n - \lambda\delta$ becomes so small that

$$I \vartriangleleft \{x \mapsto n - \lambda\delta\} \models F_4[x] \leftrightarrow F_{-\infty}[x] \text{ , so}$$
$$I \vartriangleleft \{x \mapsto n - \lambda\delta\} \models F_{-\infty}[x] \text{ .}$$

That is, $n - \lambda\delta$ is so small that the inequality literals of F_4 evaluate under $I \vartriangleleft \{x \mapsto n - \lambda\delta\}$ exactly as in the construction of $F_{-\infty}$. Now, since $F_{-\infty}$ contains only divides literals, we can choose a μ such that $n - \lambda\delta + \mu\delta \in [1, \delta]$. Let $j^* = n - \lambda\delta + \mu\delta$. Then $I \models F_{-\infty}[j^*]$, so that $I \models F_5$.   ∎

7.2.3 A Symmetric Elimination

The construction in Step 5 was biased to the left. We can just as easily define a right elimination. Construct the **right infinite projection** $F_{+\infty}[x']$ from $F_4[x']$ by replacing

(A) literals $x' < a$ by $\bot$

and

(B) literals $b < x'$ by $\top$.

The idea is that very large numbers (the right side of the "number line") satisfy **(B)** literals but not **(A)** literals.

Then define δ as before, but now define A as the set of a terms appearing in **(A)** literals. Construct

$$F_5 : \bigvee_{j=1}^{\delta} F_{+\infty}[-j] \vee \bigvee_{j=1}^{\delta} \bigvee_{a \in A} F_4[a - j] .$$

Now, instead of choosing the **left** or **right elimination** (corresponding to the left or right infinite projections, respectively) arbitrarily, choose the elimination according to the number of **(A)** and **(B)** literals. If there are fewer **(A)** literals than **(B)** literals, choose the right elimination; otherwise, choose the left elimination. This heuristic minimizes the number of disjuncts in the resulting formula F_5.

Example 7.11. In the formula

$$F : \exists x. \ (x < 13 \ \lor \ x > 15) \ \land \ x < y \ ,$$

there are two **(A)** literals but only one **(B)** literal. Hence, choose the left infinite projection to produce fewer disjuncts. ∎

7.2.4 Eliminating Blocks of Quantifiers

Consider a formula with a block of quantifiers: $\exists x_1. \ \cdots \exists x_n. \ F[x_1, \dots, x_n]$, where F is quantifier-free. Eliminating x_n produces a formula of the form

$$G_1 : \quad \exists x_1. \ \cdots \exists x_{n-1}. \quad \bigvee_{j=1}^{\delta} F_{-\infty}[x_1, \dots, x_{n-1}, j] \ \lor \ \bigvee_{j=1}^{\delta} \bigvee_{b \in B} F_4[x_1, \dots, x_{n-1}, b + j] \ .$$

Disjunction and existential quantification commute, so we can rewrite G_1 as

$$G_2 : \quad \begin{aligned} &\bigvee_{j=1}^{\delta} \exists x_1. \ \cdots \exists x_{n-1}. \ F_{-\infty}[x_1, \dots, x_{n-1}, j] \\ &\lor \ \bigvee_{j=1}^{\delta} \bigvee_{b \in B} \exists x_1. \ \cdots \exists x_{n-1}. \ F_4[x_1, \dots, x_{n-1}, b + j] \end{aligned}$$

and continue the elimination on each disjunct.

This optimization can be taken one step further. Rather than expanding the disjuncts over the iterator j, treat j as a free variable during the subsequent eliminations. Then only $1 + |B|$ formulae need be examined during the next phase: the formula $\exists x_1. \ \cdots \exists x_{n-1}. \ F_{-\infty}[x_1, \dots, x_{n-1}, j]$ and, for each $b \in B$, the formula $\exists x_1. \ \cdots \exists x_{n-1}. \ F_4[x_1, \dots, x_{n-1}, b + j]$.

Example 7.12. Consider the formula

$$\exists y. \ \exists x. \ \underbrace{x < -2 \ \land \ 1 - 5y < x \ \land \ 1 + y < 13x}_{F[x,y]} \ .$$

At Step 3,

$$\delta' = \mathsf{lcm}\{1, 13\} = 13 \ ,$$

producing

$$\exists y. \ \exists x. \ 13x < -26 \ \land \ 13 - 65y < 13x \ \land \ 1 + y < 13x$$

and then

$$\exists y. \ \exists x'. \ x' < -26 \ \land \ 13 - 65y < x' \ \land \ 1 + y < x' \ \land \ 13 \mid x' \ .$$

With $\delta = \text{lcm}\{13\} = 13$, $A = \{-26\}$, and $B = \{13 - 65y, 1 + y\}$, choose the right elimination to form:

$$\exists y. \bigvee_{j=1}^{13} \left[\begin{array}{l} -26 - j < -26 \ \wedge \ 13 - 65y < -26 - j \\ \wedge \ 1 + y < -26 - j \ \wedge \ 13 \mid -26 - j \end{array} \right] .$$

$F_{+\infty}$ simplifies to $\perp$ since F is a conjunction of both (A) and (B) literals. Now, instead of applying elimination to the entire subformula within the quantifier $\exists y$, commute the quantifier and the disjunctions:

$$G : \bigvee_{j=1}^{13} \exists y. \ j > 0 \ \wedge \ 39 + j < 65y \ \wedge \ y < -27 - j \ \wedge \ 13 \mid -j - 26 .$$

Treating j as a free variable, apply QE to the subformula

$$H : \exists y. \ j > 0 \ \wedge \ 39 + j < 65y \ \wedge \ y < -27 - j \ \wedge \ 13 \mid -j - 26$$

as usual. Then simplify to produce

$$H' : \bigvee_{k=1}^{65} (k < -66j - 1794 \ \wedge \ 13 \mid -j - 26 \ \wedge \ 65 \mid 39 + j + k) ,$$

and replace H with H' in G to produce the final formula

$$\bigvee_{j=1}^{13} \bigvee_{k=1}^{65} (k < -66j - 1794 \ \wedge \ 13 \mid -j - 26 \ \wedge \ 65 \mid 39 + j + k) .$$

This formula is $\widehat{T_{\mathbb{Z}}}$-equivalent to $\exists y, x. \ F[x, y]$.   ∎

7.2.5 ★Solving Divides Constraints

Consider a formula of the form $G : \exists x_1. \ \cdots \exists x_n. \ F[x_1, \ldots, x_n]$ without free variables. Applying Cooper's method with the block elimination optimization produces a quantifier-free $\widehat{T_{\mathbb{Z}}}$-equivalent formula of the form

$$G' : \bigvee_{j_1=1}^{\delta_1} \cdots \bigvee_{j_n=1}^{\delta_n} F'[j_1, \ldots, j_n] ,$$

also without free variables. Expanding this formula by attempting every possible combination of values for $j_1, \ldots, j_n$ produces $\delta_1 \times \delta_2 \times \cdots \times \delta_n$ disjuncts. This naive expansion is prohibitively expensive on even small problems.

Notice, however, that Step 4 introduces many divisibility literals as conjuncts. F_5 has the form

$$F_5 : \bigvee_{j_1=1}^{\delta_1} \cdots \bigvee_{j_n=1}^{\delta_n} \left(F'' \wedge \bigwedge_i k_i \mid t_i[j_1, \ldots, j_n] \right) ,$$

where the t_i are terms containing only constants and the j_i iterators. Cooper realized that the conjuncts

$$D : \bigwedge_i k_i \mid t_i[j_1, \ldots, j_n]$$

can be solved to reduce significantly the number of disjuncts to consider.

There are two steps to solving divides constraints.

Step 1: Triangulate the Constraints

The following theorem provides a means for reducing the number of literals that contain some j_i. It applies Euclid's algorithm for computing the greatest common divisor (GCD) d of two integers m and n. Euclid's algorithm also returns two integers p and q such that $pm + qn = d$.

Theorem 7.13. *Consider two divisibility constraints*

$$F : m \mid ax + b \wedge n \mid \alpha x + \beta ,$$

where $m, n \in \mathbb{Z}^+$, $a, \alpha \in \mathbb{Z} \setminus \{0\}$, and b, β are terms not containing x. Let $d, p, q = \gcd(an, \alpha m)$ be such that d is the GCD of an and αm, and p and q obey $pan + q\alpha m = d$. Then F is satisfiable iff

$$G : mn \mid dx + bpn + \beta qm \wedge d \mid \alpha b - a\beta$$

is satisfiable.

While both of the literals of F contain x, only one of the literals of G contains x. Therefore, we can apply this theorem to triangulate a set S of divisibility constraints. Let $\prec$ be a linear ordering of $j_1, \ldots, j_n$. S is in **triangular form** if for each j_i, at most one constraint of S contains j_i as the least (according to $\prec$) free variable.

The triangularization algorithm proceeds iteratively. On one iteration, perform the following steps:

1. Choose from S two constraints

   $$m \mid aj_i + b \quad \text{and} \quad n \mid \alpha j_i + \beta$$

   such that there is no $j_k \prec j_i$ that occurs in at least two divisibility constraints of S.
2. Apply Theorem 7.13 to produce the new constraints

   $$mn \mid dj_i + bpn + \beta qm \quad \text{and} \quad d \mid \alpha b - a\beta .$$

   Replace the original constraints with these constraints in S.

Example 7.14. Consider the divisibility constraints of Example 7.12:

$$13 \mid -j - 26 \ \wedge \ 65 \mid 39 + j + k \ .$$

Fix the variable order $j \prec k$. According to this order, only one constraint should have an occurrence of j, so apply Theorem 7.13:

$$
\begin{array}{ll}
m \mid aj + \quad b & n \mid \alpha j + \quad \beta \\
13 \mid -j + -26 \ \wedge \ 65 \mid \quad j + k + 39
\end{array}
$$

Compute

$$
\begin{array}{ll}
d, p, q = \gcd(an, \alpha m) & \quad pan + q\alpha m = \quad d \\
13, 0, 1 = \gcd(-65, 13) & \quad 0(-65) + 1(13) = 13
\end{array}
\quad \text{so that}
$$

and construct

$$
\begin{array}{ll}
mn \mid \quad dj + \quad bpn \quad + \quad \beta qm & d \mid \quad \alpha b - \quad a\beta \\
845 \mid 13j + (-26)(0)(65) + (k+39)13 \quad \wedge \quad 13 \mid -26 - (-1)(k+39)
\end{array}
$$

or, simplifying,

$$845 \mid 13j + 13k + 507 \ \wedge \ 13 \mid k + 13 \ .$$

As desired, only one constraint has an occurrence of j. Additionally, the simplest constraint contains only k. ∎

Step 2: Solve the Constraints

To solve the triangulated system of constraints S, consider the following theorem.

Theorem 7.15. *Consider divisibility constraint*

$$F : \ m \mid ax + b \ ,$$

for $m \in \mathbb{Z}^+$, $a \in \mathbb{Z} \backslash \{0\}$, and b a term not containing x. Let $d, p, q = \gcd(a, m)$ be such that d is the GCD of a and m, and p and q obey $pa + qm = d$. F is satisfiable iff $d \mid b$. If it is satisfiable, its solutions are

$$x = -\frac{pb}{d} + \frac{\lambda m}{d} \quad \text{for } \lambda \in \mathbb{Z} \ .$$

With S in triangular form, we need only solve the system recursively:

1. If S is empty, generate a disjunct according to the current values of $j_1, \ldots, j_n$.
2. Otherwise, choose from S a constraint

$$F : \ m \mid aj_i + b$$

such that b is an integer. Apply Theorem 7.15 to F.

3. If F is unsatisfiable, return.
4. Otherwise, instantiate the remaining constraints of S with each solution to j_i within the range $[1, \delta_i]$, and recursively solve.

Example 7.16. Consider the divisibility constraints of Example 7.12:

$$13 \mid -j - 26 \ \wedge \ 65 \mid 39 + j + k .$$

The system is already in triangular form for the variable order $k \prec j$. To solve the first constraint

$$
\begin{array}{ll}
m \mid aj + b & \\
13 \mid -j + -26 & \text{compute}
\end{array}
\quad
\begin{array}{l}
d, \ p, q = \gcd(a, m) \\
1, \ -1, 0 = \gcd(-1, 13) .
\end{array}
$$

Does $1 \mid -26$? Yes, so the solutions are given by

$$j = -(-1)\frac{-26}{1} + \lambda\frac{13}{1} = -26 + 13\lambda \quad \text{for } \lambda \in \mathbb{Z} .$$

Since $j \in [1, 13]$, only $\lambda = 3$ is relevant, providing the solution $j = 13$.
After substituting $j = 13$ into the second constraint, to solve

$$
\begin{array}{ll}
m \mid ak + b & \\
65 \mid \ k + 52 & \text{compute}
\end{array}
\quad
\begin{array}{l}
d, p, q = \gcd(a, m) \\
1, 1, 0 = \gcd(1, 65) .
\end{array}
$$

Does $1 \mid 52$? Yes, so the solutions are given by

$$k = -(1)\frac{52}{1} + \lambda\frac{65}{1} = -52 + 65\lambda \quad \text{for } \lambda \in \mathbb{Z} .$$

Since $k \in [1, 65]$, only $\lambda = 1$ is relevant, providing the solution $k = 13$. $j = 13$, $k = 13$ is the only solution to the divisibility constraints $13 \mid -j - 26 \ \wedge \ 65 \mid 39 + j + k$.
However, the additional conjunct

$$(k < -66j - 1794)\{j \mapsto 13, \ k \mapsto 13\}$$

is not true, so the formula of Example 7.12 is $\widehat{T_{\mathbb{Z}}}$-equivalent to $\perp$ and is thus $\widehat{T_{\mathbb{Z}}}$-unsatisfiable.
Alternatively, we could have enumerated all $13 \times 65 = 845$ possible disjuncts to discover that none of them simplifies to $\top$. In 844 of these disjuncts, at least one of the divisibility constraints is $\perp$.
Solve the triangulated system of Example 7.14 with variable order $j \prec k$, and verify that the solution is the same. The variable order used for triangulating the constraint system does not affect the solutions. ∎

Solving divisibility constraints significantly improves the performance of QE on purely existential and purely universal formulae. What about formulae with free variables or some quantifier alternation? For example, consider the formula

$$G : \forall y_1. \cdots \forall y_m. \exists x_1. \cdots \exists x_n. F[x_1, \ldots, x_n, y_1, \ldots, y_m] \ .$$

Eliminating the inner block produces the $\widehat{T_{\mathbb{Z}}}$-equivalent formula

$$G' : \forall y_1. \cdots \forall y_m. \bigvee_{j_1=1}^{\delta_1} \cdots \bigvee_{j_n=1}^{\delta_n} F'[j_1, \ldots, j_n, y_1, \ldots, y_m] \ .$$

Order the free variables $\mathrm{free}(F') = \{j_1, \ldots, j_n, y_1, \ldots, y_m\}$ so that the y_i's precede the j_i's. In the resulting triangulated system, as few constraints as possible contain y_i variables. Drop all resulting constraints that contain a y_i variable, and solve the remaining constraints. A variable j_i that does not appear in the final set of constraints must be instantiated to all values in its range $[1, \delta_i]$.

7.3 Quantifier Elimination over Rationals

QE for the theory of rationals $T_{\mathbb{Q}}$ is simpler than for $\widehat{T_{\mathbb{Z}}}$. Recall that $T_{\mathbb{Q}}$ has the following signature:

$$\Sigma_{\mathbb{Q}} : \{0, \ 1, \ +, \ -, \ =, \ \geq\} \ ,$$

where

- 0 and 1 are constants;
- $+$ is a binary function;
- $-$ is a unary function;
- and $=$ and $\geq$ are binary predicates.

To be consistent with our presentation of Cooper's method, we switch from weak inequality $\geq$ to strict inequality $>$. Of course, they are interchangeable:

$$x \geq y \ \Leftrightarrow \ x > y \ \vee \ x = y \quad \text{and} \quad x > y \ \Leftrightarrow \ x \geq y \ \wedge \ \neg(x = y) \ .$$

7.3.1 Ferrante and Rackoff's Method

Given a $\Sigma_{\mathbb{Q}}$-formula $\exists x. \ F[x]$ as input, where F is quantifier-free, the algorithm proceeds according to the following steps.

Step 1

Put $F[x]$ in NNF. The output $\exists x. \ F_1[x]$ is $T_{\mathbb{Q}}$-equivalent to $\exists x. \ F[x]$ and is such that F_1 is a positive Boolean combination (only $\wedge$ and $\vee$) of literals.

Step 2

Replace literals according to the following $T_{\mathbb{Q}}$-equivalences, applied from left to right:

$$\neg(s < t) \quad \Leftrightarrow \quad t < s \ \lor \ t = s$$
$$\neg(s = t) \quad \Leftrightarrow \quad t < s \ \lor \ t > s$$

The output $\exists x. \ F_2[x]$ is $T_{\mathbb{Q}}$-equivalent to $\exists x. \ F[x]$ and does not contain any negations.

Step 3

Solve for x in each atom of $F_2[x]$: for example, replace the atom

$$t < cx \ ,$$

where $c \in \mathbb{Z} \setminus \{0\}$ and t is a term not containing x, with

$$\frac{t}{c} < x \ .$$

Atoms in the output $\exists x. \ F_3[x]$ now have the form

(A) $x < a$
(B) $b < x$
(C) $x = c$

where a, b, c are terms that do not contain x. $\exists x. \ F_3[x]$ is $T_{\mathbb{Q}}$-equivalent to $\exists x. \ F[x]$.

Step 4

Construct the **left infinite projection** $F_{-\infty}$ from $F_3[x]$ by replacing

(A) atoms $x < a$ by $\top$,   **(B)** atoms $b < x$ by $\bot$,

and

(C) atoms $x = c$ by $\bot$.

Construct the **right infinite projection** $F_{+\infty}$ from $F_3[x]$ by replacing

(A) atoms $x < a$ by $\bot$,   **(B)** atoms $b < x$ by $\top$,

and

(C) atoms $x = c$ by $\bot$.

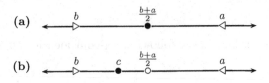

Fig. 7.2. Satisfying points: (a) $\frac{b+a}{2}$ (b) $\frac{c+c}{2}$

The left (right) infinite projection captures the case when small (large) $n \in \mathbb{Q}$ satisfy $F_3[n]$.

Let S be the set of a, b, and c terms from the **(A)**, **(B)**, and **(C)** atoms. Construct the final output

$$F_4 : F_{-\infty} \vee F_{+\infty} \vee \bigvee_{s,t \in S} F_3 \left[\frac{s+t}{2} \right] ,$$

which is $T_{\mathbb{Q}}$-equivalent to $\exists x.\ F[x]$.

The disjunct $F_{-\infty}$ captures the possibility that all rationals n less than some value a^* satisfy $F_4[n]$. The disjunct $F_{+\infty}$ captures the symmetric case for large n. Finally, the last disjunct can be seen as capturing two possibilities. First, disjuncts in which s and t are the same terms check whether any term $s \in S$ satisfies $F_4[s]$. Second, consider the remaining $O(|S|^2)$ disjuncts in which s and t are different terms. In any $T_{\mathbb{Q}}$-interpretation, $|S| - 1$ pairs $s, t \in S$ are adjacent; for such a pair, (s, t) is an interval in which no other $s' \in S$ lies. If $F_4[\frac{s+t}{2}]$, then it can be shown that every other point $n \in (s, t)$ also satisfies $F_4[n]$. In other words, $\frac{s+t}{2}$ represents the whole interval (s, t). Since no single $T_{\mathbb{Q}}$-interpretation is fixed in advance, all $O(|S|^2)$ pairs are considered (but see Exercise 7.8 for an optimization).

Figure 7.2 illustrates two cases in which a, b, and c terms are constant. Figure 7.2**(a)** visualizes the formula $b < x \wedge x < a$, for which $\frac{b+a}{2}$ is a satisfying point. Triangles represent inequalities; the solid circle represents $\frac{b+a}{2}$. All points in the interval (b, a) are satisfying, but $\frac{b+a}{2}$ is the representative of this interval. Figure 7.2**(b)** includes an additional literal, $x = c$ (the solid circle); now, $\frac{b+a}{2}$ (the open circle) is not a satisfying point, but $\frac{c+c}{2} = c$ is.

Example 7.17. Consider the $\Sigma_{\mathbb{Q}}$-formula

$$\exists x.\ \underbrace{2x = y}_{F[x]} .$$

In Step 3, solving for x produces

$$F' : \exists x.\ x = \frac{y}{2}$$

so that $S = \{\frac{y}{2}\}$. The left $F_{-\infty}$ and right $F_{+\infty}$ infinite projections are both $\bot$, as F' contains a single **(C)** atom. Hence, simplifying

$$F_4 : \bigvee_{s,t\in S} \left(\frac{s+t}{2} = \frac{y}{2}\right)$$

reveals the $T_\mathbb{Q}$-equivalent quantifier-free formula $\frac{y}{2} = \frac{y}{2}$, or $\top$. Therefore, $\exists x. \; F[x]$ is $T_\mathbb{Q}$-valid. ∎

Example 7.18. Consider the $\Sigma_\mathbb{Q}$-formula

$$\exists x. \; \underbrace{3x + 1 < 10 \; \wedge \; 7x - 6 > 7}_{F[x]} \; .$$

Solving for x gives

$$F' : \exists x. \; \underbrace{x < 3 \; \wedge \; x > \frac{13}{7}}_{F_3[x]}$$

and $S = \{3, \frac{13}{7}\}$. Since $x < 3$ is an **(A)** atom and $x > \frac{13}{7}$ is a **(B)** atom, both $F_{-\infty}$ and $F_{+\infty}$ simplify to $\bot$, leaving

$$F_4 : \bigvee_{s,t\in S} \left(\frac{s+t}{2} < 3 \; \wedge \; \frac{s+t}{2} > \frac{13}{7}\right) \; .$$

$\frac{s+t}{2}$ takes on three expressions: 3, $\frac{13}{7}$, and $\frac{\frac{13}{7}+3}{2}$. The first two expressions arise when s and t are the same terms. $F_3[3]$ and $F_3[\frac{13}{7}]$ both simplify to $\bot$ since the inequalities are strict; however,

$$F_3\left[\frac{\frac{13}{7}+3}{2}\right] : \; \frac{\frac{13}{7}+3}{2} < 3 \; \wedge \; \frac{\frac{13}{7}+3}{2} > \frac{13}{7}$$

simplifies to $\top$. Thus, $F_4 : \top$ is $T_\mathbb{Q}$-equivalent to $\exists x. \; F[x]$, so $\exists x. \; F[x]$ is $T_\mathbb{Q}$-valid. ∎

Example 7.19. Consider the $\Sigma_\mathbb{Q}$-formula

$$G : \forall x. \; x < y \; .$$

To eliminate x, consider the subformula F of

$$G' : \neg(\underbrace{\exists x. \; \neg(x < y)}_{F[x]}) \; .$$

Step 2 rewrites F as

$$\exists x. \; y < x \; \vee \; y = x \; .$$

The literals are already in solved form for x in Step 3. Then

$$F_{-\infty} : \bot \vee \bot \quad \text{and} \quad F_{+\infty} : \top \vee \bot$$

simplify to $\bot$ and $\top$, respectively. Since $F_{+\infty}$ is $\top$, we need not consider the rest of Step 4, but instead declare that $\exists x. \; F[x]$ is $T_\mathbb{Q}$-equivalent to $F_4 : \top$. Then G' is $\neg\top$, so that G is $T_\mathbb{Q}$-equivalent to $\bot$. ∎

Theorem 7.20 (Correct). *Given $\Sigma_{\mathbb{Q}}$-formula $\exists x.\ F[x]$ in which F is quantifier-free, Ferrante and Rackoff's method returns a $T_{\mathbb{Q}}$-equivalent quantifier-free formula.*

Exercise 7.9 asks the reader to prove the theorem.

A limited form of the block elimination optimization discussed in Section 7.2.4 can be adapted to this QE procedure: commute disjunction and existential quantification. This step reduces the size of the term set S in each subproblem.

7.4 ⋆Complexity

Fischer and Rabin proved the following lower bounds. The length n of a formula is the number of symbols.

Theorem 7.21 ($\widehat{T_{\mathbb{Z}}}$ Lower Bound). *There is a fixed constant $c > 0$ such that for all sufficiently large n, there is a $\widehat{\Sigma_{\mathbb{Z}}}$-formula of length n that requires at least $2^{2^{cn}}$ steps to decide its validity.*

Theorem 7.22 ($T_{\mathbb{Q}}$ Lower Bound). *There is a fixed constant $c > 0$ such that for all sufficiently large n, there is a $\Sigma_{\mathbb{Q}}$-formula of length n that requires at least 2^{cn} steps to decide its validity.*

Oppen analyzed Cooper's method to prove the following upper bound.

Theorem 7.23 ($\widehat{T_{\mathbb{Z}}}$ Upper Bound). *On a $\widehat{\Sigma_{\mathbb{Z}}}$-formula of length n, Cooper's method requires deterministic time $2^{2^{2^{pn}}}$ for some fixed constant $p > 0$.*

Ferrante and Rackoff proved the following upper bound.

Theorem 7.24 ($T_{\mathbb{Q}}$ Upper Bound). *On a $\Sigma_{\mathbb{Q}}$-formula of length n, Ferrante and Rackoff's method requires deterministic time $2^{2^{pn}}$ for some fixed constant $p > 0$.*

Closing the gap between the lower and upper bounds would require answering long-standing open questions in complexity theory.

7.5 Summary

Quantifier elimination is a standard technique for reasoning about theories in which satisfiability is decidable even with arbitrary quantification. This chapter presents the technique in the context of arithmetic over integers and over rationals or reals. It covers:

- *Quantifier elimination* in general. Based on structural induction, one only needs to consider the special case of formulae of the form $\exists x.\ F[x]$, in which F is quantifier-free but may contain free variables in addition to x; arbitrary formulae may then be treated compositionally.
- *Elimination over integers, $T_{\mathbb{Z}}$.* The basic theory of integers does not admit quantifier elimination; it must be augmented with divisibility predicates. This situation, in which additional predicates are required to develop a quantifier elimination procedure, is common. The main idea of the procedure is to identify intervals with periodic behavior induced by the divisibility predicates.
- *Elimination over rationals, $T_{\mathbb{Q}}$.* The main idea of the procedure is to partition the rationals into a finite number of points and intervals.

The optimizations of Cooper's method, particularly solving divides constraints, make the procedure acceptably fast in practice on quantifier-free $\Sigma_{\mathbb{Z}}$-formulae. However, faster decision procedures exist for deciding $\Sigma_{\mathbb{Q}}$-satisfiability of quantifier-free $\Sigma_{\mathbb{Q}}$-formulae; we study one in Chapter 8.

In addition to handling quantifiers, the algorithms of this chapter treat arbitrary Boolean combinations of literals. The decision procedures of subsequent chapters require the Boolean structure to be simple: formulae are just conjunctions of literals. Treating formulae with arbitrary Boolean structure directly avoids the potential exponential increase in size associated with converting to DNF.

Bibliographic Remarks

Presburger proves that arithmetic over the natural numbers without multiplication $T_{\mathbb{N}}$ is decidable [73]. Cooper presents the version of the quantifier-elimination procedure for $T_{\mathbb{Z}}$ that we describe [19]. Fischer and Rabin provide the lower bound on the complexity of the decision problem for $T_{\mathbb{Z}}$ [33], while Oppen analyzes Cooper's procedure to obtain an upper bound [68].

Ferrante and Rackoff describe the quantifier-elimination procedure that we present and the lower and upper complexity bounds on the problem [32].

Exercises

7.1 ($T_{\mathbb{Z}}$ does not admit QE). Prove Lemma 7.4. *Hint*: Apply structural induction; the base cases involve comparisons between ay and c, for constants a and c.

7.2 (QE for $\widehat{T_{\mathbb{Z}}}$). Apply quantifier-elimination to the following $\Sigma_{\mathbb{Z}}$-formulae.

(a) $\forall y.\ 3 < x + 2y\ \lor\ 2x + y < 3$
(b) $\exists y.\ 3 < x + 2y\ \lor\ 2x + y < 3$

(c) $\exists y.\ x = 2y\ \wedge\ y < x$
(d) $\forall x.\ (\exists y.\ x = 2y)\ \rightarrow\ (\exists y.\ 3x = 2y)$

7.3 (QE for $\widehat{T_{\mathbb{Z}}}$). Construct new $\Sigma_{\mathbb{Z}}$-formulae such that

(a) the $F_{-\infty}$ component of the elimination simplifies to $\top$;
(b) the $F_{-\infty}$ component of the elimination simplifies to $\bot$;
(c) using the right infinite projection is better than using the left infinite projections.

In each case, describe the elimination.

7.4 (Block elimination in $T_{\mathbb{Z}}$). Apply quantifier-elimination to the following $\Sigma_{\mathbb{Z}}$-formulae. Use block elimination.

(a) $\exists x.\ \exists y.\ 2x + 3y = 7\ \wedge\ x < y$
(b) $\exists x.\ \exists y.\ 2x + 3y = 7\ \wedge\ y < x$
(c) $\exists x.\ \exists y.\ 2x + 3y = 7\ \wedge\ x < y\ \wedge\ 0 < x\ \wedge\ 0 < y$
(d) $\exists x.\ \exists y.\ 3x + 3y < 8\ \wedge\ 8 < 3x + 2y$
(e) $\exists x.\ \exists y.\ x = 2y\ \wedge\ \exists z.\ x = 3z$

7.5 (Divides constraints). Apply the divides-constraints elimination to the $\Sigma_{\mathbb{Z}}$-formulae of Exercise 7.4.

7.6 (QE for $T_{\mathbb{Q}}$). Apply quantifier-elimination to the formulae of Exercise 7.2, but treat them as $\Sigma_{\mathbb{Q}}$-formula.

7.7 (QE for $T_{\mathbb{Q}}$). Construct new $\Sigma_{\mathbb{Q}}$-formulae such that

(a) the $F_{-\infty}$ and $F_{+\infty}$ components of the elimination simplify to $\top$ and $\bot$, respectively;
(b) the $F_{-\infty}$ and $F_{+\infty}$ components of the elimination simplify to $\bot$ and $\top$, respectively.

In each case, describe the elimination.

7.8 (Sufficient set). Step 4 of Ferrante and Rackoff's method examines terms $\frac{s+t}{2}$ for all $s, t \in S$, where S is the set of all a, b, and c terms. Describe a smaller set of terms that is still sufficient. According to this new definition, which terms should be examined in Example 7.18 and Exercise 7.6?

7.9 ($\star$Theorem 7.20). Prove Theorem 7.20. *Hint:* Apply the strategy employed in the proof of Theorem 7.10.

7.10 ($\star$Optimization problem). Consider the **optimization problem** $\max\{f(\overline{x}) : F[\overline{x}]\}$ in which the **objective function** $f(\overline{x})$ is a linear expression over the problem variables $\overline{x}$, and the **constraint** $F[\overline{x}]$ is a $\Sigma_{\mathbb{Z}}$-formula such that $\mathsf{free}(F[\overline{x}]) = \overline{x}$. The solution to the problem is the largest number n such that there exists some evaluation $\overline{v}$ of $\overline{x}$ for which $f(\overline{v}) = n$ and $F[\overline{v}]$ is true. Show how to use QE for $T_{\mathbb{Z}}$ to solve this optimization problem.

Quantifier-Free Linear Arithmetic

Because my mathematics has its origin in a real problem doesn't make it less interesting to me — just the other way around, I find it makes the puzzle I am working on all the more exciting. I get satisfaction out of knowing that I'm working on a relevant problem.

— George Dantzig
An Interview with George B. Dantzig:
The Father of Linear Programming, 1986

This chapter considers satisfiability in the quantifier-free fragment of the theory of rationals $T_{\mathbb{Q}}$. Addressing this fragment is motivated by two observations. First, program verification typically requires just considering formulae from the quantifier-free fragments of theories such as $T_{\mathbb{Q}}$. Second, deciding satisfiability in the full theory of $T_{\mathbb{Q}}$ is computationally expensive, while deciding satisfiability in just the quantifier-free fragment of $T_{\mathbb{Q}}$ is fast in practice when using, for example, the **simplex method** for **linear programming**.

A linear program is an optimization problem in which the goal is to find a point satisfying a set of linear *constraints* that maximizes a linear *objective function*. The linear constraints are a quantifier-free conjunctive $\Sigma_{\mathbb{Q}}$-formula in which each atom is a weak inequality. The objective function is a linear function. Deciding $T_{\mathbb{Q}}$-satisfiability can be cast as solving a linear program, so we benefit from existing algorithms for solving them.

Section 8.1 motivates studying the quantifier-free fragments of theories in general. Section 8.2 reviews concepts from linear algebra. Then Section 8.3 introduces linear programs and shows how to decide $T_{\mathbb{Q}}$-satisfiability by solving a linear program. Finally, Section 8.4 presents the simplex method for solving linear programs.

8.1 Decision Procedures for Quantifier-Free Fragments

The time complexities of the algorithms of Chapter 7 limit their practical impact. Additionally, Ferrante and Rackoff's method is not optimal for the quantifier-free fragment of $T_{\mathbb{Q}}$. For other theories, the situation is worse: satisfiability in the full theories such as equality T_E, lists T_{cons}, and arrays T_A is undecidable. Fortunately, for verification and other applications, we typically need to decide satisfiability of quantifier-free formulae rather than of arbitrarily quantified formulae.

Recall that the **quantifier-free fragment** of a theory T with signature Σ consists of the axioms of T and valid Σ-formulae of the form

$$G : \forall x_1, \ldots, x_n. \ F[x_1, \ldots, x_n] \ ,$$

where F is quantifier-free and $\mathsf{free}(F) = \{x_1, \ldots, x_n\}$. While such formulae have quantifiers, the point is that they do not have **quantifier alternations**: all quantifiers are universal. Using our conventions, we would ordinarily ask whether the formula F is T-valid — whether its universal closure $\forall * . \ F$ is T-valid. F is indeed quantifier-free.

T-validity of G corresponds to T-unsatisfiability of

$$\neg G : \exists x_1, \ldots, x_n. \ \neg F[x_1, \ldots, x_n] \ ,$$

or, using our conventions, simply T-unsatisfiability of $\neg F$. Hence, the quantifiers are "natural" for satisfiability checking: $\neg G$ is T-satisfiable iff there exists a T-interpretation I and an assignment to $x_1, \ldots, x_n$ under which $\neg F$ evaluates to true.

Fortunately, the quantifier-free fragments of many theories are decidable, often efficiently so. In Chapters 8-10, we focus on decision procedures for the quantifier-free fragments of theories.

For ease of exposition, we consider only **conjunctive** quantifier-free Σ-formulae in each theory T that we examine. Conjunctive Σ-formulae are conjunctions of Σ-literals. This restriction does not limit the scope of the decision procedures. For given arbitrary quantifier-free Σ-formula F, we can convert it into DNF Σ-formula

$$F_1 \vee \cdots \vee F_k$$

in which each F_i is conjunctive. F is T-satisfiable iff at least one F_i is T-satisfiable. Decide the T-satisfiability of F by considering each F_i.

Remark 8.1 ($\star$Complexity). This restriction does, however, affect complexity. Because satisfiability in PL is NP-complete, any decision procedure that considers arbitrary quantifier-free formulae must be at least NP-hard, as it must handle not only the theory-specific aspects of the formulae but also the combinatorial (PL) aspects. However, considering only conjunctive formulae allows us to give more insightful complexity bounds. For example, satisfiability in the conjunctive quantifier-free fragments of $T_{\mathbb{Q}}$, T_E, T_{cons}, and their union theory is in PTIME. Thus, the "hard" part of deciding satisfiability of arbitrary quantifier-free formulae in these theories is handling the underlying PL structure. Analyzing the theory-specific aspects is comparatively easy.

8.2 Preliminary Concepts and Notation

We define basic concepts and notation of linear algebra, covering only what is required for understanding the remainder of the chapter. We refer the reader interested in learning more about linear algebra to relevant texts in **Bibliographic Remarks**.

Basic Concepts and Notation

A **variable** n-**vector** $\bar{x}$ is a column of n variables $x_1, \ldots, x_n$. An n-**vector** is a column $\bar{a} \in \mathbb{Q}^n$ of n rationals, and its **transpose** $\bar{a}^\mathsf{T}$ is a row with elements listed in the same order:

$$\bar{a} = \begin{bmatrix} a_1 \\ \vdots \\ a_n \end{bmatrix} \quad \text{and} \quad \bar{a}^\mathsf{T} = \begin{bmatrix} a_1 & \cdots & a_n \end{bmatrix} .$$

An $m \times n$-**matrix** $A \in \mathbb{Q}^{m \times n}$ consists of n columns of m rationals each (alternatively, m rows of n rationals each), and its **transpose** A^T is an $n \times m$-matrix in which element a_{ij} is swapped with element a_{ji}:

$$A = \begin{bmatrix} a_{11} & \cdots & a_{1n} \\ & \vdots & \\ a_{m1} & \cdots & a_{mn} \end{bmatrix} \quad \text{and} \quad A^\mathsf{T} = \begin{bmatrix} a_{11} & \cdots & a_{m1} \\ & \vdots & \\ a_{1n} & \cdots & a_{mn} \end{bmatrix} .$$

When we refer to a row $\bar{a}_i$ of A, we mean the row vector $\begin{bmatrix} a_{i1} & \cdots & a_{in} \end{bmatrix}$, and when we refer to a column $\bar{a}_j$ of A, we mean the column vector $\begin{bmatrix} a_{1j} & \cdots & a_{mj} \end{bmatrix}^\mathsf{T}$. We use this compact notation of transposed row vectors for column vectors to save vertical space.

    Vector-vector multiplication works as follows:

$$\bar{a}^\mathsf{T}\bar{b} = \begin{bmatrix} a_1 & \cdots & a_n \end{bmatrix} \begin{bmatrix} b_1 \\ \vdots \\ b_n \end{bmatrix} = \sum_{i=1}^{n} a_i b_i .$$

Matrix-vector multiplication works as follows:

$$A\bar{x} = \begin{bmatrix} a_{11} & \cdots & a_{1n} \\ & \vdots & \\ a_{m1} & \cdots & a_{mn} \end{bmatrix} \begin{bmatrix} x_1 \\ \vdots \\ x_n \end{bmatrix} = \begin{bmatrix} \sum_{i=1}^{n} a_{1i} x_i \\ \vdots \\ \sum_{i=1}^{n} a_{mi} x_i \end{bmatrix} .$$

Each row of A multiplies (as a vector) $\bar{x}$. Finally **matrix-matrix multiplication** works as follows: the product P of AB, for $m \times n$-matrix A and $n \times \ell$-matrix B, is an $m \times \ell$-matrix in which element p_{ij} is the product of the vector-vector multiplication of row $\bar{a}_i$ of A and column $\bar{b}_j$ of B:

$$p_{ij} = \bar{a}_i \bar{b}_j = \begin{bmatrix} a_{i1} & \cdots & a_{in} \end{bmatrix} \begin{bmatrix} b_{1j} \\ \vdots \\ b_{nj} \end{bmatrix} = \sum_{k=1}^{n} a_{ik} b_{kj} \ .$$

There are several important named vectors and matrices. $\bar{0}$ is a (column) vector of 0s. Similarly, $\bar{1}$ is a vector of 1s. Their sizes depend on the context in which they are used. Combining our notation so far,

$$\bar{1}^{\mathsf{T}} \bar{x} = \sum_{i=1}^{n} x_i \ .$$

In this context, $\bar{1}$ is an n-vector. The $n \times n$-matrix I is the **identity matrix**, in which the diagonal elements are 1 and all other elements are 0. Thus,

$$IA = AI = A$$

for any $n \times n$-matrix A. Finally, the **unit vector** e_i is the vector in which the ith element is 1 and all other elements are 0. Again, the sizes of I and e_i depend on their context.

Linear Equations

A **vector space** is a set of vectors that is closed under addition and scaling of vectors: if $\bar{v}_1, \ldots, \bar{v}_k \in S$ are vectors in vector space S, then also

$$\lambda_1 \bar{v}_1 + \cdots + \lambda_k \bar{v}_k \in S$$

for $\lambda_1, \ldots, \lambda_n \in \mathbb{Q}$. $\bar{0}$ is always a member of a vector space. For example, $\mathbb{Q}^n$ is a vector space with **dimension** n; it consists of all n-vectors of rationals. In general, the dimension of a vector space is given by the minimal number of vectors required to produce all vectors of the space through addition and scaling. Such a minimal set is called a **basis**. For example, a line has dimension 1 and can be described by a single vector: the full space of the line is described simply by scaling this vector. Similarly, a plane has dimension 2 and can be described by two vectors. The vector space consisting of just $\bar{0}$ has dimension 0 and is described by the empty set of vectors.

The **linear equation**

$$F : \quad A\bar{x} = \bar{b} \ ,$$

for $m \times n$-matrix A, variable n-vector $\bar{x}$, and m-vector $\bar{b}$, compactly represents the $\Sigma_{\mathbb{Q}}$-formula

$$F : \bigwedge_{i=1}^{m} a_{i1}x_1 + \cdots + a_{in}x_n = b_i \ .$$

The satisfying points comprise a vector space.

To solve linear equations (at least on paper), we apply **Gaussian elimination**. Consider first the case when A is a **square matrix**: its numbers of columns and rows are equal. For equation $A\bar{x} = \bar{b}$ define the **augmented matrix** $[A \mid \bar{b}]$. A matrix is in **triangular form** if all of its entries below the diagonal are 0; an augmented matrix $[A \mid \bar{b}]$ is in triangular form if A is in triangular form. The goal of Gaussian elimination is to manipulate $[A \mid \bar{b}]$ into triangular form via the following **elementary row operations**:

1. Swap two rows.
2. Multiply a row by a nonzero scalar.
3. Add one row to another.

The last two operations are often combined to yield the composite operation: add the scaling of one or more rows (by nonzero scalars) to a row.

Once an augmented matrix is in triangular form, solving the equations is simple. Solve the equation of the final row, which involves only one variable. Then substitute the solution into the other rows, yielding another equation with one variable. Continue until a solution is obtained for each variable.

Example 8.2. Solve

$$\begin{bmatrix} 3 & 1 & 2 \\ 1 & 0 & 1 \\ 2 & 2 & 1 \end{bmatrix} \begin{bmatrix} x_1 \\ x_2 \\ x_3 \end{bmatrix} = \begin{bmatrix} 6 \\ 1 \\ 2 \end{bmatrix} \ .$$

Construct the augmented matrix

$$\left[\begin{array}{ccc|c} 3 & 1 & 2 & 6 \\ 1 & 0 & 1 & 1 \\ 2 & 2 & 1 & 2 \end{array} \right] \ .$$

Apply the row operations as follows:

1. Add -2 times the first row and 4 times the second row to the third row:

$$\left[\begin{array}{ccc|c} 3 & 1 & 2 & 6 \\ 1 & 0 & 1 & 1 \\ 0 & 0 & 1 & -6 \end{array} \right]$$

2. Add -1 times the first row and 2 times the second row to the second row:

$$\left[\begin{array}{ccc|c} 3 & 1 & 2 & 6 \\ 0 & -1 & 1 & -3 \\ 0 & 0 & 1 & -6 \end{array} \right]$$

This augmented matrix is in triangular form.

Now solve the final row, representing equation $x_3 = -6$, for x_3, yielding $x_3 = -6$. Substituting into the second equation yields $-x_2 - 6 = -3$, or $x_2 = -3$. Substituting the solutions for x_2 and x_3 into the first equation yields $3x_1 - 3 - 12 = 6$, or $x_1 = 7$. Hence, the solution is $\bar{x} = \begin{bmatrix} 7 & -3 & -6 \end{bmatrix}^{\mathsf{T}}$. ∎

Gaussian elimination can also be applied when A is not a square matrix. Rather than achieving a triangular form, the goal is to achieve **echelon form**, in which the first nonzero element of each row is to the right of those above it. In this case, there are multiple solutions to the equation.

Example 8.3. Suppose that an equation over variables x_1, x_2, x_3, x_4 reduces to the following echelon form:

$$\left[\begin{array}{cccc|c} 3 & 1 & 2 & 0 & 6 \\ 0 & -1 & 1 & -1 & 0 \\ 0 & 0 & 0 & 2 & -6 \end{array}\right]$$

From the last row, $x_4 = -3$. We cannot solve for x_3 because there is not a row in which the x_3 column has the first non-zero element; therefore, x_3 can take on any value. To solve the second row, $-x_2 + x_3 - x_4 = 0$, for x_2, replace x_4 with its value -3 and let x_3 be any value: $-x_2 + x_3 + 3 = 0$. Then $x_2 = 3 + x_3$. Substituting for x_2 in the first equation, solve $3x_1 + (3 + x_3) + 2x_3 = 6$ for x_1: $x_1 = 1 - x_3$. Solutions thus lie on the line described by

$$\begin{bmatrix} 1 - x_3 \\ 3 + x_3 \\ x_3 \\ -3 \end{bmatrix}$$

for any value of x_3. ∎

A square matrix A is **nonsingular** or **invertible** if its inverse A^{-1} such that $AA^{-1} = A^{-1}A = I$ exists. We can also define nonsingularity in terms of a matrix's **null space**, denoted $\mathrm{null}(A)$, which is the set of points $\bar{v}$ such that $A\bar{v} = \bar{0}$. A matrix is nonsingular iff its null space has dimension 0.

For intuition, view square matrix A as a function that maps one point $\bar{u}$ to another $\bar{v} = A\bar{u}$. Suppose that A is not nonsingular so that $\mathrm{null}(A)$ has dimension greater than 0: A sends more than one point to $\bar{0}$. In this case, one cannot construct an inverse function A^{-1}, as it would have to map $\bar{0}$ back to more than one point. It turns out that it is sufficient to consider only the points that A maps to $\bar{0}$: if A sends only $\bar{0}$ to $\bar{0}$, then the inverse A^{-1} exists. In other words, when A maps only $\bar{0}$ to $\bar{0}$, then it is a 1-to-1 map so that its inverse exists.

A's inverse can be computed (on paper) with Gaussian elimination if it exists. Construct the augmented $n \times 2n$-matrix $\begin{bmatrix} A \mid I \end{bmatrix}$, and apply the elementary row operations to it until the left half is the identity matrix. The right half is then the inverse. To find just the kth column of A^{-1}, solve $A\bar{y} = e_k$ by

Gaussian elimination for $\bar{y}$, rather than computing all of A^{-1} and extracting the kth column.

Example 8.4. To find the second column of the inverse of

$$A = \begin{bmatrix} 3 & 1 & 2 \\ 1 & 0 & 1 \\ 2 & 2 & 1 \end{bmatrix},$$

solve

$$\underbrace{\begin{bmatrix} 3 & 1 & 2 \\ 1 & 0 & 1 \\ 2 & 2 & 1 \end{bmatrix}}_{A} \begin{bmatrix} x_1 \\ x_2 \\ x_3 \end{bmatrix} = \underbrace{\begin{bmatrix} 0 \\ 1 \\ 0 \end{bmatrix}}_{e_2}.$$

Construct the augmented matrix

$$\left[\begin{array}{ccc|c} 3 & 1 & 2 & 0 \\ 1 & 0 & 1 & 1 \\ 2 & 2 & 1 & 0 \end{array} \right]$$

Apply the same row operations as in Example 8.2.

1. Add -2 times the first row and 4 times the second row to the third row:

$$\left[\begin{array}{ccc|c} 3 & 1 & 2 & 0 \\ 1 & 0 & 1 & 1 \\ 0 & 0 & 1 & 4 \end{array} \right]$$

2. Add -1 times the first row and 2 times the second row to the second row:

$$\left[\begin{array}{ccc|c} 3 & 1 & 2 & 0 \\ 0 & -1 & 1 & 3 \\ 0 & 0 & 1 & 4 \end{array} \right]$$

This augmented matrix is in triangular form.

Solving the resulting equations in reverse yields $x_1 = -3$, $x_2 = 1$, and $x_3 = 4$. Verify that $\begin{bmatrix} -3 & 1 & 4 \end{bmatrix}^T$ is indeed the second column of A^{-1}. $\blacksquare$

8.3 Linear Programs

Linear Inequalities

The **linear inequality**

$$G : A\bar{x} \leq \bar{b},$$

for $m \times n$-matrix A, variable n-vector $\bar{x}$, and m-vector $\bar{b}$, compactly represents the $\Sigma_{\mathbb{Q}}$-formula

$$G: \bigwedge_{i=1}^{m} a_{i1}x_1 + \cdots + a_{in}x_n \leq b_i \ .$$

The subset of $\mathbb{Q}^n$ (or $\mathbb{R}^n$) that this inequality describes is called a **polyhedron**. Each member of this subset corresponds to one satisfying $T_{\mathbb{Q}}$-interpretation of G. Exercises 8.3, 8.4, and 8.5 explore polyhedra in depth.

One important characteristic of the space defined by $A\bar{x} \leq \bar{b}$ is that it is **convex**. An n-dimensional space $S \subseteq \mathbb{R}^n$ is **convex** if for all pairs of points $\bar{v}_1, \bar{v}_2 \in S$,

$$\lambda\bar{v}_1 + (1 - \lambda)\bar{v}_2 \in S \quad \text{for } \lambda \in [0, 1] \ .$$

$A\bar{x} \leq \bar{b}$ defines a convex space. For suppose $A\bar{v}_1 \leq \bar{b}$ and $A\bar{v}_2 \leq \bar{b}$; then also

$$\lambda A\bar{v}_1 \leq \lambda\bar{b} \quad \text{and} \quad (1 - \lambda)A\bar{v}_2 \leq (1 - \lambda)\bar{b}$$

for $\lambda \in [0, 1]$. Summing each side of the inequalities yields

$$\lambda A\bar{v}_1 + (1 - \lambda)A\bar{v}_2 \leq \lambda\bar{b} + (1 - \lambda)\bar{b}$$
$$A(\lambda\bar{v}_1 + (1 - \lambda)\bar{v}_2) \leq \bar{b}$$

as desired.

Consider when the $m \times n$-matrix A is such that $m \geq n$. An n-vector $\bar{v}$ is a **vertex** of $A\bar{x} \leq \bar{b}$ if there is a nonsingular $n \times n$-submatrix A_0 of A and corresponding n-subvector $\bar{b}_0$ of $\bar{b}$ such that $A_0\bar{v} = \bar{b}_0$. The rows in A_0 and $\bar{b}_0$ are the set of **defining constraints** of the vertex $\bar{v}$. In general, $\bar{v}$ may have multiple sets of defining constraints. Two vertices are **adjacent** if they have defining constraints that differ in only one constraint.

Intuitively, a vertex is an extremal point, such as the three vertices of a triangle. Adjacent vertices are connected by an edge of the space defined by $A\bar{x} \leq \bar{b}$; for example, each pair of vertices is adjacent in a triangle and connected by their common edge.

Linear Programs

The **linear optimization problem**, or **linear program**,

> **max** $\bar{c}^\mathsf{T}\bar{x}$
> **subject to**
> $A\bar{x} \leq \bar{b}$

is solved by a point $\bar{v}^*$ that satisfies the **constraints** $A\bar{x} \leq \bar{b}$ and that maximizes the **objective function** $\bar{c}^\mathsf{T}\bar{x}$. That is, $A\bar{v}^* \leq \bar{b}$, and $\bar{c}^\mathsf{T}\bar{v}^*$ is maximal: $\bar{c}^\mathsf{T}\bar{v}^* \geq \bar{c}^\mathsf{T}\bar{u}$ for all $\bar{u}$ satisfying $A\bar{u} \leq \bar{b}$. If $A\bar{x} \leq \bar{b}$ is unsatisfiable, the maximum is $-\infty$ by convention. It is also possible that the maximum is unbounded, in which case the maximum is ∞ by convention.

Example 8.5. Consider the following linear program:

$$\max \underbrace{\begin{bmatrix} 1 & 1 & -1 & -1 \end{bmatrix}}_{\bar{c}^{\mathsf{T}}} \underbrace{\begin{bmatrix} x \\ y \\ z_1 \\ z_2 \end{bmatrix}}_{\bar{x}}$$

subject to

$$\underbrace{\begin{bmatrix} -1 & 0 & 0 & 0 \\ 0 & -1 & 0 & 0 \\ 0 & 0 & -1 & 0 \\ 0 & 0 & 0 & -1 \\ 1 & 1 & 0 & 0 \\ 1 & 0 & -1 & 0 \\ 0 & 1 & 0 & -1 \end{bmatrix}}_{A} \underbrace{\begin{bmatrix} x \\ y \\ z_1 \\ z_2 \end{bmatrix}}_{\bar{x}} \leq \underbrace{\begin{bmatrix} 0 \\ 0 \\ 0 \\ 0 \\ 3 \\ 2 \\ 2 \end{bmatrix}}_{\bar{b}}$$

A is a 7×4-matrix, $\bar{b}$ is a 7-vector, and $\bar{x}$ is a variable 4-vector representing the variables x, y, z_1, z_2. The objective function is

$$(x - z_1) + (y - z_2) .$$

The constraints are equivalent to the $\Sigma_{\mathbb{Q}}$-formula

$$x \geq 0 \ \wedge \ y \geq 0 \ \wedge \ z_1 \geq 0 \ \wedge \ z_2 \geq 0$$
$$\wedge \ x + y \leq 3 \ \wedge \ x - z_1 \leq 2 \ \wedge \ y - z_2 \leq 2 .$$

One vertex of the constraints is $\bar{v} = \begin{bmatrix} 2 & 1 & 0 & 0 \end{bmatrix}^{\mathsf{T}}$. Why is it a vertex? Consider the submatrix A_0 of A consisting of rows 3, 4, 5, and 6; and the subvector $\bar{b}_0$ of $\bar{b}$ consisting of the same rows. A_0 is invertible. Additionally, $A_0\bar{v} = \bar{b}_0$:

$$\underbrace{\begin{bmatrix} 0 & 0 & -1 & 0 \\ 0 & 0 & 0 & -1 \\ 1 & 1 & 0 & 0 \\ 1 & 0 & -1 & 0 \end{bmatrix}}_{A_0} \underbrace{\begin{bmatrix} 2 \\ 1 \\ 0 \\ 0 \end{bmatrix}}_{\bar{v}} = \underbrace{\begin{bmatrix} 0 \\ 0 \\ 3 \\ 2 \end{bmatrix}}_{\bar{b}_0} .$$

Rows 3-6 are **equationally satisfied** in this case. Constraints 3, 4, 5, and 6 comprise the defining constraints of $\bar{v}$.

Another vertex is simply $\begin{bmatrix} 0 & 0 & 0 & 0 \end{bmatrix}^{\mathsf{T}}$, for which the first four constraints are the defining constraints. ∎

The following theorem is fundamental for solving linear programs. It asserts that the maximum value achieved by the objective function $\bar{c}^{\mathsf{T}}\bar{x}$ over $\bar{x}$ satisfying $A\bar{x} \leq \bar{b}$ is equal to the minimum value achieved over the **dual optimization problem**.

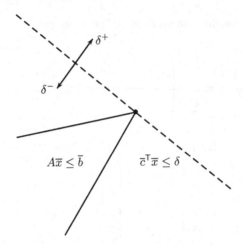

Fig. 8.1. Choosing δ

Theorem 8.6 (Duality Theorem of Linear Programming). *Consider* $A \in \mathbb{Z}^{m \times n}$, $\bar{b} \in \mathbb{Z}^m$, *and* $\bar{c} \in \mathbb{Z}^n$. *Then*

$$\max\{\bar{c}^\mathsf{T}\bar{x} \; : \; A\bar{x} \leq \bar{b}\} = \min\{\bar{y}^\mathsf{T}\bar{b} \; : \; \bar{y} \geq \bar{0} \; \wedge \; \bar{y}^\mathsf{T}A = \bar{c}^\mathsf{T}\}$$

if $A\bar{x} \leq \bar{b}$ *is satisfiable.*

By convention, when $A\bar{x} \leq \bar{b}$ is unsatisfiable, the maximum of the primal problem is $-\infty$, and the minimum of the dual form is ∞.

The left and right optimization problems of the theorem are the **primal** and **dual** forms of the same problem. The theorem states that maximizing the function $\bar{c}^\mathsf{T}\bar{x}$ over $A\bar{x} \leq \bar{b}$ is equivalent to minimizing the function $\bar{y}^\mathsf{T}\bar{b}$ over all nonnegative $\bar{y}$ such that $\bar{y}^\mathsf{T}A = \bar{c}^\mathsf{T}$.

The theorem is actually surprisingly easy to visualize. In Figure 8.1, the region labeled $A\bar{x} \leq \bar{b}$ satisfies the inequality. The objective function $\bar{c}^\mathsf{T}\bar{x}$ is represented by the dashed line. Its value increases in the direction of the arrow labeled δ^+ and decreases in the direction of the arrow labeled δ^-. Now, rather than asking for the maximum value of $\bar{c}^\mathsf{T}\bar{x}$ over $\bar{x}$ satisfying $A\bar{x} \leq \bar{b}$, let us instead seek the minimal value δ such that

$$A\bar{x} \leq \bar{b} \; \Rightarrow \; \bar{c}^\mathsf{T}\bar{x} \leq \delta \; .$$

In words, we seek the minimal δ such that $A\bar{x} \leq \bar{b}$ implies $\bar{c}^\mathsf{T}\bar{x} \leq \delta$ or — visually — the region defined by $\bar{c}^\mathsf{T}\bar{x} \leq \delta$ just covers the region defined by $A\bar{x} \leq \bar{b}$. Moving the dashed line of Figure 8.1 in the directions given by the arrows, we see that the best δ makes the dashed line just touch the $A\bar{x} \leq \bar{b}$ region (and at that "touched" point, $\bar{c}^\mathsf{T}\bar{x}$ achieves its maximum, which is δ). Decreasing δ (δ^- direction) causes the implication to fail; increasing δ (δ^+ direction) causes the region defined by $\bar{c}^\mathsf{T}\bar{x} \leq \delta$ to be unnecessarily large.

Therefore, we seek the right δ. Now consider multiplying the rows of $A\overline{x} \leq \overline{b}$ by nonnegative rationals and then summing the multiplied rows together. The resulting inequality is satisfied by any $\overline{x}$ satisfying $A\overline{x} \leq \overline{b}$; in other words, it is implied by $A\overline{x} \leq \overline{b}$. Mathematically, consider any nonnegative vector $\overline{y} \geq \overline{0}$; then

$$A\overline{x} \leq \overline{b} \;\Rightarrow\; \overline{y}^\mathsf{T} A\overline{x} \leq \overline{y}^\mathsf{T}\overline{b} \;.$$

Hence, to prove

$$A\overline{x} \leq \overline{b} \;\Rightarrow\; \overline{c}^\mathsf{T}\overline{x} \leq \delta$$

for a fixed δ, find $\overline{y} \geq \overline{0}$ such that

$$\overline{y}^\mathsf{T} A = \overline{c}^\mathsf{T} \quad\text{and}\quad \overline{y}^\mathsf{T}\overline{b} = \delta \;.$$

That is,

$$A\overline{x} \leq \overline{b} \;\Rightarrow\; \underbrace{\overline{c}^\mathsf{T}}_{\overline{y}^\mathsf{T} A}\,\overline{x} \leq \underbrace{\delta}_{\overline{y}^\mathsf{T}\overline{b}} \;.$$

But we want to find a minimal δ such that the implication holds, not just prove it for a fixed δ. Thus, choose $\overline{y} \geq \overline{0}$ such that $\overline{y}^\mathsf{T} A = \overline{c}^\mathsf{T}$ and that minimizes $\overline{y}^\mathsf{T}\overline{b}$. This equivalence between maximizing $\overline{c}^\mathsf{T}\overline{x}$ and minimizing $\overline{y}^\mathsf{T}\overline{b}$ is the one claimed by Theorem 8.6.

We refer the reader in **Bibliographic Remarks** to texts that contain the proof of this theorem.

$T_\mathbb{Q}$-Satisfiability

Consider a generic $\Sigma_\mathbb{Q}$-formula

$$F: \quad \bigwedge_{i=1}^{m} a_{i1}x_1 + \cdots + a_{in}x_n \leq b_i$$

$$\wedge \bigwedge_{i=1}^{\ell} \alpha_{i1}x_1 + \cdots + \alpha_{in}x_n < \beta_i$$

with both weak and strict inequalities. Equalities can be written as two inequalities. F is $T_\mathbb{Q}$-equivalent to the $\Sigma_\mathbb{Q}$-formula

$$F': \quad \bigwedge_{i=1}^{m} a_{i1}x_1 + \cdots + a_{in}x_n \leq b_i$$

$$\wedge \bigwedge_{i=1}^{\ell} \alpha_{i1}x_1 + \cdots + \alpha_{in}x_n + x_{n+1} \leq \beta_i$$

$$\wedge\; x_{n+1} > 0$$

with only weak inequalities except for $x_{n+1} > 0$. To decide the $T_{\mathbb{Q}}$-satisfiability of F', and thus of F, pose and solve the following linear program:

$$\textbf{max } x_{n+1}$$
$$\textbf{subject to}$$
$$\bigwedge_{i=1}^{m} a_{i1}x_1 + \cdots + a_{in}x_n \leq b_i$$
$$\bigwedge_{i=1}^{\ell} \alpha_{i1}x_1 + \cdots + \alpha_{in}x_n + x_{n+1} \leq \beta_i$$

F' is $T_{\mathbb{Q}}$-satisfiable iff the optimum is positive.

When F does not contain any strict inequality literals, the optimization problem is just a satisfiability problem because x_{n+1} is not introduced. This situation corresponds to a linear program with a constant objective value:

$$\textbf{max } 1$$
$$\textbf{subject to}$$
$$\bigwedge_{i=1}^{m} a_{i1}x_1 + \cdots + a_{in}x_n \leq b_i$$

According to convention, the optimum is $-\infty$ iff the constraints are $T_{\mathbb{Q}}$-unsatisfiable and 1 otherwise. This form of linear program is sometimes called a **linear feasibility problem**.

8.4 The Simplex Method

Consider the generic linear program

$$M : \textbf{max } \bar{c}^{\mathsf{T}}\bar{x}$$
$$\textbf{subject to}$$
$$G : \ A\bar{x} \leq \bar{b}$$

The **simplex method** solves the linear program in two main steps. In the first step, it obtains an initial vertex $\bar{v}_1$ of $A\bar{x} \leq \bar{b}$. In the second step, it iteratively traverses the vertices of $A\bar{x} \leq \bar{b}$, beginning at $\bar{v}_1$, in search of the vertex that maximizes the objective function. On each iteration of the second step, it determines if the current vertex $\bar{v}_i$ has a greater objective value than the vertices adjacent to $\bar{v}_i$. If not, it moves to one of the adjacent vertices with a greater objective value. If so, it halts and reports $\bar{v}_i$ as the optimum point with value $\bar{c}^{\mathsf{T}}\bar{v}_i$.

$\bar{v}_i$ is a **local optimum** since its adjacent vertices have lesser objective values. But because the space defined by $A\bar{x} \leq \bar{b}$ is convex, $\bar{v}_i$ is also the **global optimum**: it is the highest value attained by any point that satisfies the constraints.

How does the simplex method find the initial vertex $\overline{v}_1$? In the first step, it constructs a new linear program

$$M_0: \ \mathbf{max} \ \overline{c}'^{\mathsf{T}}\overline{x}$$
$$\mathbf{subject \ to}$$
$$G_0: \ A'\overline{x} \leq \overline{b}'$$

based only on $G: A\overline{x} \leq \overline{b}$ and for which, by construction, it has an initial vertex $\overline{v}'_1$. Moreover, by construction, M_0 achieves a certain optimal value v_G iff G is satisfiable; and if this optimal value is achieved, the point that achieves it is a vertex $\overline{v}_1$ of G. M_0 is solved by running the second step of the simplex method on M_0 itself, initialized with the known vertex $\overline{v}'_1$.

If the objective function of M is constant, then solving M_0 is the main step of the algorithm. G is satisfiable iff the optimum of M_0 is v_G. The second step is not applied to M in this case.

We now discuss the details of the simplex method.

8.4.1 From M to M_0

To find the initial vertex of M, the simplex method constructs and solves a new linear program M_0. To that end, reformulate the constraints $G: A\overline{x} \leq \overline{b}$ of M so that they have the form

$$\overline{x} \geq 0, \ A\overline{x} \leq \overline{b}$$

for new matrix A and vectors $\overline{x}$ and $\overline{b}$. A general technique is to introduce two nonnegative variables x_1, x_2 for each variable x and then to replace each instance of x with $x_1 - x_2$. Then we obtain a constraint system of the desired form that is $T_{\mathbb{Q}}$-equisatisfiable to G.

Next, separate the new constraints $A\overline{x} \leq \overline{b}$ into two sets of inequalities

$$D_1\overline{x} \leq \overline{g}_1 \quad \text{and} \quad D_2\overline{x} \geq \overline{g}_2 \quad \text{for } \overline{g}_1 \geq \overline{0}, \overline{g}_2 > \overline{0}$$

according to the signs of the b_i. That is, if b_i is nonnegative, make row i of $A\overline{x} \leq \overline{b}$ a part of $D_1\overline{x} \leq \overline{g}_1$; otherwise, multiply row i of $A\overline{x} \leq \overline{b}$ by -1 and make the result a part of $D_2\overline{x} \geq \overline{g}_2$.

Pose the following optimization problem:

$$M_0: \ \mathbf{max} \ \overline{1}^{\mathsf{T}}(D_2\overline{x} - \overline{z}) \tag{8.1}$$
$$\mathbf{subject \ to}$$
$$\overline{x}, \overline{z} \geq \overline{0} \qquad (1)$$
$$D_1\overline{x} \leq \overline{g}_1 \qquad (2)$$
$$D_2\overline{x} - \overline{z} \leq \overline{g}_2 \qquad (3)$$

The variable vector $\overline{z}$ has as many rows as D_2. The objective function is the sum of the components of the vector $D_2\overline{x} - \overline{z}$.

M_0 has several interesting characteristics:

1. The point $\bar{x} = \bar{0}$, $\bar{z} = \bar{0}$ satisfies constraints (1)-(3). It is a vertex.
   - It satisfies constraints (2) and (3), for

$$D_1\bar{0} = \bar{0} \leq \bar{g}_1 \quad \text{and} \quad D_2\bar{0} - \bar{0} = \bar{0} \leq \bar{g}_2 .$$

   The inequalities hold since $\bar{g}_1 \geq \bar{0}$ and $\bar{g}_2 > \bar{0}$ according to our construction of $\bar{g}_1$ and $\bar{g}_2$.
   - It satisfies constraints (1). Indeed, constraints (1) are its defining constraints.

2. The optimum equals $v_G = \bar{1}^{\mathsf{T}}\bar{g}_2$ iff G is $T_{\mathbb{Q}}$-satisfiable.
   - If the optimal value is $\bar{1}^{\mathsf{T}}\bar{g}_2$ at optimal point $\bar{x}^*$, $\bar{z}^*$, then $\bar{x}^*$ satisfies G. For

$$D_1\bar{x}^* \leq \bar{g}_1$$

   by (2); and

$$D_2\bar{x}^* - \bar{z}^* = \bar{g}_2$$

   by constraint (3) of M_0 and that the optimal value is $\bar{1}^{\mathsf{T}}\bar{g}_2$, so

$$D_2\bar{x}^* = \bar{g}_2 + \bar{z}^* \geq \bar{g}_2$$

   by (1). By construction of D_1, D_2, $\bar{g}_1$, and $\bar{g}_2$, we thus know that $A\bar{x}^* \leq \bar{b}$, so G is satisfiable.
   - If $\bar{x}^*$ satisfies G, then the optimal value is at least $\bar{1}^{\mathsf{T}}\bar{g}_2$. We have

$$D_1\bar{x}^* \leq \bar{g}_1 , \quad D_2\bar{x}^* \geq \bar{g}_2 , \quad \text{and} \quad \bar{x}^* \geq \bar{0} .$$

   Choose $\bar{z}^* = D_2\bar{x}^* - \bar{g}_2$. Then $\bar{z}^* \geq \bar{0}$ and $D_2\bar{x}^* - \bar{z}^* = \bar{g}_2$, so that all constraints of M_0 are satisfied. Additionally, $\bar{1}^{\mathsf{T}}(D_2\bar{x}^* - \bar{z}^*) = \bar{1}^{\mathsf{T}}\bar{g}_2$, so that the maximum of M_0 is at least $\bar{1}^{\mathsf{T}}\bar{g}_2$. Constraint (3) limits the maximum to $\bar{1}^{\mathsf{T}}\bar{g}_2$.

Because the optimum equals $\bar{1}^{\mathsf{T}}\bar{g}_2$ iff G is $T_{\mathbb{Q}}$-satisfiable, we need only solve the optimization problem M_0 to determine the satisfiability of G and to find a vertex of G if it is satisfiable. We already have a satisfying vertex $\bar{x} = \bar{0}$, $\bar{z} = \bar{0}$ of M_0 by characteristic 1.

Example 8.7. Consider the $\Sigma_{\mathbb{Q}}$-formula

$$F : \ x + y \geq 1 \ \wedge \ x - y \geq -1 .$$

Because F has only weak inequality literals, the corresponding linear program has a constant objective function:

$$M : \ \textbf{max} \ 1$$
$$\textbf{subject to}$$
$$\left. \begin{array}{l} x + y \geq 1 \\ x - y \geq -1 \end{array} \right\} G$$

Solving the corresponding linear program M_0 is sufficient to determine the $T_{\mathbb{Q}}$-satisfiability of F.

To convert F to the form $\bar{x} \geq \bar{0} \ \wedge \ A\bar{x} \leq \bar{b}$, introduce nonnegative x_1, x_2 for x and y_1, y_2 for y:

$$F' : \ (x_1 - x_2) + (y_1 - y_2) \geq 1 \ \wedge \ (x_1 - x_2) - (y_1 - y_2) \geq -1$$
$$\wedge \ x_1, x_2, y_1, y_2 \geq 0$$

F is $T_{\mathbb{Q}}$-equisatisfiable to F'. In matrix form, the first two literals of F' are

$$\underbrace{\begin{bmatrix} -1 & 1 & -1 & 1 \\ -1 & 1 & 1 & -1 \end{bmatrix}}_{A} \begin{bmatrix} x_1 \\ x_2 \\ y_1 \\ y_2 \end{bmatrix} \leq \underbrace{\begin{bmatrix} -1 \\ 1 \end{bmatrix}}_{\bar{b}}$$

Since $b_1 < 0$ and $b_2 > 0$, separating constraints yields

$$\underbrace{\begin{bmatrix} -1 & 1 & 1 & -1 \end{bmatrix}}_{D_1} \begin{bmatrix} x_1 \\ x_2 \\ y_1 \\ y_2 \end{bmatrix} \leq \underbrace{[1]}_{\bar{g}_1} \quad \text{and} \quad \underbrace{\begin{bmatrix} 1 & -1 & 1 & -1 \end{bmatrix}}_{D_2} \begin{bmatrix} x_1 \\ x_2 \\ y_1 \\ y_2 \end{bmatrix} \geq \underbrace{[1]}_{\bar{g}_2} .$$

D_2 has only one row, so $\bar{z} = [z]$. According to (8.1), pose the following optimization problem:

$$\mathbf{max} \ \begin{bmatrix} 1 & -1 & 1 & -1 \end{bmatrix} \begin{bmatrix} x_1 \\ x_2 \\ y_1 \\ y_2 \end{bmatrix} - [z]$$

subject to
$$x_1, x_2, y_1, y_2, z \geq 0$$
$$\begin{bmatrix} -1 & 1 & 1 & -1 \end{bmatrix} \begin{bmatrix} x_1 \\ x_2 \\ y_1 \\ y_2 \end{bmatrix} \leq [1]$$
$$\begin{bmatrix} 1 & -1 & 1 & -1 \end{bmatrix} \begin{bmatrix} x_1 \\ x_2 \\ y_1 \\ y_2 \end{bmatrix} - [z] \leq [1]$$

F is $T_{\mathbb{Q}}$-satisfiable iff the optimum is $v_G = \bar{1}^{\mathsf{T}} \bar{g}_2 = 1$.

We know that the point $\begin{bmatrix} x_1 & x_2 & y_1 & y_2 & z \end{bmatrix}^{\mathsf{T}} = \begin{bmatrix} 0 & 0 & 0 & 0 & 0 \end{bmatrix}^{\mathsf{T}}$ is a vertex. It satisfies all constraints and has defining constraints $x_1, x_2, y_1, y_2, z \geq 0$. ∎

The simplex method requires M_0 to be in standard form

$$\text{max } \bar{c}^T \bar{y}$$
$$\text{subject to}$$
$$A\bar{y} \leq \bar{b}$$

Let

$$\bar{y} = \begin{bmatrix} \bar{x} \\ \bar{z} \end{bmatrix} .$$

Since the objective function of M_0 is

$$\bar{1}^T (D_2 \bar{x} - \bar{z}) = \bar{1}^T \begin{bmatrix} D_2 & -I \end{bmatrix} \underbrace{\begin{bmatrix} \bar{x} \\ \bar{z} \end{bmatrix}}_{\bar{y}} ,$$

construct vector $\bar{c}$ as follows:

$$\bar{c}^T = \bar{1}^T \begin{bmatrix} D_2 & -I \end{bmatrix} .$$

The constraints have the form

$$\begin{bmatrix} -I & \\ & -I \\ D_1 & \\ D_2 & -I \end{bmatrix} \underbrace{\begin{bmatrix} \bar{x} \\ \bar{z} \end{bmatrix}}_{\bar{y}} \leq \begin{bmatrix} \bar{0} \\ \bar{0} \\ \bar{g}_1 \\ \bar{g}_2 \end{bmatrix} ,$$

where blank regions of the matrix are filled with 0s. Hence, M_0 of (8.1) in standard form is written

$$M_0 : \text{max } \underbrace{\bar{1}^T \begin{bmatrix} D_2 & -I \end{bmatrix}}_{\bar{c}^T} \underbrace{\begin{bmatrix} \bar{x} \\ \bar{z} \end{bmatrix}}_{\bar{y}} \qquad (8.2)$$

$$\text{subject to}$$

$$\underbrace{\begin{bmatrix} -I & \\ & -I \\ D_1 & \\ D_2 & -I \end{bmatrix}}_{A} \underbrace{\begin{bmatrix} \bar{x} \\ \bar{z} \end{bmatrix}}_{\bar{y}} \leq \underbrace{\begin{bmatrix} \bar{0} \\ \bar{0} \\ \bar{g}_1 \\ \bar{g}_2 \end{bmatrix}}_{\bar{b}}$$

Example 8.8. According to (8.2), rewrite the optimization problem of Example 8.7 as follows:

$$\max \underbrace{\begin{bmatrix} 1 & -1 & 1 & -1 & -1 \end{bmatrix}}_{\bar{c}^{\mathsf{T}}} \begin{bmatrix} x_1 \\ x_2 \\ y_1 \\ y_2 \\ z \end{bmatrix}$$

subject to

$$\underbrace{\begin{bmatrix} -1 & 0 & 0 & 0 & 0 \\ 0 & -1 & 0 & 0 & 0 \\ 0 & 0 & -1 & 0 & 0 \\ 0 & 0 & 0 & -1 & 0 \\ 0 & 0 & 0 & 0 & -1 \\ -1 & 1 & 1 & -1 & 0 \\ 1 & -1 & 1 & -1 & -1 \end{bmatrix}}_{A} \begin{bmatrix} x_1 \\ x_2 \\ y_1 \\ y_2 \\ z \end{bmatrix} \leq \underbrace{\begin{bmatrix} 0 \\ 0 \\ 0 \\ 0 \\ 0 \\ 1 \\ 1 \end{bmatrix}}_{\bar{b}}$$

∎

8.4.2 Vertex Traversal

Assume that we have a generic optimization problem

$$\max \quad \bar{c}^{\mathsf{T}} \bar{x} \tag{8.3}$$

subject to
$$A\bar{x} \leq \bar{b}$$

for which we have a satisfying vertex $\bar{v}_i$. The simplex method traverses vertices of $A\bar{x} \leq \bar{b}$ to find the vertex $\bar{v}^*$ that maximizes $\bar{c}^{\mathsf{T}}\bar{x}$. In particular, one iteration of this step seeks a vertex $\bar{v}_{i+1}$ adjacent to $\bar{v}_i$ such that $\bar{c}^{\mathsf{T}}\bar{v}_{i+1} > \bar{c}^{\mathsf{T}}\bar{v}_i$.

For the optimization problem M_0 of (8.2), the point $\bar{x} = \bar{0}$, $\bar{z} = \bar{0}$, which satisfies the constraints of M_0, is the initial vertex $\bar{v}_1$.

Example 8.9. The point $\bar{v}_1 = \begin{bmatrix} x_1 & x_2 & y_1 & y_2 & z \end{bmatrix}^{\mathsf{T}} = \begin{bmatrix} 0 & 0 & 0 & 0 & 0 \end{bmatrix}^{\mathsf{T}}$ is a vertex of the constraints of the optimization problem of Example 8.8. ∎

Construction of $\bar{u}$

To begin the ith iteration, we use the vertex $\bar{v}_i$ to construct a vector $\bar{u}$ such that $\bar{u}^{\mathsf{T}}A = \bar{c}^{\mathsf{T}}$. If $\bar{u} \geq \bar{0}$ then the Duality Theorem (Theorem 8.6) implies that $\bar{v}_i$ is optimal, as we discuss below, and the process terminates. However, in all but the final iteration, $\bar{u} \ngeq \bar{0}$: at least one row of $\bar{u}$ is negative.

To construct $\bar{u}$, choose one of its sets of defining constraints: choose a $n \times n$ nonsingular submatrix A_i of A with corresponding rows $\bar{b}_i$ such that

$$A_i \bar{v}_i = \bar{b}_i . \tag{8.4}$$

Let R be the indices of the rows of A in A_i. Such a subset of constraints exists because $\bar{v}_i$ is a vertex.

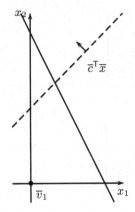

Fig. 8.2. Illustration of Example 8.10

Second, solve $\bar{u}^{\mathsf{T}} A = \bar{c}^{\mathsf{T}}$ for $\bar{u}$: solve

$$A_i{}^{\mathsf{T}} \bar{u}_i = \bar{c} \tag{8.5}$$

for $\bar{u}_i$ (which has a solution because A_i is nonsingular), and let $\bar{u}$ be $\bar{u}_i$ for indices in R with 0s added for rows with indices not in R. Thus,

$$\bar{u}^{\mathsf{T}} A = \bar{c}^{\mathsf{T}} . \tag{8.6}$$

Example 8.10. Consider the optimization problem of the form (8.3)

$$\textbf{max } \underbrace{[-1\ 1]}_{\bar{c}^{\mathsf{T}}} \bar{x}$$

subject to

$$\underbrace{\begin{bmatrix} -1 & 0 \\ 0 & -1 \\ 2 & 1 \end{bmatrix}}_{A} \bar{x} \le \underbrace{\begin{bmatrix} 0 \\ 0 \\ 2 \end{bmatrix}}_{\bar{b}}$$

for which we know that $\bar{v}_1 = \begin{bmatrix} 0 & 0 \end{bmatrix}^{\mathsf{T}}$ is a vertex.

The problem and initial vertex is visualized in Figure 8.2. The solid lines represent the constraints of the problem, and the set of satisfying points corresponds to the interior of the triangle. The dashed line indicates $\bar{c}^{\mathsf{T}}\bar{x}$; the arrow points in the direction of increasing value.

Given vertex $\bar{v}_1 = \begin{bmatrix} 0 & 0 \end{bmatrix}^{\mathsf{T}}$, the first two constraints are the defining constraints of $\bar{v}_1$, so choose $R = [1; 2]$:

$$A_1 = \begin{bmatrix} -1 & 0 \\ 0 & -1 \end{bmatrix} \quad \text{and} \quad \bar{b}_1 = \begin{bmatrix} 0 \\ 0 \end{bmatrix} .$$

From (8.5), solving

$$\underbrace{\begin{bmatrix} -1 & 0 \\ 0 & -1 \end{bmatrix}}_{A_1{}^{\mathsf{T}}} \bar{u}_1 = \underbrace{\begin{bmatrix} -1 \\ 1 \end{bmatrix}}_{\bar{c}}$$

for $\bar{u}_1$ (via, for example, Gaussian elimination; or by observing that $A_1{}^{\mathsf{T}} = -I$ and that $-I\bar{u}_1 = \bar{c}$ implies that $\bar{u}_1 = -\bar{c}$) yields $\bar{u}_1 = \begin{bmatrix} 1 & -1 \end{bmatrix}^{\mathsf{T}}$. Adding 0s for rows not in R produces

$$\bar{u} = \begin{bmatrix} 1 & -1 & 0 \end{bmatrix}^{\mathsf{T}},$$

where the first two elements are from $\bar{u}_1$. Check that this $\bar{u}$ satisfies $\bar{u}^{\mathsf{T}} A = \bar{c}^{\mathsf{T}}$ of (8.6) as desired. ∎

Example 8.11. Continuing from Examples 8.8 and 8.9, choose the first five rows of A and $\bar{b}$ ($R = [1; 2; 3; 4; 5]$) since

$$\underbrace{\begin{bmatrix} -1 & 0 & 0 & 0 & 0 \\ 0 & -1 & 0 & 0 & 0 \\ 0 & 0 & -1 & 0 & 0 \\ 0 & 0 & 0 & -1 & 0 \\ 0 & 0 & 0 & 0 & -1 \end{bmatrix}}_{A_1} \underbrace{\begin{bmatrix} 0 \\ 0 \\ 0 \\ 0 \\ 0 \end{bmatrix}}_{\bar{v}_1} = \underbrace{\begin{bmatrix} 0 \\ 0 \\ 0 \\ 0 \\ 0 \end{bmatrix}}_{\bar{b}_1}$$

as desired from (8.4). From (8.5), solving

$$\underbrace{\begin{bmatrix} -1 & 0 & 0 & 0 & 0 \\ 0 & -1 & 0 & 0 & 0 \\ 0 & 0 & -1 & 0 & 0 \\ 0 & 0 & 0 & -1 & 0 \\ 0 & 0 & 0 & 0 & -1 \end{bmatrix}}_{A_1{}^{\mathsf{T}}} \bar{u}_1 = \underbrace{\begin{bmatrix} 1 \\ -1 \\ 1 \\ -1 \\ -1 \end{bmatrix}}_{\bar{c}}$$

yields

$$\bar{u}_1{}^{\mathsf{T}} = \begin{bmatrix} -1 & 1 & -1 & 1 & 1 \end{bmatrix}.$$

Then

$$\bar{u} = \begin{bmatrix} -1 & 1 & -1 & 1 & 1 & 0 & 0 \end{bmatrix}^{\mathsf{T}},$$

where the first five elements are from $\bar{u}_1$. Check that this $\bar{u}$ satisfies $\bar{u}^{\mathsf{T}} A = \bar{c}^{\mathsf{T}}$ of (8.6) as desired. ∎

There are two cases to consider: either $\bar{u} \geq \bar{0}$ or $\bar{u} \not\geq \bar{0}$.

Case 1: $\bar{u} \geq \bar{0}$

We prove that in this case, $\bar{v}_i$ is actually the optimal point with optimal value $\bar{c}^\mathsf{T} \bar{v}_i$. The crux of the argument is the Duality Theorem (Theorem 8.6).

From equation (8.6), we have

$$\bar{c}^\mathsf{T} \bar{v}_i = \bar{u}^\mathsf{T} A \bar{v}_i .$$

We claim next that

$$\bar{u}^\mathsf{T} A \bar{v}_i = \bar{u}^\mathsf{T} \bar{b} . \tag{8.7}$$

First, from (8.4)

$$A_i \bar{v}_i = \bar{b}_i \quad \text{implies} \quad \bar{u}_i{}^\mathsf{T} A_i \bar{v}_i = \bar{u}_i{}^\mathsf{T} \bar{b}_i$$

so that equation (8.7) holds at rows R. For rows $j \notin R$, we know that $u_j = 0$ by construction, so that both

$$(\bar{u}^\mathsf{T} A \bar{v}_i)_j = 0 \quad \text{and} \quad (\bar{u}^\mathsf{T} \bar{b})_j = 0 ,$$

proving equation (8.7). Reasoning further,

$$\bar{u}^\mathsf{T} \bar{b} \geq \min\{\bar{y}^\mathsf{T} \bar{b} \ : \ \bar{y} \geq \bar{0} \ \wedge \ \bar{y}^\mathsf{T} A = \bar{c}^\mathsf{T}\}$$

since $\bar{u}$ is a member of the set by (8.6) and the case $\bar{u} \geq \bar{0}$. By duality (Theorem 8.6),

$$\min\{\bar{y}^\mathsf{T} \bar{b} \ : \ \bar{y} \geq \bar{0} \ \wedge \ \bar{y}^\mathsf{T} A = \bar{c}^\mathsf{T}\} = \max\{\bar{c}^\mathsf{T} \bar{x} \ : \ A\bar{x} \leq \bar{b}\} .$$

In summary, we have by (8.6), (8.7), and Theorem 8.6,

$$\bar{c}^\mathsf{T} \bar{v}_i = \bar{u}^\mathsf{T} A \bar{v}_i = \bar{u}^\mathsf{T} \bar{b} \geq$$
$$\min\{\bar{y}^\mathsf{T} \bar{b} \ : \ \bar{y} \geq \bar{0} \ \wedge \ \bar{y}^\mathsf{T} A = \bar{c}^\mathsf{T}\} = \max\{\bar{c}^\mathsf{T} \bar{x} \ : \ A\bar{x} \leq \bar{b}\} ,$$

which proves that $\bar{v}_i$ is actually the optimal point with optimal value $\bar{c}^\mathsf{T} \bar{v}_i$.

Figure 8.3 illustrates this case: the vertex $\bar{v}_i$ maximizes $\bar{c}^\mathsf{T} \bar{x}$. The dashed line illustrates the objective function $\bar{c}^\mathsf{T} \bar{x}$. Moving upward relative to it increases its value. In this illustration, $\bar{c}^\mathsf{T} \bar{x}$ cannot be increased without leaving the region defined by the constraints.

Case 2: $\bar{u} \not\geq \bar{0}$

In this case, $\bar{v}_i$ is not the optimal point. Thus, we need to move along an edge $\bar{y}$ to an adjacent vertex to increase the value of the objective function. In moving to an adjacent vertex, we swap one of the defining constraints of $\bar{v}_i$ for another constraint to form the defining constraints of $\bar{v}_{i+1}$.

In this second case, there exists some $u_k < 0$. Let k be the lowest index of $\bar{u}$ such that $u_k < 0$ (it must be one of the indices of R since for all other indices ℓ, $u_\ell = 0$). Let k' be the index of the row of $\bar{u}_i$ and A_i corresponding to row k of $\bar{u}$ and A_i.

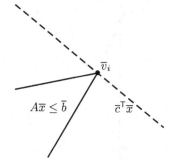

Fig. 8.3. Case 1

Construction of $\overline{y}$

Having fixed the indices k (row k of A and $\overline{b}$) and k' (the corresponding row k' of A_i and $\overline{b}_i$) of the offending constraint, we seek a direction along which to travel away from vertex $\overline{v}_i$ and, in particular, away from the plane that defines the kth constraint.

Define $\overline{y}$ to be the k'th column of $-A_i^{-1}$. To find $\overline{y}$, solve

$$A_i\overline{y} = -\mathsf{e}_{k'} \tag{8.8}$$

(where, recall, $\mathsf{e}_{k'}$ is the k'th unit vector, which consists of 0s except in position k') for $\overline{y}$. Thus,

$$\overline{a}_\ell\overline{y} = 0 \quad \text{for every row } \overline{a}_\ell \text{ of } A_i \text{ except the } k'\text{th row}$$

and

$$\overline{a}_{k'}\overline{y} = -1 \quad \text{for the } k'\text{th row } \overline{a}_{k'} \text{ of } A_i \ .$$

The vector $\overline{y}$ provides the direction along which to move to the next vertex. For all rows $\overline{a}_\ell$ but the k'th row of A_i, $\overline{a}_\ell\overline{y} = 0$ implies that moving in direction $\overline{y}$ stays on the boundary of the constraints (*i.e.*, both $\overline{a}_\ell\overline{v}_i = \overline{b}$ and, in the next step, $\overline{a}_\ell\overline{v}_{i+1} = \overline{b}$), so $\overline{a}_\ell$ will be a row in A_{i+1}. However, moving along $\overline{y}$ moves inward from the boundary of the k'th constraint because $\overline{a}_{k'}\overline{y} = -1$. This change is desirable, as this constraint is keeping $\overline{u}$ from being nonnegative.

Example 8.12. Let us examine

$$\overline{u}_1 = \begin{bmatrix} 1 & -1 \end{bmatrix}^\mathsf{T} \quad \text{and} \quad \overline{u} = \begin{bmatrix} 1 & -1 & 0 \end{bmatrix}^\mathsf{T}$$

of Example 8.10. Since the second row of $\overline{u}$ is -1, we are in Case 2 with $k = 2$, corresponding to row $k' = 2$ of $\overline{u}_1$. Let $\overline{y}$ be the second column of $-A_1^{-1}$: solve

$$\underbrace{\begin{bmatrix} -1 & 0 \\ 0 & -1 \end{bmatrix}}_{A_1} \overline{y} = \underbrace{\begin{bmatrix} 0 \\ -1 \end{bmatrix}}_{-\mathsf{e}_2}$$

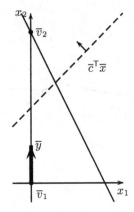

Fig. 8.4. Illustration of Example 8.12

for $\bar{y}$, yielding $\bar{y} = \begin{bmatrix} 0 & 1 \end{bmatrix}^{\mathsf{T}}$.

This $\bar{y}$ is visualized in Figure 8.4 by the dark solid arrow that points up from $\bar{v}_1$. The vertical and horizontal lines are the defining constraints of $\bar{v}_1$; in moving in the direction $\bar{y}$, we keep the vertical constraint for the next vertex $\bar{v}_2$ but drop the horizontal constraint. The diagonal constraint will become the second of $\bar{v}_2$'s defining constraints. ∎

Example 8.13. Let us examine

$$\bar{u}_1 = \begin{bmatrix} -1 & 1 & -1 & 1 & 1 \end{bmatrix}^{\mathsf{T}} \quad \text{and} \quad \bar{u} = \begin{bmatrix} -1 & 1 & -1 & 1 & 1 & 0 & 0 \end{bmatrix}^{\mathsf{T}}$$

of Example 8.11. Since the first row of $\bar{u}$ is -1, $k = 1$, corresponding to row $k' = 1$ of $\bar{u}_1$. Thus, solve

$$\underbrace{\begin{bmatrix} -1 & 0 & 0 & 0 & 0 \\ 0 & -1 & 0 & 0 & 0 \\ 0 & 0 & -1 & 0 & 0 \\ 0 & 0 & 0 & -1 & 0 \\ 0 & 0 & 0 & 0 & -1 \end{bmatrix}}_{A_1} \bar{y} = \underbrace{\begin{bmatrix} -1 \\ 0 \\ 0 \\ 0 \\ 0 \end{bmatrix}}_{-e_1}$$

for $\bar{y}$, yielding $\bar{y} = \begin{bmatrix} 1 & 0 & 0 & 0 & 0 \end{bmatrix}^{\mathsf{T}}$. ∎

Again we have two cases to consider: either the optimum is bounded (**Case 2(a)**) or it is unbounded (**Case 2(b)**).

Case 2(a): Optimum is Bounded

In this case, we move along the edge $\bar{y}$ to a better vertex $\bar{v}_{i+1}$, according to the objective function $\bar{c}^{\mathsf{T}}\bar{x}$. However, there is a set of rows of A with indices

S such that for $\ell \in S$, $\overline{a}_\ell \overline{y} > 0$. For these constraints, moving in the direction $\overline{y}$ actually moves toward leaving the satisfying region. These constraints limit how far in direction $\overline{y}$ we can move. For example, in Figure 8.4, the diagonal constraint limits how far we can move in direction $\overline{y}$.

Construction of λ_i, $\overline{v}_{i+1}$

We want to solve for the greatest $\lambda_i \geq 0$ such that

$$A(\overline{v}_i + \lambda_i \overline{y}) \leq \overline{b} \,. \tag{8.9}$$

Thus, choose $\lambda_i > 0$ such that for some row $\overline{a}_\ell$, $\ell \in S$,

$$\overline{a}_\ell(\overline{v}_i + \lambda_i \overline{y}) = b_\ell \tag{8.10}$$

and for all other rows $m \in S \setminus \{\ell\}$,

$$\overline{a}_m(\overline{v}_i + \lambda_i \overline{y}) \leq b_m \,. \tag{8.11}$$

Set

$$\overline{v}_{i+1} \stackrel{\text{def}}{=} \overline{v}_i + \lambda_i \overline{y} \,. \tag{8.12}$$

Finally, we construct the defining constraints of $\overline{v}_{i+1}$ for the next iteration. Construct submatrix A_{i+1} of A from A_i: replace row $\overline{a}_{k'}$ of A_i with row $\overline{a}_\ell$ of A. Choose the corresponding rows of $\overline{b}$ for $\overline{b}_{i+1}$. Row ℓ and the rows carried over from this iteration comprise the defining constraints of $\overline{v}_{i+1}$.

Example 8.14. Continuing from Example 8.12, choose λ_1 such that

$$A(\overline{v}_1 + \lambda_1 \overline{y}) \leq \overline{b} \,,$$

specifically

$$\begin{bmatrix} -1 & 0 \\ 0 & -1 \\ 2 & 1 \end{bmatrix} \left(\begin{bmatrix} 0 \\ 0 \end{bmatrix} + \lambda_1 \begin{bmatrix} 0 \\ 1 \end{bmatrix} \right) \leq \begin{bmatrix} 0 \\ 0 \\ 2 \end{bmatrix} \,,$$

and one constraint is equationally satisfied. Thus, choose $\lambda_1 = 2$.

Notice that the first and third constraints are equationally satisfied. The first row is already included in R; hence, focus on the third row ($\ell = 3$). From (8.12), define v_{i+1} for the next iteration:

$$\overline{v}_2 = \overline{v}_1 + \lambda_1 \overline{y} = \begin{bmatrix} 0 \\ 0 \end{bmatrix} + 2 \begin{bmatrix} 0 \\ 1 \end{bmatrix} = \begin{bmatrix} 0 \\ 2 \end{bmatrix} \,.$$

This vertex is visualized in Figure 8.4. Choosing $R = [1; 3]$ and replacing the second row of A_1 and $\overline{b}_1$ with the third row of $A\overline{x} \leq \overline{b}$ yields

$$A_2 = \begin{bmatrix} -1 & 0 \\ 2 & 1 \end{bmatrix} \quad \text{and} \quad \bar{b}_2 = \begin{bmatrix} 0 \\ 2 \end{bmatrix}.$$

In Figure 8.4, the rows of A_2 and $\bar{b}_2$ correspond to the vertical and diagonal constraints, respectively, which are the defining constraints of $\bar{v}_2$.

In the next iteration, solving $A_2{}^\mathsf{T}\bar{u}_2 = \bar{c}$ yields $\bar{u}_2 = \begin{bmatrix} 3 & 1 \end{bmatrix}^\mathsf{T}$. Adding 0s for rows not in R produces

$$\bar{u} = \begin{bmatrix} 3 & 0 & 1 \end{bmatrix}^\mathsf{T}.$$

Since $\bar{u} \geq \bar{0}$, we are in Case 1. The maximum is

$$\bar{c}^\mathsf{T}\bar{v}_2 = \begin{bmatrix} -1 & 1 \end{bmatrix} \begin{bmatrix} 0 \\ 2 \end{bmatrix} = 2$$

at vertex $\bar{v}_2$.   ∎

This move from vertex $\bar{v}_i$ to vertex $\bar{v}_{i+1}$ makes progress. For

$$\begin{aligned} \bar{c}^\mathsf{T}\bar{v}_{i+1} &= \bar{c}^\mathsf{T}(\bar{v}_i + \lambda_i\bar{y}) \\ &= \bar{c}^\mathsf{T}\bar{v}_i + \lambda_i\bar{c}^\mathsf{T}\bar{y} \\ &= \bar{c}^\mathsf{T}\bar{v}_i + \lambda_i(-u_k) \\ &> \bar{c}^\mathsf{T}\bar{v}_i. \end{aligned}$$

When considering line 3, recall from (8.5) of the construction of $\bar{u}$ that

$$\bar{u}_i{}^\mathsf{T} = \bar{c}^\mathsf{T}A_i^{-1}$$

and that the k'th column of A_i^{-1} is $-\bar{y}$ by (8.8). Hence, $\bar{c}^\mathsf{T}\bar{y} = -u_k$.

Moreover, since there are only a finite number of vertices to examine, **Case 1** (or, in the general case, possibly **Case 2(b)**) eventually occurs.

Figure 8.5(a) illustrates this case: vertex $\bar{v}_{i+1}$ is discovered by moving along ray $\bar{y}$ as far as possible without violating the constraints. Moreover $\bar{c}^\mathsf{T}\bar{v}_{i+1}$ is greater than $\bar{c}^\mathsf{T}\bar{v}_i$.

It is possible that $\lambda_i = 0$ when the vertex $\bar{v}_i$ has multiple sets of defining constraints. However, because there are only a finite number of constraints, the number of defining constraint sets is also finite. Preventing repetitions of the matrix A_i across iterations guarantees that the algorithm still halts in this case.

Case 2(b): Optimum is Unbounded

In this case, $A\bar{y} \leq \bar{0}$ and the optimum is unbounded. Since $A\bar{y} \leq \bar{0}$, for all $\lambda \geq 0$,

$$A(\bar{v}_i + \lambda\bar{y}) = \underbrace{A\bar{v}_i}_{\leq \bar{b}} + \lambda\underbrace{A\bar{y}}_{\leq \bar{0}} \leq \bar{b},$$

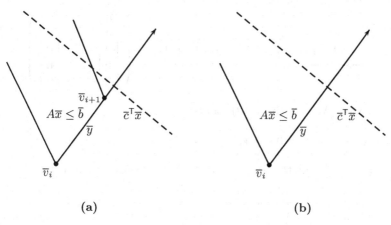

Fig. 8.5. Case 2

so all $\bar{v}_i + \lambda\bar{y}$ satisfy the constraints. In other words, moving in direction $\bar{y}$ either moves along the boundary of a constraint ($\bar{a}\bar{y} = 0$) or moves inward ($\bar{a}\bar{y} < 0$). Moreover,

$$\bar{c}^\mathsf{T}(\bar{v}_i + \lambda\bar{y}) = \bar{c}^\mathsf{T}\bar{v}_i + \lambda\bar{c}^\mathsf{T}\bar{y}$$
$$= \bar{c}^\mathsf{T}\bar{v}_i + \lambda\bar{u}^\mathsf{T}A\bar{y}$$
$$= \bar{c}^\mathsf{T}\bar{v}_i + -\lambda\underbrace{u_k}_{<0} ,$$

which grows with λ (recall $\bar{c}^\mathsf{T} = \bar{u}^\mathsf{T}A$, and $A\bar{y} = \begin{bmatrix} 0 \cdots 0 -1\,0 \cdots 0 \end{bmatrix}^\mathsf{T}$ by selection of $\bar{y}$). Thus, the maximum is unbounded. Figure 8.5(b) illustrates this case: all points along the ray labeled $\bar{y}$ satisfy the constraints, and moving along the ray increases $\bar{c}^\mathsf{T}\bar{x}$ without bound.

Example 8.15. Continuing with $\bar{y} = \begin{bmatrix} 1\,0\,0\,0\,0 \end{bmatrix}^\mathsf{T}$ from Example 8.13, compute $A\bar{y}$

$$\underbrace{\begin{bmatrix} -1 & 0 & 0 & 0 & 0 \\ 0 & -1 & 0 & 0 & 0 \\ 0 & 0 & -1 & 0 & 0 \\ 0 & 0 & 0 & -1 & 0 \\ 0 & 0 & 0 & 0 & -1 \\ -1 & 1 & 1 & -1 & 0 \\ 1 & -1 & 1 & -1 & -1 \end{bmatrix}}_{A} \underbrace{\begin{bmatrix} 1 \\ 0 \\ 0 \\ 0 \\ 0 \end{bmatrix}}_{\bar{y}} = \begin{bmatrix} -1 \\ 0 \\ 0 \\ 0 \\ 0 \\ -1 \\ 1 \end{bmatrix}$$

to find that $S = [7]$ since $\bar{a}_7\bar{y} = 1 > 0$. Thus, according to (8.10), examine the seventh row of the constraints and choose the greatest λ_1 such that

$$\underbrace{\begin{bmatrix} 1 & -1 & 1 & -1 & -1 \end{bmatrix}}_{\bar{a}_7}(\bar{v}_1 + \lambda_1 \bar{y}) = \begin{bmatrix} 1 & -1 & 1 & -1 & -1 \end{bmatrix}\left(\begin{bmatrix} 0 \\ 0 \\ 0 \\ 0 \\ 0 \end{bmatrix} + \lambda_1 \begin{bmatrix} 1 \\ 0 \\ 0 \\ 0 \\ 0 \end{bmatrix}\right) = 1 \; ;$$

that is, choose $\lambda_1 = 1$. By (8.12), define

$$\bar{v}_2 = \bar{v}_1 + \lambda_1 \bar{y} = \begin{bmatrix} 1 & 0 & 0 & 0 & 0 \end{bmatrix}^{\mathsf{T}} .$$

Form A_2 by replacing the first row ($k' = 1$) of A_1 with the seventh row ($\ell = 7$) of A:

$$A_2 = \begin{bmatrix} 1 & -1 & 1 & -1 & -1 \\ 0 & -1 & 0 & 0 & 0 \\ 0 & 0 & -1 & 0 & 0 \\ 0 & 0 & 0 & -1 & 0 \\ 0 & 0 & 0 & 0 & -1 \end{bmatrix} .$$

This move to vertex $\bar{v}_2$ makes progress:

$$\bar{c}^{\mathsf{T}}\bar{v}_1 = 0 < \bar{c}^{\mathsf{T}}\bar{v}_2 = 1 .$$

Now $R = [7; 2; 3; 4; 5]$; that is, A_2 is the submatrix of A constructed from rows 7, 2, 3, 4, and 5. Solve $A_2^{\mathsf{T}}\bar{u}_2 = \bar{c}$ for $\bar{u}_2$, yielding $\bar{u}_2 = \begin{bmatrix} 1 & 0 & 0 & 0 & 0 \end{bmatrix}^{\mathsf{T}}$. Since $\bar{u}_2 \geq 0$, we are in **Case 1**: we have found an optimum point $\bar{v}_2$ with optimal value 1.

Recall from Example 8.7 that $v_G = \bar{1}^{\mathsf{T}}\bar{g}_2 = 1$. The equality of the optimum and v_G implies that

$$F : \; x + y \geq 1 \; \wedge \; x - y \geq -1$$

is $T_{\mathbb{Q}}$-satisfiable. In particular, extract from

$$\begin{bmatrix} x_1 \\ x_2 \\ y_1 \\ y_2 \\ z \end{bmatrix} = \bar{v}_2 = \begin{bmatrix} 1 \\ 0 \\ 0 \\ 0 \\ 0 \end{bmatrix}$$

the assignment

$$x = x_1 - x_2 = 1 - 0 = 1 \quad \text{and} \quad y = y_1 - y_2 = 0 - 0 = 0 ,$$

which indeed satisfies F. ∎

Example 8.16. Consider the $\Sigma_{\mathbb{Q}}$-formula

$$F : \; x \geq 0 \; \wedge \; y \geq 0 \; \wedge \; x \geq 2 \; \wedge \; y \geq 2 \; \wedge \; x + y \leq 3 ,$$

or, in matrix form,

$$F: \begin{bmatrix} -1 & 0 \\ 0 & -1 \\ -1 & 0 \\ 0 & -1 \\ 1 & 1 \end{bmatrix} \begin{bmatrix} x \\ y \end{bmatrix} \le \begin{bmatrix} 0 \\ 0 \\ -2 \\ -2 \\ 3 \end{bmatrix}.$$

Is F $T_{\mathbb{Q}}$-satisfiable? Because F has only weak inequality literals, the corresponding linear program has a constant objective function:

$M:$ **max** 1
   subject to

$$G: \begin{bmatrix} -1 & 0 \\ 0 & -1 \\ -1 & 0 \\ 0 & -1 \\ 1 & 1 \end{bmatrix} \begin{bmatrix} x \\ y \end{bmatrix} \le \begin{bmatrix} 0 \\ 0 \\ -2 \\ -2 \\ 3 \end{bmatrix}$$

Solving the corresponding linear program M_0 is sufficient to determine the $T_{\mathbb{Q}}$-satisfiability of F.

Construction of M_0

Because x and y are already constrained to be nonnegative, we do not need to introduce new x_1, x_2, y_1, y_2. Rewrite the final three literals of F as two sets of constraints:

$$\underbrace{\begin{bmatrix} 1 & 1 \end{bmatrix}}_{D_1} \begin{bmatrix} x \\ y \end{bmatrix} \le \underbrace{\begin{bmatrix} 3 \end{bmatrix}}_{\bar{g}_1} \quad \text{and} \quad \underbrace{\begin{bmatrix} 1 & 0 \\ 0 & 1 \end{bmatrix}}_{D_2} \begin{bmatrix} x \\ y \end{bmatrix} \ge \underbrace{\begin{bmatrix} 2 \\ 2 \end{bmatrix}}_{\bar{g}_2}$$

so that $\bar{g}_1 \ge 0$ and $\bar{g}_2 > 0$. Then pose the following optimization problem of form (8.2):

$$M_0: \textbf{max } \underbrace{\begin{bmatrix} 1 & 1 & -1 & -1 \end{bmatrix}}_{\bar{c}^{\mathsf{T}}} \begin{bmatrix} x \\ y \\ z_1 \\ z_2 \end{bmatrix}$$

   subject to

$$\underbrace{\begin{bmatrix} -1 & 0 & 0 & 0 \\ 0 & -1 & 0 & 0 \\ 0 & 0 & -1 & 0 \\ 0 & 0 & 0 & -1 \\ 1 & 1 & 0 & 0 \\ 1 & 0 & -1 & 0 \\ 0 & 1 & 0 & -1 \end{bmatrix}}_{A} \begin{bmatrix} x \\ y \\ z_1 \\ z_2 \end{bmatrix} \le \underbrace{\begin{bmatrix} 0 \\ 0 \\ 0 \\ 0 \\ 3 \\ 2 \\ 2 \end{bmatrix}}_{\bar{b}}$$

in which $\bar{c}$ is computed according to

$$\bar{c}^T \bar{x} = \bar{1}^T \begin{bmatrix} D_2 & -I \end{bmatrix} \begin{bmatrix} x \\ y \\ z_1 \\ z_2 \end{bmatrix} = \begin{bmatrix} 1 & 1 \end{bmatrix} \begin{bmatrix} 1 & 0 & -1 & 0 \\ 0 & 1 & 0 & -1 \end{bmatrix} \begin{bmatrix} x \\ y \\ z_1 \\ z_2 \end{bmatrix}$$

$$= \underbrace{\begin{bmatrix} 1 & 1 & -1 & -1 \end{bmatrix}}_{\bar{c}^T} \begin{bmatrix} x \\ y \\ z_1 \\ z_2 \end{bmatrix} .$$

Use the initial vertex

$$\bar{v}_1 = \begin{bmatrix} x \\ y \\ z_1 \\ z_2 \end{bmatrix} = \begin{bmatrix} 0 \\ 0 \\ 0 \\ 0 \end{bmatrix}$$

to start the vertex traversal.

F is satisfiable iff the optimal value is equal to

$$v_G = \bar{1}^T \bar{g}_2 = \begin{bmatrix} 1 & 1 \end{bmatrix} \begin{bmatrix} 2 \\ 2 \end{bmatrix} = 4 .$$

We apply the simplex method to find the optimum.

Iteration 1

Choose rows $R = [1; 2; 3; 4]$ of A and $\bar{b}$ to form

$$A_1 = \begin{bmatrix} -1 & 0 & 0 & 0 \\ 0 & -1 & 0 & 0 \\ 0 & 0 & -1 & 0 \\ 0 & 0 & 0 & -1 \end{bmatrix} \quad \text{and} \quad \bar{b}_1 = \begin{bmatrix} 0 \\ 0 \\ 0 \\ 0 \end{bmatrix} .$$

This submatrix and subvector correspond to the defining constraints of vertex $\bar{v}_1$: $A_1 \bar{v}_1 = \bar{b}_1$.

Recall that by the Duality Theorem (Theorem 8.6), our goal is to find a vector $\bar{u}$ such that $\bar{u} \geq \bar{0}$ and $\bar{u}^T A = \bar{c}^T$. We use A_1 to solve for a $\bar{u}$ satisfying $\bar{u}^T A = \bar{c}^T$ and, through iteratively exploring a sequence of vertices, eventually find a $\bar{u}$ that also satisfies $\bar{u} \geq \bar{0}$.

Therefore, we solve for $\bar{u}$. By (8.5), solve $A_1{}^T \bar{u}_1 = \bar{c}$ to yield $\bar{u}_1 = \begin{bmatrix} -1 & -1 & 1 & 1 \end{bmatrix}^T$. Adding 0s for the rows not in R produces $\bar{u}$:

$$\bar{u} = \begin{bmatrix} -1 & -1 & 1 & 1 & 0 & 0 & 0 \end{bmatrix}^T ,$$

which satisfies $\bar{u}^T A = \bar{c}^T$ (8.6) as desired.

Since $u_1, u_2 < 0$, we are in **Case 2** with $k = k' = 1$. We have not yet found a $\bar{u} \geq \bar{0}$, so we must continue searching. In particular, constraints 1 and 2 are causing a problem (as indicated by $u_1, u_2 < 0$), so we must find a direction $\bar{y}$ and distance λ_1 to travel to a better vertex whose defining constraints do not include constraint 1. The direction is given by the first column of $-A_1^{-1}$: by (8.8), solve $A_1\bar{y} = -e_1$ to yield $\bar{y} = \begin{bmatrix} 1\ 0\ 0\ 0 \end{bmatrix}^{\mathsf{T}}$.

It remains to find the distance λ_1 to travel along $\bar{y}$. Computing $A\bar{y}$ shows that $S = [5; 6]$: the fifth and sixth rows $\bar{a}$ of A are such that $\overline{a}\bar{y} > 0$. This situation means that traveling along $\bar{y}$ too far will result in making one or both of constraints 5 and 6 unsatisfied. The other constraints will continue to be satisfied independent of λ_1.

Therefore, by (8.9), choose the largest λ_1 such that

$$A(\bar{v}_1 + \lambda_1\bar{y}) \leq \bar{b} .$$

Focusing on the fifth and sixth rows of A (since $S = [5; 6]$), choose the largest λ_1 such that

$$\underbrace{\begin{bmatrix} 1 & 1 & 0 & 0 \\ 1 & 0 & -1 & 0 \end{bmatrix}}_{\text{rows 5,6 of } A} \left(\underbrace{\begin{bmatrix} 0 \\ 0 \\ 0 \\ 0 \end{bmatrix}}_{\bar{v}_1} + \lambda_1 \underbrace{\begin{bmatrix} 1 \\ 0 \\ 0 \\ 0 \end{bmatrix}}_{\bar{y}} \right) \leq \underbrace{\begin{bmatrix} 3 \\ 2 \end{bmatrix}}_{\text{rows 5,6 of } \bar{b}}$$

according to (8.9). Namely, choose $\lambda_1 = 2$ (and $\ell = 6$).

We now have a direction ($\bar{y}$) and a distance (λ_1) to travel away from $\bar{v}_1$. By (8.12), define

$$\bar{v}_2 = \bar{v}_1 + \lambda_1\bar{y} = \begin{bmatrix} 0 \\ 0 \\ 0 \\ 0 \end{bmatrix} + 2\begin{bmatrix} 1 \\ 0 \\ 0 \\ 0 \end{bmatrix} = \begin{bmatrix} 2 \\ 0 \\ 0 \\ 0 \end{bmatrix} .$$

For the next iteration, replace the first row of A_1 (since $k' = 1$) with the sixth row of A (since $\ell = 6$) to produce

$$A_2 = \begin{bmatrix} 1 & 0 & -1 & 0 \\ 0 & -1 & 0 & 0 \\ 0 & 0 & -1 & 0 \\ 0 & 0 & 0 & -1 \end{bmatrix} \quad \text{and} \quad \bar{b}_2 = \begin{bmatrix} 2 \\ 0 \\ 0 \\ 0 \end{bmatrix} .$$

Have we made progress by moving to vertex $\bar{v}_2$? Yes, for

$$\bar{c}^{\mathsf{T}}\bar{v}_1 = 0 < 2 = \bar{c}^{\mathsf{T}}\bar{v}_2 .$$

The objective function has increased from 0 to 2.

Iteration 2

Now $R = [6; 2; 3; 4]$. Solve $A_2{}^\mathsf{T}\bar{u}_2 = \bar{c}$ to yield $\bar{u}_2 = \begin{bmatrix} 1 & -1 & 0 & 1 \end{bmatrix}^\mathsf{T}$ for rows $[6; 2; 3; 4]$. Then filling in 0s for the other rows of A produces:

$$\bar{u} = [0 \; -1 \; 0 \; 1 \; 0 \; 1 \; 0]^\mathsf{T} \; .$$
$$\text{row:} \quad 2 \; 3 \; 4 \quad 6$$

Note that $\bar{u}$ maintains the order of rows, while $\bar{u}_2$ is ordered according to R. $u_2 < 0$, so $k = 2$, which corresponds to row $k' = 2$ of $\bar{u}_2$. According to **Case 2**, let $\bar{y}$ be the second column of $-A_2^{-1}$: solve $A_2\bar{y} = -e_2$ to yield $\bar{y} = [0 \; 1 \; 0 \; 0]^\mathsf{T}$. Then the fifth and seventh rows $\bar{a}$ of A are such that $\overline{ay} > 0$ so that $S = [5; 7]$. Focusing on the fifth and seventh rows of A, choose the largest λ_2 such that

$$\underbrace{\begin{bmatrix} 1 & 1 & 0 & 0 \\ 0 & 1 & 0 & -1 \end{bmatrix}}_{\text{rows 5,7 of } A} \left(\underbrace{\begin{bmatrix} 2 \\ 0 \\ 0 \\ 0 \end{bmatrix}}_{\bar{v}_2} + \lambda_2 \underbrace{\begin{bmatrix} 0 \\ 1 \\ 0 \\ 0 \end{bmatrix}}_{\bar{y}} \right) \le \underbrace{\begin{bmatrix} 3 \\ 2 \end{bmatrix}}_{\text{rows 5,7 of } \bar{b}} \; .$$

Choose $\lambda_2 = 1$ (and $\ell = 5$). Then

$$\bar{v}_3 = \bar{v}_2 + \lambda_2\bar{y} = \begin{bmatrix} 2 \\ 0 \\ 0 \\ 0 \end{bmatrix} + 1 \begin{bmatrix} 0 \\ 1 \\ 0 \\ 0 \end{bmatrix} = \begin{bmatrix} 2 \\ 1 \\ 0 \\ 0 \end{bmatrix} \; .$$

Replace the second row of A_2 (since $k' = 2$) with the fifth row of A (since $\ell = 5$) to produce

$$A_3 = \begin{bmatrix} 1 & 0 & -1 & 0 \\ 1 & 1 & 0 & 0 \\ 0 & 0 & -1 & 0 \\ 0 & 0 & 0 & -1 \end{bmatrix} \quad \text{and} \quad \bar{b}_3 = \begin{bmatrix} 2 \\ 3 \\ 0 \\ 0 \end{bmatrix} \; .$$

Have we made progress? Yes, for

$$\bar{c}^\mathsf{T}\bar{v}_1 = 0 < \bar{c}^\mathsf{T}\bar{v}_2 = 2 < \bar{c}^\mathsf{T}\bar{v}_3 = 3 \; .$$

The objective function has increased from 2 to 3.

Iteration 3

Now $R = [6; 5; 3; 4]$. Solve $A_3{}^\mathsf{T}\bar{u}_3 = \bar{c}$, yielding $\bar{u}_3 = \begin{bmatrix} 0 & 1 & 1 & 1 \end{bmatrix}^\mathsf{T}$. Because $\bar{u}_3 \ge \bar{0}$, we are in **Case 1**: $\bar{v}_3$ is the optimum with objective value

$$\bar{c}^\mathsf{T}\bar{v}_3 = \begin{bmatrix} 1 & 1 & -1 & -1 \end{bmatrix} \begin{bmatrix} 2 \\ 1 \\ 0 \\ 0 \end{bmatrix} = 3 \ .$$

The optimal value of the constructed optimization problem is 3, which is less than the required $v_G = 4$. The constraints G of the linear program M are unsatisfiable, and thus F itself is $T_\mathbb{Q}$-unsatisfiable. ∎

8.4.3 ⋆Complexity

Theorem 8.17. $T_\mathbb{Q}$-*satisfiability of conjunctive quantifier-free $\Sigma_\mathbb{Q}$-formulae is weakly polynomial-time decidable.*

An algorithm is weakly polynomial-time if it runs in time polynomial in the actual values of the input, not just the size of the input. **Bibliographic Remarks** discusses algorithms that achieve this performance.

While efficient in practice, the simplex method actually has poor worst-case behavior for known fixed pivot rules. A **pivot rule** determines which adjacent vertex to visit next. In our presentation, no rule is fixed: the next vertex can be any of those corresponding to the negative entries in the $\bar{u}$ vector. However, for all known pivot rules, there exist classes of quantifier-free $\Sigma_\mathbb{Q}$-formulae on which the simplex method requires an exponential number of steps in the size of the formulae.

8.5 Summary

This chapter covers linear programming and the simplex method for solving linear programs. It covers:

- How decision procedures that reason only about conjunctive formulae extend to arbitrary Boolean structure by converting to DNF. Exercise 8.1 explores a more effective way of converting to DNF.
- A review of linear algebra.
- *Linear programs*, which are optimization problems with linear constraints and linear objective functions. Application to $T_\mathbb{Q}$-satisfiability.
- The *simplex method*. Finding an initial point via a new linear program. Greedy search along vertices.

The structure of the simplex method is markedly different from the structure of the quantifier elimination procedures of Chapter 7. It focuses on the structure of the set of interpretations of the given formula, rather than on the formula itself. Exercises 8.3, 8.4, and 8.5 explore these sets, which describe polyhedra.

In addition to applications in all of engineering, arithmetical reasoning is necessary for analyzing program correctness. Of course, arithmetic usually appears in the context of other data structures in software. Chapter 10 discusses a method for combining the arithmetic decision procedures of this and the previous chapter with other decision procedures.

Bibliographic Remarks

For a presentation of linear algebra, see [42]; for a comprehensive presentation of linear and integer programming, see [82].

Work on linear programming proceeded in parallel in the western hemisphere and the USSR. Dantzig is the inventor of the simplex method in the western hemisphere [22]. Earlier work by Kantorovich in the USSR also proposes the method [44]. Weakly polynomial-time algorithms were achieved by Khachian [49] in the USSR and Karmarkar [45] in the western hemisphere.

Exercises

8.1 ($\star$Conjunctive quantifier-free formulae). Converting an arbitrary quantifier-free Σ-formula to DNF and then applying a decision procedure to each disjunct can be prohibitively expensive. In practice, SAT solvers (decision procedures for propositional logic, such as DPLL) are used to extend a decision procedure for conjunctive quantifier-free Σ-formula to arbitrary quantifier-free Σ-formula.

(a) Show that the DNF of a formula F can be exponentially larger than F.

(b) Describe a procedure that, using a SAT solver, extracts conjunctive Σ-formulae from a quantifier-free Σ-formula F. Using this procedure, each discovered conjunctive formula's T-satisfiability will be decided. If it is T-satisfiable, then F is T-satisfiable, so the procedure finishes; otherwise, the procedure finds another conjunctive formula.

(c) The proposed procedure is really no more efficient than simply converting to DNF. This part explores an optimization. An **unsatisfiable core** of T-unsatisfiable conjunctive Σ-formula G is the conjunction H of a subset of literals of G such (1) H is also T-unsatisfiable, and (2) the conjunction of each strict subset of literals of H is T-satisfiable. Improve your procedure from the previous part to use a function $\mathsf{UnsatCore}_T(G)$ that returns a T-unsatisfiable core of a T-unsatisfiable conjunctive Σ-formula G.

(d) Given a decision procedure DP_T for conjunctive quantifier-free Σ-formula, describe a procedure $\mathsf{UnsatCore}(G)$ for computing an unsatisfiable core of G that takes no more than a number of DP_T calls linear in the number of literals of G. Note that G can have multiple unsatisfiable cores; your procedure need only return one.

(e) Given a decision procedure DP_T for conjunctive quantifier-free Σ-formula, describe a procedure $\mathsf{UnsatCore}(G)$ for computing an unsatisfiable core of G that takes no more than $O(m \log n)$ calls of DP_T, where m is the number of literals of the returned unsatisfiable core and n is the number of literals of G.

8.2 (DP for $T_{\mathbb{Q}}$). Apply the simplex method to decide the $T_{\mathbb{Q}}$-satisfiability of the following $\Sigma_{\mathbb{Q}}$-formulae.

(a) $x \geq 1 \ \wedge \ 2x \leq 1$
(b) $x + 2y \geq 1 \ \wedge \ 2x + y \geq 1 \ \wedge \ 2x + 2y \leq 1$
(c) $x + 2y \geq 1 \ \wedge \ 2x + y \geq 1 \ \wedge \ x + y \leq 1$

8.3 ($\star$Polyhedra & dual representation). $A\bar{x} \leq \bar{b}$ defines a subspace of $\mathbb{R}^n$ called a **polyhedron**; $A\bar{x} \leq \bar{b}$ is the **constraint representation** of this space. A polyhedron can also be described by the union of a set of vertices $V \subseteq \mathbb{R}^n$ and a set of **rays** $R \subseteq \mathbb{R}^n$; this representation is the **vertex representation**. While vertices $\bar{v} \in V$ describe points in $\mathbb{R}^n$, rays $\bar{r} \in R$ describe directions in $\mathbb{R}^n$. For example, as a vertex, $[1\ 1]^\mathsf{T} \in \mathbb{R}^2$ describes the point one unit right and one unit up from the origin on the plane. As a ray, it describes the "northeast" direction.

Represent each vertex $\bar{v} \in V$ and ray $\bar{r} \in R$ by the $(n+1)$-vectors

$$\begin{bmatrix} \bar{x} \\ 1 \end{bmatrix} \quad \text{and} \quad \begin{bmatrix} \bar{r} \\ 0 \end{bmatrix},$$

respectively. Let P be the union of V and R represented in this way. Then for every inequality $A\bar{x} \leq \bar{b}$, there exists a vertex-ray set P with k elements such that

$$A\bar{x} \leq \bar{b} \quad \text{iff} \quad \exists \lambda_1, \ldots, \lambda_k \geq 0. \ \begin{bmatrix} \bar{x} \\ 1 \end{bmatrix} = \sum_{i=1}^{k} \lambda_i \bar{p}_i \ .$$

(a) Given an element

$$\bar{p} = \begin{bmatrix} \bar{x} \\ \epsilon \end{bmatrix} \in P \ ,$$

we can evaluate $A\bar{x} \leq \epsilon \bar{b}$. If $\bar{p}$ is a vertex, it is equivalent to evaluating $A\bar{x} \leq \bar{b}$, as expected. If $\bar{p}$ is a ray, it is equivalent to evaluating $A\bar{x} \leq \bar{0}$. Explain what the ray case means.
(b) Define the **convex hull** as follows:

$$\mathsf{hull}(P) = \left\{ \bar{x} \ : \ \exists \lambda_1, \ldots, \lambda_k \geq 0. \ \begin{bmatrix} \bar{x} \\ 1 \end{bmatrix} = \sum_{i=1}^{k} \lambda_i \bar{p}_i \right\} \ .$$

Show that $\mathsf{hull}(P)$ is convex. Conclude that if $A\bar{x} \leq \epsilon \bar{b}$ for each $[\bar{x}^\mathsf{T} \ \epsilon]^\mathsf{T} \in P$, then $\mathsf{hull}(P) \subseteq \{\bar{x} \ : \ A\bar{x} \leq \bar{b}\}$.

8.4 (★Set operations). The constraint representations of two polyhedra S_1 and S_2 are $A_1 \bar{x} \le \bar{b}_1$ and $A_2 \bar{x} \le \bar{b}_2$, respectively, and their vertex representations are P_1 and P_2, respectively.

(a) Write the constraint representation of $S_1 \cap S_2$ in terms of S_1 and S_2.
(b) Write the vertex representation of $\text{hull}(S_1 \cup S_2)$ in terms of P_1 and P_2.
(c) Describe how to compute whether $S_1 \subseteq S_2$. *Hint:* Use both representations.

8.5 (★Set operations with vertex representation). The vertex representations of two polyhedra S_1 and S_2 are P_1 and P_2, respectively.

(a) Describe how to compute whether $S_1 \subseteq S_2$ using only their vertex representations. *Hint:* Use the simplex method.
(b) Given $A\bar{x} \le \bar{b}$, a **vertex enumeration algorithm** lists the corresponding vertex representation. Using a vertex enumeration algorithm, describe how to compute the vertex representation of $S_1 \cap S_2$ using only their vertex representations.

Quantifier-Free Equality and Data Structures

Almost all proofs require reasoning about equalities.
— Greg Nelson and Derek C. Oppen
Fast Decision Procedures Based on Congruence Closure, 1980

Equality is perhaps the most widely-used relation among data in programs. In this chapter, we consider equality among variables, constants, and function applications (Section 9.1); among recursive data structures (records, lists, trees, and stacks) and their elements (Section 9.4); and among elements of arrays (Section 9.5). For all three theories, we examine their quantifier-free fragments.

In the last two theories — recursive data structures and arrays — we distinguish between equality among data structures and among their elements. The quantifier-free fragment of the theory of recursive data structures can express equality among whole structures, which reduces to element-wise equality. In contrast, the quantifier-free fragment of the theory of arrays cannot express equality among entire arrays. Chapter 11 presents larger fragments of various theories of arrays that can express equality among arrays and array segments, among other properties.

Equality among variables, constants, and function applications is expressed in the theory of equality T_E. This theory is sometimes referred to as the **theory of equality with uninterpreted functions** (**EUF**). Its signature contains all predicate and function symbols, yet its axioms do not interpret (assign meaning to) the symbols other than in the context of equality. Specifically, the axioms of T_E assert that a function symbol acts like a function: if two terms t_1 and t_2 are equal, then $f(t_1)$ and $f(t_2)$ are also equal. Similarly, predicate symbols act like predicates: $p(t_1)$ is equivalent to $p(t_2)$ when t_1 is equal to t_2.

Section 9.1 presents the theory T_E and its quantifier-free fragment. Then Section 9.2 describes at a high-level the **congruence-closure algorithm** to decide T_E-satisfiability of quantifier-free Σ_E-formulae. Section 9.3 details an implementation that employs an efficient representation of Σ_E-formulae.

The congruence closure algorithm is the basis for the other decision procedures of this chapter as well. It is extended in Section 9.4 to decide satisfiability in the quantifier-free fragment of the theory of recursive data structures T_{RDS}, and in particular in the theory of lists T_{cons}. Finally, it is applied in Section 9.5 to decide satisfiability in the quantifier-free fragment of the theory of arrays T_{A}.

The quantifier-free fragment of T_{E} and its satisfiability decision procedure play a central role in combining theories that share the equality predicate. We discuss the combination of theories in Chapter 10.

9.1 Theory of Equality

Recall from Chapter 3 that the signature of T_{E},

$$\Sigma_{\text{E}} : \{=, \ a, \ b, \ c, \ \ldots, \ f, \ g, \ h, \ \ldots, \ p, \ q, \ r, \ \ldots\} \ ,$$

consists of

- $=$, a binary predicate;
- and all constant, function, and predicate symbols.

As in every other theory, Σ_{E}-formulae are constructed from symbols of the signature, variables, logical connectives, and quantifiers.

The equality predicate $=$ is interpreted, or given meaning, via the axioms of T_{E}. The axioms

1. $\forall x. \ x = x$	(reflexivity)
2. $\forall x, y. \ x = y \ \rightarrow \ y = x$	(symmetry)
3. $\forall x, y, z. \ x = y \ \wedge \ y = z \ \rightarrow \ x = z$	(transitivity)

define $=$ to be an **equivalence relation**. These axioms give $=$ the expected meaning of equality on pairs of variable terms.

However, they do not provide the full meaning for $=$ in the context of function terms, such as in $f(x) = f(g(y, z))$. The following axiom schema stands for an infinite but countable set of axioms:

4. for each positive integer n and n-ary function symbol f,

$$\forall \overline{x}, \overline{y}. \ \left(\bigwedge_{i=1}^{n} x_i = y_i \right) \ \rightarrow \ f(\overline{x}) = f(\overline{y}) \qquad \text{(function congruence)}$$

For example, two instances of this axiom schema are the following:

$$\forall x, y. \ x = y \ \rightarrow \ f(x) = f(y)$$

and

$$\forall x_1, x_2, y_1, y_2. \ x_1 = y_1 \ \wedge \ x_2 = y_2 \ \rightarrow \ g(x_1, x_2) = g(y_1, y_2) \ .$$

Then

$$x = g(y, z) \ \rightarrow \ f(x) = f(g(y, z))$$

is T_E-valid by the first instance. Alternately,

$$x = g(y, z) \ \wedge \ f(x) \neq f(g(y, z))$$

is T_E-unsatisfiable, where $t_1 \neq t_2$ abbreviates $\neg(t_1 = t_2)$. This axiom schema makes $=$ a **congruence relation**.

Finally, observe that the logical operator $\leftrightarrow$ should behave on predicate formulae similarly to the way $=$ behaves on function terms. For example, our intuition asserts that

$$x = y \ \rightarrow \ (p(x) \leftrightarrow p(y)) \tag{9.1}$$

should be T_E-valid. In Chapter 3, we list a fifth axiom schema:

5. for each positive integer n and n-ary predicate symbol p,

$$\forall \overline{x}, \overline{y}. \ \left(\bigwedge_{i=1}^{n} x_i = y_i \right) \ \rightarrow \ (p(\overline{x}) \leftrightarrow p(\overline{y})) \qquad \text{(predicate congruence)}$$

Under this axiom schema, formula (9.1) is T_E-valid.

Example 9.1. The Σ_E-formula

$$f(x) = f(y) \ \wedge \ x \neq y$$

is T_E-satisfiable: a function can evaluate unequal arguments to equal values. However,

$$x = y \ \wedge \ f(x) \neq f(y)$$

is T_E-unsatisfiable: a function evaluates each value to one value, independent of representation. Here, $x = y$, so x and y represent the same value.

Finally,

$$F : \ f(f(f(a))) = a \ \wedge \ f(f(f(f(f(a))))) = a \ \wedge \ f(a) \neq a$$

is T_E-unsatisfiable. We can make the following intuitive argument: substituting a for $f(f(f(a)))$ in $f(f(f(f(f(a))))) = a$ by the first equality yields $f(f(a)) = a$; and substituting a for $f(f(a))$ in $f(f(f(a))) = a$ according to this new equality yields $f(a) = a$, contradicting the literal $f(a) \neq a$.

Substitution, of course, rests on the axioms of T_E: in particular, the first substitution requires four steps:

1. $f(f(f(f(a)))) = f(a)$ — first literal of F, (function congruence)
2. $f(f(f(f(f(a))))) = f(f(a))$ — step 1, (function congruence)
3. $f(f(a)) = f(f(f(f(f(a)))))$ — step 2, (symmetry)
4. $f(f(a)) = a$ — step 3, second literal of F, (transitivity)

The decision procedure of this chapter reasons similarly. ∎

The (predicate congruence) axiom schema needlessly complicates our discussion. Instead, we describe by example a simple reduction of Σ_E-formulae containing uninterpreted predicates to Σ_E-formulae without predicates other than $=$. This transformation allows us to disregard the (predicate congruence) axiom schema. For example, given Σ_E-formula

$$x = y \ \rightarrow \ (p(x) \leftrightarrow p(y)) \ ,$$

introduce fresh constant $\bullet$ and fresh function f_p, and write

$$x = y \ \rightarrow \ ((f_p(x) = \bullet) \ \leftrightarrow \ (f_p(y) = \bullet)) \ .$$

Similarly, transform

$$p(x) \ \wedge \ q(x, y) \ \wedge \ q(y, z) \ \rightarrow \ \neg q(x, z)$$

into

$$f_p(x) = \bullet \ \wedge \ f_q(x, y) = \bullet \ \wedge \ f_q(y, z) = \bullet \ \rightarrow \ f_q(x, z) \neq \bullet \ .$$

In the rest of this chapter, we consider Σ_E-formulae without predicates other than $=$.

T_E-satisfiability is undecidable since satisfiability in FOL is undecidable. However, satisfiability in the quantifier-free fragment of T_E is decidable. We focus on this fragment in this chapter. Therefore, when we say "Σ_E-formula," we mean "quantifier-free Σ_E-formula" unless otherwise stated.

Additionally, as in Chapter 8, we consider only quantifier-free Σ_E-formulae that are conjunctions of literals. Satisfiability of an arbitrary quantifier-free Σ_E-formula is considered via conversion to DNF.

9.2 Congruence Closure Algorithm

Each positive literal $s = t$ of a (conjunctive quantifier-free) Σ_E-formula F asserts an equality between two terms s and t. Applying symmetry, reflexivity, transitivity, and congruence to these equalities of F produces more equalities over terms occurring in F. Since there are only a finite number of terms in F, only a finite number of equalities among these terms are possible. Hence, one of two situations eventually occurs: either some equality is formed that directly contradicts a negative literal $s' \neq t'$ of F; or the propagation of equalities ends without finding a contradiction. These cases correspond to T_E-unsatisfiability and T_E-satisfiability, respectively, of F.

This section develops the basic concepts for describing the algorithm mathematically as forming the **congruence closure** of the equality relation over terms asserted by F.

9.2.1 Relations

Binary Relations

Consider a set S and a binary relation R over S. For two elements $s_1, s_2 \in S$, either $s_1 R s_2$ or $\neg(s_1 R s_2)$.

The relation R is an **equivalence relation** if it is

- **reflexive:** $\forall s \in S.\ sRs$;
- **symmetric:** $\forall s_1, s_2 \in S.\ s_1 R s_2 \;\rightarrow\; s_2 R s_1$;
- **transitive:** $\forall s_1, s_2, s_3 \in S.\ s_1 R s_2 \;\wedge\; s_2 R s_3 \;\rightarrow\; s_1 R s_3$.

It is a **congruence relation** if it additionally obeys congruence: for every n-ary function f,

$$\forall \bar{s}, \bar{t}.\ \left(\bigwedge_{i=1}^{n} s_i R t_i \right) \;\rightarrow\; f(\bar{s}) R f(\bar{t}) .$$

In this case, function evaluation of R-related terms yields R-related results. The way we think of equality in our everyday computations is as a congruence relation.

Classes and Partitions

Consider an equivalence relation R over a set S. The **equivalence class** of $s \in S$ under R is the set

$$[s]_R \overset{\text{def}}{=} \{s' \in S \;:\; sRs'\} .$$

If R is a congruence relation over S, then $[s]_R$ is the **congruence class** of s.

Example 9.2. Consider the set $\mathbb{Z}$ of integers and the equivalence relation $\equiv_2$ such that

$$m \equiv_2 n \quad \text{iff} \quad (m \bmod 2) = (n \bmod 2) .$$

$m, n \in \mathbb{Z}$ are related iff they are both even or both odd. The equivalence class of 3 under $\equiv_2$ is

$$\begin{aligned}
[3]_{\equiv_2} &= \{n \in \mathbb{Z} \;:\; (n \bmod 2) = (3 \bmod 2)\} \\
&= \{n \in \mathbb{Z} \;:\; (n \bmod 2) = 1\} \\
&= \{n \in \mathbb{Z} \;:\; n \text{ is odd}\} .
\end{aligned}$$

A **partition** P of S is a set of subsets of S that is **total**,

$$\left(\bigcup_{S' \in P} S' \right) = S \ ,$$

and **disjoint**,

$$\forall S_1, S_2 \in P. \ S_1 \neq S_2 \ \rightarrow \ S_1 \cap S_2 = \emptyset \ .$$

The **quotient** S/R of S by the equivalence (congruence) relation R is a partition of S: it is a set of equivalence (congruence) classes

$$S/R \ = \ \{[s]_R \ : \ s \in S\} \ .$$

Example 9.3. The quotient $\mathbb{Z}/\equiv_2$ is a partition: it is the set of equivalence classes

$$\{\{n \in \mathbb{Z} \ : \ n \text{ is odd}\}, \ \{n \in \mathbb{Z} \ : \ n \text{ is even}\}\} \ .$$

∎

Just as an equivalence relation R induces a partition S/R of S, a given partition P of S induces an equivalence relation over S. Specifically, $s_1 R s_2$ iff for some $S' \in P$, both $s_1, s_2 \in S'$.

Relation Refinements

Consider two binary relations R_1 and R_2 over set S. R_1 is a **refinement** of R_2, or $R_1 \prec R_2$, if

$$\forall s_1, s_2 \in S. \ s_1 R_1 s_2 \ \rightarrow \ s_1 R_2 s_2 \ .$$

We also say that R_1 **refines** R_2. Viewing the relations as sets of pairs, $R_1 \subseteq R_2$.

Example 9.4. For $S = \{a, b\}$, $R_1 : \{a R_1 b\} \prec R_2 : \{a R_2 b, \ b R_2 b\}$.
Viewing the relations as sets of pairs, $R_1 \prec R_2$ iff $R_1 \subseteq R_2$. ∎

Example 9.5. Consider set S, the relation

$$R_1 : \{s R_1 s \ : \ s \in S\}$$

induced by the partition

$$P_1 : \{\{s\} \ : \ s \in S\} \ ,$$

and the relation

$$R_2 : \{s R_2 t \ : \ s, t \in S\}$$

induced by the partition

$$P_2 : \{S\} \ .$$

Then $R_1 \prec R_2$. ∎

Example 9.6. Consider the set $\mathbb{Z}$ and the two relations

$$R_1 : \{xR_1y \; : \; x \bmod 2 = y \bmod 2\} \text{ and } R_2 : \{xR_2y \; : \; x \bmod 4 = y \bmod 4\} \,.$$

Then $R_2 \prec R_1$. ∎

Closures

The **equivalence closure** R^E of the binary relation R over S is the equivalence relation such that

- R refines R^E: $R \prec R^E$;
- for all other equivalence relations R' such that $R \prec R'$, either $R' = R^E$ or $R^E \prec R'$.

That is, R^E is the "smallest" equivalence relation that "covers" R.

Example 9.7. If $S = \{a, b, c, d\}$ and

$$R = \{aRb, bRc, dRd\} \,,$$

then

- $aRb, bRc, dRd \in R^E$ since $R \subseteq R^E$;
- $aRa, bRb, cRc \in R^E$ by reflexivity;
- $bRa, cRb \in R^E$ by symmetry;
- $aRc \in R^E$ by transitivity;
- $cRa \in R^E$ by symmetry.

Hence,

$$R^E = \{aRb, bRa, aRa, bRb, bRc, cRb, cRc, aRc, cRa, dRd\} \,.$$

∎

The **congruence closure** R^C of R is the "smallest" congruence relation that "covers" R. Shortly, we shall illustrate the congruence closure of a term set.

9.2.2 Congruence Closure Algorithm

Having defined several abstract concepts, we now return to the theory of equality. The **subterm set** S_F of Σ_{E}-formula F is the set that contains precisely the subterms of F.

Example 9.8. The subterm set of

$$F : \; f(a, b) = a \; \wedge \; f(f(a, b), b) \neq a$$

is

$$S_F = \{a, \; b, \; f(a, b), \; f(f(a, b), b)\} \,.$$

∎

Now we relate the congruence closure of a Σ_E-formula's subterm set with its T_E-satisfiability. Given Σ_E-formula F

$$F: \; s_1 = t_1 \; \wedge \; \cdots \; \wedge \; s_m = t_m \; \wedge \; s_{m+1} \neq t_{m+1} \; \wedge \; \cdots \; \wedge \; s_n \neq t_n \;, \quad (9.2)$$

with subterm set S_F, F is T_E-satisfiable iff there exists a congruence relation $\sim$ over S_F such that

- for each $i \in \{1, \ldots, m\}$, $s_i \sim t_i$;
- for each $i \in \{m+1, \ldots, n\}$, $s_i \not\sim t_i$.

Such a congruence relation $\sim$ defines a T_E-interpretation $I : (D_I, \alpha_I)$ of F. D_I consists of $|S_F/ \sim|$ elements, one for each congruence class of S_F under $\sim$. α_I assigns elements of D_I to the terms of S_F in a way that respects $\sim$. Finally, α_I assigns to $=$ a binary relation over D_I that behaves like $\sim$. Based on this construction, we abbreviate $(D_I, \alpha_I) \models F$ with $\sim \models F$.

The goal of the **congruence closure algorithm** is to construct the congruence relation of a formula's subterm set, or to prove that no congruence relation exists. Given formula (9.2), the algorithm performs the following steps:

1. Construct the congruence closure $\sim$ of

$$\{s_1 = t_1, \ldots, s_m = t_m\}$$

over the subterm set S_F. Then

$$\sim \;\models\; s_1 = t_1 \; \wedge \; \cdots \; \wedge \; s_m = t_m \;.$$

2. If $s_i \sim t_i$ for any $i \in \{m+1, \ldots, n\}$, return unsatisfiable.
3. Otherwise, $\sim \models F$, so return satisfiable.

How do we actually construct the congruence closure in Step 1? Initially, begin with the finest congruence relation $\sim_0$ given by the partition

$$\{\{s\} \;:\; s \in S_F\}$$

in which each term of S_F is its own congruence class. Then, for each $i \in \{1, \ldots, m\}$, impose $s_i = t_i$ by merging the congruence classes

$$[s_i]_{\sim_{i-1}} \quad \text{and} \quad [t_i]_{\sim_{i-1}}$$

to form a new congruence relation $\sim_i$. To accomplish this merging, first form the union of $[s_i]_{\sim_{i-1}}$ and $[t_i]_{\sim_{i-1}}$. Then propagate any new congruences that arise within this union. In the new congruence relation $\sim_i$, $s_i \sim_i t_i$. Section 9.3 presents the details of an efficient data structure and algorithm for performing this construction.

Example 9.9. Consider the Σ_E-formula

$$F: \; f(a, b) = a \; \wedge \; f(f(a, b), b) \neq a \;.$$

Construct the following initial partition by letting each member of the subterm set S_F be its own class:

$$\{\{a\}, \{b\}, \{f(a,b)\}, \{f(f(a,b),b)\}\} .$$

According to the first literal $f(a,b) = a$, merge

$$\{f(a,b)\} \quad \text{and} \quad \{a\}$$

to form partition

$$\{\{a, f(a,b)\}, \{b\}, \{f(f(a,b),b)\}\} .$$

According to the (function congruence) axiom,

$$f(a,b) \sim a, \ b \sim b \quad \text{implies} \quad f(f(a,b),b) \sim f(a,b) ,$$

resulting in the new partition

$$\{\{a, f(a,b), f(f(a,b),b)\}, \{b\}\} .$$

This partition represents the congruence closure of S_F. Now, is it the case that

$$\{\{a, f(a,b), f(f(a,b),b)\}, \{b\}\} \models F ?$$

No, as $f(f(a,b),b) \sim a$ but F asserts that $f(f(a,b),b) \neq a$. Hence, F is T_E-unsatisfiable.   ∎

Example 9.10. Consider the Σ_E-formula

$$F : \ f(f(f(a))) = a \ \wedge \ f(f(f(f(f(a))))) = a \ \wedge \ f(a) \neq a$$

From the subterm set S_F, the initial partition is

$$\{\{a\}, \{f(a)\}, \{f^2(a)\}, \{f^3(a)\}, \{f^4(a)\}, \{f^5(a)\}\} ,$$

where, for example, $f^3(a)$ abbreviates $f(f(f(a)))$.
    According to the literal $f^3(a) = a$, merge

$$\{f^3(a)\} \quad \text{and} \quad \{a\} .$$

From the union $\{a, f^3(a)\}$, deduce the following congruence propagations:

$$f^3(a) \sim a \ \Rightarrow \ f(f^3(a)) \sim f(a) , \ i.e., \ f^4(a) \sim f(a)$$

and

$$f^4(a) \sim f(a) \ \Rightarrow \ f(f^4(a)) \sim f(f(a)) , \ i.e., \ f^5(a) \sim f^2(a) .$$

Thus, the final partition for this iteration is the following:

$$\{\{a, f^3(a)\}, \{f(a), f^4(a)\}, \{f^2(a), f^5(a)\}\} \ .$$

From the second literal, $f^5(a) = a$, merge

$$\{f^2(a), f^5(a)\} \quad \text{and} \quad \{a, f^3(a)\}$$

to form the partition

$$\{\{a, f^2(a), f^3(a), f^5(a)\}, \{f(a), f^4(a)\}\} \ .$$

Propagating the congruence

$$f^3(a) \sim f^2(a) \ \Rightarrow \ f(f^3(a)) \sim f(f^2(a)) \ , \ i.e., \ f^4(a) \sim f^3(a)$$

yields the partition

$$\{\{a, f(a), f^2(a), f^3(a), f^4(a), f^5(a)\}\} \ ,$$

which represents the congruence closure in which all of S_F are equal.
    Now, is it the case that

$$\{\{a, f(a), f^2(a), f^3(a), f^4(a), f^5(a)\}\} \ \models \ F \ ?$$

No, as $f(a) \sim a$, but F asserts that $f(a) \neq a$. Hence, F is T_E-unsatisfiable. ■

Example 9.11. Consider the Σ_E-formula

$$F: \ f(x) = f(y) \ \wedge \ x \neq y \ .$$

The subterm set S_F induces the following initial partition:

$$\{\{x\}, \{y\}, \{f(x)\}, \{f(y)\}\} \ .$$

Then $f(x) = f(y)$ indicates to merge

$$\{f(x)\} \quad \text{and} \quad \{f(y)\} \ .$$

The union $\{f(x), f(y)\}$ does not yield any new congruences, so the final partition is

$$\{\{x\}, \{y\}, \{f(x), f(y)\}\} \ .$$

Does

$$\{\{x\}, \{y\}, \{f(x), f(y)\}\} \ \models \ F \ ?$$

Yes, as $x \not\sim y$, agreeing with $x \neq y$. Hence, F is T_E-satisfiable.   ■

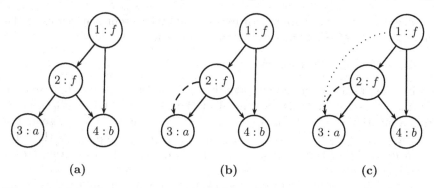

Fig. 9.1. (a) DAG representation; (b), (c) with `find`

9.3 Congruence Closure with DAGs

So far, we have considered the congruence closure algorithm at an abstract level. In this section, we describe an efficient implementation of the algorithm.

Section 9.3.1 defines a graph-based data structure for representing all members of the subterm set S_F of a Σ_E-formula F. Each node represents a subterm. Congruence classes are stored within this data structure via references between nodes. Sections 9.3.2 and 9.3.3 present algorithms that manipulate the data structure to construct the congruence closure of the relation defined by F.

9.3.1 Directed Acyclic Graphs

A **graph** $G : \langle N, E \rangle$ has a set of **nodes** $N = \{n_1, n_2, \ldots, n_k\}$ and a set of **edges** $E = \{\ldots, \langle n_i, n_j \rangle, \ldots\}$, which consists of pairs of nodes. In a **directed graph**, edges point from one node to another. For example, the edge $\langle n_3, n_5 \rangle$ is not the same edge as $\langle n_5, n_3 \rangle$: the first points to n_5, while the second points to n_3. In a directed edge $\langle m, n \rangle$, m is the **source**, and n is the **target**. A **directed acyclic graph** (**DAG**) is a directed graph in which no subset of edges forms a directed loop, or **cycle**.

Example 9.12. Consider the directed graph

$$G : \langle N : \{1, 2, 3\}, \ E : \{\langle 1, 2 \rangle, \langle 2, 3 \rangle, \langle 3, 1 \rangle\} \rangle \ .$$

It is not a DAG because it contains the loop $1 \to 2 \to 3 \to 1$. However, the directed graph

$$G : \langle N : \{1, 2, 3\}, \ E : \{\langle 1, 2 \rangle, \langle 2, 3 \rangle, \langle 1, 3 \rangle\} \rangle$$

is a DAG.   ∎

The congruence closure algorithm uses a DAG to represent terms of the subterm set. The DAG of Figure 9.1(a) represents the subterm set

$$\{a,\ b,\ f(a,b),\ f(f(a,b),b)\}\ .$$

Each node has a unique number identifying it and a text label representing the root constant or function symbol of the associated term. Edges point from a function symbol to its arguments. For example, node 3 represents the term a; node 2 represents the term $f(a,b)$; and node 1 represents the term $f(f(a,b),b)$. Node 4, representing the term b, is shared by the terms $f(a,b)$ and $f(f(a,b),b)$.

So far, the following data type is sufficient to represent subterms:

```
type node = {
    id    :  id
    fn    :  string
    args  :  id list
}
```

The id field holds the node's unique identification number; the fn field holds the constant or function symbol; and the args field holds a list of identification numbers representing the function arguments. For example, node 2 of Figure 9.1(a) has id = 2, fn = f, and args = $[3; 4]$; and node 3 has id = 3, fn = a, and args = $[]$.

To represent congruence classes, we augment the data type with one more field:

```
type node = {
    id             :  id
    fn             :  string
    args           :  id list
    mutable find   :  id
}
```

The mutable keyword indicates that the value of the field can be modified. The find field holds the identification number of another node (possibly itself) in its congruence class. Following a chain of find references leads to the **representative** of the congruence class. A representative node's find field points to the node itself.

Consider the DAG of Figure 9.1(b). The dashed edge from node 2 to node 3 indicates that node 2's find field points to node 3, and thus that nodes 2 and 3 are in the same congruence class

$$\{f(a,b),a\}\ .$$

To avoid cluttering the illustrations, we do not draw dashed lines from a node to itself when its find is set to itself. Thus, the DAG of Figure 9.1(b) represents the partition

$$\{\{f(a,b),\ a\},\ \{b\},\ \{f(f(a,b),b)\}\}\ ;$$

and, for example, the **find** field of node 1 is 1. Also, since the **find** of node 3 is 3, node 3 represents the congruence class of nodes 2 and 3.

In Figure 9.1**(c)**, the dashed and dotted edges play the same role for now, each representing the value of the source node's **find** field. The DAG represents the partition

$$\{\{f(f(a,b),b),\ f(a,b),\ a\},\ \{b\}\}\ .$$

Node 3 is the (unique) representative of its congruence class. We shall see that the algorithm maintains exactly one representative for each congruence class.

Finally, merging congruence classes requires accessing parent terms (*e.g.*, $f(a,b)$ is the parent of a and b). Thus, we add a final mutable field:

```
type node = {
    id              :  id
    fn              :  string
    args            :  id list
    mutable find    :  id
    mutable ccpar   :  id set
}
```

If a node is the representative for its congruence class, then its **ccpar** (for **congruence closure parents**) field stores the set of all parents of all nodes in its congruence class. A non-representative node's **ccpar** field is empty. In Figure 9.1**(b)**, the **ccpar**

- of 1 is $\emptyset$ because 1 is its own representative, but it lacks parents;
- of 2 is $\emptyset$ because 2 is not a representative;
- of 3 is $\{1,2\}$ because 3 represents the class $\{2,3\}$ in which the parent of 2 is 1 and the parent of 3 is 2;
- of 4 is $\{1,2\}$ because 4 represents itself and has parents $\{1,2\}$.

The DAG representation of node 2 is thus

```
{   id    = 2;
    fn    = f;
    args  = [3;4];
    find  = 3;
    ccpar = ∅;
}
```

Similarly, the DAG representation of node 3 is

```
{   id    = 3;
    fn    = a;
    args  = [];
    find  = 3;
    ccpar = {1,2};
}
```

9.3.2 Basic Operations

In this section, we define the **union-find** algorithm on the DAG data structure. Generally, a union-find algorithm provides an efficient means of manipulating sets. It represents each set by a single representative element. Calling the FIND function on any element returns its set's unique representative. Calling the UNION function on two elements unions the two elements' sets and fixes a unique representative for the union set.

The union-find algorithm on DAGs is sufficient for manipulating equivalence classes of terms. In Section 9.3.3, we extend the union-find algorithm to manipulate congruence classes.

NODE

NODE i returns the node n with id i. Thus, (NODE i).id $= i$. For example, in Figure 9.1(**b**), (NODE 2).find $= 3$.

FIND

The FIND function returns the representative of a node's equivalence class. It follows find edges until it finds a self-loop:

```
let rec FIND i =
  let n = NODE i in
  if n.find = i then i else FIND n.find
```

Example 9.13. In the DAG of Figure 9.1(**b**), FIND 2 is 3. FIND follows the find edge of 2 to 3; then it recognizes the self-loop and thus returns 3.   ■

UNION

The UNION function returns the union of two equivalence classes, given two node identities i_1 and i_2. It first finds the representatives n_1 and n_2 of i_1's and i_2's equivalence classes, respectively. Next, it sets n_1's find to n_2's representative, which is the identity of n_2 itself. Now n_2 represents the new larger equivalence class.

Finally, it combines the congruence closure parents, storing the new set in n_2's ccpar field because n_2 is the representative of the union equivalence class. This last step is not strictly part of the union-find algorithm (which, recall, computes equivalence classes); rather, it is intended for when we use the union-find algorithm to compute congruence classes. In code,

```
let UNION i₁ i₂ =
  let n₁ = NODE (FIND i₁) in
  let n₂ = NODE (FIND i₂) in
  n₁.find ← n₂.find;
  n₂.ccpar ← n₁.ccpar ∪ n₂.ccpar;
  n₁.ccpar ← ∅
```

Example 9.14. Consider the DAG of Figure 9.1(b). To compute UNION 1 2, UNION finds $n_1 = 1$ and $n_2 = 3$ as the representatives of $i_1 = 1$ and $i_2 = 2$, respectively. It sets 1's find field to 3's find, which is 3, and combines the ccpars, setting 3's ccpar to $\{1, 2\}$ and 1's ccpar to $\emptyset$. The result is Figure 9.1(c). For now, ignore the difference between dotted and dashed lines. ∎

CCPAR

The simple function CCPAR i returns the parents of all nodes in i's congruence class:

```
let CCPAR i =
  (NODE (FIND i)).ccpar
```

9.3.3 Congruence Closure Algorithm

We are ready to build the congruence closure algorithm using the basic operations. First we define the CONGRUENT function to check whether two nodes that are not in the same congruence class are in fact congruent. Then we define the MERGE function to merge two congruence classes and to propagate the effects of new congruences recursively.

CONGRUENT

CONGRUENT i_1 i_2 tests whether i_1 and i_2 are congruent. Let n_1 and n_2 be the nodes with identities i_1 and i_2, respectively. If their fn fields or their numbers of arguments are different, then they cannot be congruent, so CONGRUENT returns false. Otherwise, if any argument of n_1 is not in the congruence class of the corresponding argument of n_2, then the terms are not congruent, so CONGRUENT returns false. If both of these tests are passed, then n_1 and n_2 are congruent, so CONGRUENT returns true. Formally,

```
let CONGRUENT i₁ i₂ =
  let n₁ = NODE i₁ in
  let n₂ = NODE i₂ in
  n₁.fn = n₂.fn
  ∧ |n₁.args| = |n₂.args|
  ∧ ∀i ∈ {1,...,|n₁.args|}. FIND n₁.args[i] = FIND n₂.args[i]
```

Example 9.15. Consider the DAG of Figure 9.1(b). Are nodes 1 and 2 congruent? CONGRUENT notes that

- their fn fields are both f: $n_1.\mathtt{fn} = n_2.\mathtt{fn} = f$;
- their numbers of arguments are both 2;
- their left arguments $f(a, b)$ and a are both congruent to 3: $n_1.\mathtt{args} = [2; 4]$, $n_2.\mathtt{args} = [3; 4]$, and FIND 2 = FIND 3 = 3;

- and their right arguments b and b are both congruent to 4:
  $n_1.\text{args} = [2; 4]$, $n_2.\text{args} = [3; 4]$, and FIND $4 =$ FIND $4 = 4$.

Therefore, nodes 1 and 2 are congruent.   ∎

MERGE

Next, MERGE i_1 i_2 merges the congruence classes of i_1 and i_2. If FIND $i_1 =$ FIND i_2, then the two nodes are already in the same congruence class, so MERGE returns without changing the DAG structure. Otherwise, let P_{i_1} and P_{i_2} store the current values of CCPAR i_1 and CCPAR i_2, respectively. MERGE first calls UNION i_1 i_2 to compute the merged equivalence class. Then, for each pair of terms $t_1, t_2 \in P_{i_1} \times P_{i_2}$, it recursively calls MERGE t_1 t_2 if CONGRUENT t_1 t_2. This last step propagates the effects of new congruences according to the (function congruence) axiom schema. Upon completion, the new partition represents a congruence relation in which i_1 and i_2 are congruent. In code,

```
let rec MERGE i₁ i₂ =
  if FIND i₁ ≠ FIND i₂ then begin
    let Pᵢ₁ = CCPAR i₁ in
    let Pᵢ₂ = CCPAR i₂ in
    UNION i₁ i₂;
    foreach t₁, t₂ ∈ Pᵢ₁ × Pᵢ₂ do
      if FIND t₁ ≠ FIND t₂ ∧ CONGRUENT t₁ t₂
      then MERGE t₁ t₂
    done
  end
```

9.3.4 Decision Procedure for T_E-Satisfiability

Given Σ_E-formula

$$F: \quad s_1 = t_1 \ \wedge \ \cdots \ \wedge \ s_m = t_m \ \wedge \ s_{m+1} \neq t_{m+1} \ \wedge \ \cdots \ \wedge \ s_n \neq t_n$$

with subterm set S_F, perform the following steps:

1. Construct the initial DAG for the subterm set S_F.
2. For $i \in \{1, \dots, m\}$, MERGE s_i t_i.
3. If FIND $s_i =$ FIND t_i for some $i \in \{m+1, \dots, n\}$, return unsatisfiable.
4. Otherwise (if FIND $s_i \neq$ FIND t_i for all $i \in \{m+1, \dots, n\}$) return satisfiable.

Example 9.16. Consider the Σ_E-formula

$$F: \quad f(a, b) = a \ \wedge \ f(f(a, b), b) \neq a \ .$$

The subterm set is

$$S_F = \{a,\ b,\ f(a,b),\ f(f(a,b),b)\}\ ,$$

resulting in the initial partition

$$\{\{a\},\ \{b\},\ \{f(a,b)\},\ \{f(f(a,b),b)\}\}$$

in which each term is its own congruence class. The DAG of Figure 9.1(a) represents this initial partition.

According to the literal $f(a,b) = a$, MERGE 2 3. FIND 2 $\neq$ FIND 3, so let

$$P_2 = \text{CCPAR } 2 = \{1\} \quad \text{and} \quad P_3 = \text{CCPAR } 3 = \{2\}\ .$$

The UNION 2 3 computation results in the DAG of Figure 9.1(b) in which 2 and 3 are equivalent. This new equivalence makes 1 and 2 congruent, so MERGE 1 2 is called recursively.

In computing MERGE 1 2,

$$P_1 = \text{CCPAR } 1 = \emptyset \quad \text{and} \quad P_2 = \text{CCPAR } 2 = \{1,2\}\ ,$$

so $P_1 \times P_2 = \emptyset$. Hence, after computing UNION 1 2, the computation finishes with the DAG of Figure 9.1(c). The dotted edge distinguishes the deduced merge from the merge dictated by the equality in F, marked by the dashed edge. This final DAG represents the partition

$$\{\{a, f(a,b), f(f(a,b),b)\},\ \{b\}\}$$

and thus the congruence relation in which a, $f(a,b)$, and $f(f(a,b),b)$ are congruent. Does

$$\{\{a, f(a,b), f(f(a,b),b)\},\ \{b\}\} \models F\ ?$$

No, as $f(f(a,b),b) \sim a$, but F asserts that $f(f(a,b),b) \neq a$. Hence, F is T_E-unsatisfiable. ∎

Example 9.17. Consider the Σ_E-formula

$$F:\ f(f(f(a))) = a\ \wedge\ f(f(f(f(f(a))))) = a\ \wedge\ f(a) \neq a\ ,$$

which induces the initial partition and DAG shown in Figure 9.2(a). According to the literal $f(f(f(a))) = a$, MERGE 3 0. On this initial merge

$$P_3 = \{4\} \quad \text{and} \quad P_0 = \{1\}\ .$$

Additionally, the labels of both 4 and 1 are f, and their arguments, 3 and 0 respectively, are congruent after UNION 3 0. Thus, recursively MERGE 4 1. After UNION 4 1, their parents 5 and 2 are congruent, so MERGE 5 2. The recursion finishes after UNION 5 2 since $P_5 = \emptyset$, resulting in the DAG of Figure 9.2(b).

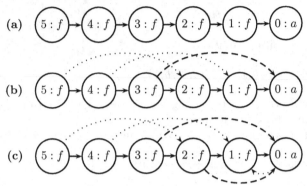

Fig. 9.2. DAGs for Example 9.17

The dotted edges distinguish deduced merges from merges dictated by F, which are marked by dashed edges. Thus, the partition is now

$$\{\{a, f^3(a)\}, \ \{f(a), f^4(a)\}, \ \{f^2(a), f^5(a)\}\} \ .$$

Next, according to the literal $f(f(f(f(f(a))))) = a$, MERGE 5 0. FIND 5 = 2 and FIND 0 = 0, so

$$P_5 = \{3\} \quad \text{and} \quad P_0 = \{1, 4\} \ .$$

After completing UNION 5 0 (by adding the dashed line from 2 to 0 in Figure 9.2(**c**)), it is the case that CONGRUENT 3 1, so MERGE 3 1. This merge causes the final UNION 3 1, resulting in the dotted line from 0 to 1 in Figure 9.2(**c**). Figure 9.2(**c**) represents the partition

$$\{\{a, f(a), f^2(a), f^3(a), f^4(a), f^5(a)\}\} \ .$$

Now, does

$$\{\{a, f(a), f^2(a), f^3(a), f^4(a), f^5(a)\}\} \models F \ ?$$

No, as $f(a) \sim a$, but F asserts that $f(a) \neq a$. Hence, F is T_E-unsatisfiable. ∎

Theorem 9.18 (Sound & Complete). *Quantifier-free conjunctive Σ_E-formula F is T_E-satisfiable iff the congruence closure algorithm returns* satisfiable.

9.3.5 ⋆Complexity

Let e be the number of edges and n be the number of nodes in the initial DAG.

Theorem 9.19 (Complexity). *The congruence closure algorithm runs in time $O(e^2)$ for $O(n)$* MERGE*s.*

However, Downey, Sethi, and Tarjan described an algorithm with $O(e \log e)$ average running time for $O(n)$ MERGEs. Computing T_E-satisfiability is inexpensive.

9.4 Recursive Data Structures

Recursive data structures include records, lists, trees, stacks, and queues. The theory T_{RDS} can model records, lists, trees, and stacks, but not queues: whereas a particular list has a single representation, queues — in which only order matters — do not. In this section, we discuss the theory of lists T_{cons} for ease of exposition. Both its axiomatization and the decision procedure for the quantifier-free fragment rely on our discussion of T_E.

Recall that the signature of T_{cons} is

$$\Sigma_{cons} : \{\text{cons, car, cdr, atom}, =\} \,,$$

where

- cons is a binary function, called the **constructor**; cons(a, b) represents the list constructed by prepending a to b;
- car is a unary function, called the **left projector**: car$(\text{cons}(a, b)) = a$;
- cdr is a unary function, called the **right projector**: cdr$(\text{cons}(a, b)) = b$;
- atom is a unary predicate;
- and $=$ is a binary predicate.

Its axioms are the following:

1. the axioms of (reflexivity), (symmetry), and (transitivity) of T_E
2. instantiations of the (function congruence) axiom schema for cons, car, and cdr:

$$\forall x_1, x_2, y_1, y_2. \ x_1 = x_2 \ \wedge \ y_1 = y_2 \ \rightarrow \ \text{cons}(x_1, y_1) = \text{cons}(x_2, y_2)$$

$$\forall x, y. \ x = y \ \rightarrow \ \text{car}(x) = \text{car}(y)$$

$$\forall x, y. \ x = y \ \rightarrow \ \text{cdr}(x) = \text{cdr}(y)$$

3. an instantiation of the (predicate congruence) axiom schema for atom:

$$\forall x, y. \ x = y \ \rightarrow \ (\text{atom}(x) \leftrightarrow \text{atom}(y))$$

4. $\forall x, y. \ \text{car}(\text{cons}(x, y)) = x$ (left projection)
5. $\forall x, y. \ \text{cdr}(\text{cons}(x, y)) = y$ (right projection)
6. $\forall x. \ \neg\text{atom}(x) \ \rightarrow \ \text{cons}(\text{car}(x), \text{cdr}(x)) = x$ (construction)
7. $\forall x, y. \ \neg\text{atom}(\text{cons}(x, y))$ (atom)

As in our discussion of T_E, we consider only quantifier-free conjunctive Σ_{cons}-formulae. Again, satisfiability of quantifier-free but non-conjunctive Σ_{cons}-formulae can be decided by converting to DNF and checking each disjunct. However, the decision procedure does not extend to the quantified case since satisfiability in the full theory T_{cons} is undecidable.

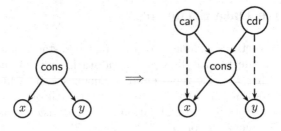

Fig. 9.3. The transformation in Step 2 of the decision procedure

Given a quantifier-free conjunctive Σ_{cons}-formula F, $\neg\text{atom}(u_i)$ literals are removed in a preprocessing step that follows from the (construction) axiom. Replace

$$\neg\text{atom}(u_i) \quad \text{with} \quad u_i = \text{cons}(u_i^1, u_i^2) .$$

Now consider Σ_{cons}-formula

$$F: \quad s_1 = t_1 \wedge \cdots \wedge s_m = t_m \wedge s_{m+1} \neq t_{m+1} \wedge \cdots \wedge s_n \neq t_n$$
$$\wedge \ \text{atom}(u_1) \wedge \cdots \wedge \text{atom}(u_\ell)$$

in which s_i, t_i, and u_i are T_{cons}-terms. To decide its T_{cons}-satisfiability, perform the following steps:

1. Construct the initial DAG for the subterm set S_F.
2. For each node n such that $n.\textbf{fn} = \text{cons}$,
   - add $\text{car}(n)$ to the DAG and MERGE $\text{car}(n)$ $n.\textbf{args}[1]$;
   - add $\text{cdr}(n)$ to the DAG and MERGE $\text{cdr}(n)$ $n.\textbf{args}[2]$
   by the (left projection) and (right projection) axioms. See Figure 9.3.
3. For $i \in \{1, \ldots, m\}$, MERGE s_i t_i.
4. For $i \in \{m+1, \ldots, n\}$, if FIND s_i = FIND t_i, return unsatisfiable.
5. For $i \in \{1, \ldots, \ell\}$ if $\exists v.$ FIND v = FIND $u_i \wedge v.\textbf{fn} = \text{cons}$, return unsatisfiable by axiom (atom).
6. Otherwise, return satisfiable.

Steps 1, 3, 4, and 6 are identical to Steps 1-4 of the decision procedure for T_{E}. Because of their similarity, it is simple to combine the two theories.

Example 9.20. Consider the $(\Sigma_{\text{cons}} \cup \Sigma_{\text{E}})$-formula

$$F: \quad \text{car}(x) = \text{car}(y) \wedge \text{cdr}(x) = \text{cdr}(y) \wedge f(x) \neq f(y)$$
$$\wedge \ \neg\text{atom}(x) \wedge \neg\text{atom}(y)$$

in which the function symbol f is in $\Sigma_{=}$. Is it $(T_{\text{cons}} \cup T_{\text{E}})$-satisfiable? According to the final two literals, x and y are non-atom structures; thus, the first two literals imply that $x = y$. Yet the third literal, $f(x) \neq f(y)$, contradicts this

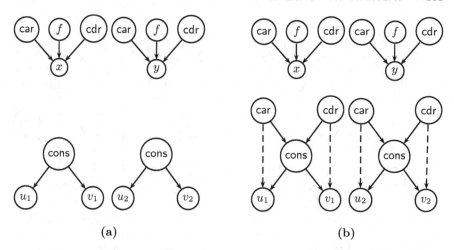

Fig. 9.4. DAG after **(a)** Step 1 and **(b)** Step 2

equality according to the (congruence) axiom of T_E. Hence, F is $(T_{cons} \cup T_E)$-unsatisfiable.

To prepare F for the decision procedure, rewrite F according to the (construction) axiom:

$$F' : \quad car(x) = car(y) \ \wedge \ cdr(x) = cdr(y) \ \wedge \ f(x) \neq f(y)$$
$$\wedge \ x = cons(u_1, v_1) \ \wedge \ y = cons(u_2, v_2) \ .$$

The first two and final two literals imply that $u_1 = u_2$ and $v_1 = v_2$ so that again $x = y$. The remaining reasoning is as for F.

Let us apply the decision procedure to F'. The initial DAG of F' is displayed in Figure 9.4(a). Figure 9.4(b) displays the DAG after Step 2.

According to the literals $car(x) = car(y)$ and $cdr(x) = cdr(y)$, compute

> MERGE $car(x)$ $car(y)$ and   MERGE $cdr(x)$ $cdr(y)$,

which add the two dashed arrows on the top of Figure 9.5(a). Then according to literal $x = cons(u_1, v_1)$,

> MERGE x $cons(u_1, v_1)$,

which adds the dashed arrow from x to cons in Figure 9.5(a). Consequently, $car(x)$ and $car(cons(u_1, v_1))$ become congruent. Since

> FIND $car(x) = car(y)$ and   FIND $car(cons(u_1, v_1)) = u_1$,

the find of $car(y)$ is set to point to u_1 during the subsequent UNION, resulting in the left dotted arrow of Figure 9.5(a). Similarly, $cdr(x)$ and $cdr(cons(u_1, v_1))$ become congruent, with similar effects (the right dotted arrow of Figure

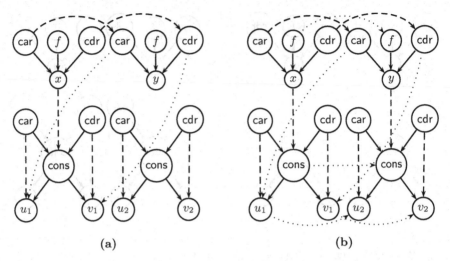

(a)   (b)

Fig. 9.5. (a) Intermediate DAG and (b) final DAG

9.5(a)). The state of the DAG after these MERGEs is shown in Figure 9.5(a). Dashed lines indicate merges that arise directly from the literals of F'; dotted lines indicate deduced merges.

Next, according to the literal $y = \text{cons}(u_2, v_2)$,

$$\text{MERGE } y \text{ cons}(u_2, v_2) \ ,$$

resulting in the new dashed line from y to $\text{cons}(u_2, v_2)$ in Figure 9.5(b). This merge produces two new congruences:

$$\text{car}(y) = \text{car}(\text{cons}(u_2, v_2)) \quad \text{and} \quad \text{cdr}(y) = \text{cdr}(\text{cons}(u_2, v_2)) \ .$$

Trace through the actions of these MERGEs to understand the addition of the two bottom dotted arrows from u_1 to u_2 and from v_1 to v_2 in Figure 9.5(b). During the computation

$$\text{MERGE } \text{cdr}(y) \text{ cdr}(\text{cons}(u_2, v_2)) \ ,$$

$\text{cons}(u_1, v_1)$ and $\text{cons}(u_2, v_2)$ become congruent; then **find** of $\text{cons}(u_1, v_1)$ is set to point to $\text{cons}(u_2, v_2)$, as represented by the new horizontal dashed line in Figure 9.5(b). This congruence causes the additional congruence

$$f(x) = f(y) \ ;$$

MERGE $f(x)$ $f(y)$ produces the final dotted edge from $f(x)$ to $f(y)$. Figure 9.5(b) displays the final DAG.

Does this DAG model F? No, as FIND $f(x)$ is $f(y)$ and FIND $f(y)$ is $f(y)$ so that $f(x) \sim f(y)$; however, F asserts that $f(x) \neq f(y)$. F is thus ($T_{\text{cons}} \cup T_{\text{E}}$)-unsatisfiable.   ∎

9.5 Arrays

Arrays are a basic nonrecursive data type in programming languages, so reasoning about them is important. In this section, we present a decision procedure for the quantifier-free fragment of T_A. This fragment is not expressive: one can assert properties only of individual elements, not of entire arrays. Chapter 11 examines a decision procedure for a more expressive fragment.

Recall from Chapter 3 that the theory of arrays T_A has signature

$$\Sigma_A : \{\cdot[\cdot], \ \cdot\langle\cdot \triangleleft \cdot\rangle, \ =\},$$

where

- $a[i]$ is a binary function: $a[i]$ represents the value of array a at position i;
- $a\langle i \triangleleft v\rangle$ is a ternary function: $a\langle i \triangleleft v\rangle$ represents the modified array a in which position i has value v;
- and $=$ is a binary predicate.

The axioms of T_A are the following:

1. the axioms of (reflexivity), (symmetry), and (transitivity) of T_E
2. $\forall a, i, j.\ i = j \ \rightarrow \ a[i] = a[j]$ (array congruence)
3. $\forall a, v, i, j.\ i = j \ \rightarrow \ a\langle i \triangleleft v\rangle[j] = v$ (read-over-write 1)
4. $\forall a, v, i, j.\ i \neq j \ \rightarrow \ a\langle i \triangleleft v\rangle[j] = a[j]$ (read-over-write 2)

We consider T_A-satisfiability in the quantifier-free fragment of T_A. As usual, we consider only conjunctive Σ_A-formulae since conversion to DNF extends the decision procedure to arbitrary quantifier-free Σ_A-formulae.

The decision procedure for T_A-satisfiability of quantifier-free Σ_A-formula F is based on a reduction to T_E-satisfiability via applications of the (read-over-write) axioms. Intuitively, if F does not contain any write terms, then the read terms can be viewed as uninterpreted function terms. Otherwise, any write term must occur in the context of a read — as a read-over-write term $a\langle i \triangleleft v\rangle[j]$ — since arrays themselves cannot be asserted to be equal or not equal. In this case, the (read-over-write) axioms can be applied to deconstruct the read-over-write terms. In detail, to decide the T_A-satisfiability of F, perform the following recursive steps.

Step 1

If F does not contain any write terms $a\langle i \triangleleft v\rangle$, perform the following steps:

1. Associate each array variable a with a fresh function symbol f_a, and replace each read term $a[i]$ with $f_a(i)$.
2. Decide and return the T_E-satisfiability of the resulting formula.

Step 2

Select some read-over-write term $a\langle i \triangleleft v\rangle[j]$ (recall that a may itself be a write term), and split on two cases:

1. According to (read-over-write 1), replace

   $$F[a\langle i \triangleleft v\rangle[j]] \quad \text{with} \quad F_1: \; F[v] \;\wedge\; i = j \;,$$

   and recurse on F_1. If F_1 is found to be T_A-satisfiable, return satisfiable.
2. According to (read-over-write 2), replace

   $$F[a\langle i \triangleleft v\rangle[j]] \quad \text{with} \quad F_2: \; F[a[j]] \;\wedge\; i \neq j \;,$$

   and recurse on F_2. If F_2 is found to be T_A-satisfiable, return satisfiable.

If both F_1 and F_2 are found to be T_A-unsatisfiable, return unsatisfiable.

Example 9.21. Consider Σ_A-formula

$$F: \; i_1 = j \;\wedge\; i_1 \neq i_2 \;\wedge\; a[j] = v_1 \;\wedge\; a\langle i_1 \triangleleft v_1\rangle\langle i_2 \triangleleft v_2\rangle[j] \neq a[j] \;.$$

Recall that $a\langle i_1 \triangleleft v_1\rangle\langle i_2 \triangleleft v_2\rangle[j]$ abbreviates the term

$$((a\langle i_1 \triangleleft v_1\rangle)\langle i_2 \triangleleft v_2\rangle)[j] \;.$$

F contains a write term, so select a read-over-write term to deconstruct:

$$a\langle i_1 \triangleleft v_1\rangle\langle i_2 \triangleleft v_2\rangle[j] \;.$$

According to (read-over-write 1), assume $i_2 = j$ and recurse on

$$F_1: \; i_2 = j \;\wedge\; i_1 = j \;\wedge\; i_1 \neq i_2 \;\wedge\; a[j] = v_1 \;\wedge\; v_2 \neq a[j] \;.$$

F_1 does not contain any write terms, so rewrite it to

$$F_1': \; i_2 = j \;\wedge\; i_1 = j \;\wedge\; i_1 \neq i_2 \;\wedge\; f_a(j) = v_1 \;\wedge\; v_2 \neq f_a(j) \;.$$

The first two literals imply that $i_1 = i_2$, contradicting the third literal, so F_1' is T_E-unsatisfiable.

Returning, we try the second case: according to (read-over-write 2), assume $i_2 \neq j$ and recurse on

$$F_2: \; i_2 \neq j \;\wedge\; i_1 = j \;\wedge\; i_1 \neq i_2 \;\wedge\; a[j] = v_1 \;\wedge\; a\langle i_1 \triangleleft v_1\rangle[j] \neq a[j] \;.$$

F_2 contains a write term, so select the only read-over-write term to deconstruct. According to (read-over-write 1), assume $i_1 = j$ and recurse on

$$F_3: \; i_1 = j \;\wedge\; i_2 \neq j \;\wedge\; i_1 = j \;\wedge\; i_1 \neq i_2 \;\wedge\; a[j] = v_1 \;\wedge\; v_1 \neq a[j] \;.$$

Clearly, following this path leads to a contradiction because of the final two terms. Thus, according to (read-over-write 2), assume $i_1 \neq j$ and recurse on

$$F_4: \; i_1 \neq j \;\wedge\; i_2 \neq j \;\wedge\; i_1 = j \;\wedge\; i_1 \neq i_2 \;\wedge\; a[j] = v_1 \;\wedge\; a[j] \neq a[j] \;.$$

But the final literal is contradictory. As all branches have been tried, F is T_A-unsatisfiable. ∎

Theorem 9.22 (Sound & Complete). *Given quantifier-free conjunctive Σ_A-formula F, the decision procedure returns* satisfiable *iff F is T_A-satisfiable; otherwise, it returns* unsatisfiable.

Theorem 9.23 (Complexity). T_A*-satisfiability of quantifier-free conjunctive Σ_A-formulae is* NP*-complete.*

The power of disjunction manifested in Steps 2(a) and 2(b) of the decision procedure results in this complexity.

Proof. That the problem is in NP is simple: for a given formula F, guess a formula like F, except that for every instance of a read-over-write term $a\langle i \lhd v\rangle[j]$, it includes as a conjunction either $i = j$ or $i \neq j$. Only a linear number of literals are added. Then check T_A-satisfiability of this formula, using the new literals to simplify read-over-write terms.

To prove NP-hardness, we reduce from satisfiability of PL formulae, which is NP-complete. Given a propositional formula F in CNF, assert

$$v_P \neq v_{\neg P}$$

for each variable P in F; v_P and $v_{\neg P}$ represent the values of P and $\neg P$, respectively. Introduce a fresh constant $\bullet$. Then consider the nth clause of F, say

$$(\neg P \lor Q \lor \neg R) .$$

In this case, assert

$$a[j_n] \neq \bullet \ \land \ a\langle i_P \lhd v_{\neg P}\rangle\langle i_Q \lhd v_Q\rangle\langle i_R \lhd v_{\neg R}\rangle[j_n] = \bullet .$$

j_n must be equal to one of the introduced values at i_P, i_Q, or i_R. Therefore, at cell j_n the corresponding value ($v_{\neg P}$, v_Q, or $v_{\neg R}$) must equal $\bullet$. In this fashion, add an assertion for each clause of F. Conjoin all assertions to form quantifier-free conjunctive Σ_A-formula G. G is equisatisfiable to F: $v_P = \bullet$ iff P is true; and $v_{\neg P}$ iff P is false. G is also of size polynomial in the size of F. Thus, deciding T_A-satisfiability of G decides propositional satisfiability of F, so T_A-satisfiability is NP-complete. ∎

9.6 Summary

This chapter presents the congruence closure algorithm and applications to deciding satisfiability in the quantifier-free fragments of T_E, T_{cons}, and T_A. It covers:

- The *congruence closure algorithm* at an abstract level. Relations, equivalence relations, congruence relations. Partitions; equivalence and congruence classes. Closures.

- The *DAG-based implementation*. Directed acyclic graph representation of formulae. The union-find algorithm. Merging.
- *Recursive data structures*. These structures include records, lists, stacks, and trees, but not queues. The decision procedure extends the congruence closure algorithm.
- *Arrays*. The decision procedure branches based on read-over-write terms according to the read-over-write axioms. When all write terms have been removed on one branch, the congruence closure algorithm is applied.

Equality is found within many first-order theories, including all the theories studied in this book. Additionally, equality and the congruence closure algorithm are the unifying components of the Nelson-Oppen combination method studied in Chapter 10. Hence, reasoning about it is fundamental. Fortunately, satisfiability is efficiently decidable using the congruence closure algorithm.

Uninterpreted functions are used to represent data structures in the context of T_{RDS} and T_{A}. In applications such as software and hardware verification, they allow abstracting away implementations of select components to simplify reasoning.

The DAG-based data structure that is the basis of the congruence closure algorithm is used whenever subformulae must be represented uniquely, either for algorithm correctness or for space and time considerations. Exercises 9.4 and 9.5 explore this data structure.

So far, we have seen three types of decision procedures. The quantifier-elimination procedures of Chapter 7 manipulate formulae to construct equivalent quantifier-free (and possibly variable-free) formulae. The simplex method of Chapter 8 works explicitly with the underlying structure of the set of satisfying interpretations. The congruence closure algorithm shares characteristics of both types of procedures: it manipulates formulae efficiently using the DAG-based algorithm; but it also represents satisfying interpretations explicitly as congruence classes of terms via the find pointers.

Bibliographic Remarks

The quantifier-free fragment of T_{E} was first proved decidable by Ackermann in 1954 [1] and later studied by various teams in the late 1970s. Shostak [83], Nelson and Oppen [66], and Downey, Sethi, and Tarjan [29] present alternate solutions to the problem. We discuss the method of Nelson and Oppen [66].

Oppen presents a theory of acyclic recursive data structures [69, 71]. The decision problem in the quantifier-free fragment of this theory is decidable in linear time, and the full theory is decidable. Our presentation is based on the work of Nelson and Oppen [66] for possibly-cyclic data structures.

McCarthy proposes the axiomatization of arrays based on read-over-write [58]. James King implemented the decision procedure for the quantifier-free fragment as part of his thesis work [50].

Exercises

9.1 (DP for T_E). Apply the decision procedure for T_E to the following Σ_E-formulae. Provide a level of detail as in Example 9.10.

(a) $f(x,y) = f(y,x) \ \wedge \ f(a,y) \neq f(y,a)$
(b) $f(g(x)) = g(f(x)) \ \wedge \ f(g(f(y))) = x \ \wedge \ f(y) = x \ \wedge \ g(f(x)) \neq x$
(c) $f(f(f(a))) = f(f(a)) \ \wedge \ f(f(f(f(a)))) = a \ \wedge \ f(a) \neq a$
(d) $f(f(f(a))) = f(a) \ \wedge \ f(f(a)) = a \ \wedge \ f(a) \neq a$
(e) $p(x) \ \wedge \ f(f(x)) = x \ \wedge \ f(f(f(x))) = x \ \wedge \ \neg p(f(x))$

9.2 (DAG-based DP for T_E). Apply the DAG-based decision procedure for T_E to the Σ_E-formulae of Exercise 9.1. Provide a level of detail as in Example 9.17.

9.3 (*Undecidable fragment). Show that allowing even one quantifier alternation (*i.e.*, $\exists x_1, \ldots, x_k. \ \forall y_1, \ldots, y_n. \ F[\overline{x}, \overline{y}]$) makes satisfiability in T_E undecidable.

9.4 (*DAG). Describe a data structure and algorithm for constructing the initial DAG in the congruence closure procedure. It should run in time approximately linear in the size of the formula.

9.5 (*PL & DAGs). This problem explores a concise representation of propositional logic formulae.

(a) Describe a DAG-based representation of PL formulae.
(b) If you have not already done so, consider that the logical connectives $\wedge$ and $\vee$ are associative and commutative. Improve your representation to exploit this observation.
(c) Modify the CNF conversion algorithm of Section 1.7.3 to operate on your DAG-based representation. How large is the resulting CNF formula relative to the DAG?

9.6 (DP for T_{cons}). Apply the decision procedure for T_{cons} to the following T_{cons}-formulae. Provide a level of detail as in Example 9.20.

(a) $\mathsf{car}(x) = y \ \wedge \ \mathsf{cdr}(x) = z \ \wedge \ x \neq \mathsf{cons}(y,z)$
(b) $\neg\mathsf{atom}(x) \ \wedge \ \mathsf{car}(x) = y \ \wedge \ \mathsf{cdr}(x) = z \ \wedge \ x \neq \mathsf{cons}(y,z)$

9.7 (Flawed DP for T_{cons}). Consider a variant of the T_{cons}-satisfiability procedure in which Steps 2 and 3 are swapped.[1] What is wrong with reversing these two steps? Identify a counterexample to its correctness: find a T_{cons}-unsatisfiable (conjunctive, quantifier-free) Σ_{cons}-formula that the incorrect procedure claims is satisfiable, and show the final DAGs for both the incorrect and the correct procedures.

---

[1] Suggested by a typo in [66].

9.8 (DP for quantifier-free T_A). Apply the decision procedure for quantifier-free T_A to the following Σ_A-formulae.

(a) $a\langle i \triangleleft e\rangle[j] = e \ \wedge \ i \neq j$

(b) $a\langle i \triangleleft e\rangle[j] = e \ \wedge \ a[j] \neq e$

(c) $a\langle i \triangleleft e\rangle[j] = e \ \wedge \ i \neq j \ \wedge \ a[j] \neq e$

(d) $a\langle i \triangleleft e\rangle\langle j \triangleleft f\rangle[k] = g \ \wedge \ j \neq k \ \wedge \ i = j \ \wedge \ a[k] \neq g$

(e) $i_1 = j \ \wedge \ a[j] = v_1 \ \wedge \ a\langle i_1 \triangleleft v_1\rangle\langle i_2 \triangleleft v_2\rangle[j] \neq a[j]$

Combining Decision Procedures

The expressions which arise in program manipulation often do not fall within any... naturally defined theories — they usually involve mixed terms containing functions and predicates from several theories.
— Greg Nelson and Derek C. Oppen
Simplification by Cooperating Decision Procedures, 1979

Chapters 7–9 consider decision procedures for theories that each formalize just one data type. Yet almost all formulae in Chapter 5 are formulae of union theories. For example, many assert facts in $T_{\mathbb{Z}} \cup T_A$ about arrays of integers indexed by integers. Additionally, the decision procedure for the array property fragment of $T_A^{\mathbb{Z}}$ that we discuss in Chapter 11 requires a procedure for the quantifier-free fragment of $T_{\mathbb{Z}} \cup T_A$. Can we reuse the decision procedures of Chapters 7–9 to decide satisfiability of formulae in union theories, or must we invent a new procedure for each combination?

Fortunately, there is a general result for quantifier-free fragments of union theories that allows us to reuse the procedures. This chapter discusses the **Nelson-Oppen combination method** for constructing decision procedures for union theories from decision procedures for individual theories. Section 10.1 introduces the method and discusses its limitations. Then Section 10.2 presents a nondeterministic version, for which correctness is proved in Section 10.4; and Section 10.3 presents the more practical deterministic version.

In this chapter, decision procedures for individual theories apply just to quantifier-free fragments. We rely on Cooper's method with all optimizations for considering quantifier-free $\Sigma_{\mathbb{Z}}$-formulae. Procedures for the other theories already apply only to their quantifier-free fragments.

10.1 Combining Decision Procedures

Consider two theories T_1 and T_2 over signatures Σ_1 and Σ_2, respectively. For the quantifier-free fragments of T_1 and T_2, we have decision procedures P_1 and P_2. How do we decide satisfiability in the quantifier-free fragment of $T_1 \cup T_2$?

Example 10.1. Consider the $(\Sigma_E \cup \Sigma_Z)$-formula

$$F : 1 \le x \ \wedge \ x \le 2 \ \wedge \ f(x) \ne f(1) \ \wedge \ f(x) \ne f(2) \ .$$

Chapter 9 describes a decision procedure for T_E, while Chapter 7 presents a decision procedure for T_Z. We would like to combine these decision procedures to decide the $(T_E \cup T_Z)$-satisfiability of F and other quantifier-free $(\Sigma_E \cup \Sigma_Z)$-formulae. ∎

The **Nelson-Oppen combination method** (**N-O** method) combines decision procedures for the quantifier-free fragments of several theories into one decision procedure for the quantifier-free fragment of the union theory. In our presentation of the N-O method, we usually discuss combining two theories and their decision procedures; however, the N-O method can combine an arbitrary number of theories and procedures. Additionally, we restrict ourselves to considering conjunctive formulae; however, the satisfiability of arbitrary (quantifier-free) formulae can be considered by converting to DNF and checking each disjunct.

Besides being restricted to quantifier-free formulae, the N-O method has two additional restrictions. First, the signatures Σ_1 and Σ_2 can only share equality $=$:

$$\Sigma_1 \cap \Sigma_2 = \{=\} \ .$$

Second, the theories T_1 and T_2 must be stably infinite.

A theory T with signature Σ is **stably infinite** if for every quantifier-free Σ-formula F, if F is T-satisfiable, then there exists some T-interpretation that satisfies F and has a domain of infinite cardinality. We illustrate this concept with two example theories.

Example 10.2. Consider the theory $T_{a,b}$ with signature

$$\Sigma_2 : \ \{a, \ b, \ =\} \ ,$$

where both a and b are constants, and axiom

1. $\forall x. \ x = a \ \vee \ x = b$ (two)

Because of axiom (two), every $T_{a,b}$-interpretation $I : (D_I, \alpha_I)$ is such that the domain D_I has at most two elements: $|D_I| \le 2$. Hence, $T_{a,b}$ is not stably infinite. ∎

Example 10.3. We prove that T_E is stably infinite. Consider the T_E-satisfiable quantifier-free Σ_E-formula F with arbitrary satisfying T_E-interpretation $I : (D_I, \alpha_I)$ in which α_I maps $=$ to $=_I$. Let A be any infinite set disjoint from D_I. Then construct new interpretation $J : (D_J, \alpha_J)$:

- $D_J = D_I \cup A$

- $\alpha_J = \{= \mapsto =_J, \ldots\}$, where for $v_1, v_2 \in D_J$,

$$v_1 =_J v_2 \stackrel{\text{def}}{=} \begin{cases} v_1 =_I v_2 & \text{if } v_1, v_2 \in D_I \\ \top & \text{if } v_1 \text{ is the same element as } v_2 \\ \bot & \text{otherwise} \end{cases}$$

J is a T_E-interpretation satisfying F with infinite domain. Hence, T_E is stably infinite. ∎

The other theories discussed in this book are also stably infinite.

Example 10.4. Consider the quantifier-free conjunctive $(\Sigma_\mathsf{E} \cup \Sigma_\mathbb{Z})$-formula

$$F : 1 \leq x \,\wedge\, x \leq 2 \,\wedge\, f(x) \neq f(1) \,\wedge\, f(x) \neq f(2) .$$

The signatures of T_E and $T_\mathbb{Z}$ only share $=$. Also, both theories are stably infinite. Hence, the N-O combination of the decision procedures for T_E and $T_\mathbb{Z}$ decides the $(T_\mathsf{E} \cup T_\mathbb{Z})$-satisfiability of F.

Intuitively, F is $(T_\mathsf{E} \cup T_\mathbb{Z})$-unsatisfiable. For the first two literals imply $x = 1 \,\vee\, x = 2$ so that $f(x) = f(1) \,\vee\, f(x) = f(2)$. Yet the last two literals contradict this conclusion. ∎

10.2 Nelson-Oppen Method: Nondeterministic Version

In this section, we discuss the nondeterministic version of the N-O method. While simple to present, it suffers from high complexity. Section 10.3 reformulates the method to be deterministic and efficient.

Consider a quantifier-free conjunctive $(\Sigma_1 \cup \Sigma_2)$-formula F. The N-O method proceeds in two steps.

10.2.1 Phase 1: Variable Abstraction

The variable abstraction phase transforms a quantifier-free conjunctive formula F into two quantifier-free conjunctive formulae, a Σ_1-formula F_1 and a Σ_2-formula F_2, such that F and $F_1 \wedge F_2$ are $(T_1 \cup T_2)$-equisatisfiable. That is, F is $(T_1 \cup T_2)$-satisfiable iff $F_1 \wedge F_2$ is $(T_1 \cup T_2)$-satisfiable. F_1 and F_2 are linked via a set of shared variables.

For term t, let $\mathsf{hd}(t)$ be the root symbol; $e.g.$, $\mathsf{hd}(f(x)) = f$. Then for $i, j \in \{1, 2\}$ and $i \neq j$, repeat the following transformations as long as possible:

1. if function $f \in \Sigma_i$ and $\mathsf{hd}(t) \in \Sigma_j$,

$$F[f(t_1, \ldots, t, \ldots, t_n)] \implies F[f(t_1, \ldots, w, \ldots, t_n)] \,\wedge\, w = t$$

2. if predicate $p \in \Sigma_i$ and $\mathsf{hd}(t) \in \Sigma_j$,

$$F[p(t_1, \ldots, t, \ldots, t_n)] \implies F[p(t_1, \ldots, w, \ldots, t_n)] \,\wedge\, w = t$$

3. if $\mathsf{hd}(s) \in \Sigma_i$ and $\mathsf{hd}(t) \in \Sigma_j$,

$$F[s = t] \quad \Longrightarrow \quad F[w = t] \ \wedge \ w = s$$

w is a fresh variable in each application of a transformation. Transformation 3 also applies to $s \neq t$ literals: replace $F[s \neq t]$ with $F[w \neq t] \ \wedge \ w = s$.

After applying the transformations, each literal of the resulting formula falls entirely within the signature of one of the two theories (or possibly within each if it is just an equality $x = y$ or a disequality $x \neq y$ between variables: such literals are in every signature since they do not have symbols other than $=$). Divide the literals into two sets, one for each theory. These sets are not disjoint when there is a literal that is an equality or disequality between variables. Then return the conjunction of each set.

Example 10.5. Consider $(\Sigma_\mathsf{E} \cup \Sigma_\mathbb{Z})$-formula

$$F : \ 1 \leq x \ \wedge \ x \leq 2 \ \wedge \ f(x) \neq f(1) \ \wedge \ f(x) \neq f(2) .$$

Since $f \in \Sigma_=$ and $1 \in \Sigma_\mathbb{Z}$, replace $f(1)$ by $f(w_1)$ and add $w_1 = 1$ by transformation 1. Similarly, replace $f(2)$ by $f(w_2)$ and add $w_2 = 2$.

Now, the literals

$$1 \leq x, \ x \leq 2, \ w_1 = 1, \ \text{and} \ w_2 = 2$$

are $T_\mathbb{Z}$-literals, while the literals

$$f(x) \neq f(w_1) \ \text{and} \ f(x) \neq f(w_2)$$

are T_E-literals. Hence, construct the $\Sigma_\mathbb{Z}$-formula

$$F_\mathbb{Z} : \ 1 \leq x \ \wedge \ x \leq 2 \ \wedge \ w_1 = 1 \ \wedge \ w_2 = 2$$

and the Σ_E-formula

$$F_\mathsf{E} : \ f(x) \neq f(w_1) \ \wedge \ f(x) \neq f(w_2) .$$

$F_\mathbb{Z}$ and F_E share the variables x, w_1, and w_2. $F_\mathbb{Z} \wedge F_\mathsf{E}$ is $(T_\mathsf{E} \cup T_\mathbb{Z})$-equisatisfiable to F. ∎

Example 10.6. Consider the $(\Sigma_\mathsf{E} \cup \Sigma_\mathbb{Z})$-formula

$$F : \ f(x) = x + y \ \wedge \ x \leq y + z \ \wedge \ x + z \leq y \ \wedge \ y = 1 \ \wedge \ f(x) \neq f(2) .$$

Intuitively, F is $(T_\mathsf{E} \cup T_\mathbb{Z})$-satisfiable: consider an interpretation in which $x = 0$, $y = 1$, $z = 1$, $f(0) = 1$, and $f(2) = 2$.

In the first literal, $\mathsf{hd}(f(x)) = f \in \Sigma_\mathsf{E}$ and $\mathsf{hd}(x + y) = + \in \Sigma_\mathbb{Z}$; thus, by transformation 3, replace the literal with

$$w_1 = x + y \ \wedge \ w_1 = f(x) .$$

In the last literal, $f \in \Sigma_E$ but $2 \in \Sigma_{\mathbb{Z}}$, so by transformation 1, replace it with

$$f(x) \neq f(w_2) \wedge w_2 = 2 .$$

Now, separating the literals results in two formulae:

$$F_{\mathbb{Z}} : w_1 = x + y \wedge x \leq y + z \wedge x + z \leq y \wedge y = 1 \wedge w_2 = 2$$

is a $\Sigma_{\mathbb{Z}}$-formula, and

$$F_E : w_1 = f(x) \wedge f(x) \neq f(w_2)$$

is a Σ_E-formula. The conjunction $F_{\mathbb{Z}} \wedge F_E$ is $(T_E \cup T_{\mathbb{Z}})$-equisatisfiable to F. ∎

10.2.2 Phase 2: Guess and Check

Phase 1 separates $(\Sigma_1 \cup \Sigma_2)$-formula F into two formulae, Σ_1-formula F_1, and Σ_2-formula F_2. F_1 and F_2 are linked by a set of shared variables. Let

$$V = \mathsf{shared}(F_1, F_2) = \mathsf{free}(F_1) \cap \mathsf{free}(F_2)$$

be the shared variables of F_1 and F_2. Let E be an equivalence relation over V. The **arrangement** $\alpha(V, E)$ of V induced by E is the formula

$$\alpha(V, E) : \bigwedge_{u,v \,\in\, V.\ uEv} u = v \wedge \bigwedge_{u,v \,\in\, V.\ \neg(uEv)} u \neq v ,$$

which asserts that variables related by E are equal and that variables unrelated by E are not equal. The formula F is $(T_1 \cup T_2)$-satisfiable iff there exists an equivalence relation E of V such that

- $F_1 \wedge \alpha(V, E)$ is T_1-satisfiable, and
- $F_2 \wedge \alpha(V, E)$ is T_2-satisfiable.

Otherwise, F is $(T_1 \cup T_2)$-unsatisfiable.

Example 10.7. Consider $(\Sigma_E \cup \Sigma_{\mathbb{Z}})$-formula

$$F : 1 \leq x \wedge x \leq 2 \wedge f(x) \neq f(1) \wedge f(x) \neq f(2) .$$

Phase 1 separates this formula into the $\Sigma_{\mathbb{Z}}$-formula

$$F_{\mathbb{Z}} : 1 \leq x \wedge x \leq 2 \wedge w_1 = 1 \wedge w_2 = 2$$

and the Σ_E-formula

$$F_E : f(x) \neq f(w_1) \wedge f(x) \neq f(w_2) ,$$

with

$$V = \mathsf{shared}(F_{\mathbb{Z}}, F_E) = \{x, w_1, w_2\} .$$

There are 5 equivalence relations to consider, which we list by stating the partitions:

1. $\{\{x, w_1, w_2\}\}$, *i.e.*, $x = w_1 = w_2$: $F_E \wedge \alpha(V, E)$ is T_E-unsatisfiable because it cannot be the case that both $x = w_1$ and $f(x) \neq f(w_1)$.
2. $\{\{x, w_1\}, \{w_2\}\}$, *i.e.*, $x = w_1$, $x \neq w_2$: $F_E \wedge \alpha(V, E)$ is T_E-unsatisfiable because it cannot be the case that both $x = w_1$ and $f(x) \neq f(w_1)$.
3. $\{\{x, w_2\}, \{w_1\}\}$, *i.e.*, $x = w_2$, $x \neq w_1$: $F_E \wedge \alpha(V, E)$ is T_E-unsatisfiable because it cannot be the case that both $x = w_2$ and $f(x) \neq f(w_2)$.
4. $\{\{x\}, \{w_1, w_2\}\}$, *i.e.*, $x \neq w_1$, $w_1 = w_2$: $F_Z \wedge \alpha(V, E)$ is T_Z-unsatisfiable because it cannot be the case that both $w_1 = w_2$ and $w_1 = 1 \wedge w_2 = 2$.
5. $\{\{x\}, \{w_1\}, \{w_2\}\}$, *i.e.*, $x \neq w_1$, $x \neq w_2$, $w_1 \neq w_2$: $F_Z \wedge \alpha(V, E)$ is T_Z-unsatisfiable because it cannot be the case that both $x \neq w_1 \wedge x \neq w_2$ and $x = w_1 = 1 \vee x = w_2 = 2$ (since $1 \leq x \leq 2$ implies that $x = 1 \vee x = 2$ in T_Z).

Hence, F is $(T_E \cup T_Z)$-unsatisfiable. ∎

Example 10.8. Consider the $(\Sigma_{\text{cons}} \cup \Sigma_Z)$-formula

$$F : \quad \text{car}(x) + \text{car}(y) = z \; \wedge \; \text{cons}(x, z) \neq \text{cons}(y, z) \; .$$

After two applications of transformation 1, Phase 1 separates F into the Σ_{cons}-formula

$$F_{\text{cons}} : \quad w_1 = \text{car}(x) \; \wedge \; w_2 = \text{car}(y) \; \wedge \; \text{cons}(x, z) \neq \text{cons}(y, z)$$

and the Σ_Z-formula

$$F_Z : \quad w_1 + w_2 = z \; ,$$

with

$$V = \text{shared}(F_{\text{cons}}, F_Z) = \{z, w_1, w_2\} \; .$$

Consider the equivalence relation E given by the partition

$$\{\{z\}, \{w_1\}, \{w_2\}\} \; .$$

The arrangement

$$\alpha(V, E) : \quad z \neq w_1 \; \wedge \; z \neq w_2 \; \wedge \; w_1 \neq w_2$$

satisfies both F_{cons} and F_Z: $F_{\text{cons}} \wedge \alpha(V, E)$ is T_{cons}-satisfiable, and $F_Z \wedge \alpha(V, E)$ is T_Z-satisfiable. Hence, F is $(T_{\text{cons}} \cup T_Z)$-satisfiable. ∎

10.2.3 Practical Efficiency

Phase 2 is formulated as "guess and check": first, guess an equivalence relation E, then check the induced arrangement. Unfortunately, the number of equivalence relations increases significantly with the number of shared variables. The number of equivalence relations is given by the sequence of **Bell numbers**, which grows super-exponentially. For example, just 12 shared variables induce over four million equivalence relations. Hence, the guess-and-check method is impractical.

However, there is no need to guess the entire equivalence relation at once; instead, construct it incrementally, as the following example illustrates:

Example 10.9. In Example 10.6, Phase 1 separates the $(\Sigma_E \cup \Sigma_\mathbb{Z})$-formula

$$F : \; f(x) = x + y \; \wedge \; x \leq y + z \; \wedge \; x + z \leq y \; \wedge \; y = 1 \; \wedge \; f(x) \neq f(2)$$

into $\Sigma_\mathbb{Z}$-formula

$$F_\mathbb{Z} : \; w_1 = x + y \; \wedge \; x \leq y + z \; \wedge \; x + z \leq y \; \wedge \; y = 1 \; \wedge \; w_2 = 2$$

and Σ_E-formula

$$F_E : \; w_1 = f(x) \; \wedge \; f(x) \neq f(w_2)$$

Then

$$V = \mathsf{shared}(F_\mathbb{Z}, F_E) = \{x, w_1, w_2\} \; .$$

We attempt to construct an arrangement.

1. Suppose $x = w_1$. But then $w_1 = x + y$ of $F_\mathbb{Z}$ implies that $y = 0$, yet $F_\mathbb{Z}$ asserts that $y = 1$. Hence, $x \neq w_1$.
2. $F_\mathbb{Z} \wedge x \neq w_1$ and $F_E \wedge x \neq w_1$ are $T_\mathbb{Z}$- and T_E-satisfiable, respectively.
3. Suppose $x = w_2$. But $f(x) \neq f(w_2)$ of F_E contradicts this supposition. Hence, $x \neq w_2$.
4. $F_\mathbb{Z} \wedge x \neq w_1 \wedge x \neq w_2$ and $F_E \wedge x \neq w_1 \wedge x \neq w_2$ are $T_\mathbb{Z}$- and T_E-satisfiable, respectively.
5. Suppose $w_1 = w_2$. No contradiction exists.

We discovered the arrangement

$$x \neq w_1 \; \wedge \; x \neq w_2 \; \wedge \; w_1 = w_2 \; ,$$

so F is $(T_E \cup T_\mathbb{Z})$-satisfiable. ∎

Readers interested in implementing a simple Nelson-Oppen-based decision procedure could consider this incremental-construction "optimization" of the nondeterministic method. However, in practice, implementations are based on the deterministic method described in the next section.

10.3 Nelson-Oppen Method: Deterministic Version

Phase 1 of the deterministic version is the same as in the nondeterministic version.

Phase 2 of the nondeterministic method (both the guess-and-check method and the optimized incremental construction) proposes a set of equalities and disequalities and then lets each decision procedure P_i check the set with the corresponding formula F_i. In contrast, Phase 2 of the deterministic version asks the decision procedures P_1 and P_2 to propagate information in the form of new equalities.

A **convex** theory is particularly well-suited for propagating equalities. Section 10.3.1 discusses convex theories. Then Section 10.3.2 presents the deterministic Nelson-Oppen method.

10.3.1 Convex Theories

If a conjunctive formula in a convex theory implies a disjunction of equalities between variables, then it actually implies a single equality. Formally, consider a quantifier-free conjunctive Σ-formula F and a disjunction

$$G: \bigvee_{i=1}^{n} u_i = v_i \,, \tag{10.1}$$

for variables u_i and v_i. Theory T is **convex** if for every such F and G, if

$$F \Rightarrow \bigvee_{i=1}^{n} u_i = v_i$$

then

$$F \Rightarrow u_i = v_i \quad \text{for some } i \in \{1, \ldots, n\} \,.$$

If F implies G, then F actually implies one of the disjuncts of G.

Intuitively, F cannot be "covered" by any disjunction of equalities — no matter how many — if no single equality covers F (F is covered by a formula if F implies it). This intuition is especially apparent for vector spaces (Section 8.2): a plane cannot be covered by a finite disjunction of lines; it cannot even be covered by a finite disjunction of other planes unless at least one of the planes is the plane itself.

Example 10.10. The theory of integers $T_{\mathbb{Z}}$ is not convex. For consider the quantifier-free conjunctive $\Sigma_{\mathbb{Z}}$-formula

$$F: 1 \leq z \wedge z \leq 2 \wedge u = 1 \wedge v = 2 \,.$$

Then

$$F \;\Rightarrow\; z = u \;\vee\; z = v \,,$$

but neither

$$F \;\Rightarrow\; z = u \quad \text{nor} \quad F \;\Rightarrow\; z = v \,.$$

■

Example 10.11. The theory of arrays T_A is not convex. For consider the quantifier-free conjunctive Σ_A-formula

$$F : \; a\langle i \triangleleft v \rangle[j] = v \,.$$

Then

$$F \;\Rightarrow\; i = j \;\vee\; a[j] = v \,,$$

but neither

$$F \;\Rightarrow\; i = j \quad \text{nor} \quad F \;\Rightarrow\; a[j] = v \,.$$

■

Example 10.12. ★ The theory of rationals $T_{\mathbb{Q}}$ is convex, as it is convex in a geometric sense (see Chapter 8).

Each equality $u_i = v_i$ of the disjunction G of (10.1) is geometrically convex, but G itself is not. Consider, for example,

$$H : \; x = y \;\vee\; x = z \,.$$

Let S_H be the set of points satisfying H. The point $(x, y, z) = (0, 0, 1)$ is included in S_H, as is the point $(1, 0, 1)$. However, the average of the two points, $(\frac{1}{2}, 0, 1)$ (choosing $\lambda = \frac{1}{2}$), is not in S_H. Indeed, choose any two points

$$(u, u, v_1) \quad \text{and} \quad (w, v_2, w)$$

from $S_{x=y}$ and $S_{x=z}$, respectively, such that neither is in their intersection $S_{x=y=z}$ (i.e., $v_1 \neq u$ and $v_2 \neq w$). Then for any $\lambda \in (0, 1)$, the point

$$(\lambda u + (1 - \lambda)w, \; \lambda u + (1 - \lambda)v_2, \; \lambda v_1 + (1 - \lambda)w)$$

is neither in $S_{x=y}$ nor in $S_{x=z}$.

Suppose, then, that $F \Rightarrow G : \bigvee_{i=1}^{n} u_i = v_i$, but for no $i \in \{1, \ldots, n\}$ does $F \Rightarrow u_i = v_i$. Then it must be the case that there are two points s_1 and s_2 of S_F in separate subsets $S_{u_i = v_i}$, $S_{u_j = v_j}$, $i \neq j$, of S_G. By the argument above, the points on the line segment between s_1 and s_2 are not in S_G and thus not in S_F. Then F is not geometrically convex, a contradiction.

Thus, $T_{\mathbb{Q}}$ is convex. ■

Exercise 10.5 asks the reader to prove that the theories T_E and T_{cons} are also convex.

10.3.2 Phase 2: Equality Propagation

Recall that the nondeterministic version guesses an equivalence relation E over the shared variables V and checks that both $F_1 \wedge \alpha(V, E)$ is T_1-satisfiable and $F_2 \wedge \alpha(V, E)$ is T_2-satisfiable. If it finds a satisfying equivalence relation E, it declares that F is $(T_1 \cup T_2)$-satisfiable. This method suffers from the enormous number of equivalence relations that are possible even over small sets of shared variables. In the deterministic version, a central manager asks the decision procedures P_1 and P_2 to report any new implied equalities between shared variables. It then adds this new information to the already discovered equalities and propagates it to the other decision procedure. This method is efficient.

In the context of already discovered equalities $\mathcal{E}$, a decision procedure P_i for a convex theory T_i discovers a new equality $u = v$, for shared variables u and v, when

$$F_i \wedge \mathcal{E} \Rightarrow u = v .$$

The central manager then propagates this new equality to the other decision procedure.

If T_j is not convex, P_j discovers a new disjunction of equalities S when

$$F_j \wedge \mathcal{E} \Rightarrow \bigvee_{u_i = v_i \ \in \ S} (u_i = v_i) ,$$

for shared variables u_i and v_i. In this case, the central manager must split the disjunction and search along multiple branches. Each branch assumes one of the disjuncts. The search along a branch ends either when a full arrangement is discovered (so the original formula is $(T_1 \cup T_2)$-satisfiable; see below) or when all sub-branches end in contradiction (T_i-unsatisfiability for some i). In the latter case, the central manager tries another branch. If no branches remain to try, then the central manager declares the original formula to be $(T_1 \cup T_2)$-unsatisfiable.

If at some point, neither P_1 nor P_2 finds a new equality (or a disjunction of equalities in the non-convex case), then the central manager concludes that the given formula is $(T_1 \cup T_2)$-satisfiable. For if $\mathcal{E}$ is the set of all learned equalities, S is the set of all possible remaining equalities, and

$$F_1 \wedge \mathcal{E} \not\Rightarrow \bigvee_{u_i = v_i \ \in \ S} (u_i = v_i) \quad \text{and} \quad F_2 \wedge \mathcal{E} \not\Rightarrow \bigvee_{u_i = v_i \ \in \ S} (u_i = v_i) ,$$

(which must hold when no new disjunctions of equalities are discovered), then

$$F_1 \wedge \mathcal{E} \wedge \bigwedge_{u_i = v_i \ \in \ S} (u_i \neq v_i) \quad \text{and} \quad F_2 \wedge \mathcal{E} \wedge \bigwedge_{u_i = v_i \ \in \ S} (u_i \neq v_i)$$

are T_1-satisfiable and T_2-satisfiable, respectively. Hence, the discovered arrangement is

$$\alpha(V, E) = \mathcal{E} \ \wedge \bigwedge_{u_i = v_i \ \in \ S} (u_i \neq v_i) \ ,$$

and F is $(T_1 \cup T_2)$-satisfiable.

Example 10.13. Consider the $(\Sigma_E \cup \Sigma_Q)$-formula

$$F : \ f(f(x) - f(y)) \neq f(z) \ \wedge \ x \leq y \ \wedge \ y + z \leq x \ \wedge \ 0 \leq z \ .$$

F is $(T_E \cup T_Q)$-unsatisfiable: the final three literals imply that $z = 0$ and $x = y$, so that $f(x) = f(y)$. But then from the first literal, $f(0) \neq f(0)$ since both $f(x) - f(y)$ and z equal 0.

Phase 1 separates F into two formulae. According to transformation 1, it replaces $f(x)$ by u, $f(y)$ by v, and $u - v$ by w, resulting in Σ_E-formula

$$F_E : \ f(w) \neq f(z) \ \wedge \ u = f(x) \ \wedge \ v = f(y)$$

and Σ_Q-formula

$$F_Q : \ x \leq y \ \wedge \ y + z \leq x \ \wedge \ 0 \leq z \ \wedge \ w = u - v \ ,$$

with

$$V = \mathsf{shared}(F_E, F_Q) = \{x, y, z, u, v, w\} \ .$$

Recall that T_E and T_Q are convex theories. The decision procedure P_Q for T_Q discovers

$$F_Q \ \Rightarrow \ x = y$$

from $x \leq y \ \wedge \ y + z \leq x \ \wedge \ 0 \leq z$, so

$$\mathcal{E}_1 : \ x = y \ .$$

Then P_E discovers the new congruence $f(x) = f(y)$ from $x = y$, so that

$$F_E \ \wedge \ \mathcal{E}_1 \ \Rightarrow \ u = v \ ,$$

yielding

$$\mathcal{E}_2 : \ x = y \ \wedge \ u = v \ .$$

But then

$$F_Q \ \wedge \ \mathcal{E}_2 \ \Rightarrow \ z = w$$

since $w = u - v = 0$, according to $u = v$, and $z = 0$. Propagating this equality back to P_E via

$$\mathcal{E}_3 : \ x = y \ \wedge \ u = v \ \wedge \ z = w$$

$$\{\}$$

$$F_{\mathbb{Q}} \models x = y$$

$$\big|$$

$$\{x = y\}$$

$$\big|$$

$$F_{\mathsf{E}} \wedge x = y \models u = v$$

$$\{x = y, \ u = v\}$$

$$F_{\mathbb{Q}} \wedge u = v \models z = w \quad \big|$$

$$\{x = y, \ u = v, \ z = w\}$$

$$\big| \qquad F_{\mathsf{E}} \wedge z = w \models \bot$$

$$\bot$$

Fig. 10.1. Summary of Example 10.13

reveals the contradiction

$$F_{\mathsf{E}} \wedge \mathcal{E}_3 \Rightarrow \bot \ ;$$

in particular, $z = w$ contradicts $f(w) \neq f(z)$. Therefore, F is $(T_{\mathsf{E}} \cup T_{\mathbb{Q}})$-unsatisfiable.

Since both T_{E} and $T_{\mathbb{Q}}$ are convex, no case splitting was required.

Figure 10.1 summarizes this argument. The left and right halves list deductions made in $T_{\mathbb{Q}}$ and T_{E}, respectively. The sets in the middle are the deduced sets of shared equalities. The deductions terminate with $\bot$, indicating that F is $(T_{\mathsf{E}} \cup T_{\mathbb{Q}})$-unsatisfiable. ∎

Example 10.14. Consider the $(\Sigma_{\mathsf{E}} \cup \Sigma_{\mathbb{Z}})$-formula

$$F : \ 1 \leq x \ \wedge \ x \leq 2 \ \wedge \ f(x) \neq f(1) \ \wedge \ f(x) \neq f(2) \ .$$

While T_{E} is convex, $T_{\mathbb{Z}}$ is not. Thus, we should expect some case splits.

According to transformation 1, Phase 1 replaces $f(1)$ by $f(w_1)$ and $f(2)$ by $f(w_2)$, resulting in the $\Sigma_{\mathbb{Z}}$-formula

$$F_{\mathbb{Z}} : \ 1 \leq x \ \wedge \ x \leq 2 \ \wedge \ w_1 = 1 \ \wedge \ w_2 = 2$$

and the Σ_{E}-formula

$$F_{\mathsf{E}} : \ f(x) \neq f(w_1) \ \wedge \ f(x) \neq f(w_2) \ ,$$

with

$$V = \mathsf{shared}(F_{\mathbb{Z}}, F_{\mathsf{E}}) = \{x, w_1, w_2\} \ .$$

Immediately, $P_{\mathbb{Z}}$ recognizes that

$$F_{\mathbb{Z}} \ \Rightarrow \ x = w_1 \ \vee \ x = w_2 \ ,$$

since $1 \leq x \leq 2$ implies that either $x = 1$ or $x = 2$. Hence, case split on these two disjuncts. For the first case, propagate

$$\{\}$$
$$x = w_1 \quad^\star\quad x = w_2$$
$$\{x = w_1\} \qquad\qquad \{x = w_2\}$$
$$F_E \wedge x = w_1 \models \bot \qquad\qquad F_E \wedge x = w_2 \models \bot$$
$$\bot \qquad\qquad\qquad \bot$$

$$\star:\ F_{\mathbb{Z}} \models x = w_1 \vee x = w_2$$

Fig. 10.2. Summary of Example 10.14

$$\mathcal{E}_1^a:\ x = w_1$$

to P_E, which discovers that

$$F_E \wedge \mathcal{E}_1^a \Rightarrow \bot\ ,$$

as $x = w_1$ contradicts $f(x) \neq f(w_1)$.
For the second case,

$$\mathcal{E}_1^b:\ x = w_2\ .$$

Again, P_E discovers that

$$F_E \wedge \mathcal{E}_1^b \Rightarrow \bot\ ,$$

as $x = w_2$ contradicts $f(x) \neq f(w_2)$.
   As all branches end in contradiction, F is $(T_E \cup T_{\mathbb{Z}})$-unsatisfiable.
   Figure 10.2 summarizes this argument. Unlike in Example 10.13 and Figure 10.1, the nonconvexity of $T_{\mathbb{Z}}$ causes the argument to branch along two possibilities. Each branch ends in a contradiction. ∎

Example 10.15. Consider the $(\Sigma_E \cup \Sigma_{\mathbb{Z}})$-formula

$$F:\ 1 \le x \wedge x \le 3 \wedge f(x) \neq f(1) \wedge f(x) \neq f(3) \wedge f(1) \neq f(2)\ .$$

Applying transformation 1 of Phase 1 three times produces the $\Sigma_{\mathbb{Z}}$-formula

$$F_{\mathbb{Z}}:\ 1 \le x \wedge x \le 3 \wedge w_1 = 1 \wedge w_2 = 2 \wedge w_3 = 3$$

and the Σ_E-formula

$$F_E:\ f(x) \neq f(w_1) \wedge f(x) \neq f(w_3) \wedge f(w_1) \neq f(w_2)\ ,$$

with

$$V = \text{shared}(F_{\mathbb{Z}}, F_{\mathsf{E}}) = \{x, w_1, w_2, w_3\} \ .$$

From $1 \leq x \leq 3$, $P_{\mathbb{Z}}$ discovers that

$$F_{\mathbb{Z}} \ \Rightarrow \ x = w_1 \ \lor \ x = w_2 \ \lor \ x = w_3 \ .$$

Recall that $T_{\mathbb{Z}}$ is not convex. On case

$$\mathcal{E}_1^a : \ x = w_1 \ ,$$

P_{E} finds that

$$F_{\mathsf{E}} \ \land \ \mathcal{E}_1^a \ \Rightarrow \ \bot$$

because of $f(x) \neq f(w_1)$. On case

$$\mathcal{E}_1^b : \ x = w_2 \ ,$$

neither $P_{\mathbb{Z}}$ nor P_{E} discovers any contradiction or new equality. That is,

$$F_{\mathbb{Z}} \ \land \ \mathcal{E}_1^b \ \nRightarrow \ x = w_1 \ \lor \ x = w_3 \ \lor \ w_1 = w_2 \ \lor \ w_1 = w_3 \ \lor \ w_2 = w_3$$

and

$$F_{\mathsf{E}} \ \land \ \mathcal{E}_1^b \ \nRightarrow \ x = w_1 \ \lor \ x = w_3 \ \lor \ w_1 = w_2 \ \lor \ w_1 = w_3 \ \lor \ w_2 = w_3 \ ;$$

or, in other words,

$$F_{\mathbb{Z}} \ \land \ \mathcal{E}_1^b \ \land \ x \neq w_1 \ \land \ x \neq w_3 \ \land \ w_1 \neq w_2 \ \land \ w_1 \neq w_3 \ \land \ w_2 \neq w_3$$

is $T_{\mathbb{Z}}$-satisfiable, and

$$F_{\mathsf{E}} \ \land \ \mathcal{E}_1^b \ \land \ x \neq w_1 \ \land \ x \neq w_3 \ \land \ w_1 \neq w_2 \ \land \ w_1 \neq w_3 \ \land \ w_2 \neq w_3$$

is T_{E}-satisfiable. Thus, F is $(T_{\mathsf{E}} \cup T_{\mathbb{Z}})$-satisfiable.

Figure 10.3 summarizes this argument. The middle branch terminates with a satisfying arrangement. We did not actually explore the right branch. ∎

10.3.3 Equality Propagation: Implementation

Equality propagation can be implemented somewhat efficiently without modifying the individual decision procedures. For convex theory T_j, test each possible equality $u_i = v_i$. Suppose that F_j is the Σ_j-formula constructed in Phase 1 and $\mathcal{E}$ is the conjunction of equalities discovered so far. Then check if any equality $u_i = v_i$ is implied:

$$F_j \ \land \ \mathcal{E} \ \Rightarrow \ u_i = v_i \ .$$

Any implied equality should be propagated to the other theories.

$$\{\}$$

$$\star:\ F_{\mathbb{Z}} \models x = w_1 \ \vee \ x = w_2 \ \vee \ x = w_3$$

Fig. 10.3. Summary of Example 10.15

This procedure is not applicable to a non-convex theory T_k. A procedure for a non-convex theory must be able to find disjunctions of equalities that are implied by a Σ_k-formula F_k. Moreover, the disjunctions should be as small as possible since the Nelson-Oppen method must branch on each disjunct. A disjunction is **minimal** if it is implied by F_k and if each smaller disjunction is not implied by F_k.

A simple procedure to find a minimal disjunction is based on the observation that any disjunction that contains a minimal disjunction — which is implied by F_k by definition — is also implied by F_k. Therefore, we can strip off extra disjuncts one-by-one. First, consider the disjunction of all equalities at once. If it is not implied, then no subset is implied either, so we are done. Otherwise, drop each equality in turn: if the remaining disjunction is still implied by F_k, continue with this smaller disjunction; otherwise, restore the equality and continue. When all equalities have been considered, the resulting disjunction is minimal. This procedure requires checking T_k-satisfiability $O(|V|^2)$ times, where V is the set of shared variables. Exercise 10.4 asks the reader to describe a procedure based on binary search that requires asymptotically fewer satisfiability checks when the final disjunction is small relative to the disjunction of all equalities.

10.4 ⋆Correctness of the Nelson-Oppen Method

In this section, we prove the correctness of the Nelson-Oppen combination method. We reason at the level of arrangements, which is more suited to the nondeterministic version of the method. However, Section 10.3 shows how to construct an arrangement in the deterministic version, as well, so the following proof can be extended to the deterministic version. We also focus on the second phase of the nondeterministic procedure, which chooses an arrangement if one exists. We thus assume that the variable abstraction phase is correct: it produces formulae F_1 and F_2 such that $F_1 \wedge F_2$ is $(T_1 \cup T_2)$-equivalent to the given $(\Sigma_1 \cup \Sigma_2)$-formula F.

A theory **has equality** (or is a theory **with equality**) if its signature includes the binary predicate $=$ and its axioms imply reflexivity, symmetry, and transitivity of equality. The **pure equality** fragment of a theory with equality is composed of formulae that are possibly quantified Boolean combinations of equalities between variables.

Theorem 10.16 (Sound & Complete). *Consider stably infinite theories T_1 and T_2 such that $\Sigma_1 \cap \Sigma_2 = \{=\}$. For conjunctive quantifier-free Σ_1-formula F_1 and conjunctive quantifier-free Σ_2-formula F_2, $F_1 \wedge F_2$ is $(T_1 \cup T_2)$-satisfiable iff there exists an arrangement $K = \alpha(\mathsf{shared}(F_1, F_2), E)$ such that $F_1 \wedge K$ is T_1-satisfiable and $F_2 \wedge K$ is T_2-satisfiable.*

Soundness is straightforward. Suppose that $F_1 \wedge F_2$ is $(T_1 \cup T_2)$-satisfiable with satisfying $(T_1 \cup T_2)$-interpretation I. Extract from I the equivalence relation E such that the arrangement $K = \alpha(\mathsf{shared}(F_1, F_2), E)$ is satisfied by I. Then $F_1 \wedge K$ and $F_2 \wedge K$ are both satisfied by I, which can be viewed as both a T_1-interpretation and a T_2-interpretation, so that they are T_1-satisfiable and T_2-satisfiable, respectively.

Completeness is more complicated. Let $K = \alpha(\mathsf{shared}(F_1, F_2), E)$ be an arrangement such that $F_1 \wedge K$ and $F_2 \wedge K$ are T_1-satisfiable and T_2-satisfiable, respectively. Suppose that $F_1 \wedge F_2$ is $(T_1 \cup T_2)$-unsatisfiable. We derive a contradiction.

The outline of the proof is the following. Because $F_1 \wedge F_2$ is $(T_1 \cup T_2)$-unsatisfiable, we know that F_1 implies $\neg F_2$ in $T_1 \cup T_2$. An adaptation of the **Craig Interpolation Lemma** (Theorem 2.38) tells us that there is a quantifier-free formula H such that F_1 implies H over all infinite T_1-interpretations (T_1-interpretations with infinite domains) and F_2 implies $\neg H$ over all infinite T_2-interpretations: H interpolates between F_1 and F_2. We then show that the arrangement K implies H, which means that F_2 implies $\neg K$ over all infinite T_2-interpretations. In other words, no infinite T_2-interpretation satisfies $F_2 \wedge K$. Yet if T_2 is stably infinite and $F_2 \wedge K$ is T_2-satisfiable as assumed, then $F_2 \wedge K$ is satisfied by some infinite T_2-interpretation, a contradiction.

We now present the details of the proof. First, because we are considering only stably infinite theories, we need only consider interpretations with infinite domains. For we can extend a T_1- or T_2-interpretation with a finite domain to a T_1- or T_2-interpretation with an infinite domain. Therefore, define $\Rightarrow^*$ as a weaker form of implication: $F \Rightarrow^* G$ iff G is true on every interpretation I that has an infinite domain and that satisfies F. Similarly, weaken $\Leftrightarrow$ to $\Leftrightarrow^*$. If $F \Rightarrow^* G$, we say that F **weakly implies** G; if $F \Leftrightarrow^* G$, we say that F is **weakly equivalent** to G.

Recall from Section 2.7.4 the following theorem.

Theorem 10.17 (Compactness Theorem). *A countable set of first-order formulae S is simultaneously satisfiable iff the conjunction of every finite subset is satisfiable.*

Since $F_1 \wedge F_2$ is $(T_1 \cup T_2)$-unsatisfiable, the Compactness Theorem tells us that there exist a conjunction S_1 of a finite subset of axioms of T_1 and a conjunction S_2 of a finite subset of axioms of T_2 such that $S_1 \wedge F_1 \wedge S_2 \wedge F_2$ is (first-order) unsatisfiable. Choose S_1 and S_2 to include the axioms that imply reflexivity, symmetry, and transitivity of equality. Then, rearranging, we have that

$$S_1 \wedge F_1 \Rightarrow \neg S_2 \vee \neg F_2 . \tag{10.2}$$

Recall from Section 2.7.4 the following theorem.

Theorem 10.18 (Craig Interpolation Lemma). *If $F_1 \Rightarrow F_2$, then there exists a formula H such that $F_1 \Rightarrow H$, $H \Rightarrow F_2$, and each free variable, function symbol, and predicate symbol of H appears in F_1 and F_2.*

Hence, from implication (10.2), there exists an interpolant H' such that $\mathsf{free}(H') = \mathsf{shared}(F_1, F_2)$ and

$$S_1 \wedge F_1 \Rightarrow H' \quad \text{and} \quad S_2 \wedge H' \Rightarrow \neg F_2 .$$

The latter implication is derived by rearranging $H' \Rightarrow \neg S_2 \vee \neg F_2$. Because $=$ is the only predicate or function shared between $S_1 \wedge F_1$ and $S_2 \wedge F_2$, H' is of a special form: its atoms are equalities between variables of $\mathsf{shared}(F_1, F_2)$. However, H' may have quantifiers. We prove next that in fact a "weak" quantifier-free interpolant H exists.

Lemma 10.19 (Weak Quantifier Elimination for Pure Equality). *Consider any stably infinite theory T with equality. For each pure equality formula F, there exists a quantifier-free pure equality formula F' such that F is weakly T-equivalent to F'.*

Proof. Consider pure equality formula $\exists x. \ G[x, \overline{y}]$, where G is quantifier-free with free variables x and $\overline{y}$. Define

$$G_0 : \ G\{x = x \mapsto \mathsf{true}, \ x = y_1 \mapsto \mathsf{false}, \ \ldots, \ x = y_n \mapsto \mathsf{false}\}$$

and, for $i \in \{1, \ldots, n\}$,

$$G_i : \ G\{x \mapsto y_i\} .$$

We claim that $\exists x. \ G$ is weakly T-equivalent to

$$G' : \ G_0 \vee G_1 \vee \cdots \vee G_n .$$

For G' asserts that x is either equal to some free variable y_i or not. Because we consider only interpretations with infinite domains, it is always possible for x not to equal any y_i.

By Section 7.1, we have a weak quantifier elimination procedure over the pure equality fragment of T. It is weak because equivalence is only guaranteed to hold on infinite interpretations. ∎

Example 10.20. Consider the pure equality formula

$$F : x \neq y \wedge (\forall z.\ z = x \vee z = y) .$$

For eliminating z, consider the negation of the second conjunct,

$$G : \exists z.\ z \neq x \wedge z \neq y ,$$

for which we have

$$G_0 : \neg\bot \wedge \neg\bot \Leftrightarrow \top$$

and

$$G_x : x \neq x \wedge x \neq y \Leftrightarrow \bot \qquad G_y : y \neq x \wedge y \neq y \Leftrightarrow \bot .$$

Then

$$G' : G_0 \vee G_x \vee G_y \Leftrightarrow \top .$$

Substituting into F, we have

$$x \neq y \wedge \neg(\top) \Leftrightarrow \bot .$$

Hence, over infinite interpretations satisfying the axioms of equality, F is equivalent to $\bot$.

However, in an interpretation with a two-element domain that satisfies the equality axioms, F is not equivalent to $\bot$, but rather to $x \neq y$. For if $x \neq y$ on such an interpretation, then every element is equal either to x or to y. ■

Continuing the main theorem, we claim that there exists a quantifier-free pure equality formula H over $\mathsf{shared}(F_1, F_2)$ such that

$$S_1 \wedge F_1 \Rightarrow^* H \quad \text{and} \quad S_2 \wedge H \Rightarrow^* \neg F_2 .$$

For by Lemma 10.19, a quantifier-free pure equality formula H exists such that H is weakly equivalent to the Craig interpolant H' in any stably infinite theory with equality.

For the next step, recall from the beginning of the proof that $F_1 \wedge K$ is T_1-satisfiable and $F_2 \wedge K$ is T_2-satisfiable, where $K = \alpha(\mathsf{shared}(F_1, F_2), E)$ is an arrangement. We thus know that

$$S_1 \wedge F_1 \wedge K \quad \text{and} \quad S_2 \wedge F_2 \wedge K$$

are (first-order) satisfiable. Moreover, as T_1 and T_2 are stably infinite, each of these formulae has an interpretation with an infinite domain.

Now, K is a conjunction of equalities and disequalities between pairs of variables of $\mathsf{shared}(F_1, F_2)$. Moreover, by the definition of an arrangement, K is as strong as possible: no additional equality literals L over $\mathsf{shared}(F_1, F_2)$

can be added to K without either K and $K \wedge L$ being equivalent in a theory with equality or $K \wedge L$ being unsatisfiable in a theory with equality. Based on this observation, construct the formula K' by conjoining additional equality literals: for each pair of variables $u, v \in \mathsf{shared}(F_1, F_2)$, conjoin either $u = v$ or $u \neq v$, depending on which maintains the satisfiability of K' in a theory with equality. Now, since $S_1 \wedge F_1 \wedge K$ is satisfiable, then so is $S_1 \wedge F_1 \wedge K'$, indeed by the same interpretations.

We claim that the DNF representation of H must include K' or a (conjunctive) subformula of K' as a disjunct. Suppose not; then every disjunct of the DNF representation of H contradicts the satisfying interpretations of $S_1 \wedge F_1 \wedge K'$, of which at least one exists. Therefore, $K' \Rightarrow H$, and — because K and K' are equivalent in a theory with equality — $K \Rightarrow H$. In other words, the discovered arrangement K is a special case of the weak interpolant H.

To finish, we have

$$S_2 \ \wedge \ H \ \Rightarrow^* \ \neg F_2 \ ,$$

or, rearranging,

$$S_2 \ \wedge \ F_2 \ \Rightarrow^* \ \neg H \ .$$

From $K \Rightarrow H$, we have $\neg H \Rightarrow \neg K$, so

$$S_2 \ \wedge \ F_2 \ \Rightarrow^* \ \neg K \ .$$

But this weak implication contradicts that $S_2 \wedge F_2 \wedge K$ is satisfied by some infinite interpretation. Thus, $F_1 \wedge F_2$ is actually $(T_1 \cup T_2)$-satisfiable, and the Nelson-Oppen method is correct.

10.5 *Complexity

Assume that T_1 and T_2 are stably infinite theories such that $\Sigma_1 \cap \Sigma = \{=\}$. Also, they have decision procedures P_1 and P_2 for their respective conjunctive quantifier-free fragments.

Theorem 10.21 (Complexity: Convex Theories). *If convex theories T_1 and T_2 have PTIME decision procedures P_1 and P_2, then the Nelson-Oppen combination based on equality propagation is a PTIME decision procedure for the conjunctive quantifier-free fragment of $T_1 \cup T_2$.*

Theorem 10.22 (Complexity: Non-Convex Theories). *If T_1 and T_2 have NPTIME decision procedures P_1 and P_2, then the Nelson-Oppen combination based on equality propagation is an NPTIME decision procedure for the conjunctive quantifier-free fragment of $T_1 \cup T_2$.*

10.6 Summary

Combining decision procedures in a general and efficient manner is crucial for most applications. This chapter covers the Nelson-Oppen combination method, in particular:

- The *nondeterministic Nelson-Oppen method*. Three requirements: the theories only share $=$; the theories are stably infinite; and the considered formula is quantifier-free. Variable abstraction, separation into theory-specific formulae. Shared variables, equivalence relations over shared variables, arrangements.
- The *deterministic Nelson-Oppen method*. Convex theories. Equality propagation.
- *Correctness* of the Nelson-Oppen method, which follows from the Craig Interpolation Lemma of Chapter 2.
- *Complexity*. When the individual decision procedures are convex and run in polynomial time, the combination procedure runs in polynomial time.

The Nelson-Oppen combination method provides a general means of reasoning simultaneously about the theories studied in this book using the individual decision procedures. Being able to reason in union theories is crucial. For example, almost all of the verification conditions of Chapters 5 and 6 are expressed in multiple signatures.

Bibliographic Remarks

Nelson and Oppen describe the Nelson-Oppen combination method [65]. Their original proof of correctness was flawed; Oppen presents a corrected proof in [70], and Nelson presents a corrected proof in [64]. Oppen also proves in [70] the complexity results that we state. Tinelli and Harandi present an alternate proof of correctness in [92]. Our correctness proof derives from that of Nelson and Oppen. See [56] for another presentation of the method and its correctness.

Another general combination method that has received much attention is that of Shostak [84]. See the work of Ruess and Shankar [78] for a correct presentation of the method.

Exercises

10.1 (DP for combinations). For each of the following formulae, identify the combination of theories in which it lies. To avoid ambiguity, prefer $T_{\mathbb{Z}}$ to $T_{\mathbb{Q}}$. Then apply the N-O method using the appropriate decision procedures. Use either the nondeterministic or deterministic version. Provide a level of detail as in the examples of the chapter.

(a) $1 \leq x \ \wedge \ x \leq 2 \ \wedge \ \mathsf{cons}(1, y) \neq \mathsf{cons}(x, y) \ \wedge \ \mathsf{cons}(2, y) \neq \mathsf{cons}(x, y)$
(b) $a[i] \geq 1 \ \wedge \ a[i] + x \leq 2 \ \wedge \ x > 0 \ \wedge \ x = i \ \wedge \ a\langle x \triangleleft 2\rangle[i] \neq 1$

10.2 (Deterministic N-O). Apply the deterministic N-O method to the following formulae. Prefer $T_{\mathbb{Q}}$ to $T_{\mathbb{Z}}$.

(a) $1 \leq x \ \wedge \ x \leq 2 \ \wedge \ \mathsf{cons}(1, y) \neq \mathsf{cons}(x, y) \ \wedge \ \mathsf{cons}(2, y) \neq \mathsf{cons}(x, y)$
(b) $x + y = z \ \wedge \ f(z) = z \ \wedge \ f(x + y) \neq z$
(c) $g(x + y, z) = f(g(x, y)) \ \wedge \ x + z = y \ \wedge \ z \geq 0 \ \wedge \ x \geq y$
    $\wedge \ g(x, x) = z \ \wedge \ f(z) \neq g(2x, 0)$

10.3 ($\star$Equality propagation in T_{E}). Section 10.3.3 explains general techniques for propagating equalities. However, some decision procedures are easily modified to propagate new equalities. Describe such a modification of the congruence closure algorithm of Chapter 9.

10.4 ($\star$Equality propagation). Consider conjunctive Σ-formula F of nonconvex theory T and the disjunction of equalities

$$G: \bigvee_{i=1}^{n} u_i = v_i$$

such that $F \Rightarrow G$. Describe a procedure based on binary search that discovers a minimal disjunction G' of the equalities of G that is implied by F. If the procedure returns a disjunction with m equalities, then it should have invoked the decision procedure for T at most $O(m \lg n)$ times. *Hint*: The solution is related to the solution of Exercise 8.1 *(e)*.

10.5 ($\star$Convex theories). Prove that the following theories are convex:

(a) T_{E}
(b) T_{cons}

10.6 ($\star$Complexity). Prove the complexity results about the N-O method.

(a) Theorem 10.21.
(b) Theorem 10.22.

11

Arrays

So let us let our ordinals start at zero: an element's ordinal (subscript) equals the number of elements preceding it in the sequence. And the moral of the story is that we had better regard — after all those centuries! — zero as a most natural number.

— Edsger W. Dijkstra
EWD831: Why Numbering Should Start at Zero, 1982

Programs rely on data structures to store and manipulate data in complex ways. Therefore, verifying these programs requires decision procedures that reason about the data structures. This chapter discusses fragments and decision procedures for reasoning about arrays and array-like data structures: arrays with anonymous or uninterpreted indices (Section 11.1), the familiar arrays of C and other imperative languages with integer indices (Section 11.2), and hashtables (Section 11.3).

Unlike the quantifier-free fragment of arrays presented in Chapter 9, the fragments of this chapter allow some quantification. Specifically, at most one **quantifier alternation** is allowed: for satisfiability, formulae may have universal quantifiers in addition to the implicit existential ones. The technique that underlies the decision procedures of this chapter is **quantifier instantiation**. A satisfiability decision procedure based on quantifier instantiation identifies a finite set of terms suggested by the given formula F; it then replaces universal quantification with finite conjunction over the set of terms. The resulting formula F' is quantifier-free and equisatisfiable to the given one. Finally, it applies to F' a satisfiability decision procedure for the quantifier-free fragment (for example, a Nelson-Oppen combination of procedures; see Chapter 10); the answer applies also to F.

Section 11.1 studies the **array property fragment** of T_A in which one (restricted) quantifier alternation is allowed. Section 11.2 examines the familiar case in which arrays are indexed by integers. Reasoning about integer indices allows making relative comparisons via $\leq$, providing more power than the case in which indices are only compared via equality.

Hashtables are another important data type. They are similar to arrays with uninterpreted indices in that their indices, or keys, can only be compared via equality. However, hashtables allow two new interesting operations: first, a key/value pair can be removed; and second, a hashtable's domain — its set of keys that it maps to values — can be read. Section 11.3 formalizes reasoning about hashtables in the theory T_H and then presents a decision procedure for the **hashtable property fragment** of T_H. The procedure operates by transforming Σ_H-formulae to Σ_A-formulae in the array property fragment such that the original formula is T_H-satisfiable iff the constructed formula is T_A-satisfiable.

11.1 Arrays with Uninterpreted Indices

The quantifier-free fragment of T_A enables basic reasoning in the presence of arrays. For verification purposes, it allows verifying properties of individual elements but not of entire arrays. However, in practice, it is useful to be able to reason about properties such as equality between arrays. Using combinations of theories (see Chapter 10), one would also like to reason about properties such as that all integer elements of an array are positive.

11.1.1 Array Property Fragment

In this section, we define a decidable fragment of T_A that allows some quantification. This fragment is called the **array property fragment** because it allows specifying basic properties of arrays, not just properties of array elements. The principal characteristic of the array property fragment is that array indices can be universally quantified with some restrictions.

Example 11.1. In the Σ_A-formula

$$\forall j.\ a\langle i \triangleleft v\rangle[j] = a[j]\ \wedge\ a[i] \neq v\ ,$$

the first conjunct asserts that $a\langle i \triangleleft v\rangle$ and a are equal. This formula is T_A-unsatisfiable.   ∎

Unfortunately, the use of universal quantification must be restricted to avoid undecidability (see Section 11.4 for further discussion). An **array property** is a Σ_A-formula of the form

$$\forall \bar{i}.\ F[\bar{i}]\ \rightarrow\ G[\bar{i}]$$

in which $\bar{i}$ is a list of variables, and $F[\bar{i}]$ and $G[\bar{i}]$ are the **index guard** and the **value constraint**, respectively. The index guard $F[\bar{i}]$ is any Σ_A-formula that is syntactically constructed according to the following grammar:

iguard $\rightarrow$ iguard $\wedge$ iguard | iguard $\vee$ iguard | atom
atom $\rightarrow$ var = var | $evar \neq$ var | var $\neq evar$ | $\top$
var $\rightarrow$ $evar$ | $uvar$

where $uvar$ is any universally quantified index variable, and $evar$ is any constant or unquantified (that is, implicitly existentially quantified) variable.

Additionally, a universally quantified index can occur in a value constraint $G[\bar{i}]$ only in a read $a[i]$, where a is an array term. The read cannot be nested; for example, $a[b[i]]$ is not allowed.

The array property fragment of T_A then consists of formulae that are Boolean combinations of quantifier-free Σ_A-formulae and array properties.

Example 11.2. The antecedent of the implication in the Σ_A-formula

$$F : \forall i. \ i \neq a[k] \ \rightarrow \ a[i] = a[k]$$

is not a legal index guard since $a[k]$ is not a variable (neither a $uvar$ nor an $evar$); however, a simple manipulation makes it conform:

$$F' : \ v = a[k] \ \wedge \ \forall i. \ i \neq v \ \rightarrow \ a[i] = a[k]$$

Here, $i \neq v$ is a legal index guard, and $a[i] = a[k]$ is a legal value constraint. F and F' are equisatisfiable.

However, no amount of manipulation can make the following formula conform:

$$G : \ \forall i. \ i \neq a[i] \ \rightarrow \ a[i] = a[k] \ .$$

Thus, G is not in the array property fragment. ∎

Example 11.3. The array property fragment allows expressing equality between arrays, a property referred to as **extensionality**: two arrays are equal precisely when their corresponding elements are equal. For given formula

$$F : \ \cdots \ \wedge \ a = b \ \wedge \ \cdots$$

with array terms a and b, rewrite F as

$$F' : \ \cdots \ \wedge \ (\forall i. \ a[i] = b[i]) \ \wedge \ \cdots \ .$$

F and F' are equisatisfiable. Moreover, the index guard in the literal is just $\top$, and the value constraint $a[i] = b[i]$ obeys the requirement that i appear only as an index in read terms.

Recall that the theory of arrays with extensionality $T_A^=$ (see Section 3.6) augments T_A with the following axiom:

$$\forall a, b. \ (\forall i. \ a[i] = b[i]) \ \leftrightarrow \ a = b \qquad \text{(extensionality)}$$

The universal quantifier of the array property fragment allows expressing equality between arrays directly.

Subsequently, where convenient, we write equality $a = b$ between arrays to abbreviate $\forall i. \ a[i] = b[i]$. ∎

Example 11.4. Reasoning about arrays is most useful when we can say something interesting about their elements. Suppose array elements are interpreted in some theory T with signature Σ. Then we can assert that all elements of an array have some property $F[x]$, where F is a quantifier-free Σ-formula: $\forall i.\ F[a[i]]$; or that all but a finite number of elements have some property $F[x]$:

$$\forall i.\ \left(\bigwedge_{k=1}^{n} i \neq j_k \right) \ \rightarrow\ F[a[i]]\ .$$

■

11.1.2 Decision Procedure

The idea of the decision procedure for the array property fragment is to reduce universal quantification to finite conjunction. It constructs a finite set of index terms such that examining only these positions of the arrays is sufficient to decide satisfiability.

Example 11.5. Consider the formula

$$F:\ a\langle i \triangleleft v \rangle = a \ \wedge\ a[i] \neq v\ ,$$

which expands to

$$F':\ \forall j.\ a\langle i \triangleleft v \rangle[j] = a[j] \ \wedge\ a[i] \neq v\ .$$

Intuitively, to determine that F' is T_A-unsatisfiable requires merely examining index i:

$$F'':\ \left(\bigwedge_{j \in \{i\}} a\langle i \triangleleft v \rangle[j] = a[j] \right) \ \wedge\ a[i] \neq v\ ,$$

or simply

$$a\langle i \triangleleft v \rangle[i] = a[i] \ \wedge\ a[i] \neq v\ .$$

Simplifying,

$$v = a[i] \ \wedge\ a[i] \neq v\ ,$$

it is clear that this formula, and thus F, is T_A-unsatisfiable.   ■

Given array property formula F, decide its T_A-satisfiability as follows.

Step 1

Put F in NNF.

Step 2

Apply the following rule exhaustively to remove writes:

$$\frac{F[a\langle i \lhd v\rangle]}{F[a'] \;\wedge\; a'[i] = v \;\wedge\; (\forall j.\; j \neq i \;\rightarrow\; a[j] = a'[j])} \text{ for fresh } a' \quad \text{(write)}$$

Rules should be read from top to bottom. For example, this rule states that given a formula F containing an occurrence of a write term $a\langle i \lhd v\rangle$, substitute every occurrence of $a\langle i \lhd v\rangle$ with a fresh variable a' and conjoin several new conjuncts.

This step deconstructs write terms in a straightforward manner, essentially encoding the (read-over-write) axioms into the new formula. After an application of the rule, the resulting formula contains at least one fewer write terms than the given formula.

Step 3

Apply the following rule exhaustively to remove existential quantification:

$$\frac{F[\exists \bar{i}.\; G[\bar{i}]]}{F[G[\bar{j}]]} \text{ for fresh } \bar{j} \quad \text{(exists)}$$

Existential quantification can arise during Step 1 if the given formula has a negated array property.

Step 4

Steps 4-6 accomplish the reduction of universal quantification to finite conjunction. The main idea is to select a set of symbolic index terms on which to instantiate all universal quantifiers. The proof of Theorem 11.7 argues that the following set is sufficient for correctness.

From the output F_3 of Step 3, construct the **index set** $\mathcal{I}$:

$$\mathcal{I} = \begin{array}{l} \{\lambda\} \\ \cup\; \{t\; :\; \cdot[t] \in F_3 \text{ such that } t \text{ is not a universally quantified variable}\} \\ \cup\; \{t\; :\; t \text{ occurs as an } evar \text{ in the parsing of index guards}\} \end{array}$$

Recall that $evar$ is any constant or unquantified variable. This index set is the finite set of indices that need to be examined. It includes all terms t that occur in some read $a[t]$ anywhere in F (unless it is a universally quantified variable) and all terms t that are compared to a universally quantified variable in some index guard. λ is a fresh constant that represents all other index positions that are not explicitly in $\mathcal{I}$.

Step 5

Apply the following rule exhaustively to remove universal quantification:

$$\frac{H[\forall \bar{i}.\ F[\bar{i}]\ \rightarrow\ G[\bar{i}]]}{H\left[\bigwedge_{\bar{i}\in\mathcal{I}^n}(F[\bar{i}]\ \rightarrow\ G[\bar{i}])\right]}\qquad\text{(forall)}$$

where n is the size of the list of quantified variables $\bar{i}$. This is the key step. It replaces universal quantification with finite conjunction over the index set. The notation $\bar{i}\in\mathcal{I}^n$ means that the variables $\bar{i}$ range over all n-tuples of terms in $\mathcal{I}$.

Step 6

From the output F_5 of Step 5, construct

$$F_6:\ F_5\ \wedge\ \bigwedge_{i\ \in\ \mathcal{I}\backslash\{\lambda\}}\ \lambda\neq i\ .$$

The new conjuncts assert that the variable λ introduced in Step 4 is indeed unique: it does not equal any other index mentioned in F_5.

Step 7

Decide the T_A-satisfiability of F_6 using the decision procedure for the quantifier-free fragment.

Suppose array elements are interpreted in some theory T with signature Σ. For deciding the $(T_A\cup T)$-satisfiability of an array property $(\Sigma_A\cup\Sigma)$-formula, use a combination decision procedure for the quantifier-free fragment of $T_A\cup T$ in Step 7. Thus, this procedure is a decision procedure precisely when the quantifier-free fragment of $T_A\cup T$ is decidable. Chapter 10 discusses deciding satisfiability in combinations of quantifier-free fragments of theories.

Example 11.6. Consider the array property formula

$$F:\ a\langle\ell\triangleleft v\rangle[k]=b[k]\ \wedge\ b[k]\neq v\ \wedge\ a[k]=v\ \wedge\ (\forall i.\ i\neq\ell\ \rightarrow\ a[i]=b[i])\ .$$

It contains one array property,

$$\forall i.\ i\neq\ell\ \rightarrow\ a[i]=b[i]\ ,$$

in which the index guard is $i\neq\ell$ and the value constraint is $a[i]=b[i]$. It is already in NNF. According to Step 2, rewrite F as

$$F_2 : \ a'[k] = b[k] \ \wedge \ b[k] \neq v \ \wedge \ a[k] = v \ \wedge \ (\forall i. \ i \neq \ell \ \rightarrow \ a[i] = b[i])$$
$$\wedge \ a'[\ell] = v \ \wedge \ (\forall j. \ j \neq \ell \ \rightarrow \ a[j] = a'[j]) \ .$$

F_2 does not contain any existential quantifiers. Its index set is

$$\mathcal{I} = \{\lambda\} \ \cup \ \{k\} \ \cup \ \{\ell\}$$
$$= \{\lambda, k, \ell\} \ .$$

According to Step 5, replace universal quantification as follows:

$$F_5 : \ a'[k] = b[k] \ \wedge \ b[k] \neq v \ \wedge \ a[k] = v \ \wedge \ \bigwedge_{i \in \mathcal{I}} (i \neq \ell \ \rightarrow \ a[i] = b[i])$$
$$\wedge \ a'[\ell] = v \ \wedge \ \bigwedge_{j \in \mathcal{I}} (j \neq \ell \ \rightarrow \ a[j] = a'[j]) \ .$$

Expanding produces

$$F_5' : \ a'[k] = b[k] \ \wedge \ b[k] \neq v \ \wedge \ a[k] = v \ \wedge \ (\lambda \neq \ell \ \rightarrow \ a[\lambda] = b[\lambda])$$
$$\wedge \ (k \neq \ell \ \rightarrow \ a[k] = b[k]) \ \wedge \ (\ell \neq \ell \ \rightarrow \ a[\ell] = b[\ell])$$
$$\wedge \ a'[\ell] = v \ \wedge \ (\lambda \neq \ell \ \rightarrow \ a[\lambda] = a'[\lambda])$$
$$\wedge \ (k \neq \ell \ \rightarrow \ a[k] = a'[k]) \ \wedge \ (\ell \neq \ell \ \rightarrow \ a[\ell] = a'[\ell]) \ .$$

Simplifying produces

$$F_5'' : \ a'[k] = b[k] \ \wedge \ b[k] \neq v \ \wedge \ a[k] = v \ \wedge \ (\lambda \neq \ell \ \rightarrow \ a[\lambda] = b[\lambda])$$
$$\wedge \ (k \neq \ell \ \rightarrow \ a[k] = b[k])$$
$$\wedge \ a'[\ell] = v \ \wedge \ (\lambda \neq \ell \ \rightarrow \ a[\lambda] = a'[\lambda])$$
$$\wedge \ (k \neq \ell \ \rightarrow \ a[k] = a'[k]) \ .$$

Step 6 distinguishes λ from other members of $\mathcal{I}$:

$$F_6 : \ a'[k] = b[k] \ \wedge \ b[k] \neq v \ \wedge \ a[k] = v \ \wedge \ (\lambda \neq \ell \ \rightarrow \ a[\lambda] = b[\lambda])$$
$$\wedge \ (k \neq \ell \ \rightarrow \ a[k] = b[k])$$
$$\wedge \ a'[\ell] = v \ \wedge \ (\lambda \neq \ell \ \rightarrow \ a[\lambda] = a'[\lambda])$$
$$\wedge \ (k \neq \ell \ \rightarrow \ a[k] = a'[k])$$
$$\wedge \ \lambda \neq k \ \wedge \ \lambda \neq \ell \ .$$

Simplifying, we have

$$F_6' : \ a'[k] = b[k] \ \wedge \ b[k] \neq v \ \wedge \ a[k] = v$$
$$\wedge \ a[\lambda] = b[\lambda] \ \wedge \ (k \neq \ell \ \rightarrow \ a[k] = b[k])$$
$$\wedge \ a'[\ell] = v \ \wedge \ a[\lambda] = a'[\lambda] \ \wedge \ (k \neq \ell \ \rightarrow \ a[k] = a'[k])$$
$$\wedge \ \lambda \neq k \ \wedge \ \lambda \neq \ell \ .$$

There are two cases to consider. If $k = \ell$, then $a'[\ell] = v$ and $a'[k] = b[k]$ imply $b[k] = v$, yet $b[k] \neq v$. If $k \neq \ell$, then $a[k] = v$ and $a[k] = b[k]$ imply $b[k] = v$, but again $b[k] \neq v$. Hence, F_6' is T_{A}-unsatisfiable, indicating that F is T_{A}-unsatisfiable.

Verify that the array decision procedure of Section 9.5 reaches the same conclusion for F_6'. ∎

Theorem 11.7 (Sound & Complete). *Consider $(\Sigma_A \cup \Sigma)$-formula F from the array property fragment of $T_A \cup T$. The output F_6 of Step 6 is $(T_A \cup T)$-equisatisfiable to F.*

Proof. Inspection proves the equivalence between the input and the output of Steps 1-3. The crux of the proof is that the index set constructed in Step 4 is sufficient for producing a $(T_A \cup T)$-equisatisfiable quantifier-free formula.

That satisfiability of F implies the satisfiability of F_6 is straightforward: Step 5 weakens universal quantification to finite conjunction. Moreover, the new conjuncts of Step 6 do not affect the satisfiability of F_6, as λ is a fresh constant.

The opposite direction is more complicated. Assume that $(T_A \cup T)$-interpretation I is such that $I \models F_6$. We construct a $(T_A \cup T)$-interpretation J such that $J \models F$.

First, define a projection function that maps Σ_A-terms to terms of the index set $\mathcal{I}$:

$$\mathsf{proj}_I : \Sigma_A\text{-terms} \;\rightarrow\; \mathcal{I} \;.$$

In particular, if $\alpha_I[i] = \mathsf{v}_i$ for $i \in \mathcal{I}$ and $\alpha_I[\lambda] = \mathsf{v}_\lambda$, then

$$\mathsf{proj}_I(t) = \begin{cases} i & \text{if } \alpha_I[t] = \mathsf{v}_i \text{ for some } i \in \mathcal{I} \\ \lambda & \text{otherwise} \end{cases}$$

Extend proj_I to vectors of variables:

$$\mathsf{proj}_I(\bar{i}) = (\mathsf{proj}_I(i_1), \;\ldots, \;\mathsf{proj}_I(i_n)) \;.$$

Define J to be like I except for its arrays. Under J, let $a[i] = a[\mathsf{proj}_I(i)]$. Technically, we are specifying how α_J assigns values to terms of F and the array read function $\cdot[\cdot]$; however, we can think in terms of arrays.

To prove that $J \models F$, we focus on a particular subformula $\forall \bar{i}. \; F[\bar{i}] \rightarrow G[\bar{i}]$. Assume that

$$I \models \bigwedge_{\bar{i} \in \mathcal{I}^n} (F[\bar{i}] \rightarrow G[\bar{i}]) \;;$$

then also

$$J \models \bigwedge_{\bar{i} \in \mathcal{I}^n} (F[\bar{i}] \rightarrow G[\bar{i}]) \tag{11.1}$$

by construction of J. We need to prove that

$$J \models \forall \bar{i}. \; F[\bar{i}] \rightarrow G[\bar{i}] \;; \tag{11.2}$$

that is, that

$$J \triangleleft \{\bar{i} \mapsto \bar{\mathsf{v}}\} \models F[\bar{i}] \rightarrow G[\bar{i}]$$

for all $\bar{v} \in D^n_{\bar{j}}$. Let $K = J \lhd \{\bar{i} \mapsto \bar{v}\}$.

To do so, we prove the two implications represented by dashed arrows in the following diagram:

$$
\begin{array}{ccc}
F[\text{proj}_K(\bar{i})] & \longrightarrow & G[\text{proj}_K(\bar{i})] \\
\uparrow & & \uparrow \\
K \models \quad (1) & & (2) \\
\vert & & \downarrow \\
F[\bar{i}] & \xrightarrow{\quad ? \quad} & G[\bar{i}]
\end{array}
$$

The top implication holds under K by assumption (11.1). If both implications (1) and (2) hold under K, then the transitivity of implication implies that the bottom implication holds under K as well.

For (1), we apply structural induction to the index guard $F[\bar{i}]$. Atoms have the form $i = e$, $i \neq e$, $e \neq i$, and $i = j$, for universally quantified variables i and j and term e without universally quantified variables. When such a literal is true under K, then so is the corresponding literal $\text{proj}_K(i) = e$, $\text{proj}_K(i) \neq e$, $e \neq \text{proj}_K(i)$, or $\text{proj}_K(i) = \text{proj}_K(j)$, respectively, by definition of proj_K. For example, if $K \models i \neq e$, then $\alpha_K[i]$ is either equal to some $\alpha_K[j]$ for some $j \in \mathcal{I}$ such that $\alpha_K[j] \neq \alpha_K[e]$ or equal to some other value v. In the latter case, $\text{proj}_K(i) = \lambda$; that $\lambda \neq e$ is asserted in F_6 implies that $\text{proj}_K(i) \neq e$.

For the inductive case, observe that conjunction and disjunction are monotonic on truth-values: each can only become "more true" as its arguments switch from false to true. Thus, (1) holds.

For (2), just note that $\alpha_K[a[i]] = \alpha_K[a[\text{proj}_K(i)]]$ by the construction of J.

The bottom implication thus holds under each variant K of J, so (11.2) holds, completing the proof. ∎

Theorem 11.8 (★Complexity). *Suppose T-satisfiability is in* NP. *For subfragments of the array property fragment in which formulae have bounded-size blocks of quantifiers, $(T_A \cup T)$-satisfiability is* NP-*complete.*

NP-hardness follows from Theorem 9.23. That the problem is in NP follows easily from the procedure: instantiating a block of n universal quantifiers quantifying subformula G over index set $\mathcal{I}$ produces $|\mathcal{I}|^n$ new subformulae, each of length polynomial in the length of G. Hence, the output of Step 6 is of length only a polynomial factor greater than the input to the procedure for fixed n.

11.2 Integer-Indexed Arrays

Software engineers usually think of arrays as integer-indexed segments of memory. Reasoning about indices as integers provides the power of comparison via $\leq$, which enables reasoning about subarrays and properties such as that a (sub)array is sorted or partitioned. In particular, reasoning about subarrays is essential for reasoning about programs that incrementally construct or manipulate arrays. See, for example, the programs BubbleSort and QuickSort of Chapters 5 and 6.

The **theory of integer-indexed arrays** $T_A^{\mathbb{Z}}$ augments the signature of T_A with the signature of $T_{\mathbb{Z}}$. It includes the axioms of both T_A and $T_{\mathbb{Z}}$.

11.2.1 Array Property Fragment

As in Section 11.1, we are interested in the **array property fragment** of $T_A^{\mathbb{Z}}$. An **array property** is again a $\Sigma_A^{\mathbb{Z}}$-formula of the form

$$\forall \bar{i}. \; F[\bar{i}] \;\rightarrow\; G[\bar{i}] \;,$$

where $\bar{i}$ is a list of integer variables, and $F[\bar{i}]$ and $G[\bar{i}]$ are the **index guard** and the **value constraint**, respectively. The form of an index guard is constrained according to the following grammar:

$$
\begin{array}{rcl}
\text{iguard} & \rightarrow & \text{iguard} \wedge \text{iguard} \mid \text{iguard} \vee \text{iguard} \mid \text{atom} \\
\text{atom} & \rightarrow & \text{expr} \le \text{expr} \mid \text{expr} = \text{expr} \\
\text{expr} & \rightarrow & uvar \mid \text{pexpr} \\
\text{pexpr} & \rightarrow & \text{pexpr}' \\
\text{pexpr}' & \rightarrow & \mathbb{Z} \mid \mathbb{Z} \cdot evar \mid \text{pexpr}' + \text{pexpr}'
\end{array}
$$

where *uvar* is any universally quantified integer variable, and *evar* is any existentially quantified or free integer variable.

The form of a *value constraint* is also constrained. Any occurrence of a quantified index variable i must be as a read into an array, $a[i]$, for array term a. Array reads may not be nested; e.g., $a[b[i]]$ is not allowed. Section 11.4 explains the need for these restrictions.

The array property fragment of $T_A^{\mathbb{Z}}$ then consists of formulae that are Boolean combinations of quantifier-free $\Sigma_A^{\mathbb{Z}}$-formulae and array properties.

Example 11.9. As in the basic arrays of Section 11.1, reasoning about arrays is most useful when we can say something interesting about their elements. Suppose array elements are interpreted in some theory T with signature Σ. Now that both indices and elements can be interpreted in theories, we list several interesting forms of properties and their definitions for various element theories.

- Array equality $a = b$ in T_A:

  $$\forall i. \; a[i] = b[i]$$

- Bounded array equality $\text{beq}(a, b, \ell, u)$ in $T_A^{\mathbb{Z}}$:

  $$\forall i. \; \ell \le i \le u \;\rightarrow\; a[i] = b[i]$$

- Universal properties $F[x]$ in $T_A \cup T$, where $F[x]$ is a Σ-formula:

$$\forall i.\ F[a[i]]$$

- Bounded universal properties $F[x]$ in $T_A^{\mathbb{Z}} \cup T$, where $F[x]$ is a Σ-formula:

$$\forall i.\ \ell \leq i \leq u \ \rightarrow\ F[a[i]]$$

- Bounded and unbounded sorted arrays $\mathsf{sorted}(a, \ell, u)$ in $T_A^{\mathbb{Z}} \cup T_{\mathbb{Z}}$ or $T_A^{\mathbb{Z}} \cup T_{\mathbb{Q}}$:

$$\forall i, j.\ \ell \leq i \leq j \leq u \ \rightarrow\ a[i] \leq a[j]$$

- Partitioned arrays $\mathsf{partitioned}(a, \ell_1, u_1, \ell_2, u_2)$ in $T_A^{\mathbb{Z}} \cup T_{\mathbb{Z}}$ or $T_A^{\mathbb{Z}} \cup T_{\mathbb{Q}}$:

$$\forall i, j,\ \ell_1 \leq i \leq u_1 < \ell_2 \leq j \leq u_2 \ \rightarrow\ a[i] \leq a[j]$$

The last two predicates are necessary for reasoning about sorting algorithms, while the first four forms of properties are useful in general. For example, bounded equality is essential for summarizing the effects of a function on an array — in particular, what parts of the array are unchanged.   ∎

11.2.2 Decision Procedure

As in Section 11.1, the idea of the decision procedure is to reduce universal quantification to finite conjunction. Given F from the array property fragment of $T_A^{\mathbb{Z}}$, decide its $T_A^{\mathbb{Z}}$-satisfiability as follows:

Step 1

Put F in NNF.

Step 2

Apply the following rule exhaustively to remove writes:

$$\frac{F[a\langle i \triangleleft e\rangle]}{F[a'] \ \wedge\ a'[i] = e \ \wedge\ (\forall j.\ j \neq i \ \rightarrow\ a[j] = a'[j])} \text{ for fresh } a' \quad \text{(write)}$$

To meet the syntactic requirements on an index guard, rewrite the third conjunct as

$$\forall j.\ j \leq i - 1 \ \vee\ i + 1 \leq j \ \rightarrow\ a[j] = a'[j]\ .$$

Step 3

Apply the following rule exhaustively to remove existential quantification:

$$\frac{F[\exists \bar{i}.\ G[\bar{i}]]}{F[G[\bar{j}]]} \text{ for fresh } \bar{j} \quad \text{(exists)}$$

Existential quantification can arise during Step 1 if the given formula has a negated array property.

Step 4

From the output of Step 3, F_3, construct the index set $\mathcal{I}$:

$$\mathcal{I} = \begin{array}{l} \{t \ : \ \cdot[t] \in F_3 \text{ such that } t \text{ is not a universally quantified variable}\} \\ \cup \ \{t \ : \ t \text{ occurs as a pexpr in the parsing of index guards}\} \end{array}$$

If $\mathcal{I} = \emptyset$, then let $\mathcal{I} = \{0\}$. The index set contains all relevant symbolic indices that occur in F_3.

Step 5

Apply the following rule exhaustively to remove universal quantification:

$$\frac{H[\forall \bar{i}.\ F[\bar{i}] \ \rightarrow \ G[\bar{i}]]}{H\left[\bigwedge_{\bar{i} \in \mathcal{I}^n} (F[\bar{i}] \ \rightarrow \ G[\bar{i}])\right]} \qquad \text{(forall)}$$

n is the size of the block of universal quantifiers over $\bar{i}$.

Step 6

F_5 is quantifier-free. Decide the $(T_A \cup T_\mathbb{Z})$-satisfiability of the resulting formula.

Suppose array elements are interpreted in some theory T with signature Σ. For deciding the $(T_A^\mathbb{Z} \cup T)$-satisfiability of an array property $(\Sigma_A^\mathbb{Z} \cup \Sigma)$-formula, use a combination decision procedure for the quantifier-free fragment of $T_A \cup T_\mathbb{Z} \cup T$ in Step 6. Thus, this procedure is a decision procedure precisely when the quantifier-free fragment of $T_A \cup T_\mathbb{Z} \cup T$ is decidable. Chapter 10 discusses deciding satisfiability in combinations of quantifier-free fragments of theories.

Example 11.10. Consider the following $\Sigma_A^\mathbb{Z}$-formula:

$$F : \ (\forall i.\ \ell \le i \le u \ \rightarrow \ a[i] = b[i])$$
$$\wedge \ \neg(\forall i.\ \ell \le i \le u + 1 \ \rightarrow \ a\langle u + 1 \lhd b[u+1]\rangle[i] = b[i]) \ .$$

In NNF, we have

$$F_1 : \ (\forall i.\ \ell \le i \le u \ \rightarrow \ a[i] = b[i])$$
$$\wedge \ (\exists i.\ \ell \le i \le u + 1 \ \wedge \ a\langle u + 1 \lhd b[u+1]\rangle[i] \ne b[i]) \ .$$

Step 2 produces

$$F_2 : \ (\forall i.\ \ell \le i \le u \ \rightarrow \ a[i] = b[i])$$
$$\wedge \ (\exists i.\ \ell \le i \le u + 1 \ \wedge \ a'[i] \ne b[i])$$
$$\wedge \ a'[u+1] = b[u+1]$$
$$\wedge \ (\forall j.\ j \le u + 1 - 1 \ \vee \ u + 1 + 1 \le j \ \rightarrow \ a[j] = a'[j]) \ .$$

Step 3 removes the existential quantifier by introducing a fresh constant k:

F_3 : $(\forall i.\ \ell \leq i \leq u \;\rightarrow\; a[i] = b[i])$
$\qquad \wedge\ \ell \leq k \leq u+1\ \wedge\ a'[k] \neq b[k]$
$\qquad \wedge\ a'[u+1] = b[u+1]$
$\qquad \wedge\ (\forall j.\ j \leq u+1-1\ \vee\ u+1+1 \leq j \;\rightarrow\; a[j] = a'[j])\ .$

Simplifying, we have

F_3' : $(\forall i.\ \ell \leq i \leq u \;\rightarrow\; a[i] = b[i])$
$\qquad \wedge\ \ell \leq k \leq u+1\ \wedge\ a'[k] \neq b[k]$
$\qquad \wedge\ a'[u+1] = b[u+1]$
$\qquad \wedge\ (\forall j.\ j \leq u\ \vee\ u+2 \leq j \;\rightarrow\; a[j] = a'[j])\ .$

The index set is thus

$$\mathcal{I} = \{k, u+1\}\ \cup\ \{\ell, u, u+2\}\ ,$$

which includes the read terms k and $u+1$ and the terms ℓ, u, and $u+2$ that occur as pexprs in the index guards. Step 5 rewrites universal quantification to finite conjunction over this set:

F_5 : $\bigwedge_{i\,\in\,\mathcal{I}} (\ell \leq i \leq u \;\rightarrow\; a[i] = b[i])$
$\qquad \wedge\ \ell \leq k \leq u+1\ \wedge\ a'[k] \neq b[k]$
$\qquad \wedge\ a'[u+1] = b[u+1]$
$\qquad \wedge\ \bigwedge_{j\,\in\,\mathcal{I}} (j \leq u\ \vee\ u+2 \leq j \;\rightarrow\; a[j] = a'[j])\ .$

Expanding the conjunctions according to the index set $\mathcal{I}$ and simplifying according to trivially true or false antecedents ($\ell \leq u+1 \leq u$ simplifies to $\bot$, while $u \leq u\ \vee\ u+2 \leq u$ simplifies to $\top$) produces:

F_5' : $(\ell \leq k \leq u \;\rightarrow\; a[k] = b[k])$
$\qquad \wedge\ (\ell \leq u \;\rightarrow\; a[\ell] = b[\ell]\ \wedge\ a[u] = b[u])$
$\qquad \wedge\ \ell \leq k \leq u+1\ \wedge\ a'[k] \neq b[k]$
$\qquad \wedge\ a'[u+1] = b[u+1]$
$\qquad \wedge\ (k \leq u\ \vee\ u+2 \leq k \;\rightarrow\; a[k] = a'[k])$
$\qquad \wedge\ (\ell \leq u\ \vee\ u+2 \leq \ell \;\rightarrow\; a[\ell] = a'[\ell])$
$\qquad \wedge\ a[u] = a'[u]\ \wedge\ a[u+2] = a'[u+2]\ .$

$(T_\mathsf{A} \cup T_\mathbb{Z})$-satisfiability of this quantifier-free $(\Sigma_\mathsf{A} \cup \Sigma_\mathbb{Z})$-formula can be decided using the techniques of Chapter 10. But let us finish the example. F_5' is $(T_\mathsf{A} \cup T_\mathbb{Z})$-unsatisfiable. In particular, note that by the third conjunct k is restricted such that $\ell \leq k \leq u+1$; that the first conjunct asserts that for most of this range ($k \in [\ell, u]$), $a[k] = b[k]$; that the third-to-last conjunct asserts that for $k \leq u$, $a[k] = a'[k]$, contradicting $a'[k] \neq b[k]$ by the fourth conjunct; and that even if $k = u+1$, $a'[k] \neq b[k] = b[u+1] = a'[u+1] = a'[k]$ by the fourth and fifth conjuncts, a contradiction. Hence, F is $T_\mathsf{A}^\mathbb{Z}$-unsatisfiable. ∎

Theorem 11.11 (Sound & Complete). *Consider $(\Sigma_A^Z \cup \Sigma)$-formula F from the array property fragment of $T_A^Z \cup T$. The output F_5 of Step 5 is $(T_A^Z \cup T)$-equisatisfiable to F.*

The proof proceeds using the same strategy as in the proof of Theorem 11.7. The main difference is that the projection function proj_I is defined so that it maps an index to its nearest neighbor in the index set. For a given interpretation I, define a projection function $\mathsf{proj}_I : \Sigma_A$-terms $\to \mathcal{I}$ that maps Σ_A^Z-terms to terms of the index set $\mathcal{I}$. Let $\mathsf{proj}_I(t) = i \in \mathcal{I}$ be such that either

- $\alpha_I[i] \leq \alpha_I[t] \;\wedge\; (\forall j \in \mathcal{I}.\; \alpha_I[j] \leq \alpha_I[t] \to \alpha_I[j] \leq \alpha_I[i])$
- or $\alpha_I[t] < \alpha_I[i] \;\wedge\; (\forall j \in \mathcal{I}.\; \alpha_I[i] \leq \alpha_I[j])$.

That is, i is the index set term that is t's nearest neighbor under I, with preference for left neighbors. Extend proj_I to vectors of variables:

$$\mathsf{proj}_I(\bar{i}) = (\mathsf{proj}_I(i_1), \; \ldots, \; \mathsf{proj}_I(i_n)) \;.$$

Using this projection function, the remainder of the proof closely follows the proof of Theorem 11.7. Exercise 11.4 asks the reader to finish the proof.

11.3 Hashtables

Hashtables are a common data structure in modern programs. In this section, we describe a theory for hashtables T_H and provide a reduction of the hashtable property fragment of Σ_H-formulae into the array property fragment of T_A.

The signature of T_H is the following:

$$\Sigma_H : \{\mathsf{get}(\cdot, \cdot), \; \mathsf{put}(\cdot, \cdot, \cdot), \; \mathsf{remove}(\cdot, \cdot), \; \cdot \in \mathsf{keys}(\cdot), \; =\} \;,$$

where

- $\mathsf{put}(h, k, v)$ is the hashtable that is modified from h by mapping key k to value v.
- $\mathsf{remove}(h, k)$ is the hashtable that is modified from h by unmapping the key k.
- $\mathsf{get}(h, k)$ is the value mapped by key k, which is undetermined if h does not map k to any value.
- $k \in \mathsf{keys}(h)$ is true iff h maps the key k.

$k \in \mathsf{keys}(h)$ is merely convenient notation for a binary predicate. However, we will exploit this notation in the following useful operations:

- **Key sets** $\mathsf{keys}(h)$ can be unioned ($k_1 \cup k_2$), intersected ($k_1 \cap k_2$), and complemented ($\overline{k}$).
- The predicate $\mathsf{init}(h)$ is true iff h does not map any key.

Each is definable using the basic signature.

The axioms of T_H are the following:

- $\forall x.\ x = x$ (reflexivity)
- $\forall x, y.\ x = y\ \rightarrow\ y = x$ (symmetry)
- $\forall x, y, z.\ x = y\ \wedge\ y = z\ \rightarrow\ x = z$ (transitivity)
- $\forall h, j, k.\ j = k\ \rightarrow\ \mathsf{get}(h, j) = \mathsf{get}(h, k)$ (hashtable congruence)
- $\forall h, j, k, v.\ j = k\ \rightarrow\ \mathsf{get}(\mathsf{put}(h, k, v), j) = v$

      (read-over-put 1)
- $\forall h, k, v.\ \forall j \in \mathsf{keys}(h).\ j \neq k\ \rightarrow\ \mathsf{get}(\mathsf{put}(h, k, v), j) = \mathsf{get}(h, j)$

      (read-over-put 2)
- $\forall h, k.\ \forall j \in \mathsf{keys}(h).\ j \neq k\ \rightarrow\ \mathsf{get}(\mathsf{remove}(h, k), j) = \mathsf{get}(h, j)$

      (read-over-remove)
- $\forall h, k, v.\ k \in \mathsf{keys}(\mathsf{put}(h, k, v))$ (keys-put)
- $\forall h, k.\ k \notin \mathsf{keys}(\mathsf{remove}(h, k))$ (keys-remove)

Notice the similarity between the first six axioms of T_H and those of T_A. Key sets complicate the (read-over-put 2) axiom compared to the (read-over-write 2) axiom, while keys sets and key removal require three additional axioms. In particular, reading a hashtable with an unmapped key is undefined.

11.3.1 Hashtable Property Fragment

A **hashtable property** has the form

$$\forall \overline{k}.\ F[\overline{k}]\ \rightarrow\ G[\overline{k}]\ ,$$

where $F[\overline{k}]$ is the **key guard**, and $G[\overline{k}]$ is the **value constraint**. Key guards are defined exactly as index guards of the array property fragment of T_A: they are positive Boolean combinations of equalities between universally quantified keys; and equalities and disequalities between universally quantified keys k and other key terms. Value constraints can use universally quantified keys k in hashtable reads $\mathsf{get}(h, k)$ and in key set membership checks. Finally, a hashtable property does not contain any init literals.

Σ_H-formulae that are Boolean combinations of quantifier-free Σ_H-formulae and hashtable properties comprise the **hashtable property fragment** of T_H.

Example 11.12. Consider the following hashtable property formula:

$$F :\ \forall k \in \mathsf{keys}(h).\ \mathsf{get}(h, k) \geq 0\ .$$

Its key guard is trivial, while its value constraint is

$$k \in \mathsf{keys}(h)\ \rightarrow\ \mathsf{get}(h, k) \geq 0\ .$$

Suppose that F annotates locations L_1 and L_2 in the following basic path:

```
@L₁ : F
assume v ≥ 0;
put(h, s, v);
@L₂ : F
```

We want to prove that if F holds at L_1, then it holds at L_2. The resulting verification condition is

$$\forall h, s, v. \left[\begin{array}{c} (\forall k \in \mathsf{keys}(h).\ \mathsf{get}(h, k) \geq 0)\ \wedge\ v \geq 0 \\ \rightarrow\ (\forall k \in \mathsf{keys}(\mathsf{put}(h, s, v)).\ \mathsf{get}(\mathsf{put}(h, s, v), k) \geq 0) \end{array} \right] .$$

The key set $\mathsf{keys}(h)$ provides a mechanism for reasoning about the incremental modification of hashtables.   ∎

Example 11.13. To express equality between key sets, $\mathsf{keys}(h_1) = \mathsf{keys}(h_2)$, in T_H, write

$$\forall k.\ k \in \mathsf{keys}(h_1)\ \leftrightarrow\ k \in \mathsf{keys}(h_2) .$$

To express equality between hashtables, $h_1 = h_2$, write

$$\mathsf{keys}(h_1) = \mathsf{keys}(h_2)\ \wedge\ \forall k \in \mathsf{keys}(h_1).\ \mathsf{get}(h_1, k) = \mathsf{get}(h_2, k) .$$

∎

11.3.2 Decision Procedure

Given F from the hashtable property fragment of T_H, the decision procedure reduces its T_H-satisfiability to T_A-satisfiability of a formula in the array property fragment. The main idea of the reduction is to represent hashtables h of F by two arrays in the Σ_A-formula: an array h for the elements and an array keys_h that indicates if a key maps to an element. In particular, $\mathsf{keys}_h[k] = \circ$ indicates that k is not mapped by h, while $\mathsf{keys}_h[k] \neq \circ$ ($\mathsf{keys}_h[k] = \bullet$) indicates that h does map h to a value given by $h[k]$.

Step 1

Construct $F\ \wedge\ \bullet \neq \circ$, for fresh constants $\bullet$ and $\circ$.

Step 2

Rewrite F_1 according to the following set of rules:

$$\begin{array}{rcl} F[\mathsf{put}(h, k, v)] & \Longrightarrow & F[h']\ \wedge\ h' = h\langle k \triangleleft v\rangle\ \wedge\ \mathsf{keys}_{h'} = \mathsf{keys}_h\langle k \triangleleft \bullet\rangle \\ F[\mathsf{remove}(h, k)] & \Longrightarrow & F[h']\ \wedge\ h = h'\langle k \triangleleft h[k]\rangle\ \wedge\ \mathsf{keys}_{h'} = \mathsf{keys}_h\langle k \triangleleft \circ\rangle \end{array}$$

for fresh variable h'. In the second rule, $h = h'\langle k \triangleleft h[k]\rangle$ expresses that position k of h' is undetermined since the mapping from k is being removed. Recall that equality $a = b$ between arrays is defined by $\forall i.\ a[i] = b[i]$.

Step 3

Rewrite F_2 according to the following set of rules:

$$
\begin{aligned}
F[\mathsf{get}(h,k)] &\implies F[h[k]] \\
F[k \in \mathsf{keys}(h)] &\implies F[\mathsf{keys}_h[k] \neq \circ] \\
F[k \in K_1 \cup K_2] &\implies F[k \in K_1 \vee k \in K_2] \\
F[k \in K_1 \cap K_2] &\implies F[k \in K_1 \wedge k \in K_2] \\
F[k \in \overline{K}] &\implies F[\neg(k \in K)] \\
F[\mathsf{init}(h)] &\implies F[\forall k.\ \neg(k \in \mathsf{keys}(h))]
\end{aligned}
$$

where K, K_1, and K_2 are constructed from union, disjunction, and comple-
mentation of key set membership atoms. The final four rules define auxiliary
operations: the right-side of each is expressible in the hashtable property fragment.

Step 4

Decide the T_A-satisfiability of F_3.

As in Sections 11.1 and 11.2, hashtable values may be interpreted in some
theory T with signature Σ. Then the above procedure is a decision procedure
precisely when there is a decision procedure for the array property fragment
of $T_A \cup T$.

Example 11.14. Consider the following Σ_H-formula:

$$
G : \forall h, s, v. \left[
\begin{array}{l}
(\forall k \in \mathsf{keys}(h).\ \mathsf{get}(h,k) \geq 0) \ \wedge \ v \geq 0 \\
\quad \rightarrow \ (\forall k \in \mathsf{keys}(\mathsf{put}(h,s,v)).\ \mathsf{get}(\mathsf{put}(h,s,v),k) \geq 0)
\end{array}
\right] .
$$

To prove its T_H-validity, prove the T_H-unsatisfiability of the following:

$$
\begin{aligned}
F : \ & (\forall k \in \mathsf{keys}(h).\ \mathsf{get}(h,k) \geq 0) \ \wedge \ v \geq 0 \\
& \wedge \ \neg(\forall k \in \mathsf{keys}(\mathsf{put}(h,s,v)).\ \mathsf{get}(\mathsf{put}(h,s,v),k) \geq 0) .
\end{aligned}
$$

Step 1 introduces $\bullet$ and $\circ$:

$$
F_1 : \ F \ \wedge \ \bullet \neq \circ .
$$

Step 2 reduces hashtable modifications to arrays:

$$
\begin{aligned}
F_2 : \ & (\forall k \in \mathsf{keys}(h).\ \mathsf{get}(h,k) \geq 0) \ \wedge \ v \geq 0 \\
& \wedge \ \neg(\forall k \in \mathsf{keys}(h').\ \mathsf{get}(h',k) \geq 0) \\
& \wedge \ h' = h\langle s \triangleleft v \rangle \ \wedge \ \mathsf{keys}_{h'} = \mathsf{keys}_h\langle s \triangleleft \bullet \rangle \\
& \wedge \ \bullet \neq \circ .
\end{aligned}
$$

Step 3 completes the reduction:

$F_3:$ $(\forall k.\ \mathsf{keys}_h[k] \neq \circ \ \rightarrow \ h[k] \geq 0) \ \wedge \ v \geq 0$
$\wedge \ \neg(\forall k.\ \mathsf{keys}_{h'}[k] \neq \circ \ \rightarrow \ h'[k] \geq 0)$
$\wedge \ (\forall i.\ h'[i] = h\langle s \triangleleft v\rangle[i]) \ \wedge \ (\forall j.\ \mathsf{keys}_{h'}[j] = \mathsf{keys}_h\langle s \triangleleft \bullet\rangle[j])$
$\wedge \ \bullet \neq \circ .$

F_3 is T_A-unsatisfiable. In particular, $\mathsf{keys}_{h'} = \mathsf{keys}_h\langle s \triangleleft \bullet\rangle$ and $h' = h\langle s \triangleleft v\rangle$, so that for all keys of h (k such that $\mathsf{keys}_h[k] \neq \circ$), $h'[k] = h[k] \geq 0$. For the one new key s of h', we know that $h'[s] = h\langle s \triangleleft v\rangle[s] = v \geq 0$. Therefore, no key k of h' exists at which $h[k] < 0$, a contradiction. Hence, G is T_H-valid.

The decision procedure of Section 11.1 also proves the T_A-unsatisfiability of F_3. ∎

Theorem 11.15 (Sound & Complete). *Consider $(\Sigma_H \cup \Sigma)$-formula F from the hashtable property fragment of $T_H \cup T$. The rewriting procedure terminates, and its output F_3 of Step 3 is equisatisfiable to F and in the array property fragment of $(T_A \cup T)$.*

Proof. Inspection shows that if F is a $(\Sigma_H \cup \Sigma)$-formula from the hashtable property fragment, then F_3 is a Σ_A-formula from the array property fragment.

The rewrite system terminates: the rules of Step 2 and the first two rules of Step 3 remove instances of $(\Sigma_H \cup \Sigma)$-literals and $(\Sigma_H \cup \Sigma)$-terms without introducing more; and the final four rules of Step 3 clearly terminate with a finite number of applications of the first two rules of Step 3.

We must show that F has a satisfying $(T_H \cup T)$-interpretation precisely when F_3 has a satisfying $(T_A \cup T)$-interpretation. Suppose that $(T_H \cup T)$-interpretation I satisfies F. Construct the $(T_A \cup T)$-interpretation J satisfying F_3 as follows:

- if h maps k to v in I, set $\mathsf{keys}_h[k] = \bullet$ in J and $h[k] = v$;
- otherwise, set $\mathsf{keys}_h[k] = \circ$ and $h[k] = v$ for some arbitrary value v.

This J satisfies the conjuncts added in Step 2; also, $h[k]$ is the same value under J as $\mathsf{get}(h, k)$ under I, and $\mathsf{keys}_h[k] \neq \circ$ under J iff $k \in \mathsf{keys}(h)$ under I, showing the correctness of the first two rules of Step 3. The remaining rules are auxiliary and reduce to the first two.

Similarly, a $(T_A \cup T)$-interpretation J satisfying F_3 corresponds to a $(T_H \cup T)$-interpretation I satisfying F. Construct I as follows:

- if $\mathsf{keys}_h[k] \neq \circ$ and $h[k] = v$ in J, assert $\mathsf{get}(h, k) = v$ and $k \in \mathsf{keys}(h)$ in I;
- otherwise, assert $\neg(h \in \mathsf{keys}(h))$ in I.

Again, the correspondence between the two sides of each rule is clear. ∎

11.4 Larger Fragments

Why does this chapter focus on the array property fragments of T_A and $T_A^{\mathbb{Z}}$? Why not examine more expressive fragments? In fact, the following theorem states that extending the array property fragments in natural ways produces fragments for which satisfiability is undecidable.

Theorem 11.16. *Consider the following extensions to the array property fragment of $T_A^{\mathbb{Z}}$ (T_A, where appropriate):*

- *Permit an additional quantifier alternation.*
- *Permit nested reads (e.g., $a_1[a_2[i]]$, where i is universally quantified).*
- *Permit array reads by a universally quantified variable in the index guard.*
- *Permit general Presburger arithmetic expressions over universally quantified index variables (even just addition of 1: $i + 1$) in the index guard or in the value constraint.*
- *Permit strict comparison $<$ between universally quantified variables.*
- *Augment the theory with a predicate expressing that one array is a permutation of another.*

For each resulting fragment, there exists an element theory T such that satisfiability in the array property fragment of $T_A^{\mathbb{Z}} \cup T$ ($T_A \cup T$) is decidable, yet satisfiability in the resulting fragment of $T_A^{\mathbb{Z}} \cup T$ ($T_A \cup T$) is undecidable.

Bibliographic Remarks refers the interested reader to texts that contain the proof of this theorem.

11.5 Summary

This chapter presents several decision procedures for reasoning about array-like data structures with some quantification. It covers:

- The *array property fragment* of T_A, which allows expressing properties of arrays themselves, rather than just their elements. Elements may be interpreted in some theory.
- The *array property fragment* of $T_A^{\mathbb{Z}}$, which allows expressing properties of arrays and subarrays with indices interpreted within $T_{\mathbb{Z}}$.
- Quantifier instantiation as a basis for decision procedures, which allows the direct application of decision procedures for quantifier-free fragments.
- *Hashtables.* The decision procedure rewrites a Σ_H-formula into a Σ_A-formula in which each hashtable is represented by two arrays. Reductions of this form extend decision procedures to reason about theories similar to the originally targeted theory.

Reasoning about data structures is crucial for considering the correctness of programs. The decision procedures of Chapter 9 for reasoning about recursive data structures and arrays without quantifiers provide a means of accessing elements of data structures. Additionally, equality in T_{RDS} extends to data structures. The decision procedures for the array property fragments of T_A and $T_A^{\mathbb{Z}}$ facilitate reasoning about whole or segments of arrays, not just individual elements.

Bibliographic Remarks

Theories of arrays have been studied for over four decades. McCarthy proposes
the axiomatization based on read-over-write in [58]. James King implemented
the decision procedure for the quantifier-free fragment as part of his thesis
work [50]. Several authors discuss the quantifier-free fragment of a theory
with predicates useful for reasoning about sorting algorithms [57, 43, 89].
Suzuki and Jefferson present a permutation predicate in a more restricted
fragment [89]. The approximation to reasoning about the weak permutation
predicate of Exercise 6.5 captures a similar fragment, though for a weaker form
of permutation. Stump, Barrett, Dill, and Levitt describe a decision procedure
for the quantifier-free fragment of an extensional theory of arrays [88]. Bradley,
Manna, and Sipma [9] and Bradley [6] explore the array property fragment,
including the proof of Theorem 11.16, that is the basis for the presentation of
this chapter.

Exercises

11.1 (DP for array property fragment of T_A). Apply the decision procedure for the array property fragment of T_A to the following T_A-formulae.

(a) $\forall i.\ a\langle k \triangleleft e\rangle[i] \neq e$
(b) $a[k] = b[k]\ \wedge\ \forall i.\ a[i] \neq b[i]$
(c) $a[k] \neq b[k]\ \wedge\ \forall i.\ a[i] = b[i]$

11.2 (DP for array property fragment of $T_A^{\mathbb{Z}}$). Apply the decision procedure for the array property fragment of $T_A^{\mathbb{Z}}$ to the following $\Sigma_A^{\mathbb{Z}}$-formulae.

(a) $\mathsf{sorted}(a, \ell, u)\ \wedge\ a[\ell] > a[u]$
(b) $\mathsf{sorted}(a, \ell, u)\ \wedge\ e \leq a[\ell]\ \wedge\ \neg\mathsf{sorted}(a\langle \ell - 1 \triangleleft e\rangle, \ell - 1, u)$

11.3 (DP for array property fragment of $T_A^{\mathbb{Z}}$). Apply the decision procedure for the array property fragment of $T_A^{\mathbb{Z}}$ to the following $\Sigma_A^{\mathbb{Z}}$-formula:

$\mathsf{sorted}(a\langle 0 \triangleleft 7\rangle\langle 5 \triangleleft 9\rangle,\ 0,\ 5)\ \wedge\ \mathsf{sorted}(a\langle 0 \triangleleft 11\rangle\langle 5 \triangleleft 13\rangle,\ 0,\ 5)\ .$

11.4 ($\star$Correctness of procedure for $T_A^{\mathbb{Z}}$). Prove Theorem 11.11 using
the strategy suggested following the statement of the theorem.

11.5 ($\star$Arrays with extensionality). Consider the extensional theory of
arrays $T_A^{=}$ (see Section 3.6). Describe a decision procedure for the quantifier-
free fragment of $T_A^{=}$ using the methods of this chapter. *Hint:* Does the index
set require a fresh λ variable? Why or why not?

12

Invariant Generation

It is easier to write an incorrect program than [to] understand a correct one.

— Alan Perlis
Epigrams on Programming, 1982

While applying the inductive assertion method of Chapters 5 and 6 certainly requires insights from the programmer, algorithms that examine programs can discover many simple properties. This chapter describes a form of **static analysis** called **invariant generation**, whose task is to discover inductive assertions of programs. A static analysis is a procedure that operates on the text of a program. An invariant generation procedure is a static analysis that produces inductive program annotations as output.

Section 12.1 discusses the general context of invariant generation and describes a methodology for constructing invariant generation procedures. Applying this methodology, Section 12.2 describes **interval analysis**, an invariant generation procedure that discovers invariants of the form $c \leq v$ or $v \leq c$, for program variable v and constant c. Section 12.3 describes **Karr's analysis**, an invariant generation procedure that discovers invariants of the form $c_0 + c_1 x_1 + \cdots + c_n x_n = 0$, for program variables $x_1, \ldots, x_n$ and constants $c_0, c_1, \ldots, c_n$.

Many other invariant generation algorithms are studied in the literature, including analyses to discover linear inequalities $c_0 + c_1 x_1 + \cdots + c_n x_n \leq 0$, polynomial equalities and inequalities, and facts about memory and variable aliasing. **Bibliographic Remarks** refers the interested reader to example papers on these topics.

12.1 Invariant Generation

After revisiting the **weakest precondition** and defining the **strongest postcondition** in Sections 12.1.1 and 12.1.2, Section 12.1.3 describes the general

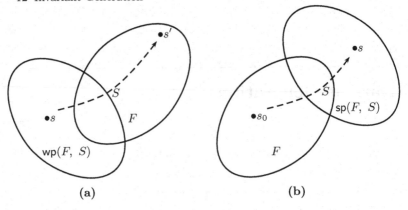

Fig. 12.1. (a) Weakest precondition and (b) strongest postcondition

forward propagation procedure for discovering inductive assertions. In general, this procedure is not an algorithm: it can run forever without producing an answer. Hence, Section 12.1.4 presents a methodology for constructing **abstract interpretations** of programs, which focus on particular elements of programs and apply a heuristic to guarantee termination. Subsequent sections examine particular instances of this methodology.

12.1.1 Weakest Precondition and Strongest Postcondition

Recall from Section 5.2.4 that a **predicate transformer** p is a function

$$p : \text{FOL} \times \text{stmts} \rightarrow \text{FOL}$$

that maps a FOL formula $F \in$ FOL and program statement $S \in$ stmts to a FOL formula. The weakest precondition predicate transformer $\text{wp}(F,\ S)$ is defined on the two types of program statements that occur in basic paths:

- $\text{wp}(F, \text{assume } c) \Leftrightarrow c \rightarrow F$, and
- $\text{wp}(F[v], v := e) \Leftrightarrow F[e]$;

and inductively on sequences of statements $S_1; \ldots; S_n$:

$$\text{wp}(F,\ S_1; \ldots; S_n) \Leftrightarrow \text{wp}(\text{wp}(F,\ S_n),\ S_1; \ldots; S_{n-1})\ .$$

The weakest precondition $\text{wp}(F,\ S)$ has the defining characteristic that if state s is such that

$$s \models \text{wp}(F,\ S)$$

and if statement S is executed on state s to produce state s', then

$$s' \models F\ .$$

In other words, the weakest precondition moves a formula backward over a sequence of statements: for F to hold after executing $S_1; \ldots; S_n$, the formula $\mathsf{wp}(F, S_1; \ldots; S_n)$ must hold before executing the statements.

This situation is visualized in Figure 12.1(a). The region labeled F is the set of states that satisfy F; similarly, the region labeled $\mathsf{wp}(F, S)$ is the set of states that satisfy $\mathsf{wp}(F, S)$. Every state s on which executing statement S leads to a state s' in the F region must be in the $\mathsf{wp}(F, S)$ region.

For reasoning in the opposite direction, we define the **strongest post-condition** predicate transformer. The strongest postcondition $\mathsf{sp}(F, s)$ has the defining characteristic that if s is the current state and

$$s \models \mathsf{sp}(F, S)$$

then there exists a state s_0 such that executing S on s_0 results in state s and

$$s_0 \models F .$$

Figure 12.1(b) visualizes this characteristic. Executing statement S on any state s_0 in the F region must result in a state s in the $\mathsf{sp}(F, S)$ region.

Define $\mathsf{sp}(F, S)$ as follows. On `assume` statements,

$$\mathsf{sp}(F, \texttt{assume } c) \Leftrightarrow c \wedge F ,$$

for if program control makes it past the statement, then c must hold.

Unlike in the case of wp, there is no simple definition of sp on assignments:

$$\mathsf{sp}(F[v], \ v := e[v]) \Leftrightarrow \exists v^0. \ v = e[v^0] \wedge F[v^0] .$$

Let s_0 and s be the states before and after executing the assignment, respectively. v^0 represents the value of v in state s_0. Every variable other than v maintains its value from s_0 in s. Then $v = e[v^0]$ asserts that the value of v in state s is equal to the value of e in state s_0. $F[v^0]$ asserts that $s_0 \models F$. Overall, $\mathsf{sp}(F, \ v := e)$ describes the states that can be obtained by executing $v := e$ from F-states, states that satisfy F.

Finally, define sp inductively on a sequence of statements $S_1; \ldots; S_n$:

$$\mathsf{sp}(F, \ S_1; \ldots; S_n) \Leftrightarrow \mathsf{sp}(\mathsf{sp}(F, \ S_1), \ S_2; \ldots; S_n) .$$

sp progresses forward through the statements.

Example 12.1. Compute

$$\mathsf{sp}(i \geq n, \ i := i + k)$$
$$\Leftrightarrow \exists i^0. \ i = i^0 + k \wedge i^0 \geq n$$
$$\Leftrightarrow i - k \geq n$$

since $i^0 = i - k$.

Compute

$$\mathsf{sp}(i \geq n, \; \mathsf{assume} \; k \geq 0; \; i := i + k)$$
$$\Leftrightarrow \; \mathsf{sp}(\mathsf{sp}(i \geq n, \; \mathsf{assume} \; k \geq 0), \; i := i + k)$$
$$\Leftrightarrow \; \mathsf{sp}(k \geq 0 \; \wedge \; i \geq n, \; i := i + k)$$
$$\Leftrightarrow \; \exists i^0. \; i = i^0 + k \; \wedge \; k \geq 0 \; \wedge \; i^0 \geq n$$
$$\Leftrightarrow \; k \geq 0 \; \wedge \; i - k \geq n$$

∎

Example 12.2. Let us prove that

$$\mathsf{sp}(\mathsf{wp}(F, \; S), \; S) \; \Rightarrow \; F \; \Rightarrow \; \mathsf{wp}(\mathsf{sp}(F, \; S), \; S) \; ;$$

that is, the strongest postcondition of the weakest precondition of F on statement S implies F, which implies the weakest precondition of the strongest postcondition of F on S. We prove the first implication and leave the second implication as Exercise 12.1.

Suppose that S is the statement $\mathsf{assume} \; c$. Then

$$\mathsf{sp}(\mathsf{wp}(F, \; \mathsf{assume} \; c), \; \mathsf{assume} \; c)$$
$$\Leftrightarrow \; \mathsf{sp}(c \to F, \; \mathsf{assume} \; c)$$
$$\Leftrightarrow \; c \; \wedge \; (c \to F)$$
$$\Leftrightarrow \; c \; \wedge \; F$$
$$\Rightarrow \; F$$

Now suppose that S is an assignment statement $v := e$. Then

$$\mathsf{sp}(\mathsf{wp}(F[v], \; v := e[v]), \; v := e[v])$$
$$\Leftrightarrow \; \mathsf{sp}(F[e[v]], \; v := e[v])$$
$$\Leftrightarrow \; \exists v^0. \; v = e[v^0] \; \wedge \; F[e[v^0]]$$
$$\Leftrightarrow \; \exists v^0. \; v = e[v^0] \; \wedge \; F[v]$$
$$\Rightarrow \; F$$

∎

Recall the definition of a verification condition in terms of wp:

$$\{F\}S_1; \ldots; S_n\{G\} : \; F \; \Rightarrow \; \mathsf{wp}(G, \; S_1; \ldots; S_n) \; .$$

We can similarly define a verification condition in terms of sp:

$$\{F\}S_1; \ldots; S_n\{G\} : \; \mathsf{sp}(F, \; S_1; \ldots; S_n) \; \Rightarrow \; G \; .$$

Typically, we prefer working with the weakest precondition because of its syntactic handling of assignment statements. However, in the remainder of this chapter, we shall see the value of the strongest postcondition.

12.1.2 ★General Definitions of wp and sp

Section 12.1.1 defines the wp and sp predicate transformers for our simple language of assumption (**assume** c) and assignment ($v := e$) statements. This section defines these predicate transformers more generally.

Describe program statements with FOL formulae over the program variables $\overline{x}$, the **program counter** pc, and the **primed variables** $\overline{x}'$ and pc'. The program counter ranges over the locations of the program. The primed variables represent the values of the corresponding unprimed variables in the next state. For example, the statement

$$L_i : \textbf{assume } c;$$
$$L_j :$$

is captured by the relation

$$\rho_1[pc, \overline{x}, pc', \overline{x}'] : \quad pc = L_i \ \wedge \ pc' = L_j \ \wedge \ c \ \wedge \ \overline{x}' = \overline{x} . \tag{12.1}$$

To execute this statement, the program counter must be L_i and c must be true. Executing the statement sets the program counter to L_j and leaves the variables $\overline{x}$ unchanged. Similarly, the assignment

$$L_i : \ x_i := e;$$
$$L_j :$$

is captured by the relation

$$\rho_2[pc, \overline{x}, pc', \overline{x}'] : \quad pc = L_i \ \wedge \ pc' = L_j \ \wedge \ x_i' = e \ \wedge \ \textsf{pres}(\overline{x} \setminus \{x_i\}) , \tag{12.2}$$

where $\textsf{pres}(V)$, for a set of variables V, abbreviates the assertion that each variable in V remains unchanged:

$$\bigwedge_{v \in V} v' = v .$$

Formulae (12.1) and (12.2) are called **transition relations**. The expressiveness of FOL allows many more constructs to be encoded as transition relations than can be encoded in either pi or the simple language of assumptions and assignments.

Let us consider the **weakest precondition** and the **strongest postcondition** in this general context. For convenience, let $\overline{y}$ be all the variables of the program including the program counter pc. The weakest precondition of F over transition relation $\rho[\overline{y}, \overline{y}']$ is given by

$$\textsf{wp}(F, \ \rho[\overline{y}, \overline{y}']) \ \Leftrightarrow \ \forall \overline{y}'. \ \rho[\overline{y}, \overline{y}'] \ \rightarrow \ F[\overline{y}'] .$$

Notice that $\textsf{free}(\textsf{wp}(F, \ \rho)) = \overline{y}$. A satisfying $\overline{y}$ represents a state from which all ρ-successors, which are states $\overline{y}'$ that ρ relates to $\overline{y}$, are F-states. Technically, such a state might not have any successors at all; for example, ρ could describe a guard that is false in the state described by $\bar{y}$.

Consider the transition relation (12.1) corresponding to assume c:

$$\mathsf{wp}(F,\ pc = L_i \wedge pc' = L_j \wedge c \wedge \bar{x}' = \bar{x})$$
$$\Leftrightarrow \forall pc', \bar{x}'.\ pc = L_i \wedge pc' = L_j \wedge c \wedge \bar{x}' = \bar{x} \rightarrow F[pc', \bar{x}']$$
$$\Leftrightarrow pc = L_i \wedge c \rightarrow F[L_j, \bar{x}]$$

Disregarding the program counter, we have recaptured our original definition of wp on assume statements:

$$\mathsf{wp}(F,\ \mathsf{assume}\ c) \Leftrightarrow c \rightarrow F\ .$$

Similarly,

$$\mathsf{wp}(F,\ pc = L_i \wedge pc' = L_j \wedge x_i' = e \wedge \mathsf{pres}(\bar{x} \setminus \{x_i\}))$$
$$\Leftrightarrow \forall pc', \bar{x}'.\ pc = L_i \wedge pc' = L_j \wedge x_i' = e \wedge \mathsf{pres}(\bar{x} \setminus \{x_i\})$$
$$\rightarrow F[pc', x_1', \ldots, x_i', \ldots, x_n']$$
$$\Leftrightarrow pc = L_i \rightarrow F[L_j, x_1, \ldots, e, \ldots, x_n]$$

Again, disregarding the program counter reveals our original definition:

$$\mathsf{wp}(F[v],\ v := e) \Leftrightarrow F[e]\ .$$

The general form of the strongest postcondition is the following:

$$\mathsf{sp}(F,\ \rho) \Leftrightarrow \exists \bar{y}_0.\ \rho[\bar{y}_0, \bar{y}] \wedge F[\bar{y}_0]\ .$$

Notice that $\mathsf{free}(\mathsf{sp}(F,\ \rho)) = \bar{y}$. It describes all states $\bar{y}$ that have some ρ-predecessor $\bar{y}_0$ that is an F-state; or, in other words, it describes all ρ-successors of F-states.

Exercise 12.2 asks the reader to specialize this definition of sp to the case of assumption and assignment statements. Exercise 12.3 asks the reader to reproduce the arguments of Example 12.2 and Exercise 12.1 in this more general setting.

12.1.3 Static Analysis

We now turn to the task of generating inductive information about programs. Throughout this chapter, we consider programs with just a single function. Exercise 12.6 asks the reader to generalize the methods to treat programs with multiple, possibly recursive, functions.

Consider a function with locations $\mathcal{L}$ forming a cutset including the initial location L_0. A **cutset** is a set of locations such that every path that begins and ends at a pair of **cutpoints** — a location in the cutset — without including another cutpoint is a basic path. An **assertion map**

$$\mu : \mathcal{L} \rightarrow \mathsf{FOL}$$

is a map from the set $\mathcal{L}$ to first-order assertions. Assertion map μ is an **inductive assertion map**, also called an **inductive map**, if for each basic path

---

$L_i :$ @ $\mu(L_i)$
$S_i;$

$\vdots$

$S_j;$
$L_j :$ @ $\mu(L_j)$

---

for $L_i, L_j \in \mathcal{L}$, the verification condition

$$\{\mu(L_i)\}S_i; \ldots; S_j\{\mu(L_j)\} \tag{12.3}$$

is valid. The task of invariant generation is to find inductive assertion maps μ. Viewing each $\mu(L_i)$ as a variable that ranges over FOL formulae, the task of invariant generation is to find solutions to the constraints imposed by the verification conditions (12.3) for all basic paths. To avoid trivial solutions, we require that at function entry location L_0 with function precondition F_{pre}, $F_{\mathsf{pre}} \Rightarrow \mu(L_0)$.

How can we solve constraints (12.3) for μ? One common technique is to perform a **symbolic execution** of the function using the strongest postcondition predicate transformer. This process is also called **forward propagation** because information flows forward through the function. The idea is to represent sets of states by formulae over the program variables. sp provides a mechanism for executing the function over formulae, and thus over sets of states.

Suppose that the function has function precondition F_{pre} at initial location L_0. Define the initial assertion map μ: let

$$\mu(L_0) := F_{\mathsf{pre}} , \quad \text{and for } L \in \mathcal{L} \setminus \{L_0\}, \quad \mu(L) := \bot .$$

This configuration represents entering the function with some values satisfying its precondition.

Maintain a set $S \subseteq \mathcal{L}$ of locations that still need processing. Initially, let $S = \{L_0\}$. Terminate when $S = \emptyset$.

Suppose that we are on iteration i, having constructed the intermediate assertion map μ. Choose some location $L_j \in S$ to process, and remove it from S. For each basic path

---

$L_j :$ @ $\mu(L_j)$
$S_j;$

$\vdots$

$S_k;$

```
let FORWARDPROPAGATE F_pre L =
    S := {L_0};
    μ(L_0) := F_pre;
    μ(L) := ⊥ for L ∈ L \ {L_0};
    while S ≠ ∅ do
        let L_j = CHOOSE S in
        S := S \ {L_j};
        foreach L_k ∈ succ(L_j) do
            let F = sp(μ(L_j), S_j;...;S_k) in
            if F ⇏ μ(L_k)
            then μ(L_k) := μ(L_k) ∨ F;
                 S := S ∪ {L_k};
        done;
    done;
    μ
```

Fig. 12.2. FORWARDPROPAGATE

$$L_k : \quad @ \ \mu(L_k)$$

starting at L_j, compute if

$$\mathsf{sp}(\mu(L_j), \ S_j;\ldots;S_k) \ \Rightarrow \ \mu(L_k) \ . \tag{12.4}$$

If the implication holds, then $\mathsf{sp}(\mu(L_j), \ S_j;\ldots;S_k)$ does not represent any states that are not already represented by $\mu(L_k)$, so do nothing. Otherwise, set

$$\mu(L_k) := \mu(L_k) \ \lor \ \mathsf{sp}(\mu(L_j), \ S_j;\ldots;S_k) \ .$$

In other words, assign $\mu(L_k)$ to be the union of the set of states represented by $\mathsf{sp}(\mu(L_j), \ S_j;\ldots;S_k)$ with the set of states currently represented by $\mu(L_k)$. Additionally, add L_k to S so that future iterations propagate the effect of the new states. For all other locations $L_\ell \in L$, assign $\mu(L_\ell) := \mu(L_\ell)$.

This procedure is summarized in Figure 12.2. Given a function's precondition F_{pre} and a cutset L of its locations, FORWARDPROPAGATE returns the inductive map μ if the main loop finishes. In the code, $L_k \in \mathsf{succ}(L_j)$ is a **successor** of L_j if there is a basic path from L_j to L_k.

If at some point S is empty, then implication (12.4) and the policy for adding locations to S guarantees that all VCs (12.3) are valid, so that μ is now an inductive map. For the initialization of μ ensures that

$$F_{\mathsf{pre}} \ \Rightarrow \ \mu(L_0) \ ,$$

while the check in the inner loop and the emptiness of S guarantees that

$$\mathsf{sp}(\mu(L_j), \ S_j;\ldots;S_k) \ \Rightarrow \ \mu(L_k) \ ,$$

which is precisely the verification condition

$$\{\mu(L_j)\}S_j; \ldots; S_k\{\mu(L_k)\} \ .$$

However, there is no guarantee that S ever becomes empty.

Example 12.3. The forward propagation procedure is an algorithm when analyzing hardware circuits: it always terminates. In particular, if a circuit has n Boolean variables, then the set of possible states has cardinality 2^n. Since each state set $\mu(L_i)$ can only grow, it must eventually be the case (within $|\mathcal{L}| \times 2^n$ iterations) that no new states are added to any $\mu(L_i)$, so S eventually becomes empty. ∎

12.1.4 Abstraction

Two elements of the forward propagation procedure prohibit it from terminating in the general case. First, as we know from Chapter 2, checking the implication

$$\mathsf{sp}(\mu(L_j), \ S_j; \ldots; S_k) \ \Rightarrow \ \mu(L_k)$$

of the inner loop is undecidable for FOL. Second, even if this check were decidable — for example, if we restricted $\mu(L_k)$ to be in a decidable theory or fragment — the while loop itself may not terminate, as the following example shows.

Example 12.4. Consider the following loop with integer variables i and n:

```
@L₀ : i = 0  ∧  n ≥ 0;
while
    @L₁ : ?
    (i < n) {
      i := i + 1;
}
```

There are two basic paths to consider:

———————————————— (1) ————————————————

```
@L₀ :  i = 0  ∧  n ≥ 0;
@L₁ : ?;
```

and

———————————————— (2) ————————————————

```
@L₁ : ?;
assume i < n;
i := i + 1;
@L₁ : ?;
```

To obtain an inductive assertion at location L_1, apply the procedure of Figure 12.2. Initially,

$$\mu(L_0) \Leftrightarrow i = 0 \land n \geq 0$$
$$\mu(L_1) \Leftrightarrow \bot .$$

Following path (1) results in assigning

$$\mu(L_1) := \mu(L_1) \lor (i = 0 \land n \geq 0) .$$

$\mu(L_1)$ was $\bot$, so that it becomes

$$\mu(L_1) \Leftrightarrow i = 0 \land n \geq 0 .$$

On the next iteration, following path (2) yields

$$\mu(L_1) := \mu(L_1) \lor \mathsf{sp}(\mu(L_1), \text{assume } i < n; \ i := i + 1) .$$

Currently $\mu(L_1) \Leftrightarrow i = 0 \land n \geq 0$, so

$$F: \ \mathsf{sp}(i = 0 \land n \geq 0, \text{assume } i < n; \ i := i + 1)$$
$$\Leftrightarrow \mathsf{sp}(i < n \land i = 0 \land n \geq 0, \ i := i + 1)$$
$$\Leftrightarrow \exists i^0. \ i = i^0 + 1 \land i^0 < n \land i^0 = 0 \land n \geq 0$$
$$\Leftrightarrow i = 1 \land n > 0 .$$

Since the implication

$$\underbrace{i = 1 \land n > 0}_{F} \Rightarrow \underbrace{i = 0 \land n \geq 0}_{\mu(L_1)}$$

is invalid,

$$\mu(L_1) \Leftrightarrow (i = 0 \land n \geq 0) \lor \underbrace{(i = 1 \land n > 0)}_{F}$$

at the end of the iteration.

At the end of the next iteration,

$$\mu(L_1) \Leftrightarrow (i = 0 \land n \geq 0) \lor (i = 1 \land n > 0) \lor (i = 2 \land n > 1) ,$$

and at the end of the kth iteration,

$$\mu(L_1) \Leftrightarrow (i = 0 \land n \geq 0) \lor (i = 1 \land n \geq 1)$$
$$\lor \cdots \lor (i = k \land n \geq k) .$$

Because the implication

$$i = k \land n \geq k$$
$$\Downarrow$$
$$(i = 0 \land n \geq 0) \lor (i = 1 \land n \geq 1) \lor \cdots \lor (i = k - 1 \land n \geq k - 1)$$

is invalid for any k, the main loop of FORWARDPROPAGATE never finishes.
However, it is obvious that

$$0 \le i \le n$$

is an inductive annotation of the loop.   ∎

The problem is that FORWARDPROPAGATE attempts to compute the exact set of reachable states. A state s is **reachable** if s appears in some computation. Inductive annotations usually over-approximate the set of reachable states: every reachable state s satisfies the annotation, but other unreachable states can also satisfy the annotation. Cleverly over-approximating the reachable state set can force the main loop of FORWARDPROPAGATE to terminate.

The method of **abstract interpretation** addresses these problems. An abstract interpretation makes two compromises to guarantee termination. First, it manipulates an artificially constrained form of state sets so that implication checking is decidable. The constrained form cannot express every possible state set. Rather, the form is chosen to focus on a particular aspect of programs, such as relationships among numerical variables or aliasing in programs with pointers. Second, it introduces a heuristic step, called **widening**, in which it guesses a limit over-approximation to a sequence of state sets. We describe how to construct an abstract interpretation in six steps.

Step 1: Choose an abstract domain D.

In the first step, we choose the form of state sets that the abstract interpretation manipulates. The **abstract domain** D is a syntactic class of Σ-formulae of some theory T; each member Σ-formula represents a particular set of states (those that satisfy it). In Section 12.2, the **interval abstract domain** D_I consists of conjunctions of $\Sigma_{\mathbb{Q}}$-literals of the forms

$$c \le v \quad \text{and} \quad v \le c \,,$$

for constant c and program variable v. In Section 12.3, we fix **Karr's abstract domain** D_K to consist of conjunctions of $\Sigma_{\mathbb{Q}}$-literals of the form

$$c_0 + c_1 x_1 + \cdots + c_n x_n = 0 \,,$$

for constants $c_0, c_1, \ldots, c_n$ and program variables $x_1, \ldots, x_n$.

Step 2: Construct a map from FOL formulae to D.

It is useful to glean as much information from existing annotations, such as the function precondition, as possible. Additionally, Step 3 requires interpreting conditions of **assume** statements in D. Hence, define a function

$$\nu_D : \mathsf{FOL} \to D$$

to map a FOL formula F to element $\nu_D(F)$ of D. For example, the assertion

$$F : \quad i = 0 \ \wedge \ n \geq 0$$

at L_0 of the loop of Example 12.4 can be represented in the interval abstract domain by

$$\nu_{D_1}(F) : \quad 0 \leq i \ \wedge \ i \leq 0 \ \wedge \ 0 \leq n$$

and in Karr's abstract domain by

$$\nu_{D_K}(F) : \quad i = 0$$

with some loss of information.

The map should have the property that for any F,

$$F \ \Rightarrow \ \nu_D(F) \ .$$

Step 3: Define an abstract sp.

Define an **abstract strongest postcondition** operator $\overline{sp}_D$ for assumption and assignment statements such that

$$sp(F, \ S) \ \Rightarrow \ \overline{sp}_D(F, \ S) \quad \text{and} \quad \overline{sp}_D(F, \ S) \in D$$

for statement S and $F \in D$.

Consider first the statement `assume c`. Conjunction is used in computing the strongest postcondition of assumption statements:

$$sp(F, \ \texttt{assume } c) \ \Leftrightarrow \ c \wedge F \ .$$

Define abstract conjunction $\sqcap_D$ for this purpose such that

$$F_1 \wedge F_2 \ \Rightarrow \ F_1 \sqcap_D F_2 \quad \text{and} \quad F_1 \sqcap_D F_2 \in D$$

for $F_1, F_2 \in D$. Then for $F \in D$,

$$\overline{sp}_D(F, \ \texttt{assume } c) \ \Leftrightarrow \ \nu_D(c) \ \sqcap_D \ F \ .$$

Often, the abstract domain D consists of conjunctions of literals of some form; in this case, $\sqcap_D$ is just the usual conjunction $\wedge$.

Defining $\overline{sp}$ for assignment statements is more complex. For suppose that we use the standard definition

$$sp(F[v], \ v := e[v]) \ \Leftrightarrow \ \underbrace{\exists v^0. \ v = e[v^0] \ \wedge \ F[v^0]}_{G} \ ,$$

which requires existential quantification. Then, later, when we compute the validity of an implication

$$G \Rightarrow \mu(L) \,,$$

$\mu(L)$ can contain existential quantification, resulting in a quantifier alternation. However, most decision procedures apply only to quantifier-free formulae, including the procedures of Chapters 8-10. Therefore, introducing existential quantification in $\overline{\mathsf{sp}}$ is undesirable.

We look at specific instances in Sections 12.2 and 12.3.

Step 4: Define abstract disjunction.

Disjunction is applied in FORWARDPROPAGATE to grow the formulae $\mu(L)$ representing the state sets at locations $L \in \mathcal{L}$. Define abstract disjunction $\sqcup_D$ for this purpose, such that

$$F_1 \vee F_2 \;\Rightarrow\; F_1 \sqcup_D F_2 \quad \text{and} \quad F_1 \sqcup_D F_2 \in D$$

for $F_1, F_2 \in D$.

Unlike conjunction, exact disjunction is usually not represented in the domain D. We examine specific instances in Sections 12.2 and 12.3.

Step 5: Define abstract implication checking.

On each iteration of the inner loop of FORWARDPROPAGATE, validity of the implication

$$\mathsf{sp}(\mu(L_j),\ S_j; \ldots; S_k) \;\Rightarrow\; \mu(L_k)$$

is checked to determine whether $\mu(L_k)$ has changed. A proper selection of D ensures that this validity check is decidable. Additionally, some domains admit a simpler check than querying a full decision procedure, as we see in Sections 12.2 and 12.3.

Step 6: Define widening.

While some abstract domains D and abstract strongest postconditions $\overline{\mathsf{sp}}_D$ guarantee that the forward propagation procedure terminates, defining an abstraction is not sufficient to guarantee termination in general; we exhibit such a case in Example 12.10 of Section 12.2. Thus, abstractions that do not guarantee termination are equipped with a widening operator $\triangledown_D$.

A **widening operator** $\triangledown_D$ is a binary function

$$\triangledown_D : D \times D \to D$$

such that

$$F_1 \vee F_2 \;\Rightarrow\; F_1 \triangledown_D F_2 \,.$$

```
let ABSTRACTFORWARDPROPAGATE F_pre L =
    S := {L_0};
    μ(L_0) := ν_D(F_pre);
    μ(L) := ⊥ for L ∈ L \ {L_0};
    while S ≠ ∅ do
        let L_j = CHOOSE S in
        S := S \ {L_j};
        foreach L_k ∈ succ(L_j) do
            let F = sp̄_D(μ(L_j), S_j; ...; S_k) in
            if F ⇏ μ(L_k)
            then if WIDEN()
                then μ(L_k) := μ(L_k) ▽_D (μ(L_k) ⊔_D F);
                else μ(L_k) := μ(L_k) ⊔_D F;
                S := S ∪ {L_k};
        done;
    done;
    μ
```

Fig. 12.3. ABSTRACTFORWARDPROPAGATE

for $F_1, F_2 \in D$. It obeys the following property. Let $F_1, F_2, F_3, \ldots$ be an infinite sequence of elements $F_i \in D$ such that for each i,

$$F_i \Rightarrow F_{i+1} \ .$$

Define the sequence

$$G_1 = F_1 \quad \text{and} \quad G_{i+1} = G_i \ \triangledown_D \ F_{i+1} \ .$$

Notice that $F_i \Rightarrow G_i$. For some i^* and for all $i \geq i^*$,

$$G_i \Leftrightarrow G_{i+1} \ .$$

That is, the sequence G_i converges even if the sequence F_i does not converge. Intuitively, the widening operator "guesses" an over-approximation to the limit of a sequence of formulae. Of course, a widening operator could always return ⊤; however, better widening operators make more precise guesses.

A proper strategy of applying widening guarantees that the forward propagation procedure terminates.

Abstract Forward Propagation

Figure 12.3 applies the operators defined in these six steps in the **abstract forward propagation algorithm**. Given a function's precondition F_{pre} and a cutset L of its locations, ABSTRACTFORWARDPROPAGATE returns the inductive map μ. When WIDEN() determines that widening should be applied,

$\mu(L_k)$ is updated to be the widening of $\mu(L_k)$ and $\mu(L_k) \sqcup_D F$. A proper definition of WIDEN() ensures that the procedure terminates. For example, a simple strategy is that after some predetermined number of iterations, WIDEN() always evaluates to **true**.

Subsequent sections examine instances of this framework.

12.2 Interval Analysis

In this section, we describe the **interval abstract interpretation**, which finds inductive assertions that are conjunctions of $\Sigma_{\mathbb{Q}}$-literals of the forms

$$v \leq c \quad \text{and} \quad c \leq v \,,$$

for $c \in \mathbb{Q}$. This analysis is useful for generating simple bounds on variables. Although the abstract domain reasons about rational variables, the analysis is applicable to integer variables: the generated invariants hold whether the program variables range over integers or rationals. Our presentation is fairly simple; one could improve some of the operations to provide better invariants.

Example 12.5. In the loop

$$@L_0 : i = 0 \ \wedge \ n \geq 0;$$
```
while
    @L₁ : ?
    (i < n) {
    i := i + 1;
}
```

the interval analysis discovers the inductive invariant $0 \leq i \ \wedge \ 0 \leq n$ at L_1. ■

Step 1: Construct the domain D_{I}.

Fix the domain D_{I} to consist of $\bot$, $\top$, and conjunctions of literals of the form

$$c \leq v \quad \text{and} \quad v \leq c \,,$$

for $c \in \mathbb{Q}$ and (program) variable v. Throughout our discussion, we assume that formulae are maintained in a **canonical form** according to the following rules:

- Simplify $\bot \wedge F$ to $\bot$.
- Simplify $\top \wedge F$ to F.
- Simplify $c_1 \leq v \ \wedge \ c_2 \leq v$ to $\max(c_1, c_2) \leq v$.
- Simplify $v \leq c_1 \ \wedge \ v \leq c_2$ to $v \leq \min(c_1, c_2)$.
- If $c_1 > c_2$, simplify $c_1 \leq v \ \wedge \ v \leq c_2$ to $\bot$.

Maintaining formulae in canonical form guarantees that no two syntactically-unequal formulae in canonical form are equivalent.

While the domain is a syntactic class of $\Sigma_{\mathbb{Q}}$-formulae, we can represent elements in a way that is suitable for computation. A useful representation is based on **interval arithmetic**. Let $[\ell, u]$ represent the interval from ℓ to u, inclusive. The sum of two intervals is

$$[\ell_1, u_1] + [\ell_2, u_2] = [\ell_1 + \ell_2, u_1 + u_2] \; .$$

The sum of an interval and a scalar c is found by treating c as the interval $[c, c]$.

For scalar multiplication, compute

$$c\,[\ell, u] = \begin{cases} [c\ell, cu] & \text{if } c \geq 0 \\ [0, 0] & \text{if } c = 0 \\ [cu, c\ell] & \text{if } c < 0 \end{cases}$$

It is convenient to allow lower and upper bounds to be $-\infty$ or ∞. Define

$$-\infty + c = -\infty \; , \quad \infty + c = \infty \; , \quad c \cdot -\infty = -\infty \; , \quad \text{and} \quad c \cdot \infty = \infty$$

for $c \geq 0$, and

$$-\infty + c = -\infty \; , \quad \infty + c = \infty \; , \quad c \cdot -\infty = \infty \; , \quad \text{and} \quad c \cdot \infty = -\infty \; ,$$

for $c < 0$. Also, define the empty interval as

$$[\infty, -\infty] \; ;$$

multiplying it by scalar c or summing it with other intervals yields the empty interval.

Consider set operations:

- Interval intersection:

$$\begin{aligned} & [\ell_1, u_1] \sqcap [\ell_2, u_2] \\ & = \begin{cases} [\infty, -\infty] & \text{if } \max(\ell_1, \ell_2) > \min(u_1, u_2) \\ [\max(\ell_1, \ell_2), \ \min(u_1, u_2)] & \text{otherwise} \end{cases} \end{aligned}$$

Intersection is exact: the computed interval represents the set that is the set intersection of the two sets represented by the given intervals.

- Interval union:

$$[\ell_1, u_1] \sqcup [\ell_2, u_2] = [\min(\ell_1, \ell_2), \ \max(u_1, u_2)]$$

The result is called the **interval hull**. It over-approximates the true union: the computed interval represents a set that may include more elements than the set union of the two sets represented by the given intervals.

For predicates,

$$[\ell_1, u_1] \leq [\ell_2, u_2] \quad \text{if } \ell_1 \leq u_2 \ ,$$

and

$$[\ell_1, u_1] = [\ell_2, u_2] \quad \text{if } [\ell_1, u_1] \sqcap [\ell_2, u_2] \neq [\infty, -\infty] \ .$$

Like interval union, these predicates are over-approximations: if any pair of points in $[\ell_1, u_1]$ and $[\ell_2, u_2]$ satisfy the predicate, then the predicate holds on the intervals.

These definitions are enough to define interval arithmetic over linear arithmetic. For example, let each variable x_i range in the interval $[\ell_i, u_i]$. Then

$$c_0 + c_1 x_1 + \cdots + c_n x_n \ ,$$

for $c_i \in \mathbb{Q}$, ranges in the interval

$$c_0 + c_1 [\ell_1, u_1] + \cdots + c_n [\ell_n, u_n] \ .$$

The correspondence of interval arithmetic with D_l is the following. $F \in D_\mathsf{l}$, which is a conjunction of literals of the form $c \leq v$ and $v \leq c$, asserts that $x_i \in [\ell_i, u_i]$, for variable x_i, where

- $\ell_i = \infty$ and $u_i = -\infty$ if F is the formula $\bot$;
- $\ell_i = d$ if $d \leq x_i$ is a literal of F, and $\ell_i = -\infty$ otherwise;
- $u_i = e$ if $x_i \leq e$ is a literal of F, and $u_i = \infty$ otherwise.

Example 12.6. The formula

$$F : \ 0 \leq i \ \wedge \ i \leq 0 \ \wedge \ 0 \leq n$$

is an element of D_l. It asserts that $i \in [0, 0]$ and $n \in [0, \infty]$. Given F, compute

$$i + 2n = [0, 0] + 2[0, \infty] = [0, \infty] \ ,$$

and

$$i - 2n = [0, 0] + -2[0, \infty] = [0, 0] + [-\infty, 0] = [-\infty, 0] \ .$$

∎

Step 2: Construct the map ν_{D_l}.

Define the map ν_{D_l} as follows. Consider literal F; then

$$\nu_{D_\mathsf{l}}(F) = \begin{cases} \bot & \text{if } F \Leftrightarrow \bot \\ \frac{b}{a} \leq v \ \wedge \ v \leq \frac{b}{a} & \text{if } F \Leftrightarrow av = b \\ v \leq \frac{b}{a} & \text{if } F \Leftrightarrow av \leq b \\ \frac{b}{a} \leq v & \text{if } F \Leftrightarrow b \leq av \\ \top & \text{otherwise} \end{cases}$$

for $a, b \in \mathbb{N}$ such that $a > 0$. Define

$$\nu_{D_l} \left(\bigwedge_i F_i \right) = \bigwedge_i \nu_{D_l}(F_i) \ .$$

This definition of ν_{D_l} is not as precise as it could be. For consider the case in which we know $G \in D_l$; then it is possible to evaluate the truth-value of, for example,

$$H : \ c_0 + c_1 x_1 + \cdots + c_n x_n \leq 0 \ ,$$

even when $n > 1$. Define $\nu_{D_l}(H, G)$ to equal the interval evaluation (either $\top$ or $\bot$) of H in the context of G. For all other literals F, define $\nu_{D_l}(F, G) = \nu_{D_l}(F)$. When F has several literals, it is sometimes more precise to compute

$$\nu_{D_l}(F, \ G \wedge \nu_{D_l}(F)) \ ,$$

which uses as much information from F as possible.

Example 12.7. Consider

$$F : \ i = 0 \ \wedge \ n \geq 0 \ \wedge \ \underbrace{j + 2n \leq 4}_{H} \ .$$

Then

$$\nu_{D_l}(F) = 0 \leq i \ \wedge \ i \leq 0 \ \wedge \ 0 \leq n \ .$$

Note that $\nu_{D_l}(H) = \top$. Now, given

$$G : \ 5 \leq j \ ,$$

compute $G \wedge \nu_{D_l}(F)$:

$$G' : \ 5 \leq j \ \wedge \ 0 \leq i \ \wedge \ i \leq 0 \ \wedge \ 0 \leq n \ .$$

Then compute

$$\nu_{D_l}(H, G') = \bot$$

since in the context G',

$$j + 2n = [5, \infty] + 2[0, \infty] = [5, \infty] \nleq [4, 4] \ .$$

Hence,

$$\nu_{D_l}(F, \ G \wedge \nu_{D_l}(F)) = \bot \ .$$

Compare this result to the weaker $\nu_{D_l}(F)$.

Simply computing $\nu_{D_l}(F, G)$ yields

$$\nu_{D_l}(F, G) : \ 0 \leq i \ \wedge \ i \leq 0 \ \wedge \ 0 \leq n \ ,$$

since in the context G,

$$j + 2n = [5, \infty] + 2[-\infty, \infty] = [-\infty, \infty] \leq [4, 4] \ .$$

Step 3: Define $\overline{\mathsf{sp}}$.

Conjunction is natural in D_{I}, so $\sqcap_{D_{\mathsf{I}}}$ is simply normal conjunction $\wedge$.

For `assume` statements, define

$$\overline{\mathsf{sp}}_{D_{\mathsf{I}}}(F, \texttt{assume } c) \Leftrightarrow \nu_{D_{\mathsf{I}}}(c, F) \wedge F .$$

That is, compute the element of D_{I} corresponding to c in the context F, and conjoin it to F.

If c is a conjunction of several literals, the following may compute a more precise formula:

$$\overline{\mathsf{sp}}_{D_{\mathsf{I}}}(F, \texttt{assume } c) \Leftrightarrow \nu_{D_{\mathsf{I}}}(c, F \wedge \nu_{D_{\mathsf{I}}}(c)) \wedge F .$$

It uses information from c to form a more precise context.

Example 12.8. Consider

$$F : 0 \leq i \wedge i \leq 0 \wedge 0 \leq n .$$

Compute

$$\overline{\mathsf{sp}}_{D_{\mathsf{I}}}(F, \texttt{assume } i \leq n)$$
$$\Leftrightarrow \nu_{D_{\mathsf{I}}}(i \leq n, \ 0 \leq i \wedge i \leq 0 \wedge 0 \leq n \wedge \nu_{D_{\mathsf{I}}}(i \leq n)) \wedge F$$
$$\Leftrightarrow \nu_{D_{\mathsf{I}}}(i \leq n, \ 0 \leq i \wedge i \leq 0 \wedge 0 \leq n) \wedge F$$
$$\Leftrightarrow [0,0] \leq [0,\infty] \wedge F$$
$$\Leftrightarrow F$$

The context F asserts that $i \in [0,0]$ and $n \in [0,\infty]$, resulting in the comparison of intervals of the fourth line. ∎

Assignment statements are handled via interval arithmetic. Compute $\overline{\mathsf{sp}}_{D_{\mathsf{I}}}(F, \ v := e)$ as follows. Let G be the conjunction of all the literals of F except those referring to v (at most two refer to v: $c_1 \leq v$ and $v \leq c_2$). If e is a linear expression, let $[\ell, u]$ be the interval evaluation of e in the context F, and

$$\overline{\mathsf{sp}}_{D_{\mathsf{I}}}(F, \ v := e) \Leftrightarrow \ell \leq v \wedge v \leq u \wedge G ,$$

where $-\infty \leq v$ and $v \leq \infty$ both simplify to $\top$. If e is not a linear expression, then let

$$\overline{\mathsf{sp}}_{D_{\mathsf{I}}}(F, \ v := e) \Leftrightarrow G .$$

According to G, v can have any value.

Example 12.9. Consider

$$F : \ 0 \le i \ \wedge \ i \le 0 \ \wedge \ 0 \le n \ .$$

To compute $\overline{\mathsf{sp}}_{D_\mathsf{I}}(F, \ i := i + 1)$, let G be the literals of F not involving i,

$$G : \ 0 \le n \ ,$$

and compute the interval evaluation of $i + 1$ in context F:

$$i + 1 = [0, 0] + [1, 1] = [1, 1] \ .$$

Then

$$\overline{\mathsf{sp}}_{D_\mathsf{I}}(F, \ i := i + 1) \ \Leftrightarrow \ 1 \le i \ \wedge \ i \le 1 \ \wedge \ 0 \le n \ .$$

∎

Step 4: Define interval disjunction, $\sqcup_{D_\mathsf{I}}$.

Define $F_1 \sqcup_{D_\mathsf{I}} F_2$ as follows. For each variable x, let F_1 assert that $x \in [\ell_1, u_1]$ and F_2 assert that $x \in [\ell_2, u_2]$. Then $F_1 \sqcup_{D_\mathsf{I}} F_2$ asserts that x is in the interval hull of $[\ell_1, u_1]$ and $[\ell_2, u_2]$: $x \in [\ell_1, u_1] \sqcup [\ell_2, u_2]$. The interval hull is defined in **Step 1**.

Step 5: Define interval implication checking.

Validity of the $\Sigma_{\mathbb{Q}}$-formula $F \to G$ is decidable for $F, G \in D_\mathsf{I}$. However, we can define a more efficient check: let F assert $x_i \in [\ell_i, u_i]$ and G assert $x_i \in [m_i, v_i]$ for each variable x_i. Then $F \Rightarrow G$ iff for each x_i

$$[\ell_i, u_i] \subseteq [m_i, v_i] \ , \quad \text{i.e., } m_i \le \ell_i \ \wedge \ u_i \le v_i \ .$$

Step 6: Define interval widening, ∇_{D_I}.

Interval analysis does not naturally terminate, as the following example illustrates.

Example 12.10. Consider again the loop

```
@L_0 : i = 0 ∧ n ≥ 0;
while
    @L_1 : ?
    (i < n) {
    i := i + 1;
}
```

of Example 12.4 with paths

――――――――――――――――――― **(1)** ―――――――――――――

$@L_0 : i = 0 \ \land \ n \geq 0;$
$@L_1 : ?;$

and

――――――――――――――――――― **(2)** ―――――――――――――

$@L_1 : ?;$
assume $i < n;$
$i := i + 1;$
$@L_1 : ?;$

Initially,

$$\mu(L_0) \ \Leftrightarrow \ \nu_{D_1}(i = 0 \ \land \ n \geq 0) \ \Leftrightarrow \ 0 \leq i \ \land \ i \leq 0 \ \land \ 0 \leq n .$$

After one iteration, following path **(1)**, $\mu(L_1) \ \Leftrightarrow \ \mu(L_0).$
   Following path **(2)** on the next iteration yields

$$\mu(L_1) := \mu(L_1) \ \sqcup_{D_1} \ \overline{sp}_{D_1}(\mu(L_1), \ \textbf{assume } i < n; \ i := i + 1) .$$

Currently $\mu(L_1) \ \Leftrightarrow \ 0 \leq i \ \land \ i \leq 0 \ \land \ 0 \leq n$, so

$$sp(0 \leq i \ \land \ i \leq 0 \ \land \ 0 \leq n, \ \textbf{assume } i < n; \ i := i + 1)$$
$$\Leftrightarrow \ sp(0 \leq i \ \land \ i \leq 0 \ \land \ 0 \leq n, \ i := i + 1)$$
$$\Leftrightarrow \ 1 \leq i \ \land \ i \leq 1 \ \land \ 0 \leq n$$

Then the new $\mu(L_1)$ is

$$\mu(L_1) := \mu(L_1) \ \sqcup_{D_1} \ \overline{sp}_{D_1}(\cdots)$$
$$\Leftrightarrow \ (0 \leq i \ \land \ i \leq 0 \ \land \ 0 \leq n) \ \sqcup_{D_1} \ (1 \leq i \ \land \ i \leq 1 \ \land \ 0 \leq n)$$
$$\Leftrightarrow \ 0 \leq i \ \land \ i \leq 1 \ \land \ 0 \leq n$$

Since the implication

$$\underbrace{0 \leq i \ \land \ i \leq 1 \ \land \ 0 \leq n}_{\text{new } \mu(L_1)} \ \Rightarrow \ \underbrace{0 \leq i \ \land \ i \leq 0 \ \land \ 0 \leq n}_{\text{old } \mu(L_1)}$$

is invalid,

$$\mu(L_1) \ \Leftrightarrow \ 0 \leq i \ \land \ i \leq 1 \ \land \ 0 \leq n$$

at the end of the iteration.
   At the end of the kth iteration,

$$\mu(L_1) \ \Leftrightarrow \ 0 \leq i \ \land \ i \leq k \ \land \ 0 \leq n .$$

It is never the case that the implication

$$0 \le i \,\wedge\, i \le k \,\wedge\, 0 \le n \,\Rightarrow\, 0 \le i \,\wedge\, i \le k - 1 \,\wedge\, 0 \le n$$

is valid, so the main loop of ABSTRACTFORWARDPROPAGATE never finishes.
∎

Hence, we need to define a widening operator $\triangledown_{D_I}$. First, for any $F \in D_I$,

$$F \,\triangledown_{D_I}\, \bot \,\Leftrightarrow\, F \quad \text{and} \quad \bot \,\triangledown_{D_I}\, F \,\Leftrightarrow\, F \,.$$

Otherwise, let $F, G \in D_I$ be other than $\bot$. For each variable v, suppose that F asserts $v \in [\ell_1, u_1]$ and G asserts $v \in [\ell_2, u_2]$. Then $F \,\triangledown_{D_I}\, G$ asserts that $v \in [\ell, u]$, where

- $\ell = -\infty$ if $\ell_2 < \ell_1$, and otherwise $\ell = \ell_1$;
- $u = \infty$ if $u_2 > u_1$, and otherwise $u = u_1$.

Intuitively, $F \,\triangledown_{D_I}\, G$ drops bounds that grow from F to G. Since at most only twice as many finite bounds as variables exist, widening can only be applied a finite number of times before all bounds become stable.

Example 12.11. On the kth iteration (for some small k, say, $k = 3$) of the analysis in Example 12.10, compute

$$\mu(L_1) := \mu(L_1) \,\triangledown_{D_I}\, (\mu(L_1) \,\sqcup_{D_I}\, \overline{\mathrm{sp}}_{D_I}(\mu(L_1), \,\texttt{assume}\ i < n;\ i := i + 1)) \,.$$

That is,

$$(0 \le i \,\wedge\, i \le k - 1 \,\wedge\, 0 \le n) \,\triangledown_{D_I}\, (0 \le i \,\wedge\, i \le k \,\wedge\, 0 \le n)$$
$$\Leftrightarrow\; 0 \le i \,\wedge\, 0 \le n$$

because the upper bound on i increases from $k - 1$ to k. Then

$$\mu(L_1) \,\Leftrightarrow\, 0 \le i \,\wedge\, 0 \le n \,.$$

While this new $\mu(L_1)$ does not imply the previous one,

$$0 \le i \,\wedge\, 0 \le n \,\not\Rightarrow\, 0 \le i \,\wedge\, i \le k - 1 \,\wedge\, 0 \le n \,,$$

one more iteration yields the same $\mu(L_1)$, finishing the analysis. Thus,

$$0 \le i \,\wedge\, 0 \le n$$

is an inductive assertion at L_1.

Unfortunately, the interval abstract domain is incapable of representing the more interesting invariant $i \le n$. ∎

12.3 Karr's Analysis

Karr's analysis discovers inductive assertions of the form

$$c_0 + c_1 x_1 + \cdots + c_n x_n = 0 \; ,$$

for $c_i \in \mathbb{Z}$ and program variables x_i. Such assertions are called **affine assertions**. They are useful for tracking the relationship among program variables and loop counters. Karr's analysis can be implemented efficiently, with running time polynomial in the program size.

In this section, we present a simplified version of the analysis that Michael Karr originally proposed. In particular, our analysis ignores guards of loops and if statements. We use the notation and concepts from Section 8.2.

Example 12.12. Consider the loop

```
@L₀ : ⊤;
i := 0;
j := 0;
k := 0;
while
    @L₁ : ?
    (∗) {
    k := k + 1;
    if (∗) i := i + 1;
    else j := j + 1;
}
```

The guard $*$ denotes nondeterministic choice: either branch can be taken. Karr's analysis discovers the inductive invariant $i + j = k$ at L_1. ∎

Step 1: Construct the domain D_K.

D_K consists of $\bot$, $\top$, and conjunctions of literals of the form

$$c_0 + c_1 x_1 + \cdots + c_n x_n = 0 \; ,$$

which define affine spaces. An **affine space** is a point, a line, a plane, *etc.* An affine space can be specified by a set of equations

$$A\bar{x} = \bar{b} \; , \quad \text{abbreviating} \quad \bigwedge_i a_{i1} x_1 + \cdots + a_{in} x_n = b_i \; ,$$

so that the space is given by points $\bar{v}$ satisfying $A\bar{v} = \bar{b}$; or by a finite set of points $V = \{\bar{v}_1, \ldots, \bar{v}_k\}$, so that the space is given by

$$\mathsf{affine}(V) = \left\{ \sum_i \lambda_i \bar{v}_i \; : \; \sum_i \lambda_i = 1 \right\} \; ,$$

that is, the set of affine combinations of vectors in V. An **affine combination** of vectors V is a weighted sum

$$\sum_i \lambda_i \bar{v}_i \quad \text{such that} \quad \sum_i \lambda_i = 1 \ .$$

For example, the affine combination of two disjoint points is a line passing through both. These two representations are the **constraint representation** and the **vertex representation**, respectively.

Example 12.13. The affine space represented in constraint form by

$$i + j = k$$

has vertex representation

$$\left\{ \begin{bmatrix} 0 \\ 0 \\ 0 \end{bmatrix}, \begin{bmatrix} 1 \\ 0 \\ 1 \end{bmatrix}, \begin{bmatrix} 0 \\ 1 \\ 1 \end{bmatrix} \right\} \ ,$$

where vectors represent values for $\begin{bmatrix} i & j & k \end{bmatrix}^T$. Confirm that each vertex satisfies $i + j = k$.

The point

$$\begin{bmatrix} 1 \\ 1 \\ 2 \end{bmatrix} = (-1) \begin{bmatrix} 0 \\ 0 \\ 0 \end{bmatrix} + (1) \begin{bmatrix} 1 \\ 0 \\ 1 \end{bmatrix} + (1) \begin{bmatrix} 0 \\ 1 \\ 1 \end{bmatrix}$$

is in the affine space because $\lambda_1 + \lambda_2 + \lambda_3 = -1 + 1 + 1 = 1$: it is an affine combination of the vertices. ∎

The vertex representation is best suited for the version of Karr's analysis that we present. Recall, though, that the abstract domain is really the set of $\Sigma_\mathbb{Q}$-formulae that are conjunctions of literals of the form

$$c_0 + c_1 x_1 + \cdots + c_n x_n = 0 \ .$$

The vertex representation of domain elements is convenient for computation.

Step 2: Construct the map ν_{D_κ}.

This step is trivial, as this version of Karr's analysis does not use information from annotations or assumption statements. Hence,

$$\nu_{D_\kappa}(F) = \top \ .$$

Step 3: Define $\overline{sp}$.

Let

$$\overline{sp}_{D_K}(F, \texttt{assume } c) \Leftrightarrow F$$

for any F and c. That is, ignore assumption statements. Ignoring assumption statements is not a terrible loss in precision: at best, only affine guards $c : A\bar{x} = \bar{b}$ could be interpreted within D_K. Such guards are uncommon in practice.

Consider assignment $x_k := e$, where e is an affine expression

$$e_0 + e_1 x_1 + \cdots + e_n x_n \ ,$$

for $e_i \in \mathbb{Q}$. Construct the **affine transformation**

$$A\bar{x} + \bar{b} : \begin{bmatrix} 1 & & & & \\ & 1 & & & \\ & & \vdots & & \\ e_1 & e_2 & \cdots & e_n & \\ & & \vdots & & \\ & & & & 1 \end{bmatrix} \begin{bmatrix} x_1 \\ \vdots \\ \vdots \\ x_n \end{bmatrix} + \begin{bmatrix} 0 \\ 0 \\ \vdots \\ e_0 \\ \vdots \\ 0 \end{bmatrix}$$

where the row with $\bar{e}$ is the kth row, corresponding to x_k, and the rest of the matrix is the identity matrix. Abbreviate this transformation with the notation $[\![x_k := e]\!]$.

Now consider an affine space F represented by a set of vertices V_F. To compute the effect of applying the assignment $x_k := e$, apply $[\![x_k := e]\!]$:

$$[\![x_k := e]\!]F \ = \ [\![x_k := e]\!]\texttt{affine}(V_F) \ = \ \texttt{affine}\{[\![x_k := e]\!]\bar{v} \ : \ \bar{v} \in V_F\} \ .$$

The transformed affine space is given by applying $[\![x_k := e]\!]$ to each of the vertices of V_F. Then

$$\overline{sp}_{D_K}(F, \ x_k := e) \Leftrightarrow [\![x_k := e]\!]F$$

for affine expression e.

Example 12.14. Consider the affine space given by vertex representation

$$V = \left\{ \begin{bmatrix} 1 \\ 0 \\ 1 \end{bmatrix} \right\} \ ,$$

for variables $\begin{bmatrix} i & j & k \end{bmatrix}^T$, and assignment $i := 2i + j + 3$. The assignment corresponds to transformation

$$
\begin{bmatrix} 2 & 1 & 0 \\ 0 & 1 & 0 \\ 0 & 0 & 1 \end{bmatrix} \begin{bmatrix} i \\ j \\ k \end{bmatrix} + \begin{bmatrix} 3 \\ 0 \\ 0 \end{bmatrix} .
$$

Then

$$
[\![i := 2i + j + 3]\!] V = \left\{ \begin{bmatrix} 2 & 1 & 0 \\ 0 & 1 & 0 \\ 0 & 0 & 1 \end{bmatrix} \begin{bmatrix} 1 \\ 0 \\ 1 \end{bmatrix} + \begin{bmatrix} 3 \\ 0 \\ 0 \end{bmatrix} \right\} = \left\{ \begin{bmatrix} 5 \\ 0 \\ 1 \end{bmatrix} \right\} .
$$

∎

For assignments $x_k := e$ in which e is not an affine expression, define the **affine hull** $\sqcup_{D_K}$ of two affine spaces F_1 and F_2 with vertex representations V and W, respectively, as

$$
F_1 \sqcup_{D_K} F_2 = \left\{ \sum_i \lambda_i \bar{v}_i + \sum_j \mu_j \bar{w}_j \ : \ \sum_i \lambda_i + \sum_j \mu_j = 1 \right\} .
$$

To implement this definition, simply let $U = V \cup W$ be the vertex representation of $F_1 \sqcup_{D_K} F_2$. Then

$$
F_1 \sqcup_{D_K} F_2 = \mathsf{affine}(U) = \left\{ \sum_i \lambda_i \bar{u}_i \ : \ \sum_i \lambda_i = 1 \right\} ,
$$

which is equivalent to the definition in terms of V and W, as desired. For example, the affine hull of two disjoint points is a line; and the affine hull of a line and a point not on the line is a plane. Clearly, the affine hull vastly over-approximates the union of two affine spaces; however, it is the most precise affine space that includes their union.

Now define

$$
\overline{\mathsf{sp}}_{D_K}(F, \ x_k := e) \ \Leftrightarrow \ [\![x_k := 0]\!] F \ \sqcup_{D_K} \ [\![x_k := 1]\!] F
$$

when e is not an affine expression. In the new affine space, x_k can have any value. Exercise 12.5 asks the reader to prove this claim.

Example 12.15. Consider affine space given by vertex representation

$$
V = \left\{ \begin{bmatrix} 1 \\ 0 \\ 1 \end{bmatrix} \right\} ,
$$

for variables $\begin{bmatrix} i & j & k \end{bmatrix}^{\mathsf{T}}$, and non-affine assignment $i := f(i, j, k)$. Compute

$[\![i := 0]\!]V \ \sqcup_{D_K} \ [\![i := 1]\!]V$

$$= \left\{ \begin{bmatrix} 0\,0\,0 \\ 0\,1\,0 \\ 0\,0\,1 \end{bmatrix} \begin{bmatrix} 1 \\ 0 \\ 1 \end{bmatrix} + \begin{bmatrix} 0 \\ 0 \\ 0 \end{bmatrix} \right\} \cup \left\{ \begin{bmatrix} 0\,0\,0 \\ 0\,1\,0 \\ 0\,0\,1 \end{bmatrix} \begin{bmatrix} 1 \\ 0 \\ 1 \end{bmatrix} + \begin{bmatrix} 1 \\ 0 \\ 0 \end{bmatrix} \right\}$$

$$= \left\{ \begin{bmatrix} 0 \\ 0 \\ 1 \end{bmatrix} \right\} \cup \left\{ \begin{bmatrix} 1 \\ 0 \\ 1 \end{bmatrix} \right\}$$

$$= \left\{ \begin{bmatrix} 0 \\ 0 \\ 1 \end{bmatrix}, \begin{bmatrix} 1 \\ 0 \\ 1 \end{bmatrix} \right\}$$

The final set of vertices represents the set of states in which $j = 0$, $k = 1$, and i is any value. ∎

Step 4: Define affine disjunction, $\sqcup_{D_K}$.

The affine hull $\sqcup_{D_K}$, defined in **Step 3**, over-approximates disjunction.

Step 5: Define affine implication checking.

For $F_1, F_2 \in D_K$, whether $F_1 \Rightarrow F_2$ is decidable. But a more efficient test relies on the vertex representations V and W of F_1 and F_2, respectively. For each $\overline{v} \in V$, check if $\overline{v} \in \mathsf{affine}(W)$: determine if there is a $\overline{\lambda}$ such that

$$\overline{v} = \sum_j \lambda_j \overline{w}_j \quad \text{and} \quad \sum_j \lambda_j = 1 .$$

In other words, determine if there is some affine combination of the elements of W that equals $\overline{v}$. More concisely, determine if there is some $\overline{\lambda}$ such that, for A_W a matrix with columns $\overline{w} \in W$,

$$\begin{bmatrix} A_W \\ \overline{1}^\mathsf{T} \end{bmatrix} \overline{\lambda} = \begin{bmatrix} \overline{v} \\ 1 \end{bmatrix} ; \text{ that is, } \overline{1}^\mathsf{T}\overline{\lambda} = 1 \quad \text{and} \quad A_W \overline{\lambda} = \overline{v} .$$

This query can be decided efficiently using algorithms for solving linear equations, such as Gaussian elimination.

Then $F_1 \Rightarrow F_2$ iff for all $\overline{v} \in V$, $\overline{v} \in \mathsf{affine}(W)$.

Example 12.16. Consider affine space F_1 given by vertex representation

$$V_1 = \left\{ \begin{bmatrix} 1 \\ 1 \\ 2 \end{bmatrix} \right\}$$

and affine space F_2 given by vertex representation

$$V_2 = \left\{ \begin{bmatrix} 0 \\ 0 \\ 0 \end{bmatrix}, \begin{bmatrix} 1 \\ 0 \\ 1 \end{bmatrix}, \begin{bmatrix} 0 \\ 1 \\ 1 \end{bmatrix} \right\}.$$

Is the implication $F_1 \Rightarrow F_2$ valid? Yes, as

$$\begin{bmatrix} 1 \\ 1 \\ 2 \end{bmatrix} = (-1) \begin{bmatrix} 0 \\ 0 \\ 0 \end{bmatrix} + (1) \begin{bmatrix} 1 \\ 0 \\ 1 \end{bmatrix} + (1) \begin{bmatrix} 0 \\ 1 \\ 1 \end{bmatrix}$$

and $-1 + 1 + 1 = 1$, so the vertex is in $\mathsf{affine}(V_2)$. ∎

Step 6: Define affine widening.

With each growth of a $\mu(L)$, its dimension increases by at least 1 by definition of the affine hull. As each $\mu(L)$ can be at most n-dimensional, for n the number of program variables, the procedure ABSTRACTFORWARDPROPAGATE termi-nates even without the use of widening. Hence, we do not define a widening operator.

Example 12.17. Consider the loop

```
@L₀ : T;
i := 0;
j := 0;
k := 0;
while
    @L₁ : ?
    (*) {
    k := k + 1;
    if (*) i := i + 1;
    else j := j + 1;
}
```

which has three basic paths:

$$\text{————————— (1) —————————}$$

```
@L₀ : T;
i := 0;
j := 0;
k := 0;
@L₁ : ?;
```

which is summarized by transformation

$$\tau_1 : \begin{bmatrix} 0 & 0 & 0 \\ 0 & 0 & 0 \\ 0 & 0 & 0 \end{bmatrix} \begin{bmatrix} i \\ j \\ k \end{bmatrix} + \begin{bmatrix} 0 \\ 0 \\ 0 \end{bmatrix},$$

────────────────────────────── **(2)** ──────────────────────────────

$@L_1 : ?;$
$k := k + 1;$
$i := i + 1;$
$@L_1 : ?;$

───

which is summarized by transformation

$$\tau_2 : \ I \begin{bmatrix} i \\ j \\ k \end{bmatrix} + \begin{bmatrix} 1 \\ 0 \\ 1 \end{bmatrix}$$

where, recall, I is the identity matrix, and

────────────────────────────── **(3)** ──────────────────────────────

$@L_1 : ?;$
$k := k + 1;$
$j := j + 1;$
$@L_1 : ?;$

───

which is summarized by transformation

$$\tau_3 : \ I \begin{bmatrix} i \\ j \\ k \end{bmatrix} + \begin{bmatrix} 0 \\ 1 \\ 1 \end{bmatrix} \ .$$

Initially, $\mu(L_0) \Leftrightarrow \top$, so its vertex representation is the set of unit vectors

$$\left\{ \begin{bmatrix} 1 \\ 0 \\ 0 \end{bmatrix}, \begin{bmatrix} 0 \\ 1 \\ 0 \end{bmatrix}, \begin{bmatrix} 0 \\ 0 \\ 1 \end{bmatrix}, \begin{bmatrix} 0 \\ 0 \\ 0 \end{bmatrix} \right\} ,$$

while $\mu(L_1) \Leftrightarrow \bot$, represented by $\emptyset$. Then

$$\mu(L_1) := \mu(L_1) \ \sqcup_{D_K} \ \tau_1 \mu(L_0) = \emptyset \ \cup \ \left\{ \begin{bmatrix} 0 \\ 0 \\ 0 \end{bmatrix} \right\} .$$

For the next iteration, consider the two transitions τ_2 and τ_3:

$$\mu(L_1) := \mu(L_1) \ \sqcup_{D_K} \ \tau_2 \mu(L_1) = \left\{ \begin{bmatrix} 0 \\ 0 \\ 0 \end{bmatrix} \right\} \cup \left\{ \tau_2 \begin{bmatrix} 0 \\ 0 \\ 0 \end{bmatrix} \right\}$$

$$= \left\{ \begin{bmatrix} 0 \\ 0 \\ 0 \end{bmatrix}, \begin{bmatrix} 1 \\ 0 \\ 1 \end{bmatrix} \right\} .$$

Next,

$$\mu(L_1) := \mu(L_1) \sqcup_{D_K} \tau_3\mu(L_1) = \left\{ \begin{bmatrix} 0 \\ 0 \\ 0 \end{bmatrix}, \begin{bmatrix} 1 \\ 0 \\ 1 \end{bmatrix} \right\} \cup \left\{ \tau_3 \begin{bmatrix} 0 \\ 0 \\ 0 \end{bmatrix}, \tau_3 \begin{bmatrix} 1 \\ 0 \\ 1 \end{bmatrix} \right\}$$

$$= \left\{ \begin{bmatrix} 0 \\ 0 \\ 0 \end{bmatrix}, \begin{bmatrix} 1 \\ 0 \\ 1 \end{bmatrix}, \begin{bmatrix} 0 \\ 1 \\ 1 \end{bmatrix} \right\} .$$

The new vertex $\begin{bmatrix} 0 & 1 & 1 \end{bmatrix}^{\mathsf{T}}$ is obtained from $\tau_3 \begin{bmatrix} 0 & 0 & 0 \end{bmatrix}^{\mathsf{T}}$. Note that τ_3 is applied to $\begin{bmatrix} 1 & 0 & 1 \end{bmatrix}^{\mathsf{T}}$ as well; however

$$\tau_3 \begin{bmatrix} 1 \\ 0 \\ 1 \end{bmatrix} = \begin{bmatrix} 1 \\ 1 \\ 2 \end{bmatrix} = (-1) \begin{bmatrix} 0 \\ 0 \\ 0 \end{bmatrix} + (1) \begin{bmatrix} 1 \\ 0 \\ 1 \end{bmatrix} + (1) \begin{bmatrix} 0 \\ 1 \\ 1 \end{bmatrix} ,$$

and $-1 + 1 + 1 = 1$. Hence, $\begin{bmatrix} 1 & 1 & 2 \end{bmatrix}^{\mathsf{T}}$ is redundant.

On the next iteration, we obtain convergence. For

$$\tau_2 \begin{bmatrix} 0 \\ 0 \\ 0 \end{bmatrix} = \begin{bmatrix} 1 \\ 0 \\ 1 \end{bmatrix}, \quad \tau_2 \begin{bmatrix} 1 \\ 0 \\ 1 \end{bmatrix} = \begin{bmatrix} 2 \\ 0 \\ 2 \end{bmatrix} = (-1) \begin{bmatrix} 0 \\ 0 \\ 0 \end{bmatrix} + (2) \begin{bmatrix} 1 \\ 0 \\ 1 \end{bmatrix} ,$$

and

$$\tau_2 \begin{bmatrix} 0 \\ 1 \\ 1 \end{bmatrix} = \begin{bmatrix} 1 \\ 1 \\ 2 \end{bmatrix} = (-1) \begin{bmatrix} 0 \\ 0 \\ 0 \end{bmatrix} + (1) \begin{bmatrix} 1 \\ 0 \\ 1 \end{bmatrix} + (1) \begin{bmatrix} 0 \\ 1 \\ 1 \end{bmatrix} ,$$

so that τ_2 does not modify $\mu(L_1)$. Additionally,

$$\tau_3 \begin{bmatrix} 0 \\ 0 \\ 0 \end{bmatrix} = \begin{bmatrix} 0 \\ 1 \\ 1 \end{bmatrix}, \quad \tau_3 \begin{bmatrix} 1 \\ 0 \\ 1 \end{bmatrix} = \begin{bmatrix} 1 \\ 1 \\ 2 \end{bmatrix} = (-1) \begin{bmatrix} 0 \\ 0 \\ 0 \end{bmatrix} + (1) \begin{bmatrix} 1 \\ 0 \\ 1 \end{bmatrix} + (1) \begin{bmatrix} 0 \\ 1 \\ 1 \end{bmatrix} ,$$

and

$$\tau_3 \begin{bmatrix} 0 \\ 1 \\ 1 \end{bmatrix} = \begin{bmatrix} 0 \\ 2 \\ 2 \end{bmatrix} = (-1) \begin{bmatrix} 0 \\ 0 \\ 0 \end{bmatrix} + (2) \begin{bmatrix} 0 \\ 1 \\ 1 \end{bmatrix} ,$$

so that τ_3 does not modify $\mu(L_1)$, either.

Hence, the final vertex representation of $\mu(L_1)$ is

$$V = \left\{ \begin{bmatrix} 0 \\ 0 \\ 0 \end{bmatrix}, \begin{bmatrix} 1 \\ 0 \\ 1 \end{bmatrix}, \begin{bmatrix} 0 \\ 1 \\ 1 \end{bmatrix} \right\} .$$

To obtain the constraint representation of this affine space, solve

$$[V^{\mathsf{T}} \ -\bar{\mathrm{I}}] \begin{bmatrix} a_1 \\ \vdots \\ a_n \\ b \end{bmatrix} = \bar{0} \; ;$$

that is,

$$\begin{bmatrix} 0 & 0 & 0 & -1 \\ 1 & 0 & 1 & -1 \\ 0 & 1 & 1 & -1 \end{bmatrix} \begin{bmatrix} a_1 \\ a_2 \\ a_3 \\ b \end{bmatrix} = \begin{bmatrix} 0 \\ 0 \\ 0 \end{bmatrix} \; .$$

In this case, we find the inductive assertion

$$i + j = k$$

at L_1.   ∎

12.4 ★Standard Notation and Concepts

Our presentation of abstract interpretation differs markedly from the standard presentation in the literature. To facilitate the reader's foray into the literature, we discuss here the standard notation and concepts and relate it to our presentation. The main idea is to describe an abstract interpretation in terms of a set of operations over two lattices.

Lattices

A **partially ordered set** $(S, \preceq)$, also called a **poset**, is a set S equipped with a **partial order** $\preceq$, which is a binary relation that is

- **reflexive:** $\forall s \in S.\ s \preceq s$;
- **antisymmetric:** $\forall s_1, s_2.\ s_1 \preceq s_2 \ \wedge \ s_2 \preceq s_1 \ \rightarrow \ s_1 = s_2$;
- **transitive:** $\forall s_1, s_2, s_3 \in S.\ s_1 \preceq s_2 \ \wedge \ s_2 \preceq s_3 \ \rightarrow \ s_1 \preceq s_3$.

A **lattice** $(S, \sqcup, \sqcap)$ is a set equipped with **join** $\sqcup$ and **meet** $\sqcap$ operators that are

- **commutative:**
    - $\forall s_1, s_2.\ s_1 \sqcup s_2 = s_2 \sqcup s_1,$
    - $\forall s_1, s_2.\ s_1 \sqcap s_2 = s_2 \sqcap s_1;$
- **associative:**
    - $\forall s_1, s_2, s_3.\ s_1 \sqcup (s_2 \sqcup s_3) = (s_1 \sqcup s_2) \sqcup s_3,$
    - $\forall s_1, s_2, s_3.\ s_1 \sqcap (s_2 \sqcap s_3) = (s_1 \sqcap s_2) \sqcap s_3;$
- **idempotent:**
    - $\forall s.\ s \sqcup s = s,$

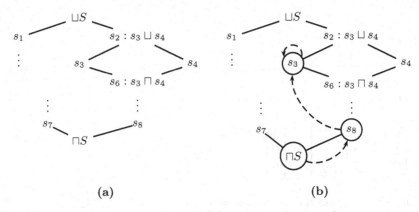

Fig. 12.4. (a) A complete lattice with (b) monotone function f

- $\forall s.\ s \sqcap s = s$.

Additionally, they satisfy the **absorption laws**:

- $\forall s_1, s_2.\ s_1 \sqcup (s_1 \sqcap s_2) = s_1$;
- $\forall s_1, s_2.\ s_1 \sqcap (s_1 \sqcup s_2) = s_1$.

One can define a partial order $\preceq$ on S:

$$\forall s_1, s_2.\ s_1 \preceq s_2 \ \leftrightarrow\ s_1 = s_1 \sqcap s_2 \ ,$$

or equivalently

$$\forall s_1, s_2.\ s_1 \preceq s_2 \ \leftrightarrow\ s_2 = s_1 \sqcup s_2 \ .$$

A lattice is **complete** if for every subset $S' \subseteq S$ (including infinite subsets), both the join, or **supremum**, $\sqcup S'$ and the meet, or **infimum**, $\sqcap S'$ exist. In particular, a complete lattice has a least element $\sqcap S$ and a greatest element $\sqcup S$. Figure 12.4(a) visualizes a complete lattice.

A function f on elements of a lattice is **monotone** in the lattice if

$$\forall s_1, s_2.\ s_1 \preceq s_2 \ \rightarrow\ f(s_1) \preceq f(s_2) \ .$$

A **fixpoint** of f is any element $s \in S$ such that $f(s) = s$. The dashed lines of Figure 12.4(b) visualize the iterative application of monotone function f from $\sqcap S$ until it reaches the fixpoint s_3.

The following theorem is an important classical result for monotone functions on complete lattices.

Theorem 12.18 (Knaster-Tarski Theorem). *The fixpoints of a monotone function on a complete lattice comprise a complete lattice.*

Since complete lattices are nonempty, a fixpoint of a monotone function on a complete lattice always exists. More, the Knaster-Tarski theorem guarantees the existence of the **least fixpoint** and the **greatest fixpoint** of f, which are the least and greatest elements, respectively, of the complete lattice defined by f's fixpoints.

Abstract Interpretation

An important complete lattice for our purposes is the lattice defined by the sets of a program P's possible states S: the join is set union, the meet is set intersection, and the partial order is set containment. The greatest element is the set of all states; the least element is the empty set. The lattice is thus represented by $(2^S, \cup, \cap)$, where 2^S is the powerset of S. Call this lattice C_P.

Treat P as a function on S: $P(s)$ is the successor state of s during execution. Define the strongest postcondition on subsets S' of states S and program P:

$$\mathsf{sp}(S',\ P) \overset{\text{def}}{=} \{P(s)\ :\ s \in S'\}\ ,$$

which we abbreviate as $P(S')$. Now define the function

$$F_P(S') \overset{\text{def}}{=} S' \cup P(S')\ ;$$

F_P is a monotone function on C_P. Hence, by the Knaster-Tarski theorem, the least fixpoint of F_P exists on C_P: it is the set of reachable states of P. The lattice C_P and the monotone function F_P define the **concrete semantics** of program P. For this reason, the elements 2^S of C_P comprise the **concrete domain**.

The FORWARDPROPAGATE algorithm of Figure 12.2 can be described as applying F_P to the set of states satisfying the function precondition until the least fixpoint is reached.

However, the least fixpoint of F_P usually cannot be computed in practice (see Section 12.1.4). Therefore, consider another lattice, $A_P : (A, \sqcup, \sqcap)$, whose elements A are "simpler" than those of C_P. Its elements A might be intervals or affine equations, for example, and thus comprise the **abstract domain**. Define two functions

$$\alpha : 2^S \to A \quad \text{and} \quad \gamma : A \to 2^S\ ,$$

the **abstraction function** and the **concretization function**, respectively. These functions should preserve order:

$$\forall S_1, S_2 \subseteq S.\ S_1 \subseteq S_2\ \rightarrow\ \alpha(S_1) \preceq \alpha(S_2)\ ,$$

and

$$\forall a_1, a_2 \in A.\ a_1 \preceq a_2\ \rightarrow\ \gamma(a_1) \subseteq \gamma(a_2)\ .$$

A monotone function $\overline{F}_P$ on A_P is a **valid abstraction** of F_P if

$$\forall a \in A.\ F_P(\gamma(a)) \subseteq \gamma(\overline{F}_P(a))\ ,$$

that is, if the set of program states represented by abstract element $\overline{F}_P(a)$ is a superset of the application of F_P to the set of states represented by abstract element a. One possible abstraction is given by applying F_P to the concretization of a and then abstracting the result:

$$\overline{F}_P(a) \stackrel{\text{def}}{=} \alpha(F_P(\gamma(a)))\ .$$

A valid abstraction $\overline{F}_P$ provides a means for approximating the least fixpoint of F_P in C_P: the concretization $\gamma(a)$ of any fixpoint a of $\overline{F}_P$ in A_P is a superset of the least fixpoint of F_P in C_P.

Lattice A_P need not be any better behaved than C_P, though. A well-behaved lattice satisfies the **ascending chain condition**: every nondecreasing sequence of elements eventually converges. Consequently, computing the least fixpoint of a monotone function in such a lattice requires only a finite number of iterations. The lattice defined by the affine spaces of Karr's analysis trivially satisfies this condition: it is of finite height because the number of dimensions is finite. But, for example, the lattice defined by intervals does not satisfy the ascending chain condition. In this case, one must define a widening operator on the abstract domain.

Relating Notation and Concepts

In our presentation, we take as our concrete set not 2^S but rather FOL representations of sets of states. The concrete lattice is thus $(\mathsf{FOL}, \vee, \wedge)$ with partial order $\Rightarrow$. This lattice is not complete: there need not be a finite first-order representation of the conjunction of an infinite number of formulae. But not surprisingly, there need not be a finite represension of a set of infinite cardinality, either, so the completeness of C_P is not of practical value.

Our abstract domains are given by syntactic restrictions on the form of FOL formulae. The abstraction function is ν_D, and the concretization function is just the identity. $\overline{\mathsf{sp}}_D$ is a valid abstraction of sp, and both are monotone in their respective lattices.

12.5 Summary

This chapter describes a methodology for developing algorithms to reason about program correctness. It covers:

- *Invariant generation* in a general setting. The forward propagation algorithm based on the strongest postcondition. The need for abstraction. Issues: decidability and convergence. Abstract interpretations.

- *Interval analysis*, an abstract interpretation with a domain describing intervals. It is appropriate for reasoning about simple bounds on variables.
- *Karr's analysis*, an abstract interpretation with a domain describing affine spaces. It discovers equations among rational or real variables.
- Notation and concepts in the standard presentation of abstract interpretation.

This chapter provides just an introduction to a widely studied area of research.

Bibliographic Remarks

We present a simplified version of the abstract interpretation framework of Cousot and Cousot, who also describe a version of the interval domain that we present [20].

Karr developed his analysis a year before the abstract interpretation framework was presented [46]. For background on linear algebra, see [42]. Our presentation of Karr's analysis is based on that of Müller-Olm and Seidl [63].

Many other domains of abstract interpretation have been studied. The most widely known is the domain of polyhedra, which Cousot and Halbwachs describe in [21]. Exercise 12.4 explores the octagon domain of Miné [61]. As an example of a non-numerical domain, see the work of Sagiv, Reps, and Wilhelm on shape analysis [96].

Exercises

12.1 (wp and sp). Prove the second implication of Example 12.2; that is, prove that

$$F \Rightarrow \mathsf{wp}(\mathsf{sp}(F,\ S),\ S) \ .$$

12.2 (General sp). Compute $\mathsf{sp}(F,\ \rho_1)$ and $\mathsf{sp}(F,\ \rho_2)$ for transition relations ρ_1 and ρ_2 of (12.1) and (12.2), respectively. Show that disregarding pc reveals the original definition of sp.

12.3 (General wp and sp). For the general definitions of wp and sp, prove that

$$\mathsf{sp}(\mathsf{wp}(F,\ S),\ S) \ \Rightarrow \ F \ \Rightarrow \ \mathsf{wp}(\mathsf{sp}(F,\ S),\ S) \ .$$

12.4 (Octagon Domain). Design an abstract interpretation for the octagon domain. That is, extend the interval domain to include literals of the form

$$c \leq v_1 + v_2 \ , \quad v_1 + v_2 \leq c \ , \quad c \leq v_1 - v_2 \ , \quad \text{and} \quad v_1 - v_2 \leq c \ .$$

Apply it to the loop of Example 12.4. Because i and n are integer variables, the loop guard $i < n$ is equivalent to $i \leq n - 1$.

12.5 (Non-affine assignments). Consider affine spaces F and

$$G: \; [\![x_k := 0]\!]F \; \sqcup_{D_k} \; [\![x_k := 1]\!]F \; .$$

Prove the following:

(a) If $[x_1 \cdots x_k \cdots x_n] \in F$, then $[x_1 \cdots m \cdots x_n] \in G$ for all $m \in \mathbb{R}$.
(b) If $[x_1 \cdots x_k \cdots x_n] \in G$, then $[x_1 \cdots m \cdots x_n] \in F$ for some $m \in \mathbb{R}$.

Hint: Use the definition of the affine hull.

12.6 (*Analyzing programs).

(a) Describe how to use ABSTRACTFORWARDPROPAGATE to analyze programs with many functions, some of which may be recursive. *Hints*: First, include a location in each function to collect information for the function postcondition. Consider that this information might include function variables other than rv and the parameters, so define an abstract operator elim to eliminate these variables. Then recall that function calls in basic paths are replaced by function summaries constructed from the function postconditions. Therefore, ABSTRACTFORWARDPROPAGATE need not be modified to handle function calls. But in which order should functions be analyzed? What about recursive functions?
(b) Describe an instance of this generalization for interval analysis. In particular, define elim.
(c) Describe an instance of this generalization for Karr's analysis. In particular, define elim.

13

Further Reading

Do not seek to follow in the footsteps of the men of old; seek what they sought.

— Matsuo Basho
Kyoroku Ribetsu no Kotoba, 1693

In this book we have presented a classical method of specifying and verifying sequential programs (Chapters 5 and 6) based on first-order logic (Chapters 1–3) and induction (Chapter 4). We then focused on algorithms for automating the application of this method: decision procedures for reasoning about verification conditions (Chapters 7–11), and invariant generation procedures for deducing inductive facts about programs (Chapter 12). This material is fundamental to all modern research in verification. In this chapter, we indicate topics for further reading and research.

First-Order Logic

Other texts on first-order logic include [87, 31, 55]. Smullyan [87], on which the presentation of Section 2.7 is partly based, concisely presents the main results in first-order logic. Enderton [31] provides a comprehensive discussion of theories of arithmetic and Gödel's first incompleteness theorem. Manna and Waldinger [55] explore additional first-order theories.

Decision Procedures

We covered three forms of decision procedures: quantifier elimination (Chapter 7) for full theories, decision procedures for quantifier-free fragments of theories with equality (Chapters 8–10), and instantiation-based procedures for limited quantification (Chapter 11). New decision procedures in each of these styles are discovered regularly (see, for example, the proceedings of the *IEEE Symposium on Logic in Computer Science* [51]).

Proofs of correctness in Chapters 7 and 11 appeal to the structure of interpretations. *Model theory* studies logic from the perspective of models (interpretations), and decision procedures can be understood in model-theoretic terms. Hodges covers this topic comprehensively [40].

The combination result of Chapter 10 is not the only one known, although it is the simplest general result. For example, Shostak's method treats a subclass of fragments with greater speed [84, 78]. Current efforts aim to extend combination methods to require fewer or different restrictions [93, 99, 94, 4]. However, most theories cannot be combined in a general way, particularly when quantification is allowed, so logicians develop special combination procedures [100].

Decision procedures for PL ("SAT solvers") and combination procedures ("SMT", for *SAT Modulo Theories*) have received much practical attention recently, even in the form of annual competitions [81, 86]. Motivating applications include software and hardware verification.

Automated Theorem Proving

While satisfiability/validity decision procedures have obvious advantages — speed; the guarantee of an answer in theory and often in practice; and, typically, the ability to produce counterexamples — not all theories or interesting fragments are decidable. For example, reasoning about permutations of arrays is undecidable in certain contexts (see Exercise 6.5 and [77, 6]), yet we would like to prove, for example, that sorting functions return permutations of their input.

Because FOL is complete, semi-decision procedures (see Section 2.6.2) are possible: the procedure described before the proof of Lemma 2.31 is such a procedure. More relevant are widely-used procedures with tactics [76, 67, 47]. Recent work has looked at effectively incorporating decision procedures into general theorem proving [48]. The specification language for verified programming is more expressive using these procedures. However, proving verification conditions sometimes requires user intervention.

FOL may not be sufficiently expressive for some applications. Second-order logic extends first-order logic with quantification over predicates. Despite being incomplete, researchers continue to investigate heuristics for partly automating second-order reasoning [67]. Separation logic is another incomplete logic designed for reasoning about mutable data structures [75].

Static Analysis

Static analysis is one of the most active areas of research in verification. Classically, static analyses of the form presented in Chapter 12 have been studied in two areas: compiler development and research [62] and verification [20].

Important areas of current research include fast numerical analyses for discovering numerical relations among program variables [80], precise alias and shape analyses for discovering how a program manipulates memory [96], and predicate abstraction and refinement [5, 37, 16, 24].

Static analyses of the form in Chapter 12 solve a set of implications for a fixpoint (an inductive assertion map is a fixpoint) by forward propagation. Other methods exist for finding fixpoints, including constraint-based static analysis [2, 17].

Static analyses also address total correctness by proving that loops and functions halt [18, 7, 8]. Their structure is different than the analyses of Chapter 12 as they seek ranking functions.

Concurrent Programs

We focus on specifying and verifying sequential programs in this book. Just as concurrent programs are more complex than sequential programs, specification and verification methodologies for concurrent programs are more complex than for sequential programs. Fortunately, many of the same methods, including the inductive assertion method and the ranking function method, are still of fundamental importance in concurrent programming. Manna and Pnueli provide a comprehensive introduction to this topic [53, 54]. Milner describes a calculus of concurrent systems in which both the system and its specification is written [60].

Temporal Logic

Because functions of pi do not have side effects, specifying function behavior through function preconditions and postconditions is sufficient. However, reactive and concurrent systems, such as operating systems, web servers, and computer processors, exhibit remarkably complex behavior. Temporal logics are typically used for specifying their behavior.

A temporal logic extends PL or FOL with temporal operators that express behavior over time. Canonical behaviors include *invariance*, in which some condition always holds; *progress*, in which a particular event eventually occurs; and *reactivity*, in which a condition causes a particular event to occur eventually.

Temporal logics are divided into logics over linear-time structures (Linear Temporal Logic (LTL)) [53]; branching-time structures (Computational Tree Logic (CTL), CTL*) [14]; and alternating-time structures (Alternating-time Temporal Logic (ATL), ATL*) [3].

Model Checking

A finite-state model checker [15, 74] is an algorithm that checks whether finite-state systems such as hardware circuits satisfy given temporal properties.

An explicit-state model checker manipulates sets of actual states as vectors of bits. A symbolic model checker uses a formulaic representation to represent sets of states, just as we use FOL to represent possibly infinite sets of states in Chapters 5 and 6. The first symbolic model checker was for CTL [12]; it represents sets of states with Reduced Ordered Binary Decision Diagrams (ROBDDs, or just BDDs) [10, 11].

LTL model checking is based on manipulating automata over infinite strings [95]. A rich literature exists on such automata; see [91] for an introduction.

Predicate abstraction and refinement [5, 37, 16, 24] has allowed model checkers to be applied to software and represents one of the many intersections between areas of research (model checking and static analysis in this case).

Clarke, Grumberg, and Peled discuss model checking in detail [14].

References

1. W. Ackermann. Solvable cases of the decision problem. *The Journal of Symbolic Logic*, 22(1):68–72, March 1957.
2. A. Aiken. Introduction to set constraint-based program analysis. *Science of Computer Programming*, 35(2-3):79–111, November 1999.
3. R. Alur, T. Henzinger, and O. Kupferman. Alternating-time temporal logic. *Journal of the ACM*, 49:672–713, 2002.
4. F. Baader, S. Ghilardi, and C. Tinelli. A new combination procedure for the word problem that generalizes fusion decidability results in modal logics. *Information and Computation*, 204(10):1413–1452, 2006.
5. N. S. Bjørner, A. Browne, and Z. Manna. Automatic generation of invariants and intermediate assertions. *Theoretical Computer Science*, 173(1):49–87, 1997.
6. A. R. Bradley. *Safety Analysis of Systems*. PhD thesis, Stanford University, June 2007.
7. A. R. Bradley, Z. Manna, and H. B. Sipma. Linear ranking with reachability. In *Computer Aided Verification*, volume 3576 of *LNCS*, pages 491–504. Springer-Verlag, 2005.
8. A. R. Bradley, Z. Manna, and H. B. Sipma. Termination of polynomial programs. In *Verification, Model Checking and Abstract Interpretation*, volume 3385 of *LNCS*, pages 113–129. Springer-Verlag, 2005.
9. A. R. Bradley, Z. Manna, and H. B. Sipma. What's decidable about arrays? In *Verification Model Checking and Abstract Interpretation*, volume 3855 of *LNCS*, pages 427–442. Springer-Verlag, January 2006.
10. R. E. Bryant. Graph-based algorithms for Boolean function manipulation. *IEEE Transactions on Computers*, 35(8):677–691, August 1986.
11. R. E. Bryant. Symbolic Boolean manipulation with ordered binary-decision diagrams. *ACM Computing Surveys*, 24(3):293–318, September 1992.
12. J. R. Burch, E. M. Clarke, K. L. McMillan, D. L. Dill, and L. J. Hwang. Symbolic model checking: 10^{20} states and beyond. *Information and Computation*, 98(2):142–170, 1992.
13. A. Church. A note on the Entscheidungsproblem. *Journal of Symbolic Logic*, 1, 1936.
14. E. Clarke, O. Grumberg, and D. Peled. *Model Checking*. MIT Press, 2000.
15. E. M. Clarke and E. A. Emerson. Design and synthesis of synchronization skeletons using branching-time temporal logic. In *Logic of Programs*, pages 52–71. Springer-Verlag, 1982.

16. E. M. Clarke, O. Grumberg, S. Jha, Y. Lu, and H. Veith. Counterexample-guided abstraction refinement. In *Computer Aided Verification*, volume 1855 of *LNCS*, pages 154–169. Springer-Verlag, 2000.

17. M. Colón, S. Sankaranarayanan, and H. B. Sipma. Linear invariant generation using non-linear constraint solving. In *Computer Aided Verification*, volume 2725 of *LNCS*, pages 420–433. Springer-Verlag, 2003.

18. M. Colón and H. B. Sipma. Synthesis of linear ranking functions. In *Tools and Algorithms for the Construction and Analysis of Systems*, volume 2031 of *LNCS*, pages 67–81. Springer-Verlag, April 2001.

19. D. C. Cooper. Theorem proving in arithmetic without multiplication. *Machine Intelligence*, 7:91–99, 1972.

20. P. Cousot and R. Cousot. Abstract interpretation: A unified lattice model for static analysis of programs by construction or approximation of fixpoints. In *Principles of Programming Languages*, pages 238–252. ACM Press, 1977.

21. P. Cousot and N. Halbwachs. Automatic discovery of linear restraints among the variables of a program. In *Principles of Programming Languages*, pages 84–96. ACM Press, 1978.

22. G. B. Dantzig. *Programming in a Linear Structure*. USAF, February 1948.

23. G. B. Dantzig. Maximization of linear function of variables subject to linear inequalities. In *Cowles Commission for Research in Economics*, volume 13, pages 339–347. Wiley, 1951.

24. S. Das and D. L. Dill. Successive approximation of abstract transition relations. In *Logic in Computer Science*, page 51. IEEE Computer Society, 2001.

25. M. Davis, G. Logemann, and D. Loveland. A machine program for theorem-proving. *Communications of the ACM*, 5(7):394–397, July 1962.

26. M. Davis and H. Putnam. A computing procedure for quantification theory. *Journal of the ACM*, 7(3):201–215, July 1960.

27. D. L. Detlefs, K. R. M. Leino, G. Nelson, and J. B. Saxe. Extended static checking. Technical Report 159, Compaq SRC, December 1998.

28. E. W. Dijkstra. Guarded commands, nondeterminacy and formal derivation of programs. *Communications of the ACM*, 18(8):453–457, August 1975.

29. P. J. Downey, R. Sethi, and R. E. Tarjan. Variations on the common subexpressions problem. *Journal of the ACM*, 27(4):758–771, 1980.

30. B. Dreben and H. Putnam. The Craig interpolation lemma. *Notre Dame Journal of Formal Logic*, 8(3):229–233, July 1967.

31. H. B. Enderton. *A Mathematical Introduction to Logic*. Academic Press, 1972.

32. J. Ferrante and C. Rackoff. A decision procedure for the first order theory of real addition with order. *SIAM Journal on Computing*, 4(1):69–76, 1975.

33. M. J. Fischer and M. O. Rabin. Super-exponential complexity of Presburger arithmetic. In R. M. Karp, editor, *Complexity of Computation*, volume 7 of *SIAM-AMS Proceedings*, pages 27–42. American Mathematical Society, 1974.

34. R. W. Floyd. Assigning meanings to programs. In *Symposia in Applied Mathematics*, volume 19, pages 19–32. American Mathematical Society, 1967.

35. K. Gödel. *Über die Vollständigkeit des Logikkalküls*. PhD thesis, University of Vienna, 1929.

36. K. Gödel. Über formal unentscheidbare Sätze der Principia Mathematica und verwandter Systeme I. *Monatshefte für Mathematik und Physik*, 38:173–198, 1931.

37. S. Graf and H. Saidi. Construction of abstract state graphs with PVS. In *Computer Aided Verification*, volume 1254 of *LNCS*, pages 72–83. Springer-Verlag, 1997.

38. D. Hilbert. Die Grundlagen der Mathematik. *Abhandlungen aus dem Seminar der Hamburgischen Universität*, 6:65–85, 1928.

39. C. A. R. Hoare. An axiomatic basis for computer programming. *Communications of the ACM*, 12(10):576–580, October 1969.

40. W. Hodges. *A Shorter Model Theory*. Cambridge University Press, 1997.

41. J. E. Hopcroft, R. Motwani, and J. D. Ullman. *Automata Theory, Languages, and Computation*. Addison-Wesley, 3rd edition, 2006.

42. R. A. Horn and C. R. Johnson. *Matrix Analysis*. Cambridge University Press, 1985.

43. J. Jaffar. Presburger arithmetic with array segments. *Information Processing Letters*, 12(2):79–82, 1981.

44. L. Kantorovich. Mathematical methods of organizing and planning production. *Management Science*, 6:366–422, 1960. In Russian, Leningrad University, 1939.

45. N. Karmarkar. A new polynomial-time algorithm for linear programming. *Combinatorica*, 4:373–395, 1984.

46. M. Karr. Affine relationships among variables of a program. *Acta Informatica*, 6:133–151, 1976.

47. M. Kaufmann, P. Manolios, and J. S. Moore. *Computer-Aided Reasoning: An Approach*. Kluwer Academic Publishers, 2000.

48. M. Kaufmann, J. S. Moore, S. Ray, and E. Reeber. Integrating external deduction tools with ACL2. In *Workshop on the Implementation of Logics*, volume 212, pages 7–26, 2006.

49. L. G. Khachian. A polynomial algorithm in linear programming. *Soviet Math. Dokl.*, 20:191–194, 1979. In Russian, *Dokl. Akad. Nauk SSSR* 244, 1093–1096, 1979.

50. J. King. *A Program Verifier*. PhD thesis, Carnegie Mellon University, September 1969.

51. IEEE Symposium on Logic in Computer Science. `http://www2.informatik.hu-berlin.de/lics`.

52. Z. Manna. *Mathematical Theory of Computation*. McGraw-Hill, 1974. Also Dover, 2004.

53. Z. Manna and A. Pnueli. *The Temporal Logic of Reactive and Concurrent Systems: Specification*. Springer-Verlag, 1991.

54. Z. Manna and A. Pnueli. *Temporal Verification of Reactive Systems: Safety*. Springer-Verlag, 1995.

55. Z. Manna and R. Waldinger. *The Deductive Foundations of Computer Programming*. Addison-Wesley, 1993.

56. Z. Manna and C. G. Zarba. Combining decision procedures. In *Formal Methods at the Cross Roads: From Panacea to Foundational Support*, volume 2757 of *LNCS*, pages 381–422. Springer-Verlag, 2003.

57. P. Mateti. A decision procedure for the correctness of a class of programs. *Journal of the ACM*, 28(2), 1981.

58. J. McCarthy. Towards a mathematical science of computation. In *International Federation for Information Processing*, pages 21–28, 1962.

59. J. McCarthy. A basis for a mathematical theory of computation. *Computer Programming and Formal Systems*, 1963.

60. R. Milner. *Communication and Concurrency*. Prentice Hall, 1989.

61. A. Miné. The octagon abstract domain. In *Analysis, Slicing and Transformation (part of Working Conference on Reverse Engineering)*, IEEE, pages 310–319. IEEE Computer Society, October 2001.

62. S. S. Muchnick. *Advanced Compiler Design and Implementation*. Morgan Kaufmann Publishers Inc., 1997.

63. M. Müller-Olm and H. Seidl. A note on Karr's algorithm. In *International Colloquium on Automata, Languages and Programming*, volume 3142 of *LNCS*, pages 1016–1027. Springer-Verlag, 2004.

64. G. Nelson. Combining satisfiability procedures by equality-sharing. *Contemporary Mathematics*, 29:201–211, 1984.

65. G. Nelson and D. C. Oppen. Simplification by cooperating decision procedures. *ACM Transactions on Programming Languages and Systems*, 1(2):245–257, October 1979.

66. G. Nelson and D. C. Oppen. Fast decision procedures based on congruence closure. *Journal of the ACM*, 27(2):356–364, April 1980.

67. T. Nipkow, L. C. Paulson, and M. Wenzel. *Isabelle/HOL: A Proof Assistant for Higher-Order Logic*, volume 2283 of *LNCS*. Springer-Verlag, 2002.

68. D. C. Oppen. A $2^{2^{2^{pn}}}$ upper bound on the complexity of Presburger arithmetic. *Journal of Computer and System Sciences*, 16(3):323–332, 1978.

69. D. C. Oppen. Reasoning about recursively defined data structures. In *Principles of Programming Languages*, pages 151–157. ACM Press, 1978.

70. D. C. Oppen. Complexity, convexity and combinations of theories. *Theoretical Computer Science*, 12:291–302, 1980.

71. D. C. Oppen. Reasoning about recursively defined data structures. *Journal of the ACM*, 27(3):403–411, July 1980.

72. C. H. Papadimitriou. *Computational Complexity*. Addison-Wesley, 1993.

73. M. Presburger. Über die Vollständigkeit eines gewissen Systems der Arithmetik ganzer Zahlen, in welchen die Addition als einzige Operation hervortritt. In *Comptes Rendus du Premier Congrés des Mathématicienes des Pays Slaves*, pages 92–101, 1929.

74. J. P. Queille and J. Sifakis. Specification and verification of concurrent systems in CESAR. In *International Symposium on Programming*, volume 137 of *LNCS*. Springer-Verlag, 1982.

75. J. C. Reynolds. Separation logic: A logic for shared mutable data structures. In *Logic in Computer Science*, pages 55–74. IEEE Computer Society, 2002.

76. A. Riazanov and A. Voronkov. The design and implementation of VAMPIRE. *AI Communications*, 15(2):91–110, September 2002.

77. L. E. Rosier. A note on Presburger arithmetic with array segments, permutation and equality. *Information Processing Letters*, 22(1):33–35, 1986.

78. H. Ruess and N. Shankar. Deconstructing Shostak. In *Logic in Computer Science*. IEEE Computer Society, 2001.

79. B. Russell. *Philosophy of Logical Atomism*, 1918.

80. S. Sankaranarayanan, M. Colón, H. Sipma, and Z. Manna. Efficient strongly relational polyhedral analysis. In *Verification, Model Checking, and Abstract Interpretation*, volume 3855 of *LNCS*, pages 111–125, 2006.

81. The international SAT competitions web page. http://www.satcompetition.org.

82. A. Schrijver. *Theory of Linear and Integer Programming*. Wiley, 1986.

83. R. E. Shostak. An algorithm for reasoning about equality. *Communications of the ACM*, 21(7):583–585, July 1978.

84. R. E. Shostak. Deciding combinations of theories. *Journal of the ACM*, 31(1):1–12, January 1984.

85. M. Sipser. *Introduction to the Theory of Computation*. Course Technology, 1996.

86. SMT-LIB: SMT solver competition. `http://goedel.cs.uiowa.edu/smtlib`.

87. R. M. Smullyan. *First-Order Logic*. Dover, 1968.

88. A. Stump, C. W. Barrett, D. L. Dill, and J. Levitt. A decision procedure for an extensional theory of arrays. In *Logic in Computer Science*, pages 29–37. IEEE Computer Society, 2001.

89. N. Suzuki and D. Jefferson. Verification decidability of Presburger array programs. *Journal of the ACM*, 27(1):191–205, January 1980.

90. A. Tarski. *A Decision Method for Elementary Algebra and Geometry*. University of California Press, 1951.

91. W. Thomas. Automata on infinite objects. In J. van Leeuwen, editor, *Handbook of Theoretical Computer Science*, volume B, pages 133–191. Elsevier North-Holland, Inc., 1990.

92. C. Tinelli and M. T. Harandi. A new correctness proof of the Nelson-Oppen combination procedure. In *Frontiers of Combining Systems*, pages 103–120. Kluwer Academic Publishers, 1996.

93. C. Tinelli and C. Ringeissen. Unions of non-disjoint theories and combinations of satisfiability procedures. *Theoretical Computer Science*, 290(1):291–353, January 2003.

94. C. Tinelli and C. Zarba. Combining non-stably infinite theories. Technical Report TinZar-RR-03, University of Iowa, 2003.

95. M. Y. Vardi. An automata-theoretic approach to linear temporal logic. In *Logics for Concurrency: Structure versus Automata*, pages 238–266. Springer-Verlag, 1996.

96. R. Wilhelm, S. Sagiv, and T. W. Reps. Parametric shape analysis via 3-valued logic. *Transactions on Programming Languages and Systems*, 24(3):217–298, May 2002.

97. M. Yadegari. The use of mathematical induction by Abu Kamil Shuja' Ibn Aslam (850-930). *Isis*, 69(2):259–262, June 1978.

98. R. Zach. Hilbert's program. In E. N. Zalta, editor, *The Stanford Encyclopedia of Philosophy*. The Metaphysics Research Lab, Fall 2003. `http://plato.stanford.edu/archives/fall2003/entries/hilbert-program`.

99. C. Zarba, Z. Manna, and H. B. Sipma. Combining theories sharing dense orders. In *Automated Reasoning with Analytic Tableaux and Related Methods: Position Papers and Tutorials*, pages 83–98, 2003.

100. T. Zhang, H. B. Sipma, and Z. Manna. Decision procedures for term algebras with integer constraints. *Information and Computation*, 204(10):1526–1574, October 2006.

Index